COGNITION,
AGING, AND
SELF-REPORTS

COGNITION, AGING, AND SELF-REPORTS

Edited by
Norbert Schwarz
Denise C. Park
Bärbel Knäuper
Seymour Sudman

USA	Publishing Office:	PSYCHOLOGY PRESS
		A member of the Taylor & Francis Group
		325 Chestnut Street
		Philadelphia, PA 19106
		Tel: (215) 265-8900
		Fax: (215) 265-2940
	Distribution Center:	PSYCHOLOGY PRESS
		A member of the Taylor & Francis Group
		47 Runway Road, Suite G
		Levittown, PA 19057-4700
		Tel: (215) 629-0400
		Fax: (215) 629-0363
UK		PSYCHOLOGY PRESS
		A member of the Taylor & Francis Group
		27 Church Road
		Hove
		E. Sussex, BN3 2FA
		Tel: +44 (0)1273 207411
		Fax: +44 (0)1273 205612

COGNITION, AGING, AND SELF-REPORTS

1 2 3 4 5 6 7 8 9 0

Printed by Edwards Brothers, Ann Arbor, MI, 1998.

A CIP catalog record for this book is available from the British Library.
∞ The paper in this publication meets the requirements of the ANSI Standard Z39.48-1984 (Permanence of Paper)

Library of Congress Cataloging-in-Publication Data

Cognition, aging, and self-reports / edited by Norbert Schwarz . . .
 [et al.]
 p. cm.
 Includes index.

 1. Cognition in old age—United States. 2. Memory in old age—United States. 3. Cognition—Age factors—United States. 4. Memory—Age factors—United States. 5. Aged—Self-rating of—United States. 6. Social surveys—United States. I. Schwarz, Norbert, Dr. Phil.
BF724.85.C64C63 1998
155.67'13—dc21   98-19790
                                                                        CIP

ISBN 1-56032-780-4 (hardcover : alk. paper)

CONTENTS

PART IV
SURVEYING OLDER RESPONDENTS

CONTRIBUTORS

The Editors:

Norbert Schwarz, Professor of Psychology and Senior Research Scientist, Survey Research Center, Institute for Social Research, University of Michigan, Ann Arbor

Denise Park, Professor of Psychology and Director of the Center for Applied Research in Cognitive Aging, University of Michigan, Ann Arbor

Bärbel Knäuper, Assistant Professor of Psychology, Free University of Berlin, Germany

Seymour Sudman, Walter Stellner Distinguished Professor of Marketing and Deputy Director of the Survey Research Laboratory, University of Illinois at Urbana-Champaign

---

Duane F. Alwin, Department of Sociology and Institute for Social Research, University of Michigan, USA

Paul Beatty, Office of Research and Methodology, National Center for Health Statistics, USA

Robert F. Belli, Institute for Social Research, University of Michigan, USA

Jane Burris, Survey Research Laboratory, University of Illinois at Urbana-Champaign, USA

John C. Cavanaugh, Office of Graduate Studies, University of Delaware, USA

Fergus I. M. Craik, Department of Psychology, University of Toronto, Canada

Roger A. Dixon, Department of Psychology, University of Victoria, Canada

Lynn Hasher, Department of Psychology, Duke University, USA

A. Regula Herzog, Institute for Social Research, University of Michigan, USA

Timothy Johnson, Survey Research Institute, University of Illinois at Chicago, USA

Susan Kemper, Department of Psychology, University of Kansas, USA

Karen Kemtes, Department of Psychology, University of Kansas, USA

Sheree T. Kwong See, Department of Psychology, University of Alberta, Canada

James M. Lepkowski, Institute for Social Research, University of Michigan, USA

Cynthia P. May, Department of Psychology, University of Arizona, USA

Diane O'Rourke, Survey Research Laboratory, University of Illinois at Urbana-Champaign, USA

Willard L. Rodgers, Institute for Social Research, University of Michigan, USA

David C. Rubin, Department of Experimental Psychology, Duke University, USA

Ellen Bouchard Ryan, Department of Psychiatry, McMaster University, Canada

Timothy A. Salthouse, School of Psychology, Georgia Institute of Technology, USA

Susan Schechter, Office of Research and Methodology, National Center for Health Statistics, USA

Paul S. Weiss, Institute for Social Research, University of Michigan, USA

Gordon B. Willis, Office of Research and Methodology, National Center for Health Statistics, USA

Arthur Wingfield, Department of Psychology and Volen National Center for Complex Systems, Brandeis University, USA

Carolyn Yoon, Management Department, University of Toronto, Canada

ACKNOWLEDGMENTS

The plan for this book was developed at a conference held at the University of Michigan in February 1997. We gratefully acknowledge the support of the Survey Research Center and the Center for Applied Cognitive Research on Aging (supported by the National Institute on Aging) at the University of Michigan, and the Walter Stellner Endowment in the Department of Business Administration of the University of Illinois at Urbana-Champaign.

Norbert Schwarz
Denise C. Park
Bärbel Knäuper
Seymour Sudman

Cognition, Aging, and Self-Reports: Editors' Introduction

Self-reports of behaviors and attitudes are the dominant source of data in the social sciences. From the dynamics of attitude change to consumer behavior or health problems, and from the styles of parenting to the nation's unemployment rate or the prevalence of crime, psychologists and social scientists rely on respondents' self-reports as their major database for testing theories of human behavior and offering advice on public policy. Unfortunately, self-reports are a fallible source of data, and minor variations in question wording or question order can strongly affect the obtained answers and hence the conclusions drawn about the phenomenon under study. It is therefore important to understand how respondents arrive at answers to the questions we pose in self-administered questionnaires, survey interviews, and the psychological laboratory. Since the early 1980s, psychologists and survey methodologists have addressed the cognitive and communicative processes underlying self-reports in an interdisciplinary program of experimental research. Drawing on psychological theories of language comprehension, memory, judgment, and communication, this work has identified numerous sources of context effects in self-reports and has provided conceptual frameworks that promise to improve data-collection strategies (see Sudman, Bradburn, & Schwarz, 1996, for a review).

The present book extends this work by exploring how age-related changes in cognitive and communicative functioning influence the processes underlying self-reports. This issue is of considerable theoretical and applied relevance. On the theoretical side, self-reports of attitudes

1

and behaviors provide a challenging arena for testing theories of cognitive aging in real-world domains, thus advancing basic theorizing about cognitive aging. Similarly, understanding how age-related changes in cognitive functioning affect the accuracy of self-reports will advance basic theorizing about the processes underlying self-reports. On the applied side, understanding age-related changes in the response process is of utmost importance across a broad range of the social sciences. Older adults are the fastest growing segment of the population in most industrialized nations. In the United States, adults aged 65 and older represented 6.8% of the population in 1950, but will represent 12.6% by the year 2000 and 22.9% by the year 2050 (U.S. Bureau of the Census, 1989). Hence, social scientists will increasingly face the challenge of collecting data from older adults, a trend that will be compounded when the social problems of an aging population receive increased attention. It is therefore important to understand how research instruments need to be adapted to meet the requirements posed by older respondents.

Of particular note are several findings reported in the present book that indicate that older and younger adults are differentially affected by question context and question format, resulting in complex interactions of respondents' age and the features of the research instrument. To give just one example, survey researchers have long been aware that the order in which different response alternatives are presented may strongly influence the obtained results. For example, Schuman and Presser (1981) asked respondents in a telephone interview, "Should divorce in this country be easier to obtain, more difficult to obtain, or stay as it is now?" Depending on conditions, the response alternative "more difficult" was read to respondents as the second or as the last alternative. Overall, respondents were somewhat more likely to select the response alternative "more difficult" when presented last, a so-called recency effect. However, secondary analyses reported by Knäuper (Chapter 17) indicate a dramatic age difference: As shown in Figure 1, the size of the recency effect increased with respondents' age, ranging from a nonsignificant 5% for those aged 54 and younger to a whopping 36.3% for those aged 70 and older. Note also that we would draw different substantive conclusions about the relationship of age and attitudes towards divorce, depending on the order in which the response alternatives are presented: While attitudes towards divorce seem to become much more conservative with age under one order condition, no reliable age differences are obtained under the other order condition. Findings of this type illustrate how age-related differences in the response process may threaten conclusions about age-related differences in the reported opinion or behavior. Unless we want to run the

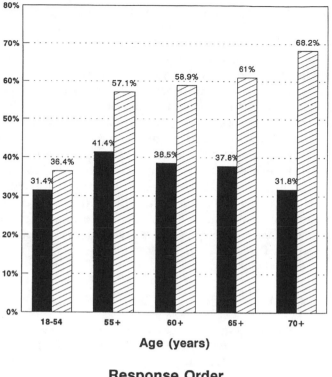

FIGURE 1. Percentage of respondents who reported that divorce should be "more difficult" to obtain when this alternative was presented in the middle position ("easier," "more difficult," "stay as is") or in the last position ("easier," "stay as is," "more difficult"). Data from Schuman & Presser (1981).

risk of misinterpreting age-related differences in response behavior as age-related differences in the substantive phenomenon under study, we need to understand how older and younger respondents differ in the cognitive and communicative processes underlying self-reports.

To address these challenging issues, we need to understand how cognitive and communicative functioning changes over the life-span and we need to relate this knowledge to the processes underlying self-reports. Fortunately, psychologists have made considerable progress in understanding both of these components over the last two decades. Cognitive aging psychologists have identified key age-related changes in basic cognitive mechanisms, memory, language comprehension, speech processing, and communication. Survey methodologists and cognitive social psychologists have illuminated the cognitive and communicative processes underlying self-reports. What is missing from these two research domains is cross-talk between them and an attempt to relate these bodies of research to one another. The present book is designed to fill this gap. It presents tutorial reviews of what has been learned in both fields, as well as research that addresses the interface by exploring differences between older and younger respondents. In combination, the contributions in this volume set the stage for the development of a stimulating and systematic program of research that integrates the knowledge base of cognitive aging researchers with self-report research. We hope that as a result of reading this volume, more researchers will begin to address how age-related changes in cognition and communication interact with features of the research instrument, thus differentially influencing older and younger respondents' answers to the questions we ask.

☐ Overview

This book is organized in four parts. Part I provides an overview of the general issues the book will address with respect to self-reports, aging, and cognition. Part II reviews age-related changes in cognitive functioning, and Part III addresses age-related changes in language processing and communication. Whereas these three parts can draw on extensive experimental research programs, we know considerably less about the interface of age-related changes in cognition and communication on the one hand and the dynamics of self-reports on the other hand. The contributions in Part IV begin to address these issues by reporting on recent empirical studies into age differences in self-reports.

Self-Reports and Cognitive Aging

In Chapter 2, Norbert Schwarz provides an introduction to the cognitive and communicative processes involved in answering a question. Drawing on research into context effects on self-reports, he addresses how respondents arrive at an interpretation of the question posed to them, retrieve relevant information from memory, form a judgment, and report this judgment to the researcher. Importantly, respondents' performance at each of these steps is highly context dependent, and the underlying processes are likely to be age sensitive, as many research examples illustrate.

In Chapter 3, Denise Park reviews the major cognitive mechanisms accounting for age-related decline in cognitive function. She discusses the implications of decreases in speed of processing, working memory function, and inhibitory function for self-report situations. Additionally, she addresses the paradox of older adults who evidence substantial cognitive decline in the laboratory but perform quite adequately on complex tasks in their work environment or in managing their health. She argues that automatic processes, familiarity, and world knowledge that are useful in the everyday environment frequently offset the negative impact of declining processing mechanisms.

In Chapter 4, Roger Dixon considers the possibility that cognitive development in late adulthood is not characterized entirely by losses, but that there are also gains in some domains of cognitive function. He addresses the prospect that stability in cognition, or relatively small losses with age, are viewed as gains by the older adult.

These three chapters provide a broad foundation for the subsequent chapters in the volume that are focused on specific domains of research.

Age-Related Changes in Cognitive Functioning

In Chapter 5, Fergus Craik provides a classic overview of what is known about memory and aging. He discusses the major subsystems of memory and provides a detailed discussion of working memory, episodic memory, spatial memory, and memory for remote events. He provides suggestions about the implications of memory decline in these subsystems for self-report. He reviews as well the truth effect (the tendency to believe that something one heard before is true) and argues that this effect is more powerful for older than for younger adults.

The focus of Chapter 6, by Carolyn Yoon, Cynthia May, and Lynn Hasher, is also on memory. They discuss a fascinating body of research, conducted primarily in their laboratories, indicating that older and young adults have peak cognitive performance at different times of day. They present data indicating that older adults' cognitive performance is best early in the morning, whereas younger adults' performance is best in the afternoons and evenings. Such findings have profound implications for survey researchers who may find that older adults are more likely to behave comparably to young adults (thus minimizing survey error) if interviewed in the morning.

In Chapter 7, John Cavanaugh discusses metacognition and aging. How does what we believe to be true about our cognitive function affect our performance? The primary focus is on metamemory. He presents a review of theoretical perspectives guiding the study of self-report data about memory function, and particularly addresses the relationship between memory self-efficacy and performance. He then discusses metamemory as a type of social cognition, and concludes by suggesting productive avenues for future research.

In Chapter 8, David Rubin presents the complex relationship between aging and autobiographical memory (memory for our personal life histories). He discusses the accuracy of autobiographical memory as we age and provides a wealth of information about age distributions in the content and regularity of autobiographical memory.

Part II concludes with a provocative commentary by Tim Salthouse on the pressing issues in cognitive aging research (Chapter 9). He argues that research in cognitive aging has focused on process, and that we have a relatively good understanding of how processes change with age. At the same time, we know relatively little about why they change. He suggests as well that we have a relatively good idea of the products of cognition or the content of knowledge as we age (the "what" of cognitive aging). What is lacking, however, is an understanding of the interaction between product and process. Salthouse argues for the importance of an understanding of the interactive relationship between these two constructs in cognitive aging.

Language Comprehension and Communication

Following this review of basic cognitive processes, the next set of chapters addresses age-related changes in speech processing, message production and comprehension, and communication. In Chapter 10, Arthur Wingfield reviews what we know about age-related changes in speech processing. Adult aging is often accompanied by declines in auditory acuity that affect the sensory processing of others' utterances. As a result, older adults have to rely to a higher degree on the context of the utterance to fill gaps in the sensory input. Moreover, older adults' reduced processing speed (discussed in Chapters 3 and 9) and susceptibility to working memory overload (see Chapters 3 and 4) make it imperative that the speaker's utterances do not place a heavy burden on memory capacity. Unfortunately, many attempts to facilitate older adults' speech comprehension do more harm than good and may be experienced as patronizing (as also emphasized in Chapters 11 and 12). Thus, exaggerated prosody (intonation, timing, and stress) and a slow overall speed of delivery hurt speech comprehension for young as well as old adults, whereas normal prosody and the thoughtful use of pauses facilitate speech comprehension for both age groups. These observations lead Wingfield to conclude that speakers need to "respect processing limitations for adult listeners regardless of age." The principles discussed in his chapter "may take on more importance for some individuals than others, but they will be important to all." From an applied point of view, Wingfield's recommendations are of particular importance for telephone interviews, a mode of data collection that poses particular demands on respondents.

Extending Wingfield's discussion, Susan Kemper and Karen Kemtes review message production and comprehension over the life-span in Chapter 11. With regard to message production, they note that some discourse skills, such as storytelling, increase with age, whereas other discourse skills decrease with age, in particular those that require keeping track of the previously established common ground of the conversation. With regard to message comprehension, the available evidence suggests that older adults' language performance "does not show an inevitable decline under normal discourse conditions." However, "older adults' comprehension is compromised when the structure of the discourse is complex and when it is presented at very rapid rates," conditions that also impair comprehension for younger adults, although to a lesser degree. Importantly, younger adults are likely to change their discourse style when they speak to older adults and may use exaggerated pitch and intonation, simplified grammar, limited vocabulary, and a slow rate of delivery. The authors refer to this speech register as "elderspeak." Research into the consequences of elderspeak indicates that its use may improve older addressees' performance on some tasks, yet this improvement comes at a cost: "Elderspeak appeared to trigger older adults' perceptions of themselves as communicatively impaired and led to increased self-report of expressive and receptive problems."

In Chapter 12, Sheree Kwong See and Ellen Bouchard Ryan extend the discussion of intergenerational communication. Drawing on a classic model of the survey interview, originally proposed in 1968 by Cannell and Kahn, and their own "communicative predicament of aging" model, Kwong See and Ryan propose a framework of intergenerational communication in the context of survey interviews. Their model emphasizes the impact of communicators' stereotypical beliefs about older adults' cognitive and communicative abilities on the course of the unfolding conversation. Much of the empirical work they review has been conducted in contexts that are less standardized than the typical survey interview. Hence, the extent to which the observed dynamics of intergenerational communication apply to standardized interviews is currently unknown. The findings reported by Belli, Weiss, and Lepkowski (Chapter 15) indicate, however, that interviewers are indeed more likely to deviate from standard procedures when interviewing older rather than younger respondents. Kwong See and Ryan's discussion provides a useful framework for conceptualizing the nature of such deviations in future research.

Surveying Older Respondents

The chapters in Part IV address age-related differences in response behavior as observed in sample surveys. Their arrangement follows the sequence of respondents' tasks, from understanding the questions posed to them to retrieving information from memory, forming a judgment, and reporting the answer. Over the last decade, survey researchers have increasingly adapted methods developed in the psychological laboratory for pretesting questionnaires (for reviews, see DeMaio & Rothgeb, 1996, and the contributions in Schwarz & Sudman, 1996). These methods, summarily referred to as "cognitive interviewing," include the use of think-aloud protocols and extensive probing to identify respondents' interpretation of a question and the strategies used in arriving at an answer. In Chapter 13, Susan Schechter, Paul Beatty, and Gordon Willis use these methods to explore the problems that older adults encounter when answering questions about their health status. Extending this discussion to questions designed to assess cognitive functioning, Diane O'Rourke, Seymour Sudman, Timothy Johnson, and Jane Burris (Chapter 14) report on older respondents' difficulties with memory questions. In combination, these chapters illustrate how cognitive interviewing techniques can be used in applied settings to identify problematic questions at an early stage of the research process. Unfortunately, the use of these techniques in many survey research centers is geared towards making a specific set of questions "work," rather than towards understanding the underlying processes. As a result, relevant comparison groups are often missing and the research is less cumulative than would seem desirable from a basic research point of view (see O'Muircheartaigh, in press, and Schwarz, in press, for critical discussions). Hopefully, the developing collaboration between survey methodologists and cognitive psychologists will provide future opportunities for combining applied questionnaire development efforts with basic theoretical work.

Whereas the preceding assessments of respondents' difficulties with survey questions were based on pretests conducted in a laboratory setting, an alternative approach to identifying respondents' difficulties is based on the coding of tape-recorded interviews conducted as part of ongoing surveys. Known as *behavior coding*, this technique, developed by Charles Cannell and his associates (Cannell, Miller, & Oksenberg, 1981; see Fowler & Cannell, 1996, for an introduction), identifies sequences of problematic interviewer and respondent behaviors. Robert Belli, Paul Weiss, and James Lepkowski applied this technique to 455 interviews with younger and older respondents and report their findings in Chapter 15. They observe that older respondents encounter more difficulties in understanding questions and are more likely to provide inadequate answers than younger respondents. Partially in response to these difficulties, interviewers "tailor" the questions to meet older respondents' needs, and hence deviate from the standardized wordings they are supposed to use. This differential degree of tailoring implies that older respondents are less likely to be exposed to the standard version of the question than younger respondents, thus introducing additional variability into the interview process. Whether or not such tailoring is desirable is an issue of considerable debate in survey research (cf. Fowler & Mangione, 1990; Schober, in press; Suchman & Jordan, 1990), which typically places a premium on standardized interviewing. Obviously, deviations from standardized interviewing might seem more justifiable if they increased the accuracy of respondents' reports. To address this issue, Belli and colleagues checked the accuracy of respondents' reports of health care visits against medical records. Surprisingly, they find that tailoring actually decreases the accuracy of older respondents' reports, in contrast to the interviewers' good intentions. Given the observational nature of their data, however, it is conceivable that a given respondent's low cognitive abilities may be responsible for both the observed low accuracy of behavioral reports and the observed increase in interviewer tailoring. Addressing these issues in controlled experiments that manipulate interviewer tailoring and assess respondents' cognitive abilities provides a promising avenue for further research in light of Kwong See and Ryan's (Chapter 12) discussion of intergenerational communication.

As highlighted in the section on cognitive aging (Part I), age per se is an imperfect indicator of individuals' cognitive functioning, and age-related declines in cognitive resources show considerable variation. Therefore, it may often be useful to assess respondents' cognitive status as part of a survey interview. In Chapter 16, Regula Herzog and Willard Rodgers report on the development of cognitive performance measures that have been employed in large-scale sample surveys, including measures of long-term and working memory, speed of processing, vocabulary, and general knowledge. Such measures allow the collection of cognitive function data from representative samples, thus enabling inferences to the population that are impossible on the basis of small-scale laboratory studies. Herzog and Rodgers address the methodological challenges posed by this work and relate cognitive performance data to a variety of respondent characteristics, as well as to respondents' ability to master the instrumental activities of daily living. They also observe that respondents with low cognitive ability are more likely to provide inconsistent answers to related questions. The availability of short measures of cognitive functioning that can be administered as part of a survey interview will greatly facilitate future work in this area, including work into the issues addressed in the final two chapters.

Two phenomena that have been of considerable interest to survey researchers are question order and response order effects (for research examples, see Schuman & Presser, 1981; Schwarz & Sudman, 1992). As Bärbel Knäuper demonstrates in Chapter 17, the emergence and size of these effects is highly age sensitive. In general, the influence of question order is less pronounced for older than for younger respondents, whereas the impact of response order is more pronounced for older than for younger respondents. Both of these observations can be traced to age-related declines in working memory, which decrease the likelihood that respondents can keep previously presented material in mind. As a result, older respondents are particularly likely to choose the last response alternative presented to them in a survey interview, and are unlikely to be influenced by questions presented earlier in the interview.

Whereas Knäuper's (Chapter 17) secondary analyses are based on question order and response order experiments embedded in sample surveys, Duane Alwin, in Chapter 18, draws on longitudinal data collected as part of the 1956–58–60 and 1972–74–76 National Election Study, a panel study that involves repeated interviews of the same respondents. Using the reliability of respondents' answers to factual questions and opinion questions as an estimate of measurement error, Alwin employs structural-equation modeling to test if measurement errors increase with age or if apparent age effects can be traced to cohort differences in formal education. Consistent with earlier findings (e.g., Rodgers & Herzog, 1987), his results indicate that there are no age differences in the reliability of factual reports, such as reports of respondents' amount of schooling or family income. For attitudes and beliefs, the emerging picture is more complicated. When cohort differences in education are not taken into account, older adults' reports of attitudes and beliefs show more measurement error than younger adults' reports. Yet, this pattern reverses when cohort differences are controlled for: "Once age groups are statistically equated with respect to levels of schooling . . ., reliability of measurement increases with age, rather then decreases."

On the methodological side, Alwin's findings highlight the potential pitfalls of comparing age groups without proper control for variables that are likely to be confounded with age (cf. Riley, 1973). On the theoretical side, they challenge the simple notion that measurement error is likely to increase with age, due to older respondents' cognitive limitations. As numerous findings in the present volume illustrate, this apparently straightforward notion is indeed too simple. For example, one of the sources of measurement unreliability is the emergence of context effects: When the same question is asked in different contexts, respondents are likely to give different answers (see Schwarz, Chapter 2). Yet, as Knäuper (Chapter 17) demonstrates, question context effects decrease with age, presumably because the content of preceding questions is less accessible in older respondents' memories. As a result, older respondents' answers would be less influenced by changes in the preceding questions, potentially resulting in higher retest reliability in reinterviews. On the other hand, Knäuper also demonstrates that the influence of response order increases with age, with older respondents being more likely to endorse the last response alternative read to them. Importantly, the order in which response alternatives are presented is held constant in the repeated interviews of panel surveys. Hence, the increased response order effects observed for older respondents would increase the likelihood that these respondents endorse the same response alternative in both interviews, thus contributing to the retest reliability of their reports. As these examples illustrate, reliability is an imperfect measure of data quality, and high reliability may sometimes be obtained for undesirable reasons. Future research may fruitfully combine experimental manipulations of question context and response order with a longitudinal design to illuminate the processes that underlie Alwin's provocative observation that the reliability of respondents' reports increases with age.

☐ Future Developments

In combination, the contributions to the present volume highlight the importance of age-related changes in cognitive and communicative functioning for the processes underlying self-reports of attitudes and behaviors. While we have achieved a reasonably good understanding of age-related changes on the one hand and of the dynamics of self-reports on the other hand, we have only begun to explore the interface. What is needed are systematic programs of experimental research that document age differences in the response process and trace their emergence to specific age-related changes in cognitive and communicative functioning, thus going beyond age per se as the crucial explanatory variable. On the theoretical side, such programs of research would contribute to our understanding of cognitive aging, memory, judgment, language comprehension, and communication and would extend the testing ground of basic theories beyond their traditional domains. On the applied side, this research would help us in designing research instruments that meet the needs of younger as well as older respondents. Most importantly, a better understanding of age-related differences in the processes underlying self-reports is of utmost importance for all disciplines that rely on self-reports—without it, we run the risk of systematically misinterpreting age-related differences in the response process as age-related differences in the substantive phenomenon under study. Hopefully, the contributions to the present book will set the stage for this endeavor.

☐ References

Cannell, C. F., & Kahn, R. L. (1968). Interviewing. In G. Lindzey & E. Aronson (Eds.), *The handbook of social psychology* (Vol. 2, 2nd ed.; pp. 526–295). Reading, MA: Addison-Wesley.

Cannell, C. F., Miller, P. V., & Oksenberg, L. (1981). Research on interviewing techniques. In S. Leinhardt (Ed.), *Sociological methodology 1981*. San Francisco: Jossey-Bass.

DeMaio, T. J., & Rothgeb, J. M. (1996). Cognitive interviewing techniques: In the lab and in the field. In N. Schwarz & S. Sudman (Eds.), *Answering questions: Methodology for determining cognitive and communicative processes in survey research* (pp. 177–196). San Francisco: Jossey-Bass.

Fowler, F. J., & Cannell, C. F. (1996). Using behavioral coding to identify cognitive problems with survey questions. In N. Schwarz & S. Sudman (Eds.), *Answering questions: Methodology for determining cognitive and communicative processes in survey research* (pp. 15–36). San Francisco: Jossey-Bass.

Fowler, F. J., & Mangione, T. W. (1990). *Standardized survey interviewing: Minimizing interviewer-related error*. Newbury Park, CA: Sage.

O'Muircheartaigh, C. (in press). CASM: Successes, failures, and potential. In M. Sirken, D. Hermann, S. Schechter, N. Schwarz, J. Tanur, & R. Tourangeau (Eds.), *Cognition and survey research*. New York: Wiley.

Riley, M. W. (1973). Aging and cohort succession: Interpretations and misinterpretations. *Public Opinion Quarterly, 37,* 35–49.

Rodgers, W. L., & Herzog, A. R. (1987). Interviewing older adults: The accuracy of factual information. *Journal of Gerontology, 42,* 387–394.

Schober, M. F. (in press). Making sense of questions: An interactional approach. In M. Sirken, D. Hermann, S. Schechter, N. Schwarz, J. Tanur, & R. Tourangeau (Eds.), *Cognition and survey research*. New York: Wiley.

Schuman, H., & Presser, S. (1981). *Questions and answers in attitude surveys*. New York: Academic Press.

Schwarz, N. (in press). Cognitive research into survey measurement: Its impact on cognitive theory and survey methodology. In M. Sirken, D. Hermann, S. Schechter, N. Schwarz, J. Tanur, & R. Tourangeau (Eds.), *Cognition and survey research*. New York: Wiley.

Schwarz, N., & Sudman, S. (Eds.). (1992). *Context effects in social and psychological re-search.* New York: Springer-Verlag.

Schwarz, N., & Sudman, S. (Eds.). (1996). *Answering questions: Methodology for determin-ing cognitive and communicative processes in survey research.* San Francisco: Jossey-Bass.

Suchman, L., & Jordan, B. (1990). Interactional troubles in face-to-face interviews. *Jour-nal of the American Statistical Association, 85,* 232–241.

Sudman, S., Bradburn, N., & Schwarz, N. (1996). *Thinking about answers: The application of cognitive processes to survey methodology.* San Francisco: Jossey-Bass.

U.S. Bureau of the Census. (1989). *Current population reports* (Series P-25, No. 1018). Washington, DC: Census Bureau.

PART

I

SELF-REPORTS AND COGNITIVE AGING

Norbert Schwarz

Self-Reports of Behaviors and Opinions: Cognitive and Communicative Processes

Social scientists have long been aware that minor changes in question wording, question format, or question order may profoundly affect the answers that research participants provide. In the survey literature, these influences of the research instrument are usually referred to as response effects or context effects. Over the last decade, researchers have made considerable progress in understanding the cognitive and communicative processes underlying the emergence of context effects, and this chapter provides an introduction to what has been learned. It draws on the collaborative work of cognitive psychologists, social psychologists, and survey methodologists, which was initiated in the early 1980s and has grown into an active field of basic and applied cognitive research (for a comprehensive review, see Sudman, Bradburn, & Schwarz, 1996; for research examples, see the contributions in Hippler, Schwarz, & Sudman, 1987; Jabine, Straf, Tanur, & Tourangeau, 1984; Jobe & Loftus, 1991; Schwarz & Sudman, 1992, 1994, 1996; Sirken, Hermann, Schechter, Schwarz, Tanur, & Tourangeau, in press; Tanur, 1992). Initially, this research was based on general information processing models developed in cognitive psychology (cf. Lachman, Lachman, & Butterfield, 1979). As the work progressed, however, it became increasingly clear that the information processing paradigm could only capture some of the key aspects of survey interviews. Most importantly, mainstream information processing models share an exclusive focus on individual thought processes. As many critics noted, this concentration on individuals as isolated information processors fostered a neglect of the social context in which human judgment occurs (cf. Forgas, 1981). The survey interview, however, is best considered as an ongoing conversation in which respondents conduct their own share of thinking and question answering in a specific social and conversational context. Hence, conceptualizations of the question-answering process need to consider conversational as well as cognitive processes and need to pay close attention to the complex interplay of social communication and individual thought processes (for more detailed discussions, see Clark & Schober, 1992; Schober, in press; Schwarz, 1994, 1996; Strack, 1992; Strack & Schwarz, 1992).

In the present chapter, I review key lessons from this interdisciplinary research. As will become apparent, this work has rarely addressed age-related differences in cognition and communication. Yet, the accumulating evidence pertaining to age-related changes in cognitive resources (Park, Chapter 3), memory (Craik, Chapter 5; Rubin, Chapter 8; Yoon, May, & Hasher, Chapter 6), metacognition (Cavanaugh, Chapter 7), and text comprehension (Kemper & Kemtes, Chapter 11) suggests that the cognitive components of the question-answering process are likely to be age sensitive. Similarly, research into age-related changes in speech processing (Wingfield, Chapter 10) and communication (Kwong See & Ryan, Chapter 12) indicates that at least some of the communicative components of the question-answering process are also likely to change over the life-span. If so, we may expect that older and younger respondents are differentially affected by our research instruments, and numerous findings reported in this book suggest that this is the case. This possibility has tremendous methodological implications for social research: If older and younger respondents are indeed differentially affected by the research instrument, any emerging age differences in the obtained data may reflect differential context effects rather than, or in addition to, actual age-related differences in the attitudes or behaviors under study. Unless we want to run the risk of misinterpreting age-sensitive context effects as evidence of substantive cohort differences or developmental changes, we therefore need to understand how changes in cognitive and communicative functioning over the life-span influence the response process. As a first step towards this goal, this chapter reviews the cognitive and communicative processes underlying self-reports to set the stage for the more detailed treatment of age-related changes in component processes in Chapters 3–12, and selected research examples in Chapters 13–18.

☐ Respondents' Tasks

From a cognitive perspective, answering a survey question requires that respondents solve several tasks. First, they need to interpret the question to understand what is meant. If the question is an opinion question, they may either retrieve a previously formed opinion from memory, or they may "compute" an opinion on the spot. While survey researchers have typically hoped for the former, the latter is far more likely even when respondents have previously formed an opinion that may still be accessible in memory. This reflects that their previously formed judgment may not match the specifics of the question asked. To compute a judgment that pertains to the question, respondents need to retrieve relevant information from memory to form a mental representation of the target that they are to evaluate. In most cases, they will also need to retrieve or construct some standard against which the target is evaluated. Once a "private" judgment is formed in their mind, respondents have to communicate it to the researcher. To do so, they may need to format their judgment to fit the response alternatives provided as part of the question. Moreover, respondents may wish to edit their response before they communicate it, due to influences of social desirability and situational adequacy.

Similar considerations apply to behavioral questions. Again, respondents first need to understand what the question refers to and which behavior they are supposed to report on. Next, they have to recall or reconstruct relevant instances of this behavior from memory. If the question specifies a reference period, they must also determine if the recalled instances occurred during this reference period or not. Similarly, if the question refers to their "usual" behavior, respondents have to determine if the recalled or reconstructed instances are reasonably representative or if they reflect a deviation from their usual behavior. If they cannot recall or reconstruct specific instances of the behavior, or are not sufficiently motivated to engage in this effort, respondents may rely on their general knowledge or other salient information that may bear on their task to compute an estimate. Finally, respondents have to provide their estimate to the researcher. They may need to map their estimate onto a response scale provided to them, and they may want to edit it for reasons of social desirability.

Accordingly, interpreting the question, generating an opinion or a representation of the relevant behavior, formatting the response, and editing the answer are the main psychological components of a process that starts with respondents' exposure to a survey question and ends with their overt report (Strack & Martin, 1987; Tourangeau, 1984). Although it is useful to present these tasks in a sequential order, respondents may not always follow this sequence, as we shall see below. Next, I address each of these steps in more detail.

Question Comprehension

The key issue at the question comprehension stage is whether the respondent's understanding of the question does or does not match what the researcher had in mind: Is the attitude object, or the behavior, that the respondent identifies as the target of the question the one that the researcher intended? Does the respondent's understanding tap the same facet of the issue and the same evaluative dimension? From a psychological point of view, question comprehension reflects the operation of two intertwined processes (see Clark & Schober, 1992; Strack & Schwarz, 1992).

The first refers to the semantic understanding of the utterance. Comprehending the literal meaning of a sentence involves the identification of words, the recall of lexical information from semantic memory, and the construction of a meaning of the utterance, which is constrained by its context. Not surprisingly, survey textbooks urge researchers to write simple questions and to avoid unfamiliar or ambiguous terms (e.g., Sudman & Bradburn, 1983). However, understanding the words is not sufficient to answer a question. For example, if respondents are asked "What have you done today?", they are likely to understand the meaning of the words. Yet, they still need to determine what kind of activities the researcher is interested in. Should they report, for example, that they took a shower, or not? Hence, understanding a question in a way that allows an appropriate answer requires not only an understanding of the literal meaning of the question, but involves inferences about the questioner's intention to determine the pragmatic meaning of the question.

To understand how respondents infer the intended meaning of a question, we need to consider the assumptions that govern the conduct of conversation in everyday life. These tacit assumptions were systematically described by Paul Grice (1975), a philosopher of language (see Clark & Schober, 1992; Schober, in press; Hilton, 1995; Schwarz, 1994, 1996; Strack, 1994; Strack & Schwarz, 1992, for applications to survey research and psychological experimentation). According to Grice's analysis, conversations proceed according to a cooperativeness principle. This principle can be expressed in the form of four maxims. There is a maxim of quality that enjoins speakers not to say anything they believe to be false or lack adequate evidence for, and a maxim of relation that enjoins speakers to make their contribution relevant to the aims of the ongoing conversation. In addition, a maxim of quantity requires speakers to make their contribution as informative as is required, but not more informative than is required, while a maxim of manner holds that the contribution should be clear rather than obscure, ambiguous, or wordy. In other words, speakers should try to be informative, truthful, relevant, and clear. As a result, "communicated information comes with a guarantee of relevance" (Sperber & Wilson, 1986, p. vi) and listeners interpret the speakers' utterances "on the assumption that they are trying to live up to these ideals" (Clark & Clark, 1977, p. 122). These tacit assumptions imply that all contributions of the researcher are considered relevant to the ongoing "conversation." These contributions include the content of preceding questions as well as apparently formal features of the questionnaire.

Formal Features of Questionnaires

Open vs. Closed Question Formats.   Suppose, for example, that respondents are asked in an open response format, "What have you done today?" To give a meaningful answer, respondents have to determine which activities may be of interest to the researcher. In an attempt to be informative, respondents are likely to omit activities that the researcher is obviously aware of (e.g., "I gave a survey interview") or may take for granted anyway (e.g., "I took a shower"). If respondents were given a list of activities that included giving an interview and taking a shower, most respondents would endorse them. At the same time, however, such a list would reduce the likelihood that respondents report activities that are not represented on the list (see Schuman & Presser, 1981; Schwarz & Hippler, 1991, for a review of relevant studies). Both of these question form effects reflect that response alternatives can clarify the intended meaning of a question, in the present example by specifying the activities the researcher is interested in, and may remind respondents of activities they may otherwise not consider. Whereas this example may seem rather obvious, more subtle influences are frequently overlooked.

Frequency Scales.   Suppose that respondents are asked how frequently they felt "really irritated" recently. To answer this question, they again have to determine what the researcher means by "really irritated." Does this term refer to major or to minor annoyances? To identify the intended meaning of the question, they may consult the response alternatives provided by the researcher. If the response alternatives present low-frequency categories, e.g., ranging from "less than once a year" to "more than once a month," they may conclude that the researcher has relatively rare events in mind and that the question cannot refer to minor irritations, which are likely to occur more often. In line with this assumption, Schwarz, Strack, Müller, and Chassein (1988) observed that respondents who had to report the frequency of irritating experiences on a low-frequency scale assumed that the question referred to major annoyances, whereas respondents who had to give their report on a high-frequency scale assumed that the question referred to minor annoyances. Thus, respondents identified different experiences as the target of the question, depending on the frequency range of the response alternatives provided to them.

The Numeric Values of Rating Scales. Similarly, Schwarz and Hippler (1995a; see also Schwarz, Knäuper, Hippler, Noelle-Neumann, & Clark, 1991) observed that respondents may use the specific numeric values provided as part of a rating scale to interpret the meaning of the scale's verbal endpoints. In their study, German adults were asked to evaluate politicians along an 11-point rating scale, ranging from "don't think very highly of this politician" (0 or –5) to "think very highly of this politician" (11 or +5). To answer this question, respondents have to determine the meaning of "don't think very highly of this politician": does this imply the absence of positive thoughts or the presence of negative thoughts? To do so, respondents draw on the numeric values of the rating scale, inferring that the label pertains to the presence of negative thoughts ("I have unfavorable thoughts about him") when accompanied by the numeric value –5, but to the absence of positive thoughts ("I have no particularly favorable thoughts about him") when accompanied by the numeric value 0. These differential interpretations of the verbal scale anchor are reflected in markedly different ratings: Whereas only 29.3% reported a rating below the midpoint along the –5 to +5 scale, fully 40.2% did so along the 0 to 10 scale, resulting in a difference of 11.5%. Obviously, politicians interested in high approval ratings would fare much better on the former scale.

Age-Related Differences. In combination, the above findings demonstrate that respondents use the response alternatives in interpreting the meaning of a question. In doing so, they proceed on the tacit assumption that every contribution is relevant to the aims of the ongoing conversation. In research situations, the researcher's contributions include apparently formal features of questionnaire design, such as the numeric values given on a rating scale. Hence, identically worded questions may acquire different meanings depending on the response alternatives by which they are accompanied (see Schwarz, 1996, for a more extensive discussion).

Are these processes likely to be affected by age-related changes in cognitive functioning? On the one hand, we can safely assume that older respondents share the tacit assumptions that underlie the conduct of conversation and are hence likely to draw on formal features of the questionnaire in much the same way as younger respondents. On the other hand, using these features to disambiguate the meaning of a question requires that respondents relate the text presented in the body of the question to the accompanying response alternatives, potentially requiring considerable cognitive resources. Given age-related decline in cognitive resources (see Park, Chapter 3), older respondents may therefore be less likely to arrive at an interpretation that reflects the integration of question wording and response alternatives.

Some preliminary data (Schwarz, Park, Knäuper, Davidson, & Smith, 1998) support the latter possibility. In a replication of Schwarz and Hippler's (1995a) experiment on the numeric values of rating scales, described above, younger and older respondents were asked to rate Bob Dole, the Republican candidate in the 1996 U.S. Presidential elections. Replicating the previous findings, younger respondents rated Bob Dole more positively when the verbal label "don't think highly of this politician" was accompanied by the numeric value –5 rather than the numeric value 0. Respondents aged 70 and older, however, provided the same ratings independent of the type of numeric values offered. This suggests that they did not draw on the numeric values in interpreting the meaning of the verbal labels, presumably because their limited cognitive resources did not allow them to relate the wording of the question and the numeric values to one another. Supporting this interpretation, we observed that the impact of numeric values varied as a function of respondents' reading span, a measure of cognitive resource. As expected, respondents high in cognitive resource related the text to the numeric values, whereas respondents low in cognitive resource did not.

Question Context

Respondents' interpretation of a question's intended meaning is further influenced by the context in which the question is presented. Not surprisingly, this influence is more pronounced, the more ambiguous the wording of the question is. As an extreme case, consider research in which respondents are asked to report their opinion about a highly obscure—or even completely fictitious—issue, such as the "Agricultural Trade Act of 1978" (e.g., Bishop, Oldendick, & Tuchfarber, 1986; Schuman & Presser, 1981). Questions of this type reflect the concern of public opinion researchers that the "fear of appearing uninformed" may induce "many respondents to conjure up opinions even when they had not given the particular issue any thought prior to the interview" (Erikson, Luttberg, & Tedin, 1988, p. 44). To explore how meaningful respondents' answers are, survey researchers introduced questions about issues that don't exist. Presumably, respondents' willingness to report an opinion on a fictitious issue casts some doubt on the reports provided in survey interviews in general. In fact, about 30% of the respondents do typically provide an answer to issues that are invented by the researcher. This has been interpreted as evidence of the operation of social pressure that induces respondents to give meaningless answers in the absence of any knowledge.

From a conversational point of view, however, the sheer fact that a question about some issue is asked presupposes that this issue exists; otherwise, asking a question about it would violate every norm of conversational conduct. But respondents have no reason to assume that the researcher would ask a meaningless question and will hence try to make sense of it. If the interviewer does not provide additional clarification, respondents are likely to turn to the context of the ambiguous question to determine its meaning, much as they would be expected to do in any other conversation. Once respondents have assigned a particular meaning to the issue, thus transforming the fictitious issue into a better defined issue that makes sense in the context of the interview, they may have no difficulty reporting a subjectively meaningful opinion. Even if they have not given the particular issue much thought, they may easily identify the broader set of issues to which it apparently belongs. They may then use their general attitude toward the broader set of issues to determine their attitude toward this particular one.

Supporting this assumption, Strack, Schwarz, and Wänke (1991, Experiment 1) observed that German university students reported different attitudes towards the introduction of a fictitious "educational contribution," depending on the nature of a preceding question. Specifically, some students were asked to estimate the average tuition fees that students have to pay at U.S. universities (in contrast to Germany, where university education is free), whereas others had to estimate the amount of money that the Swedish government pays every student as financial support. As expected, many of the respondents interpreted the subsequent question about the fictitious "educational contribution" to refer to students having to pay money in the former case, but to students receiving money in the latter case. Reflecting this differential interpretation, respondents reported a more favorable attitude toward the introduction of an "educational contribution" in Germany when the preceding question pertained to stipends students receive in Sweden than to tuition students have to pay in the United States.

Age-Related Differences.   Using the content of a preceding question in interpreting a subsequent one obviously requires that the preceding question is still accessible in memory. Secondary analyses of question order experiments, reviewed by Knäuper (Chapter 17), indicate that this often may not be the case for older respondents. As her data demonstrate, the size of question order effects decreases with increasing age. If this is true, older respondents may be less likely to draw on preceding questions than younger respondents, resulting in differential interpretations of subsequent questions, much as we have observed above for the numeric values of rating scales (Schwarz, Park, et al., 1998). This should be particularly likely in face-to-face and telephone interviews, where respondents cannot go back to earlier questions. In contrast, such age differences may be less pronounced in self-administered questionnaires, where respondents can deliberately return to previous questions when they encounter an ambiguous one (cf. Schwarz & Hippler, 1995b). Accordingly, the emergence of age-related differences in context-dependent question interpretation may to some extent depend on the mode of data collection (see Schwarz, Strack, Hippler, & Bishop, 1991, for a comparison of self-administered questionnaires, face-to-face interviews, and telephone interviews).

In addition, survey researchers have frequently observed that older respondents are more likely to offer a "don't know" (DK) response than younger respondents (e.g., Colsher & Wallace, 1989; Gergen & Back, 1966; Rodgers & Herzog, 1987). This may, in part, reflect that older respondents are less likely to draw on contextual information to arrive at an answer. Moreover, they may find it more legitimate that they "don't know" and hence may be not only more likely to volunteer this response, but also less motivated to invest considerable effort in drawing on contextual information. Finally, the hypothesis that older adults are more "cautious" (Botwinick, 1984) in their inferences and behavior suggests that they may also employ higher thresholds of certainty before they offer an opinion. The relative contribution of these factors to older adults' response behavior awaits empirical analysis.

Summary

As the preceding examples illustrate, question comprehension is not primarily an issue of understanding the literal meaning of an utterance. Rather, question comprehension involves extensive inferences about the speaker's intentions to determine the pragmatic meaning of the question. To make these inferences, respondents draw on the nature of preceding questions as well as the response alternatives. The limited available evidence suggests that older respondents may be less likely to make use of contextual information than younger respondents, resulting in systematic age-related differences in question interpretation—a possibility that renders the comparison of answers across age groups fraught with uncertainty.

Recalling or Computing a Judgment

Once respondents determine what the researcher is interested in, they need to recall relevant information from memory. In some cases, respondents may have direct access to a previously formed relevant judgment that they can offer as an answer. In most cases, however, they will not find an appropriate answer readily stored in memory and will need to compute a judgment on the spot. The processes involved in doing so are somewhat different for behavioral questions and attitude questions, and will be discussed in the respective sections below.

Formatting the Response

Once respondents have formed a judgment, they cannot typically report it in their own words. Rather, they are supposed to report it by endorsing one of the response alternatives provided by the researcher. This requires that they format their response in line with the options given. Accordingly, the researcher's choice of response alternatives may strongly affect the obtained results (see Schwarz & Hippler, 1991, for a review): First, respondents are more likely to endorse a response alternative presented in a closed-response format than to volunteer it in an open-response format, as discussed in the section on question comprehension. Second, the order in which response alternatives are presented affects the likelihood of their endorsement. This issue is addressed in detail by Knäuper (Chapter 17), who documents pronounced age differences in the emergence of response order effects.

Finally, the context in which a stimulus is rated affects respondents' use of rating scales (e.g., Ostrom & Upshaw, 1968; Parducci, 1983). Specifically, respondents use the most extreme stimuli to anchor the endpoints of a rating scale. As a result, a given stimulus will be rated as less extreme if presented in the context of a more extreme one than if presented in the context of a less extreme one. In Parducci's model, this impact of the range of stimuli is referred to as the "range effect." In addition, if the number of stimuli to be rated is sufficiently large, respondents attempt to use all categories of the rating scale about equally often. Accordingly, the specific ratings given also depend on the frequency distribution of the presented stimuli, an effect that is referred to as the "frequency effect." Daamen and de Bie (1992) provide an introduction to the logic of these processes and report several studies that illustrate their impact on survey results.

At present, the data bearing on age-related differences in response formatting are limited to the emergence of response order effects, discussed by Knäuper (Chapter 17). It seems likely, however, that the impact of contextual stimuli on the use of rating scales is also age dependent. Specifically, older respondents may be less likely to keep track of numerous stimuli presented to them, and of the ratings they assigned to each one. If so, we may expect that range as well as frequency effects are attenuated for older respondents, again raising the possibility that researchers may misinterpret differences in scale use as differences in the substantive opinion reported.

Editing the Response

Finally, respondents may want to edit their response before they communicate it, reflecting considerations of social desirability and self-presentation. DeMaio (1984) reviews the survey literature on this topic. Not surprisingly, the impact of self-presentation concerns is more pronounced in face-to-face interviews than in self-administered questionnaires.

It is important to emphasize, however, that influences of social desirability are limited to potentially threatening questions and are typically modest in size. Moreover, what constitutes a socially desirable response depends on the specifics of the situation. For example, several researchers (see Smith, 1979, for a review) observed that respondents report higher levels of happiness and satisfaction in face-to-face interviews than in self-administered questionnaires. In contrast, Strack, Schwarz, Chassein, Kern, and Wagner (1990) obtained a reversal of this effect under specific conditions. In their study, respondents reported deflated levels of happiness when they were interviewed by a handicapped interviewer, presumably because it seemed inappropriate to tell an unfortunate other how wonderful one's own life is. In contrast, the sheer presence of a handicapped confederate while respondents filled out a self-administered questionnaire resulted in increased reports of happiness, indicating that the handicapped person served as a salient standard of comparison, thus inflating respondents' private judgments. As this example illustrates, understanding issues of social desirability requires close attention to the actual social situation, which determines what is desirable and what is not.

Age-Related Differences. The observation that older respondents receive higher scores on social desirability scales (e.g., Gove & Geerken, 1977; Lewinsohn, Rohde, Seeley, & Fischer, 1993) suggests that socially desirable responding may increase with age. If so, this would have important methodological implications. Specifically, it suggests that differences in the obtained substantive responses may to some extent depend on the specific technique of data collection used: Older respondents may provide more socially acceptable answers in face-to-face interviews, but this difference may disappear under more anonymous modes of data collection. In the latter regard, survey researchers have developed a number of different technical procedures designed to ensure the confidentiality of respondents' reports and/or reduce respondents' concerns about their self-presentation. These procedures range from appropriate question wordings and sealed envelopes to complicated randomized response procedures, which allow the researcher to estimate the frequency of an undesirable behavior in the population without linking a given response to a given individual. Sudman and Bradburn (1983) review the various procedures in their chapter on threatening questions and provide detailed advice on how to use them. To what extent the use of such procedures affects age differences in the obtained reports, however, is an open issue.

Summary

This section reviewed what respondents must do to answer a question. For ease of exposition, respondents' tasks were presented in a sequential order. Although this order is plausible, respondents may obviously go back and forth between different steps, revising, for example, their initial question interpretation once the response alternatives suggest a different meaning. In any case, however, they have to determine the intended meaning of the question, recall relevant information from memory, form a judgment, and format the judgment to fit the response alternatives provided to them. Moreover, they may want to edit their private judgment before they communicate it. Next, I turn to specific considerations that pertain to behavioral reports and attitude questions.

☐ Answering Questions about Behaviors

Most survey questions about respondents' behavior are frequency questions, pertaining, for example, to how often the respondent has bought something, seen a doctor, or missed a day at work during some specified period of time. Researchers who ask these questions would ideally like the respondent to identify the behavior of interest, scan the reference period, retrieve all instances that match the target behavior, and count these instances to determine the overall frequency of the behavior. This, however, is the route that respondents are least likely to take.

In fact, except for rare and very important behaviors, respondents are unlikely to have detailed representations of numerous individual instances of a behavior stored in memory. Rather, the details of various instances of closely related behaviors blend into one global representation (Linton, 1982; Neisser, 1986). Thus, many individual episodes become indistinguishable or irretrievable, due to interference from other similar instances (Wagenaar, 1986; Baddeley & Hitch, 1977), fostering the generation of knowledge-like representations that "lack specific time or location indicators" (Strube, 1987, p. 89). The finding that a single spell of unemployment is more accurately recalled than multiple spells (Mathiowetz, 1986), for example, suggests that this phenomenon does not apply only to mundane and unimportant behaviors, but also to repeated experiences that profoundly affect an individual's life. Accordingly, a "recall and count" model does not capture how people answer questions about frequent behaviors or experiences. Rather, their answers are likely to be based on some fragmented recall and the application of inference rules to compute a frequency estimate (see Bradburn, Rips, & Shevell, 1987; Schwarz, 1990; Sudman et al., 1996, for extensive reviews and the contributions in Schwarz & Sudman, 1994, for research examples).

Estimation Strategies

The most important estimation strategies involve the decomposition of the recall problem into subparts, reliance on subjective theories of stability and change, and the use of information provided by the response alternatives.

Decomposition Strategies

Many recall problems become easier when the recall task is decomposed into several subtasks (e.g., Blair & Burton, 1987). To estimate how often she has been eating out during the last three months, for example, a respondent may determine that she eats out about every weekend and had dinner at a restaurant this Wednesday, but apparently not the week before. Thus, she may infer that this makes 4 times a month for the weekends, and let's say twice for other occasions, resulting in about "eighteen times during the last three months." Estimates of this type are likely to be accurate if the respondent's inference rule is adequate and if exceptions to the usual behavior are rare.

In the absence of these fortunate conditions, however, decomposition strategies are likely to result in overestimates. This reflects that people usually overestimate the occurrence of low-frequency events and underestimate the occurrence of high-frequency events (see Fiedler & Armbruster, 1994). As a result, asking for estimates of a global, and hence frequent, category (e.g., "eating out") is likely to elicit an underestimate, whereas asking for estimates of a narrow, and hence rare, category (e.g., "eating at a Mexican restaurant") is likely to elicit an overestimate. Therefore, the observation that decomposition usually results in higher estimates does not necessarily reflect better recall. To what extent the use of decomposition strategies is age dependent is currently unknown.

Subjective Theories

A particularly important inference strategy is based on subjective theories of stability and change (see Ross, 1989, for a review). In answering retrospective questions, respondents often use their current behavior or opinion as a benchmark and invoke an implicit theory of self to assess whether their past behavior or opinion was similar to, or different from, their present behavior or opinion. Assuming, for example, that one's political beliefs become more conservative over the life-span, older adults may infer that they held more liberal political attitudes as teenagers than they do now (Markus, 1986). The resulting reports of previous opinions and behaviors are correct to the extent that the implicit theory is accurate.

In many domains, individuals assume a rather high degree of stability, resulting in underestimates of the degree of change that has occurred over time. Accordingly, retrospective estimates of income (Withey, 1954), or of tobacco, marijuana, and alcohol consumption (Collins, Graham, Hansen, & Johnson, 1985) were found to be heavily influenced by respondents' income or consumption habits at the time of interview. On the other hand, when respondents have reason to believe in change, they will detect change, even though none has occurred. For example, participants in a study skills training inferred that their skills prior to training were much poorer than after training, even though the training had no measurable effect on actual performance (see Ross, 1989).

As this discussion indicates, retrospective reports of changes across the life-span will crucially depend on respondents' subjective theories. At present, we know relatively little about these subjective theories, nor do we know how these theories themselves change across the life-span. This provides a promising avenue for future research, which may greatly improve our understanding of retrospective reports.

Response Alternatives

A particularly important source of information that respondents use in arriving at an estimate is provided by the questionnaire itself. In many studies, respondents are asked to report their behavior by checking the appropriate alternative from a list of response alternatives of the type shown in Table 1. While the selected alternative is assumed to inform the researcher about the respondent's behavior, it is frequently overlooked that a given set of response alternatives may be far more than a simple "measurement device." Rather, it may also constitute a source of information for the respondent (see Schwarz, 1996; Schwarz & Hippler, 1991, for reviews), as we have already seen in the section on question comprehension.

Specifically, respondents assume that the range of the response alternatives provided to them reflects the researcher's knowledge of, or expectations about, the distribution of the behavior in the "real world." Accordingly, they assume that the values in the middle range of the scale reflect the "average" or "usual" behavioral frequency, whereas the extremes of the scale correspond to the extremes of the distribution. Given this assumption, respondents can use the range of the

TABLE 1.   REPORTED DAILY TV CONSUMPTION AS A FUNCTION OF RESPONSE ALTERNATIVES

Reported Daily TV Consumption			
Low Frequency Alternatives		**High Frequency Alternatives**	
Up to ½ h	7.4%	Up to 2½ h	62.5%
½ h to 1 h	17.7%	2½ h to 3 h	23.4%
1 h to 1½ h	26.5%	3 h to 3½ h	7.8%
1½ h to 2 h	14.7%	3½ h to 4 h	4.7%
2 h to 2½ h	17.7%	4 h to 4½ h	1.6%
More than 2½ h	16.2%	More than 4½ h	0.0%

Note. N = 132. Adapted from Schwarz, N., Hippler, H.J., Deutsch, B., and Strack, F. (1985). Response categories: Effects of category range on reported behavior and comparative judgments. *Public Opinion Quarterly, 49,* 388–395. Reprinted by permission.

response alternatives as a frame of reference in estimating their own behavioral frequency.

This strategy results in higher estimates along scales that present high- rather than low-frequency response alternatives, as shown in Table 1. In this study (Schwarz, Hippler, Deutsch, & Strack, 1985), only 16.2% of a sample of German respondents reported watching TV for more than 2½ hours a day when the scale presented low-frequency response alternatives, whereas 37.5% reported doing so when the scale presented high-frequency response alternatives. Similar results have been obtained for a wide range of different behaviors (see Schwarz, 1990, in press, for reviews).

Age-Related Differences. Not surprisingly, the impact of response alternatives is more pronounced the less well the behavior is represented in memory, thus forcing respondents to rely on an estimation strategy (Menon, Raghubir, & Schwarz, 1995). This suggests that the impact of response alternatives may typically be more pronounced for older than for younger respondents. The available data support this prediction with some qualifications. As shown in Table 2, Schwarz,

TABLE 2.   THE IMPACT OF RESPONSE ALTERNATIVES ON BEHAVIORAL REPORTS AS A FUNCTION OF CONTENT AND RESPONDENTS' AGE

	Frequency Scale		
	Low	High	Difference
Mundane behaviors			
Eating red meat			
Young	24%	43%	19%
Old	19%	63%	44%
Buying brithday presents			
Young	42%	49%	7%
Old	46%	61%	15%
Physical symptoms			
Headaches			
Young	37%	56%	19%
Old	11%	10%	1%
Heartburn			
Young	14%	33%	19%
Old	24%	31%	7%

Note. Younger respondents are age 29–40, older respondents, 60–90. Shown is the percentage of respondents reporting eating red meat more than 10 times a month or more often, buying birthday presents more than 5 times a year or more often, and having headaches or heartburn twice a month or more often.

Park, and Knäuper (reported in Schwarz, in press) observed that older respondents were more affected by the frequency range of the response scale when asked to report the frequency of mundane events, such as buying a birthday present. On the other hand, older respondents were less affected than younger respondents when the question pertained to the frequency of physical symptoms. In combination, these findings suggest that respondents of all ages draw on the response alternatives when they need to form an estimate. Yet, whether they need to form an estimate depends on how much attention they pay to the respective behavior, which itself is age dependent.

Importantly, we would again draw different conclusions about age-related differences in actual behavior from these reports, depending on the scale format used. We would conclude, for example, that age differences in red meat consumption (a health-relevant dietary behavior) or the purchase of birthday presents (an indicator of social integration) are minor when a low-frequency scale is used, but rather pronounced when a high-frequency scale is used. To avoid systematic influences of response alternatives, and the age-related differences in their impact, it is advisable to ask frequency questions in an open-response format, such as, "How many hours a day do you watch TV? ___ hours per day." Note that such an open format needs to specify the relevant units of measurement, e.g., "hours per day" to avoid answers like "a few." While the reports obtained under an open format are far from error-free, they are at least not systematically biased by the instrument (see Schwarz, 1990, for a discussion).

Summary

The findings reviewed in this section emphasize that retrospective behavioral reports are rarely based on adequate recall of relevant episodes. Rather, the obtained reports are to a large degree theory driven: Respondents are likely to begin with some fragmented recall of the behavior under study and to apply various inference rules to arrive at a reasonable estimate. Moreover, if quantitative response alternatives are provided, they are likely to use them as a frame of reference, resulting in systematic biases. Although researchers have developed a number of strategies to facilitate recall (which are described in Sudman et al., 1996, and the contributions in Schwarz & Sudman, 1994), it is important to keep in mind that the best we can hope for is a reasonable estimate, unless the behavior is rare and of considerable importance to respondents.

☐ Answering Attitude Questions

Like retrospective behavioral reports, respondents' answers to attitude questions are highly context dependent. As seen in the discussion of respondents' tasks, respondents' interpretation of a question, or the information they draw on in forming a judgment, may be strongly influenced by the specific wording of the question or by the content of preceding questions (see Schuman & Presser, 1981; Schwarz & Sudman, 1992; Tourangeau & Rasinski, 1988, for research examples and reviews). Sudman et al. (1996, Chaps. 3–6) provide a detailed discussion of different sources of context effects in the light of psychological theorizing. Unfortunately, a full discussion of this material is beyond the scope of the present chapter. Instead, I draw on one selected example to introduce basic theoretical principles and to illustrate the impact of question context on the results obtained in surveys as well as in the psychological laboratory.

Information Accessibility and Use

As many psychological experiments have documented, individuals are unlikely to retrieve all information that may potentially bear on a judgment, but truncate the search process as soon as enough information has come to mind to form a judgment with sufficient subjective certainty (see Bodenhausen & Wyer, 1987; Higgins, 1996; Schwarz, 1995, for reviews). Accordingly, their judgments strongly reflect the impact of the information that is most accessible in memory at the time of judgment. This is usually the information that has been used most recently, e.g., for the purpose of answering a preceding question.

The specific impact of the information that comes to mind depends on how it is used. In general, evaluative judgments require a mental representation of the target (i.e., the object of judgment) as well as a mental representation of some standard, against which the target is evaluated. If the information that comes to mind is included in the representation formed of the target, it results in an assimilation effect. That is, including a piece of information that has positive (negative) implications results in a more positive (negative) judgment. If the accessible information is excluded from the representation of the target, it may be used in constructing a representation of the standard. In this case, it results in a contrast effect. This reflects that the inclusion of some very positive (or negative) information in the representation of the standard results in a more positive (or negative) standard, relative to which the target is evaluated more negatively (or more positively, respectively). Schwarz and Bless's (1992) inclusion/exclusion model of evaluative judgment provides a detailed conceptualization of these processes.

Marital Satisfaction and the Quality of One's Life

Suppose that respondents are asked to evaluate how satisfied they are with their life as a whole. To answer this question, respondents may draw on a variety of different aspects of their lives and may evaluate them against a variety of different standards. Which aspects they actually draw on, however, may be influenced by which aspects were brought to mind by preceding questions.

In a test of this possibility, Schwarz, Strack, and Mai (1991; see also Strack, Martin, & Schwarz, 1988) asked respondents to report their marital satisfaction and their general life satisfaction and varied the order in which these questions were asked. The results are shown in Table 3. When the general satisfaction question preceded the marital satisfaction question, both questions were correlated $r = .32$, suggesting that marital satisfaction contributes moderately to one's overall well-being. When the question order was reversed, however, this correlation increased to $r = .67$, suggesting that marital satisfaction is a major determinant of overall well-being. This increase in correlation reflects that answering the marital satisfaction question brought information about one's marriage to mind, which respondents included in the representation that they formed of their lives in general.

If so, the increase in correlation should be less pronounced when the

---

TABLE 3.   CORRELATION OF GENERAL LIFE-SATISFACTION AND MARITAL SATISFACTION

Condition	
Life-marriage	.32
Marriage-life	.67
Work, leisure, marriage-life	.46
Marriage-life, with joint lead-in	.18
Marriage-life, "aside . . ."	.20

Note. Shown are Pearson correlations. $N = 50$ per cell. Adapted from Schwarz, N., Strack, F., and Mai, H. P. (1991). Assimilation and contrast effects in part-whole question sequences: A conversational logic analysis. *Public Opinion Quarterly, 55,* 3–23. Reprinted by permission.

preceding questions bring a more varied set of information to mind, as may be the case when respondents are asked to report on their work and leisure time in addition to their marriage. Consistent with this assumption, the observed increase in the correlation of marital satisfaction and general life satisfaction was less pronounced ($r = .46$) and not significant, when questions about several specific life-domains preceded the general one. This reflects that the impact of a given piece of information, e.g., pertaining to one's marriage, decreases as the amount of accessible competing information increases (see Schwarz & Bless, 1992).

However, highly accessible information is not always included in the representation formed of the target (in the present case, the target "my life"). One of the many variables that discourages inclusion (see Schwarz & Bless, 1992, for a discussion of other variables) is the conversational norm of nonredundancy. Specifically, one of the principles that govern the conduct of conversation in everyday life (Grice, 1975) requests speakers to make their contribution as informative as is required for the purpose of the conversation, but not more informative than is required. In particular, speakers are not supposed to be redundant and to provide information that the respondent already has. Hence, respondents may hesitate to reiterate information that they have already provided in response to a preceding question. Accordingly, respondents who have just reported their marital happiness may consider the subsequent question about their happiness with life as a whole to be a request for new information. They may therefore interpret the general question to refer to other aspects of their life, much as if it were worded, "Aside from your marriage, how happy do you feel about the other aspects of your life?"

To test this possibility, Schwarz, Strack, and Mai (1991; see also Strack et al., 1988) explicitly assigned both questions to the same conversational context, by introducing them with a joint lead-in that read, "Now, we would like to learn about two areas of life that may be important for people's overall well-being: (a) happiness with marriage; and (b) happiness with life in general." Subsequently, both happiness questions were asked in the specific–general order, which had resulted in a correlation of $r = .67$ without this introduction. When both questions were introduced by a joint lead-in, however, this correlation dropped to a nonsignificant $r = .18$. This reflects that respondents deliberately ignored information that they had already provided in response to a specific question when making a subsequent general judgment when the joint lead-in evoked the conversational norm of nonredundancy. In this case, respondents apparently interpreted the general question as if it referred to aspects of their life that they had not yet reported on. In line with this interpretation, a condition in which respondents were explicitly asked how satisfied they are with "other aspects" of their life, "aside from their relationship," yielded a nearly identical correlation of $r = .20$. As the range of obtained correlations, from $r = .18$ to $r = .67$, illustrates, we would draw very different conclusions from the answers given to two identically worded questions, depending on the order in which they were asked and whether or not they were introduced by a joint lead-in.

Moreover, this impact of question order is not limited to the obtained correlations but is also reflected in respondents' mean reported life satisfaction. For example, unhappily married respondents (i.e., the 1/3 of the sample that reported the lowest marital satisfaction) reported a mean general life satisfaction of $M = 6.8$ (with 11 = "very satisfied") when the general question was asked first. When a preceding question about their marital satisfaction brought their unhappy marriage to mind, however, their reported general life satisfaction dropped to $M = 5.8$. Yet, when the joint lead-in induced them to disregard their marriage, the rest of life didn't seem so bad, resulting in a markedly increased report of $M = 8.0$ for general life satisfaction. The reports of happily married respondents (i.e., the 1/3 of the sample reporting the highest marital satisfaction) provided a mirror image of these findings.

Age-Related Differences

Although relevant data bearing on the above example are not available, it is informative to consider how age-related changes in cognitive functioning (see Park, Chapter 3) may affect the obtained results. As a first possibility, the findings reviewed by Knäuper (Chapter 17) suggest that the information brought to mind by preceding questions may decay quickly from memory, thus eliminating the question order effects observed above. If so, answering the marital satisfaction question first would not result in an increased correlation of marital and general life satisfaction for older respondents, potentially leading researchers to conclude that the importance of marriage decreases with increasing age.

As a second possibility, suppose that the marriage-related information remains accessible for older respondents, for example, because the topic is involving and of high personal relevance. Would age-related differences in cognitive functioning affect how respondents use this accessible information? Should we expect, for example, that older respondents are as likely as younger respondents to avoid redundancy when both questions are presented with a joint lead-in? Several lines of arguments suggest that we may obtain pronounced age differences in this respect.

First, avoiding redundancy requires that a respondent (a) keep track of the content of preceding questions and answers, (b) recognize their relatedness and possible redundancy, (c) partial out the previously provided information, and (d) base the judgment on "new" information. Some research in the domain of interpersonal communication suggests that older respondents may already encounter difficulties at the first step, namely, keeping track of the common ground established earlier in the conversation. For example, Hupet, Chantraine, and Neff (1993) studied how older and younger respondents arrive at mutually agreed upon references for abstract objects and use these references in subsequent exchanges. They observed that younger respondents were "more collaborative in the sense that they were more likely to take previously shared information into account in the referencing process" (p. 345). In contrast, older respondents were less likely to draw on the previously shared information, suggesting that they found it more difficult to keep track of the already established common ground and to take the recipient's perspective.

At present, it is unclear to what extent this difficulty reflects that memory limitations render it difficult to (a) track previous contributions or (b) mentally represent the requirements of the communication partner. In either case, the observation that older adults are less likely to pay attention to the previously established common ground suggests that they may also be less likely to recognize potential redundancy in extended question-answer sequences. Moreover, when they do recognize the potential redundancy, they may find it difficult to partial out the previously provided information. Finally, they may not have the cognitive capacity to retrieve additional "new" information to arrive at a nonredundant judgment. If so, corrections for potential redundancy may not be obtained with older respondents.

Another line of reasoning leads to the same prediction. Survey interviewers frequently report that they find it more difficult to keep older respondents focused on the task. In many ways, older respondents seem more likely to treat the interview as a social event rather than a task-oriented exchange of information. As Higgins (1981) noted, however, the type of social encounter influences the extent to which Gricean conversational norms are adhered to. When we try to entertain one another, for example, we may deliberately repeat information that is not new to the recipient. If older respondents are more likely to pursue social goals in the interview, they may find reiterations less inappropriate than younger respondents, who consider the interview a task-oriented exchange of information and who may be more motivated to get done with it as quickly as possible. If so, redundancy avoidance may again be less likely for older respondents.

If such age-related differences in redundancy avoidance emerged, they could again lead us to rather different substantive conclusions: In the above study (Schwarz, Strack, & Mai, 1991), redundancy avoidance resulted in low correlations of marital satisfaction and life satisfaction. If older respondents were less likely to make these adjustments, the resulting higher correlation might easily lead a researcher to conclude that the contribution of marital satisfaction to overall well-being increases over the life-span.

☐ Conclusions

As the reviewed examples illustrate, minor differences in question wording, question format, and question order may greatly influence the obtained results in representative sample surveys as well as in the psychological laboratory. Over the last decade, researchers have made considerable progress in understanding the cognitive and communicative processes underlying the emergence of context effects in self-reports of behaviors and attitudes. Despite this progress, however, we know little about the impact of age-related changes in cognitive and communicative functioning on the question-answering process. The little we do know, however, is cause for considerable concern: Not surprisingly, age-related differences in cognitive resources, memory, text comprehension, speech processing, and communication can have a profound impact on the components of the question-answering process, resulting in differential context effects for older and younger respondents. Several research examples illustrate that age-sensitive context effects may lead us to conclude that older and younger respondents differ in their attitudes or behaviors under one question format or question order, yet, we would conclude that no age difference exists under another question format or question order. If we want to avoid the misinterpretation of age-sensitive methods effects as substantive findings, we need to understand how age-related changes in cognitive and communicative functioning interact with the features of our research instruments in shaping respondents' reports. Exploring this thorny issue provides a challenging avenue for future interdisciplinary research that promises to advance our theoretical understanding of human cognition and communication across the life-span and to improve the methodology of social research.

☐ Acknowledgments

Preparation of this chapter was supported by grant AG14111-01 from the National Institute of Aging to N. Schwarz, D. Park, and B. Knäuper. I thank Bärbel Knäuper and Denise Park for helpful comments on a previous draft.

☐ References

Baddeley, A. D., & Hitch, G. J. (1977). Recency examined. In S. Dornic (Ed.), *Attention and performance* (Vol. 6, pp. 647–667). Hillsdale, NJ: Erlbaum.

Bishop, G. F., Oldendick, R. W., & Tuchfarber, R. J. (1986). Opinions on fictitious issues: The pressure to answer survey questions. *Public Opinion Quarterly, 50,* 240–250.

Blair, E., & Burton, S. (1987). Cognitive processes used by survey respondents to answer behavioral frequency questions. *Journal of Consumer Research, 14,* 280–288.

Bodenhausen, G. V., & Wyer, R. S. (1987). Social cognition and social reality: Information acquisition and use in the laboratory and the real world. In H. J. Hippler, N. Schwarz, & S. Sudman (Eds.), *Social information processing and survey methodology* (pp. 6–41). New York: Springer-Verlag.

Botwinick, J. (1984). *Aging and behavior* (3rd ed.). New York: Springer-Verlag.

Bradburn, N. M., Rips, L. J., & Shevell, S. K. (1987). Answering autobiographical questions: The impact of memory and inference on surveys. *Science, 236,* 157–161.

Clark, H. H., & Clark, E. V. (1977). *Psychology and language.* New York: Harcourt, Brace, Jovanovich.

Clark, H. H., & Schober, M. F. (1992). Asking questions and influencing answers. In J. M. Tanur (Ed.), *Questions about questions* (pp. 15–48). New York: Russell Sage.

Collins, L. M., Graham, J. W., Hansen, W. B., & Johnson, C. A. (1985). Agreement between retrospective accounts of substance use and earlier reported substance use. *Applied Psychological Measurement, 9,* 301–309.

Colsher, P. L., & Wallace, R. B. (1989). Data quality and age. *Journal of Gerontology: Psychological Sciences, 44,* P45–P52.

Daamen, D. D. ,L., & de Bie, S. E. (1992). Serial context effects in survey items. In N. Schwarz & S. Sudman (Eds.), *Context effects in social and psychological research* (pp. 97–114). New York: Springer-Verlag.

DeMaio, T. J. (1984). Social desirability and survey measurement: A review. In C. F. Turner & E. Martin (Eds.), *Surveying subjective phenomena* (Vol. 2, pp. 257–281). New York: Russell Sage.

Erikson, R. S., Luttberg, N. R., & Tedin, K. T. (1988). *American public opinion* (3rd ed.). New York: Macmillan.

Fiedler, K., & Armbruster, T. (1994). Two halfs may be more than one whole: Category-split effects on frequency illusions. *Journal of Personality and Social Psychology, 66,* 633–645.

Forgas, J. P. (1981). What is social about social cognition? In J. P. Forgas (Ed.), *Social cognition. Perspectives on everyday understanding* (pp. 1–26). New York: Academic Press.

Gergen, K. J., & Back, K. W. (1966). Communication in the interview and the disengaged respondent. *Public Opinion Quarterly, 30,* 385–398.

Gove, W. R., & Geerken, M. R. (1977). Response bias in surveys of mental health: An empirical investigation. *American Journal of Sociology, 82,* 1289–1317.

Grice, H. P. (1975). Logic and conversation. In P. Cole, & J. L. Morgan (Eds.), *Syntax and semantics, Vol. 3: Speech acts* (pp. 41–58). New York: Academic Press.

Higgins, E. T. (1981). The 'communication game': Implications for social cognition and communication. In E. T. Higgins, M. P. Zanna, & C. P. Herman (Eds.), *Social cognition: The Ontario Symposium* (Vol. 1, pp. 343–392). Hillsdale, NJ: Erlbaum.

Higgins, E. T. (1996). Knowledge activation: Accessibility, applicability, and salience. In E. T. Higgins & A. Kruglanski (Eds.), *Social psychology: Handbook of basic principles* (pp. 133–168). New York: Guilford Press.

Hilton, D. J. (1995). The social context of reasoning: Conversational inference and rational judgment. *Psychological Bulletin, 118,* 248–271.

Hippler, H. J., Schwarz, N., & Sudman, S. (Eds.). (1987). *Social information processing and survey methodology.* New York: Springer-Verlag.

Hupet, M., Chantraine, Y., & Neff, F. (1993). Changes in repeated references: Collaboration or repetition effects? *Psychology and Aging, 8,* 339–346.

Jabine, T. B., Straf, M. L., Tanur, J. M., & Tourangeau, R. (Eds.). (1984). *Cognitive aspects of survey methodology: Building a bridge between disciplines.* Washington, DC: National Academy Press.

Jobe, J., & Loftus, E. (Eds.). (1991). Cognitive aspects of survey methodology. [Special issue]. *Applied Cognitive Psychology, 5.*

Lachman, R., Lachman J. T., & Butterfield, E. C. (1979). *Cognitive psychology and information processing.* Hillsdale, NJ: Erlbaum.

Lewinsohn, P. M., Rohde, P., Seeley, J. R., & Fischer, S. A. (1993). Age-cohort changes in the lifetime occurrence of depression and other mental disorders. *Journal of Abnormal Psychology, 102,* 110–120.

Linton, M. (1982). Transformations of memory in everyday life. In U. Neisser (Ed.), *Memory observed: Remembering in natural contexts* (pp. 77–91). San Francisco: Freeman.

Markus, G. B. (1986). Stability and change in political attitudes: Observed, recalled, and explained. *Political Behavior, 8,* 21–44.

Mathiowetz, N. A. (1986, June). *Episodic recall and estimation: Applicability of cognitive theories to survey data.* Paper presented at the Social Science Research Council Seminar on Retrospective Data, New York.

Menon, G., Raghubir, P., & Schwarz, N. (1995). Behavioral frequency judgments: An accessibility-diagnosticity framework. *Journal of Consumer Research, 22,* 212–228.

Neisser, U. (1986). Nested structure in autobiographical memory. In D. C. Rubin (Ed.), (1986). *Autobiographical memory* (pp. 71–88). Cambridge, UK: Cambridge University Press.

Ostrom, T. M., & Upshaw, H. S. (1968). Psychological perspective and attitude change. In A. C. Greenwald, T. C. Brock, & T. M. Ostrom (Eds.), *Psychological foundations of attitudes.* New York: Academic Press.

Parducci, A. (1983). Category ratings and the relational character of judgment. In H. G. Geissler, H. F. J. M. Bulfart, E. L. H. Leeuwenberg, and V. Sarris (Eds.), *Modern issues in perception* (pp. 262–282). Berlin: VEB Deutscher Verlag der Wissenschaften.

Rodgers, W. L., & Herzog, A. R. (1987). Interviewing older adults: The accuracy of factual information. *Journal of Gerontology, 42,* 387–394.

Ross, M. (1989). The relation of implicit theories to the construction of personal histories. *Psychological Review, 96,* 341–357.

Schober, M. F. (in press). Making sense of questions: An interactional approach. In M. Sirken, D. Hermann, S. Schechter, N. Schwarz, J. Tanur, & R. Tourangeau (Eds.), *Cognition and survey research.* New York: Wiley.

Schuman, H., & Presser, S. (1981). *Questions and answers in attitude surveys*. New York: Academic Press.

Schwarz, N. (1990). Assessing frequency reports of mundane behaviors: Contributions of cognitive psychology to questionnaire construction. In C. Hendrick & M. S. Clark (Vol. Eds.), *Review of personality and social psychology: Vol. 11. Research methods in personality and social psychology* (pp. 98–119). Beverly Hills, CA: Sage.

Schwarz, N. (1994). Judgment in a social context: Biases, shortcomings, and the logic of conversation. In M. Zanna (Ed.), *Advances in experimental social psychology* (Vol. 26, pp. 123–162). San Diego, CA: Academic Press.

Schwarz, N. (1995). Social cognition: Information accessibility and use in social judgment. In D. N. Osherson & E. E. Smith (Eds.), *Thinking. An invitation to cognitive science* (Vol. 3, 2nd ed., pp. 345–376). Cambridge, MA: MIT Press.

Schwarz, N. (1996). *Cognition and communication: Judgmental biases, research methods and the logic of conversation*. Hillsdale, NJ: Erlbaum.

Schwarz, N. (in press). Frequency reports of physical symptoms and health behaviors: How the questionnaire determines the results. In D. C. Park, R. W Morrell, & K. Shifren (Eds.), *Processing medical information in aging patients: Cognitive and human factors perspectives*. Mahwah, NJ: Erlbaum.

Schwarz, N., & Bless, H. (1992). Constructing reality and its alternatives: Assimilation and contrast effects in social judgment. In L. L. Martin & A. Tesser (Eds.), *The construction of social judgments* (pp. 217–245). Hillsdale, NJ: Erlbaum.

Schwarz, N., & Hippler, H. J. (1991). Response alternatives: The impact of their choice and ordering. In P. Biemer, R. Groves, N. Mathiowetz, & S. Sudman (Eds.), *Measurement error in surveys* (pp. 41–56). Chichester, UK: Wiley.

Schwarz, N., & Hippler, H. J. (1995a). The numeric values of rating scales: A comparison of their impact in mail surveys and telephone interviews. *International Journal of Public Opinion Research, 7*, 72–74.

Schwarz, N., & Hippler, H. J. (1995b). Subsequent questions may influence answers to preceding questions in mail surveys. *Public Opinion Quarterly, 59*, 93–97.

Schwarz, N., Hippler, H. J., Deutsch, B. & Strack, F. (1985). Response categories: Effects on behavioral reports and comparative judgments. *Public Opinion Quarterly, 49*, 388–395.

Schwarz, N., Knäuper, B., Hippler, H. J., Noelle-Neumann, E., & Clark, F. (1991). Rating scales: Numeric values may change the meaning of scale labels. *Public Opinion Quarterly, 55*, 570–582.

Schwarz, N., Park, D. C., Knäuper, B., Davidson, N., & Smith, P. (1998, April). *Aging, cognition, and self-reports: Age-dependent context effects and misleading conclusions about age-differences in attitudes and behavior*. Paper presented at Cognitive Aging Conference, Atlanta, GA.

Schwarz, N., Strack, F., Hippler, H. J., & Bishop, G. (1991). The impact of administration mode on response effects in survey measurement. *Applied Cognitive Psychology, 5*, 193–212.

Schwarz, N., Strack, F., & Mai, H. P. (1991). Assimilation and contrast effects in part-whole question sequences: A conversational logic analysis. *Public Opinion Quarterly, 55*, 3–23.

Schwarz, N., Strack, F., Müller, G., & Chassein, B. (1988). The range of response alternatives may determine the meaning of the question: Further evidence on informative functions of response alternatives. *Social Cognition, 6*, 107–117.

Schwarz, N., & Sudman, S. (Eds.). (1992). *Context effects in social and psychological research*. New York: Springer-Verlag.

Schwarz, N. & Sudman, S. (1994). *Autobiographical memory and the validity of retrospective reports*. New York: Springer-Verlag.

Schwarz, N., & Sudman, S. (1996). *Answering questions: Methodology for determining cognitive and communicative processes in survey research.* San Francisco: Jossey-Bass.

Sirken, M., Hermann, D., Schechter, S., Schwarz, N., Tanur, J., & Tourangeau, R. (Eds.). (in press). *Cognition and survey research.* New York: Wiley.

Smith, T. W. (1979). Happiness. *Social Psychology Quarterly, 42,* 18–30.

Sperber, D., & Wilson, D. (1986). *Relevance: Communication and cognition.* Cambridge, MA: Harvard University Press.

Strack, F. (1992). Order effects in survey research: Activative and informative functions of preceding questions. In N. Schwarz & S. Sudman (Eds.), *Context effects in social and psychological research* (pp. 23–34). New York: Springer-Verlag.

Strack, F. (1994). *Zur Psychologie der standardisierten Befragung.* Heidelberg, FRG: Springer Verlag.

Strack, F., & Martin, L. (1987). Thinking, judging, and communicating: A process account of context effects in attitude surveys. In H.J. Hippler, N. Schwarz, & S. Sudman (Eds.), *Social information processing and survey methodology* (pp. 123–148). New York: Springer-Verlag.

Strack, F., Martin, L. L., & Schwarz, N. (1988). Priming and communication: The social determinants of information use in judgments of life-satisfaction. *European Journal of Social Psychology, 18,* 429–442.

Strack, F., & Schwarz, N. (1992). Implicit cooperation: The case of standardized questioning. In G. Semin & F. Fiedler (Eds.), *Social cognition and language* (pp. 173–193). Beverly Hills, CA: Sage.

Strack, F., Schwarz, N., Chassein, B., Kern, D., & Wagner, D. (1990). The salience of comparison standards and the activation of social norms: Consequences for judgments of happiness and their communication. *British Journal of Social Psychology, 29,* 303–314.

Strack, F., Schwarz, N., & Wänke, M. (1991). Semantic and pragmatic aspects of context effects in social and psychological research. *Social Cognition, 9,* 111–125.

Strube, G. (1987). Answering survey questions: The role of memory. In H. J. Hippler, N. Schwarz, & S. Sudman (Eds.), *Social information processing and survey methodology* (pp. 86–101). New York: Springer-Verlag.

Sudman, S., & Bradburn, N. M. (1983). *Asking questions.* San Francisco: Jossey-Bass.

Sudman, S., Bradburn, N., & Schwarz, N. (1996). *Thinking about answers: The application of cognitive processes to survey methodology.* San Francisco, CA: Jossey-Bass.

Tanur, J. M. (Ed.). (1992). *Questions about questions.* New York: Russell Sage.

Tourangeau, R. (1984). Cognitive science and survey methods: A cognitive perspective. In T. Jabine, M. Straf, J. Tanur, & R. Tourangeau (Eds.), *Cognitive aspects of survey methodology: Building a bridge between disciplines* (pp. 73–100). Washington, DC: National Academy Press.

Tourangeau, R., & Rasinski, K. A. (1988). Cognitive processes underlying context effects in attitude measurement. *Psychological Bulletin, 103,* 299–314.

Wagenaar, W. A. (1986). My memory: A study of autobiographical memory over six years. *Cognitive Psychology, 18,* 225–252.

Withey, S. B. (1954). Reliability of recall of income. *Public Opinion Quarterly, 18,* 31–34.

CHAPTER **3**

Denise C. Park

Cognitive Aging, Processing Resources, and Self-Report

What are the implications of an aging cognitive system for providing accurate answers to questions—questions about one's health, one's life, one's opinions about politicians and public policy? In raising this question, the issue of primary concern is not whether accuracy at answering questions simply declines with age, but more importantly, whether the nature of biases present in question answering is interactive with age. This chapter provides an overview of cognitive mechanisms that are age sensitive and that may cause older people to answer questions differently from young adults due to capacity limitations. In this chapter, I will initially describe age differences in fundamental cognitive mechanisms that are indices of how much mental processing power or cognitive resource an individual might bring to bear in a situation. I hypothesize that age-related decline in these fundamental mechanisms has substantial implications for performance of many everyday activities, including survey responses, the use of technology, driving in unfamiliar environments, managing finances, managing medications, and making medical decisions (Park, 1997, in press).

The conceptualization of what is meant by cognitive resources is empirically well defined in the cognitive aging literature. Before discussing empirical measures of the construct, it is worthwhile to point out what a pervasive and intuitive construct it is. The concept of resource permeates our everyday discourse about our cognitive processes. Statements from older adults to the effect that "I'm not as sharp as I used to be"; "I'm much fresher in the morning and don't think as well at night"; "I just don't have it today"; or "I didn't feel well and couldn't remember what you told me" are all reflections of a socially shared cognitive metaphor about the need for cognitive resources to perform mental tasks. Implicit in the metaphor is that there is a pool of mental energy that can be brought to bear in situations to help solve problems or manipulate information, and that this resource somehow declines as one gets older, becomes tired, or is ill. Although notions of fatigue, illness, and low energy have all been applied in the past to views of what cognitive aging might be like (Craik & Byrd, 1982), resource models of aging are actually considerably more precise than this. Generally, all resource views of cognitive aging have as a common element that as one gets older, one has less on-line ability and that this limits one's ability to perform mental tasks. What is at issue among different conceptualizations is what underlying mechanism accounts for this apparent limitation on processing capacity or resource. This is an extraordinarily important issue in cognitive aging, because many cognitive aging scientists believe that these fundamental mechanisms drive all subsequent cognitive function (e.g., Salthouse, 1996).

The focus of this chapter is on aging and processing mechanisms. This chapter might be viewed as the "bad news" of cognitive aging given that there is compelling evidence that these processing mechanisms decline with age. Despite the present focus on bad news, there is also some "good news." It is naive to think of older adults' cognitive system only in terms of processing mechanisms and capabilities. It is also important to recognize that older adults bring vast stores of knowledge and experiences to situations and that there is considerable evidence that access to much of this information is maintained across the lifespan, and even grows as one continues to have experiences and learn new information. Perhaps a useful analogy is to conceptualize the aging cognitive system as a computer with a large hard disk that has an enormous amount of information stored on it, but the hard disk is part of a computer with limited random access memory. In this situation, we all know that the computer will behave in a slow and somewhat labored manner, despite its vast informational resources, because the processing capacity of the computer is not sufficient to use all of the information stored on it in an efficient manner. The computer works, but perhaps a little less efficiently than one would like.

One of the major challenges of cognitive aging research that has not necessarily been met by researchers to date is to understand the meaning of simultaneous growth of knowledge and decline of processing efficiency, particularly in everyday life. This would seem to be an issue that is very important for understanding changes in the nature of self-report data or survey responses with age. There is a strong resource-based processing component to answering questions, but answering questions also requires accessing existing knowledge stores to construct experiences, attitudes, feelings, and past autobiographical behaviors. Aspects of this issue are addressed in the next chapter by Roger Dixon as well as in Chapter 8 by David Rubin on autobiographical memories.

Before launching into a detailed discussion of the construct of processing resources, I will characterize cognitive function across the life-span by providing an overview of performance on a range of cognitive tasks. Then I will present four different but related views of mechanisms hypothesized to account for these cognitive aging effects, and discuss how the constructs associated with each view are related to one another. I will discuss how each mechanism could potentially have important effects on the responses of older adults in self-report situations, as well as more generally in other daily tasks. The final section of the chapter will describe a range of findings from our laboratory demonstrating that age-related declines in processing resource limitations sometimes have important implications for function in everyday life, but there are also cases where experience and practice minimize the impact of resource limitations.

☐ Overview of Findings from the Cognitive Aging Literature

In a recent study, we collected multiple measures of cognitive function from a life-span sample of 301 older adults aged 20–90 (Park et al., 1996). We measured performance on a broad range of cognitive tasks including speed of processing, working memory, free recall, cued recall, and vocabulary knowledge. Speed of processing is a measure of how rapidly individuals can make simple same/different comparisons of symbols, patterns, or letters in a short period of time. Working memory measures subjects' ability to simultaneously manipulate and store information in an on-line fashion, by asking subjects to answer a question about a sentence or an equation while at the same time remembering an element of the sentence or equation. In free recall tasks, subjects are presented with words to study and asked to remember as many as they can in any order, whereas in cued recall they are presented with word pairs for study and must recall the target word in the pair when later presented with the cue item. Figure 1 provides evidence for systematic declines in performance across the life-span on speed of processing, working memory, and free and cued recall tasks. The declines are regular, generally linear, and of considerable

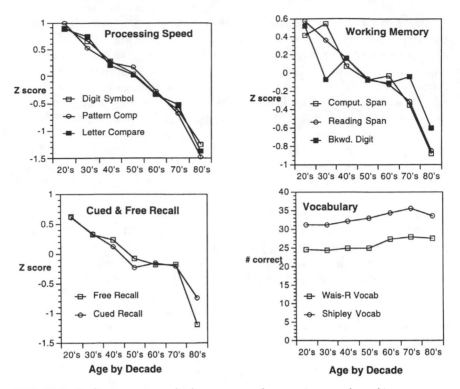

FIGURE 1. Performance on multiple measures of processing speed, working memory, cued and free recall, and vocabulary across the life-span from a sample of 301 community-dwelling adults. Adapted from Park et al. (1996).

magnitude. Notice, however, that the measure of world knowledge presented in Figure 1 (vocabulary) does not show age-related decline. It appears that measures of knowledge or crystallized intelligence are somewhat more stable across the life-span.

Generally, age differences are not found on memory tasks that are less effortful in terms of their cognitive resource requirements. Figure 2 shows that when young and old subjects are asked to recognize pictures that they studied earlier, there are no age differences in their ability to recognize these meaningful pictures (Park, Puglisi, & Smith, 1986). This age-invariance in recognition occurs both when the pictures are relatively simple drawings of objects and when they are drawings of rich complex scenes. Picture recognition is a relatively passive process that may be based on feelings of familiarity or automatic processes rather than active, effortful retrieval. Jacoby (1991) has demonstrated convincingly that the familiarity component of memory is age invariant. In a similar vein, Park and Shaw (1992) have demonstrated that there are

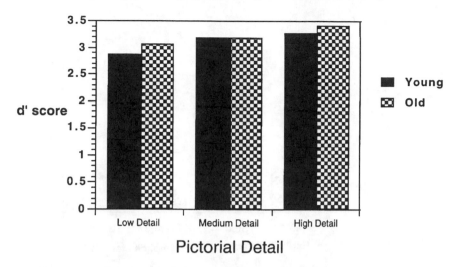

Pictorial Detail

FIGURE 2. The effects of three levels of pictorial detail on picture recognition as measured by d' scores. Adapted from Park, Puglisi, and Smith (1986).

large differences in explicit memory for words but not in implicit memory, as depicted in Figure 3. In the explicit recall task, subjects studied words and were later shown word stems that included the first three or four letters of the studied words. Subjects were told to recall words that they had studied. Under these conditions of deliberate retrieval, large age differences emerged in recall. However, when subjects were told to complete the word stems with any words that came to mind, an indirect retrieval task, young and old adults showed equivalent amounts of word-stem completion with studied words. The indirect retrieval task is a situation that does not require a directed, effortful memory search. The data presented in Figures 1–3 are typical of the laboratory findings in cognitive aging. Generally, studies indicate that there are declines in tasks that require a great deal of self-initiated processing (Craik & Jennings, 1992) but age-invariance on less effortful retrieval tasks (see Light, 1991 for more discussion of these issues) or on tasks that rely more on acquired world knowledge (e.g., vocabulary scores) rather than active cognitive processing. These are the patterns of data that theories of cognitive aging must explain.

☐ Mechanisms of Cognitive Aging

There are four important mechanisms that have been hypothesized to account for age differences in cognitive functioning: (a) the speed at

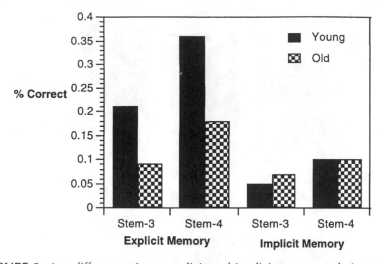

FIGURE 3. Age differences in an explicit and implicit stem completion task as a function of stem length. Adapted from Park and Shaw (1992).

which information is processed, (b) working memory function, (c) inhibitory function, and (d) sensory function. Each of these mechanisms can be conceptualized as a type of cognitive or processing resource, and some authors have suggested that combinations of these mechanisms may be an even better estimate of cognitive resource (Salthouse, 1991). It is important to note at the outset that we are not necessarily interested in explaining all of the variance on a cognitive task with these mechanisms. Rather, we are interested in understanding if the age-related variance that occurs on any given cognitive task can be explained or is mediated by one of these mechanisms. It is, of course, logically possible that age-related variance has multiple causes and that more than one of these mechanisms will account for age-related differences in performance on a cognitive task. Thus, I think that it is important to recognize that evidence in favor of one mechanism being an important underlying influence accounting for aging effects is not necessarily evidence against another.

The Processing Speed Theory

Salthouse (1991, 1996) has proposed a well-developed theory building on earlier work by Birren (1965) and others, suggesting that the fundamental mechanism that accounts for age-related variance in performance is a generalized, decreased speed of performing mental operations. Salthouse (1996) marshals an impressive amount of evidence indicating that nearly all age-related variance on almost any kind of cognitive task, ranging from memory to reasoning, can be explained by knowledge of the rate at which the individual makes speeded comparisons on perceptual speed tasks. Perceptual speed tasks are simple paper-and-pencil measures that require the individual to make rapid perceptual same/different judgments about pairs of digit or letter strings, or two similar symbols. Speed of processing is measured by the number of comparisons correctly made in a fixed period of time, typically somewhere between one and three minutes.

Salthouse (1996) hypothesizes that there are two important mechanisms responsible for the relationship between speed of processing and cognition. The "limited time mechanism" suggests that "the time to perform later operations is greatly restricted when a large proportion of the available time is occupied by the execution of earlier operations" (p. 404) and the simultaneity mechanism suggests that "the products of earlier processing may be lost by the time that later processing is completed" (p. 405). Thus, performance deteriorates on cognitive tasks with age because older adults are slow to perform early steps or stages in complex cognitive tasks, and this slowing can also result in older adults never reaching the later stages because the products of earlier operations are not available to them. The speed-of-processing construct has proven itself to be very powerful when used as an individual difference measure to explain age-related variance on a cognitive task.

The important point with respect to this mechanism for survey researchers is not that older adults will be slower to answer questions, although that is likely to be the case. Of greater importance is that this mechanism suggests that older adults, due to slowed speed of processing, will not necessarily have the products of earlier mental operations available to them and may not complete mental operations that they have begun in the same manner as young adults. Thus, older adults may give profoundly different answers from young adults to survey questions that require judgment and reasoning. The differences do not occur because they have fundamentally different opinions or attitudes from young adults on the question at hand, but rather because, due to slowed mental operations, they retrieve less or different information than young adults and process it less extensively, issues elaborated upon in Schwarz (Chapter 2 in this volume). The more complex the mental operations required to answer a question, the more likely it is that the processes they engage in to answer the question will be quite different from the processes younger adults engage in due to constraints imposed by age-related slowing. Such a finding suggests that older adults will perform most differently from young adults when survey materials are presented auditorily, as they will not be able to refer to a written text to provide information about the questions or response alternatives that is lost due to slowing of mental operations.

Working Memory

Craik and Byrd (1982) developed an important framework that relates to the construct of working memory. They suggested that older adults were deficient in the ability to engage in what they called "self-initiated processing." What Craik and Byrd refer to as "processing resource" is best measured by working memory tasks. Working memory can be conceptualized as the amount of on-line cognitive resources available at any given moment to process information and can involve storage, retrieval, and transformation of information. It is the total amount of mental energy available to perform on-line mental operations (Baddeley, 1986). We typically measure working memory by asking subjects to both store and process information simultaneously. For example, in a computational span task (a task represented in Figure 1), subjects are asked to solve a series of simple addition problems, but also to remember the second number in each equation. Working memory is measured by how many equations subjects can solve while remembering the relevant number in the equations without error.

Despite this age-related deficiency in processing resource operationalized as working memory, Craik and Byrd (1982) make the important suggestion that this can be repaired by the provision of "environmental supports" for older adults. Environmental supports are elements of a cognitive task that decrease the processing requirements of the memory task. In other words, although older adults may have a more limited working memory capacity, cognitive tasks can be structured that require somewhat less capacity to perform. For example, a survey question that is presented auditorily with alternatives also presented auditorily would be quite low in environmental support and have high processing demands, as the respondent has to hold the questions and response alternatives in working memory as well as simultaneously perform the judgments and comparisons required to answer the question. In contrast, a written question with all answers simultaneously visible and available to the respondent would be very high in environmental support because the respondent would not have to hold any information in working memory to answer the questions, and would merely have to perform judgments and comparisons. Using the Craik and Byrd model, one would expect larger differences in the kinds of responses old and young might endorse when the questions were presented auditorily compared to visually.

A research group at the University of Michigan consisting of Norbert Schwarz, Bärbel Knäuper, Natalie Davidson, Pam Smith, and myself has collected preliminary data on this topic, and we have found that patterns of responses between old and young differ substantially more for auditorily presented questions than visually presented questions. That is, older adults appear more likely to endorse the latest or most recent alternatives presented to them in multiple-choice format questions (as Knäuper reports in Chapter 17 in this volume) when the questions are presented auditorily. We also find that the pattern of differences between young and old is smaller or nonexistent when the same questions are presented visually. It is of considerable interest to us whether these differences are controlled by processing resources, and we are conducting individual differences analyses based on measures of working memory to address this question. The hypothesis is that the quantity of processing resources an individual has as measured by working memory function will predict response patterns on auditorily presented questions, where working memory is highly relevant, but not on visually presented questions, where subjects can refer back to the material presented as much as desired.

The importance of environmental support in mitigating age differences is illustrated by a number of studies in the literature. Park, Smith, Morrell, Puglisi, and Dudley (1990) presented young and old adults with pictures of concrete objects in the presence of either an unrelated cue (e.g., "cherry-spider") or a related cue (e.g., "ant-spider"). The subjects' task was to recall the word "spider" when presented with one of these two cues. Park et al. (1990) reported that older adults profited more from the conceptually related cue compared to the unrelated cue than did young adults. The related cue provided a memory support that was automatically activated (i.e., word meaning), and this support was more beneficial in improving recall for older adults because the use of it was not resource intensive. In contrast, the presentation of a target picture with an unrelated cue required active integration of target with cue, a process that is resource intensive, so that older adults were more disadvantaged in using the cue to support recall than were young adults.

In another study, Cherry, Park, Frieske, and Smith (1996) presented subjects with a task where they were to learn a critical adjective that was imbedded in a sentence. Subjects studied (a) the adjective in a simple base sentence (e.g., "The grimacing man held the cheese"); (b) the adjective presented in a simple sentence but with a complex picture present that elaborated the relationship of the adjective to the sentence (e.g., the grimacing man was depicted with his hand in a mousetrap); or (c) a sentence and a picture that were both complex and that matched one another (e.g., the elaborated picture was presented along with the sentence "The grimacing man held the cheese while the mousetrap sprang on his finger"). Figure 4 shows that age differences were large in the condition where subjects studied only the base sentence, but that the inclusion of an elaborative picture acted as an environmental support, improving the recall of both groups, but with a greater facilitation effect for old compared to young. When the elaborated picture was presented along with a complex sentence so that sentence and picture were redundant, age differences became smaller and older adults' recall was more than three times greater than in the control base picture condition. The addition of the picture elaborated the relationships described by the sentences, limiting the self-initiated processing required of older adults.

These studies suggest that when designing a survey, it is critically important to keep in mind the working memory load associated with the format and the design of the questions. It is always in the best interest of the survey researcher to keep the load as low as possible, to the extent that a question can be presented with sufficient clarity in a concise format in which it can be comprehended. To the extent that format and question structure results in a high working memory load, age dif-

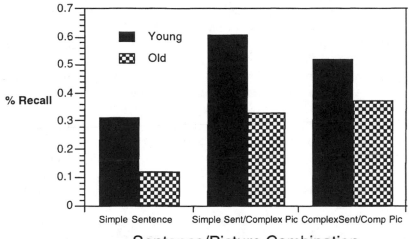

Sentence/Picture Combination

FIGURE 4. Proportion of recall for a target adjective embedded in a sentence which was sometimes accompanied by an elaborative picture at encoding. Adapted from Cherry, Park, Frieske, and Smith (1996).

ferences in patterns of responding are increasingly likely to be due to age differences in cognitive function rather than to age differences on the substantive topic about which a respondent is being queried.

Relationship Between Speed of Processing and Working Memory

One question that has not received much attention in the literature until recently is the nature of the relationship between speed and working memory. How can both of them be explanatory mechanisms for age-related declines in cognitive function? The use of structural equation modeling and path analysis permits us to determine the interrelationships among these constructs. In a recent study, we investigated this relationship (Park et al., 1996). We were also interested in verifying the ideas advanced earlier in this chapter that some types of memory did indeed require more cognitive resources than others, and that age differences would be largest on the memory tasks that proved to be the most resource intensive in structural equation modeling. We studied a sample of 301 adults, aged 20–90, with roughly equivalent numbers at each decade. Subjects were given a complete cognitive battery that included measures of speed of processing (pattern comparison, letter comparison, and digit-symbol tasks), working memory (reading span, computational span, and backward digits), verbal ability, and a number of other tasks as well. These resource constructs were used to explain the age-related variance in three different types of memory: free recall, cued recall, and spatial memory. Typically, free recall is hypothesized to be the most effortful type of memory, as there is little environmental support at encoding or retrieval in a free recall task (Craik & Jennings, 1992); spatial recall would be viewed as the least effortful task (Hasher & Zacks, 1979), with cued recall hypothesized to be intermediate in its resource demands. We hypothesized that (a) age-related variance would be mediated by speed of processing and working memory, (b) speed would be a more fundamental mechanism than working memory and would be related to all types of memory, and (c) working memory would have a stronger relationship to free recall than to spatial recall.

All of these hypotheses were verified in the model presented in Figure 5. Figure 5 shows that all significant age-related variance is mediated by speed. Additionally, speed operates through working memory but working memory has a direct path only to the two more effortful types of memory, free recall and cued recall. The model demonstrates the fundamental importance of the constructs of speed and working memory to long-term memory function because there is no significant

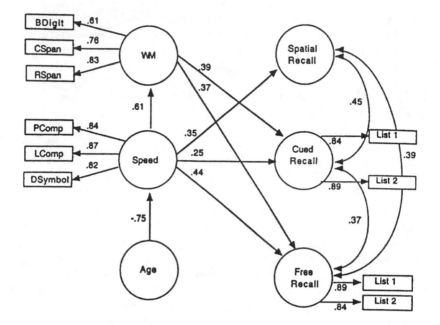

FIGURE 5. A structural equation model of free recall, cued recall, and spatial recall, portraying the relationships of age, speed, and working memory to these constructs. For each path, the standardized path coefficient is presented. All paths shown are statistically significant. N = 301. BDigit = Backward Digit Span; CSpan = Computational Span; RSpan = Reading Span; PComp = Pattern Comparison; LComp = Letter Comparison; DSymbol = Digit Symbol; List 1 = Recall List 1; List 2 = Recall List 2. Reproduced from Park et al. (1996).

amount of age-related variance remaining to be explained in the model when the speed construct is included. Moreover, because the working memory construct is related only to the two more effortful measures of recall, free and cued recall, but not to the less effortful measure of spatial recall, the model provides independent verification of the importance of speed of processing and working memory constructs in explaining the age-related variance that occurs on memory tasks. Because of the differential relationship of speed and working memory to the different memory measures, the model illustrates that some constructs might be more important for one type of memory than for another. The model supports the theorizing of both Salthouse (1996) and Craik and Jennings (1992), demonstrating that both speed and working memory are important for understanding age differences in memory and that age differences are largest on memory tasks that we have independently verified require more mental effort.

Inhibition

A third important construct in the cognitive aging literature is inhibition. Hasher and Zacks (1988) have proposed that, with age, we have more trouble focusing on target information and inhibiting attention to irrelevant material. According to this view, inefficient inhibitory processes permit "the initial entrance into working memory of information that is off the goal path. It will also result in the prolonged maintenance of such information in working memory" (p. 213). Thus, according to this model, although the contents of working memory appear to decrease or shrink with age, the mechanisms underlying this apparent loss is due to the maintenance of a considerable amount of irrelevant information in working memory at the expense of target information due to inefficient inhibitory function. Hasher and Zacks's (1988) model is particularly apt for the processing of discourse. They present compelling data suggesting that older adults are more likely to maintain disconfirmed antecedent information in memory. In a later study, Hasher, Stoltzfus, Zacks, and Rypma (1991) demonstrated that older adults responded more quickly when a response that should have been inhibited on Trial 1 became the basis for a correct response on Trial 2 (negative priming paradigm), providing evidence for less inhibitory function in older adults at early attentional stages. Unfortunately, the finding of more negative priming in older adults (evidenced by an inability to suppress the effects of the stimulus from the previous trial) reported by Hasher et al. (1991) has not proven to be easily replicable, as there have been a number of studies where negative priming has proven to be age invariant across the life-span (Earles, Connor, Frieske, Park, Smith, & Zwahr, 1997). The importance of the inhibition construct for understanding cognitive aging phenomena at this time is not clear.

Some theorists have argued that the overall phenomenon of inhibition is not reliable and that other mechanisms and constructs provide a better account of the extant data on language and discourse processing (Burke, 1997) and on attention (McDowd, 1997). In response to these criticisms, Zacks and Hasher (1997) have argued that the inhibition mechanism is important and fundamental to understanding cognitive aging. They marshal considerable support to suggest that inhibition operates in language production situations. Although they agree that alternative explanations are possible for individual studies where the inhibition construct has been invoked as the explanatory mechanism, they argue that inhibition is the most parsimonious explanation for the corpus of data that exist, and that it is thus the preferred explanation. More discussion of the inhibition construct occurs in this volume in Chapter 6, by Yoon, May, and Hasher.

The notion of poor inhibitory function may be of great importance for survey researchers, particularly given the element of on-line speech production that is involved in many survey response situations. Thus, even if the inhibition construct proves to be of limited utility for cognitive aging in general and is specific to language production, it will be of great importance to understanding age-related differences in responses to surveys. The inhibition view would suggest that older adults, in forced choice situations, may have difficulty abandoning or inhibiting the first alternative presented to them on a question, and considering the later alternatives. Hence, they should be more likely to endorse early responses compared to young adults. This hypothesis contrasts with a working memory view described earlier which argues for endorsement of the last response, as that might be all that an older adult could hang onto with limited capacity. Norbert Schwarz, Bärbel Knäuper, Natalie Davidson, Pam Smith, and myself are currently conducting research to differentiate between these explanations. Additionally, the inhibition argument would be quite important for survey situations where subjects are required to access a great deal of personalistic information or provide the surveyor with open-ended responses. The theory would predict that considerably more off-goal-path musing would be generated in older adults that they would have more difficulty abandoning. Moreover, the musing and off-goal-path thoughts that would occur as a result of earlier questions would result in considerably less capacity available for later questions and/or alternatives.

We know considerably less about inhibitory function and aging than we do about speed and working memory. There have been some methodological limitations to developing this construct, as it has proven to be difficult to develop a reliable individual difference measure of inhibitory function. We had hoped to examine the relative contributions of inhibition to memory function in the model presented in Figure 5, but could not develop a reliable measure of the construct. Thus, at this point, the attenuation of age-related variance through inhibitory function on cognitive tasks has yet to be demonstrated. Nevertheless, the rich theorizing that surrounds this construct, the existence of inhibitory neural circuits, and the considerable amount of data supporting the Hasher and Zacks argument suggest inhibition to be a construct that will continue to be invoked as an explanation for cognitive aging and one meritorious of continued investigation.

Sensory Function

Startling data on mechanisms underlying cognitive function in old age have recently emerged from the Berlin Aging Study. Lindenberger and

Baltes (1994) collected extensive medical, sensory, cognitive, and social measures from a large sample of elderly adults in Berlin aged 70–103, with equal representation of subjects at each decade, even for the very old. Lindenberger and Baltes (1994) reported compelling evidence indicating that nearly all of the age-related variance in 14 tests of cognitive ability (including measures of speed of processing, reasoning, memory, world knowledge, and verbal fluency) was mediated by sensory functioning as measured by simple tests of visual and auditory acuity. The sensory measures appeared to be a more fundamental index of cognitive resource than even speed of processing, as the sensory measures mediated all of the variance in speed of processing but the reverse was not true, adding credence to the notion that sensory function may be a fundamental index of cognitive aging. Lindenberger and Baltes (1994) argue that sensory function is a crude measure of brain integrity. They propose the "common cause" hypothesis, which is that sensory function, as a general index of physiological architecture, is fundamental to cognitive function and is thus a powerful mediator of cognitive abilities. In a later study, Baltes and Lindenberger (1997) conducted analyses similar to those just described, but with a life-span sample that included subjects ranging in age from 25 to 103 years. As shown in Figure 6, they demonstrate systematic decline across the life-span in all aspects of cognitive function including, somewhat surprisingly, measures of world knowledge and verbal fluency, domains that have typically been considered to be more resistant to age-related decline (e.g., see Figure 1). The decline functions did not change when old adults in early stages of dementia were excluded from the sample. In addition, there was strong evidence in this life-span sample for mediation of cognitive decline by sensory function, both with demented subjects included and with them excluded. Finally, Lindenberger and Baltes (1997) demonstrated that the slope of the decline gradient did not vary as a function of education, occupation, social class, and income, suggesting that the declines are indeed based on biology rather than social history, adding some confidence to the notion that the sensory measures provide an index of neuronal integrity which in turn mediates cognitive function. It should also be noted that it is plausible that Figure 6 underestimates age-related decline in these functions due to selective survival or mortality (Baltes & Smith, 1997). It is likely that individuals who survive into very late adulthood may be healthier and cognitively more elite than those who do not survive. Extensive analyses by Baltes and Smith (1997) relative to individuals for whom they had cognitive data but who died or declined to continue to participate indicated that the Berlin Aging Sample was positively selected on all 25 variables that they examined.

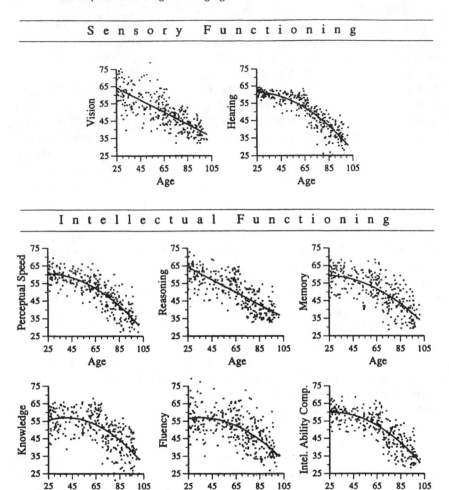

FIGURE 6. Declines in sensory and intellectual functioning across the life-span (N = 315). Taken from Baltes and Lindenberger (1997).

The findings from the Berlin Aging Study have substantial implications for the conduct of survey research and self-report interviews. The primary message is that sampling from select groups of elderly cannot correct for age-related decline. In other words, the finding that socio-biographical variables such as social class and education did not mitigate age effects suggests that age biases in responding are operating in survey situations, and that sampling from high socioeconomic and educational categories will not apparently correct for these biases. At the same time, data from Baltes and Lindenberger (1997) as well as from Cherry and Park (1993) clearly indicate that more educated individuals have higher levels of cognitive resource. Despite the uniform decline in cognitive ability for all socioeconomic groups, sociobiographical variables could nevertheless be interactive with age. The reason for this is that in a high-ability sample, age-related declines may not have too many implications for a self-report task that has modest working memory requirements. For example, presenting young and old adults with relatively simple questions with three one- or two-word alternatives should be a task of sufficiently low load that age might not be a factor in a sample of highly educated adults. Despite experiencing substantial cognitive decline, these high-ability respondents would likely still have adequate cognitive resources to perform like young adults on this relatively easy task. Age effects would only manifest themselves in this group when the overall load of the question was higher. For a less-educated sample that was lower in cognitive resource, however, age might well manifest its effects on even a simple question. Thus, the initial level of cognitive resource from which an older adult has declined may become quite relevant in understanding the impact of age on self-report. The absolute level of resource available to any given respondent is more important than the amount of decline that respondent has experienced. Cognitive aging effects are likely to manifest themselves on self-report tasks more profoundly for less educated subjects despite the fact that highly educated subjects experience the same amount of relative decline in their cognitive abilities.

☐ Cognitive Resources in Everyday Life

Despite a wealth of evidence that cognitive resources decline with age and are critically important in understanding performance on cognitive tasks, surprisingly little is known about their importance for function in everyday life. The global nature of the decline in speed of processing and working memory that occurs with age might lead one to expect that older adults would have substantial difficulties in managing the affairs of everyday life or maintaining a good level of performance on the job. However, there is considerable evidence (as well as our own personal observations) that older adults function well and that the cognitive declines documented in the lab do not impact as negatively as one would expect on everyday domains of behavior. The reasons for this are complex and not entirely understood. There are two important aspects of the aging cognitive system that likely play an important role in maintaining demanding cognitive behaviors in the everyday environment despite substantial declines in processing resource. These are that acquired knowledge is relatively impervious to age-related decline and that complex, everyday behaviors are frequently governed by automatic rather than controlled processes (Park, 1997).

As shown by the vocabulary scores shown in the lower right-hand panel of Figure 1, there is considerable evidence that knowledge is maintained across the life-span or even continues to grow. Thus, much of what has been learned throughout an older adult's life is preserved, providing older adults with access to an extensive knowledge base that can be useful in solving problems and addressing the needs of everyday life. Perhaps of even greater importance in understanding older adults' strong performance on complex cognitive tasks in everyday life is the fact that frequent and familiar behaviors become automatized; that is, they require little cognitive resource or effort to perform. Jacoby (1991) has developed a process dissociation procedure whereby he is able to separate the effortful, resource-based components of memory from the effects of familiarity which drive automatic processes. Jacoby, Jennings, and Hay (1996) have demonstrated that, although the effortful component of memory declines with age, the familiarity-based, automatic component is age invariant. The implications of this finding are that in situations that are highly familiar and where the contributions of familiarity and automaticity are high, older adults are relatively unimpaired. However, in situations that are demanding of controlled processing and mental effort, the age-related declines in processing resources will be of great importance and older adults will evidence impairment in the behavior.

If one considers everyday situations, although they may superficially appear to be cognitively demanding, they are often based more on automatic processing than effortful processing. For example, let us consider an elderly adult who lives in the suburbs of a large city like Boston and has subscribed to the Boston Symphony for 20 years. She does not hesitate to drive into Boston to see the symphony on a Sunday afternoon. Automatic processes and acquired knowledge would play a large role in her route selection and in finding her way. She simply knows how to get to the symphony with little thought and she easily negotiates complex traffic interchanges due to their high familiarity. Little controlled processing is required on her part to arrive at the destination, park the car, and find her way to the concert hall. Contrast this with another elderly adult who has flown into the same Boston suburb for a weekend to see friends who are busy on Sunday afternoon. She would also like to go to the symphony. For her, the task of driving to the symphony through Boston traffic is one that requires considerable engagement of processing resources and has a very small familiarity component. It is in this second situation, but not the first, where age-related declines in cognitive function would play an important role in the everyday behavior of driving to the symphony. Driving to the symphony for the out-of-town guest would have a high working memory load in terms of keeping the directions in mind. Speeded processing would also become important in making rapid decisions about exit selection off of the freeway and deciding how to negotiate roundabouts in moving traffic. Acquired knowledge and familiarity would not contribute much to this drive. There are few elderly adults who would attempt the second drive described (as well as many younger adults who would also be daunted) based on the likely correct perception that the processing demands of driving in Boston exceeded their level of cognitive resource.

Two domains of everyday behavior where it is important to understand the relationship of processing resource to successful performance are those of work and health. In both of these domains, I will present evidence that, despite substantial declines in processing resources, the expected relationship between cognitive function and the everyday behavior does not occur.

Work

There is a well-documented relationship between cognitive ability and work performance. Even the lowest level jobs show a positive relationship between cognitive function and rated excellence on the job (Hunter & Hunter, 1984; Schmidt, Hunter, & Outerbridge, 1986). The decline of processing resource and cognitive abilities in older adults, combined with the ability/job performance finding suggests that one could expect to find a negative relationship between aging and work performance. Meta-analyses, however, have consistently failed to find such a relationship (Rhodes, 1993; Waldman & Avolio, 1986). In general, there is a preponderance of evidence suggesting that there is no relationship between age and job performance. Park (1994) has hypothesized that there are four possibilities that can account for this relationship. One is that older adults have jobs characterized by maintenance functions and that they rarely encounter resource-demanding transition phases. As a result, age deficits in cognition are not very important in job performance. This hypothesis is in some ways an automatization hypothesis, since one of the reasons maintenance functions can be performed so effectively in the face of declining resources is the high familiarity component of such behaviors, which are also low in the effortful, controlled processing component. A second possibility is that experience protects against decline in the cognitive abilities used in the workplace. Careful work by Salthouse, Babcock, Mitchell, Skovronek, and Palmon (1990) on aging architects and by Salthouse (1984) on aging typists shows clearly that declines in component behaviors such as spatial visualization in architects and interval to respond between key strokes in typists does decline with age. Thus, there is little evidence that practice protects against declines in the basic cognitive mechanisms underlying the work behavior. A third possibility is that complex knowledge structures about a job increase with age and compensate for decline in basic cognitive abilities. There are a number of studies showing that older workers in various professions have as much or more domain-specific knowledge about aspects of their job than younger workers (Baltes & Smith, 1990; Stumpf & Rabinowitz, 1981; Taylor, 1975), so there is some legitimacy to this hypothesis. Finally, a fourth reason that the relationship between age and job performance may be null is that older adults increasingly use environmental supports to compensate for declining cognition. There is evidence that older adults consult with younger colleagues, collaborate extensively, and gravitate towards positions that require knowledge and judgment and move away from positions that have high cognitive resource requirements (e.g., a position as a university administrator, which is typical for older academics, requires more judgment and less intensive processing resource compared to that of a bench scientist, which is more typical of younger academics). The data on aging, work, and cognition point to the fact that although basic declines in cognitive function would appear to be critically important in performing a demanding job, environmental supports and the elaborated knowledge structures and experiences of the older adult worker may serve as compensatory mechanisms in this familiar, everyday environment.

Health

Older adults must frequently make complex health decisions, and it is likely that limited cognitive resources play a role in the decisions they make (Park, in press). In general, there is evidence that older adults' limited processing resources result in them seeking less information about medical conditions, making important treatment decisions faster than young adults (due to the limited information they have and reliance on authorities), and showing less sophisticated reasoning about the decisions made (Meyer, Russo, & Talbot, 1995; Yates & Patalano, in press; Zwahr, in press; Zwahr, Park, & Shifren, 1998). The literature on aging and health decision-making is one that requires additional exploration. Park (in press) discusses the possible interaction of controlled and automatic processes in the health domain.

One area where the controlled/automatic distinction may be of particular importance is in the area of medication adherence. Medication adherence is a behavior that has a substantial cognitive component, particularly when an individual is taking a complex medication regimen of four or more medications, as many elderly adults do. In order to adhere accurately to a complex regimen, an older adult has to comprehend instructions on each medication, use working memory to integrate those instructions into a daily plan, then use long-term memory to remember what the plan is, and finally, engage prospective memory to remember to take the medication (Park, 1992; Park & Jones, 1996; Park & Kidder, 1996). Park, Morrell, Frieske, and Kincaid (1992) presented evidence that very old adults did show deficits in medication adherence compared to adults aged 60–77 years and that these deficits were remedied by providing the very old with medication organizers and charts that were designed to relieve the working memory burden associated with taking medications. The medication adherence was recorded via microelectronic monitors, so that accurate data on medication usage was obtained. One surprising aspect of this work was that adults aged 60–77 made almost no errors in their medication-taking behaviors, despite the fact that they were experiencing substantial age-related decline in cognitive function. The finding that older adults do not make many medication errors was also reported by Morrell, Park, Kidder, and Martin (1997). They found that in a sample of hypertensive adults aged 35–75, older adults from 65 to 75 made fewer errors than any other age group.

In a recent study, Park et al. (1998) reported a similar finding: adults aged 60–75 with rheumatoid arthritis made the fewest medication errors of any age group. Forty-seven percent of the older adults, all of whom were taking four or more medications, made no errors at all with their medications in a one-month period. Middle-aged adults made the most errors, despite strong evidence for markedly superior cognitive function in the middle-aged subjects. The use of individual difference measures that assessed not only cognitive function but also socioemotional status and contextual variables revealed that the best predictor of medication errors was self-report of a busy, highly engaged lifestyle. Such a lifestyle rarely characterized older adults. Moreover, older adults had frequently been taking medications for many years and medication adherence behaviors were highly familiar and routinized to these adults. Thus, the apparent high cognitive investment that medication adherence would seem to require was off-set by highly practiced automatic behaviors, where the daily environment served as a cue for taking medications. In contrast, younger adults who led less routinized lives where context was frequently changing did not have the same environmental stimuli to serve as automatic cues for taking medications, and as a result, this group made more errors. One lesson to be learned from this pattern of findings is that even tasks that may appear to be highly cognitive and resource-driven, such as remembering to take medications, may operate very differently than one would expect in a real-world, everyday environment.

Implications for Collecting Data on Surveys

The data presented suggest that the role of processing resources may vary dramatically as a function of context. It seems likely that the role played by cognitive factors with age will increase in a survey situation to the extent that respondents are questioned about domains with which they are unfamiliar. Questions about an unfamiliar domain will require reliance almost exclusively on controlled processing. For example, providing older adults with information about two novel products with which they weren't familiar and asking them to make evaluations would likely be a situation where question complexity, structure, and format would be particularly important, due to the high processing demands. However, if questions focused on highly familiar, everyday aspects of products (like Tide or Coca Cola), older adults might provide relatively quick responses based on familiarity and automatically activated information. In these cases, one might expect question structure to have a less salient or more blunted effect. Finally, the present discussion should sensitize the survey researcher to the importance of the environment in which the respondent completes a survey. An unusual, unfamiliar environment may result in some of the respondents' resources being directed toward the environment and away from the question. The unfamiliar environment could result in more limited resources available to devote to answering the question and would magnify aging effects on questions.

☐ Summary

In the present chapter, I have detailed the declines that occur in the cognitive system with age. As we age, there are deficits in speed of information processing, working memory function, and sensory function. These deficits can have a substantial impact on the responses made by survey respondents such that age differences reflect differences in the ability to process and respond to the question rather than reflecting opinions and beliefs regarding a given survey question. It is important, as well, to recognize that a respondent's behavior occurs in a context and that the meaning of resource declines for everyday life will be somewhat blunted for highly familiar situations where older adults can rely on familiarity and automatic processes to guide their behaviors.

☐ Acknowledgments

This work was supported by the National Institute on Aging through several grants. Grant R01AG14111, entitled "Aging, Cognition, and Self-Report," was awarded to Norbert Schwarz, Denise Park, and Bärbel Knäuper. The Center for Applied Cognitive Research on Aging also supported this research (Grant P50AG11715) as did Grant R01AG062651, "Effects of Context on the Aging Memory." The author gratefully acknowledges this assistance. A web site with more information about related research is located at http://www.isr.umich.edu/rcgd/parklab/.

☐ References

Baddeley, A. (1986). *Working memory.* Oxford, England: Clarendon Press.

Baltes, P. B., & Lindenberger, U. (1997). Emergence of powerful connection between sensory and cognitive functions across the adult life span: A new window to the study of cogntive aging? *Psychology and Aging, 12,* 12–21.

Baltes, P. B., & Smith, J. (1990). The psychology of wisdom and its ontogenesis. In R.J. Sternberg (Ed.), *Wisdom: Its nature, origins, and development* (pp. 87–120). Cambridge, England: Cambridge University Press.

Baltes, P. B., & Smith, J. (1997). A systemic-wholistic view of psychological functioning in very old age: Introduction to a collection of articles from the Berlin Aging Study. *Psychology and Aging, 12,* 395 409.

Birren, J. E. (1965). Age changes in speed of behavior: Its central nature and physiological correlates. In A. T. Welford & J. E. Birren (Eds.), *Behavior, aging, and the nervous system* (pp. 191–216). Springfield, IL: Charles C. Thomas.

Burke, D. M. (1997). Language, aging and inhibitory deficits: Evaluation of a theory. *Journal of Gerontology: Psychological Science, 52b,* 254–264.

Cherry, K. E., & Park, D. C. (1993). Individual difference and contextual variables influence spatial memory in younger and older adults. *Psychology and Aging, 8,* 517–526.

Cherry, K. E., Park, D. C., Frieske, D. A., & Smith, A. D. (1996). Verbal and pictorial elaborations enhance memory in young and older adults. *Aging, Neuropsychology, and Cognition, 3,* 15–29.

Craik, F. I. M., & Byrd, M. (1982). Aging and cognitive deficits: The role of attentional resources. In F. I. M. Craik & S. Trehub (Eds.), *Aging and cognitive processes* (pp. 191–211). New York: Plenum Press.

Craik, F. I. M., & Jennings, J. M. (1992). Human memory. In F. I. M. Craik & T. A. Salthouse (Eds.), *The handbook of aging and cognition* (pp. 51–110). Hillsdale, NJ: Erlbaum.

Earles, J. L., Connor, L. T., Frieske, D. A., Park, D. C., Smith, A. D., & Zwahr, M. (1997). Age differences in inhibition: Possible causes and consequences. *Aging, Neuropsychology, and Cognition, 4,* 45–57.

Hasher, L., Stoltzfus, E. R., Zacks, R. T., & Rypma, B. (1991). Age and inhibition. *Journal of Experimental Psychology: Learning, Memory, and Cognition, 17,* 163–169.

Hasher, L., & Zacks, R. T. (1979). Automatic and effortful processes in memory. *Journal of Experimental Psychology: General, 108,* 356–388.

Hasher, L., & Zacks, R. T. (1988). Working memory, comprehension, and aging: A review and a new view. In G. H. Bower (Ed.), *The psychology of learning and motivation* (Vol. 22, pp. 193–225). San Diego, CA: Academic Press.

Hunter, J. E., & Hunter, R. F. (1984). Validity and utility of alternative predictors of job performance. *Psychological Bulletin, 96,* 72–98.

Jacoby, L. L. (1991). A process dissociation framework: Separating automatic from intentional uses of memory. *Journal of Memory and Language, 30,* 513–541.

Jacoby, L. L., Jennings, J. M., & Hay, J. F. (1996). Dissociating automatic and consciously-controlled processes: Implications for diagnosis and rehabilitation of memory deficits. In D. J. Hermann, C. L. McEvoy, C. Hertzog, P. Hertel, & M. K. Johnson (Eds.), *Basic and applied memory research: Theory in context* (Vol. 1, pp. 161–193). Hillsdale, NJ: Erlbaum.

Light, L. L. (1991). Memory and aging: Four hypothesis in search of data. In M. R. Rosenweig (Ed.), *Annual review of psychology, 42,* 333–376.

Lindenberger, U., & Baltes, P. B. (1994). Sensory functioning and intelligence in old age: A strong connection. *Psychology and Aging, 9,* 339–355.

Lindenberger, U., & Baltes, P. (1997). Intellectual functioning in old and very old age: Cross-sectional results from the Berlin Aging Study. *Psychology and Aging, 12,* 410–432.

McDowd, J. M. (1997). Inhibition in attention and aging. *Journal of Gerontology: Psychological Sciences, 52b,* 265–273.

Meyer, B. J. F., Russo, C., & Talbot, A. (1995). Discourse comprehension and problem solving: Decisions about the treatment of breast cancer by women across the life span. *Psychology and Aging, 10,* 84–103.

Morrell, R. W., Park, D. C., Kidder, D. P., & Martin, M. (1997). Adherence to anti-hypertensive medications over the lifespan. *The Gerontologist, 37,* 609–619.

Park, D. C. (1992). Applied cognitive aging research. In F. I. M. Craik & T. A. Salthouse (Eds.), *Handbook of cognition and aging* (pp. 449–493), Mahwah, NJ: Erlbaum.

Park, D. C. (1994). Aging, cognition, and work. *Human Performance, 7,* 181–205.

Park, D. C. (1997). Psychological issues related to competence: Cognitive aging and instrumental activities of daily living. In W. Schaie and S. Willis (Eds.), *Social structures and aging* (pp. 66–82). Mahwah, NJ: Erlbaum.

Park, D. C. (in press). Aging and the controlled and automatic processing of medical information and medical intentions. In D. C. Park, R. W. Morrell, & K. Shifren (Eds.), *Processing of medical information in aging patients: Cognitive and human factors perspectives.* Mahwah, NJ: Erlbaum.

Park, D. C., Hertzog, C., Leventhal, H., Morrell, R. W., Leventhal, E., Birchmore, D., Martin, M., & Bennett, J. (1998). *Medication adherence in rheumatoid arthitis patients: Older is wiser.* Unpublished manuscript.

Park, D. C., & Jones, T. R. (1996). Medication adherence and aging. In A. D. Fiske &

W. A. Rogers (Eds.), *Handbook of human factors and the older adult* (pp. 257–288). San Diego, CA: Academic Press.

Park, D. C., & Kidder, D. (1996). Prospective memory and medication adherence. In M. Brandimonte, G. Einstein, & M. McDaniel (Eds.), *Prospective memory: Theory and applications* (pp. 369–390). Mahwah, NJ: Erlbaum.

Park, D. C., Morrell, R. W., Frieske, D., Blackburn, A. B., & Birchmore, D. (1991). Cognitive factors and the use of over-the counter medication organizers by arthritis patients. *Human Factors, 31* (3), 57–67.

Park, D. C., Morrell, R. W., Frieske, D., & Kinkaid, D. (1992). Medication adherence behaviors in older adults: Effects of external cognitive supports. *Psychology & Aging, 7,* 252–256.

Park, D. C., Puglisi, J. T., & Smith, A. D. (1986). Memory for pictures: Does an age-related decline exist? *Psychology and Aging, 1,* 11–17.

Park, D. C., & Shaw, R. J. (1992). Effect of environmental support on implicit and explicit memory in younger and older adults. *Psychology and Aging, 7,* 632–642.

Park, D. C., Smith, A. D., Lautenschlager, G., Earles, J., Frieske, D., Zwahr, M., & Gaines, C. (1996). Mediators of long-term memory performance across the life span. *Psychology and Aging, 11,* 621–637.

Park, D. C., Smith, A. D., Morrell, R. W., Puglisi, J. T., & Dudley, W. N. (1990). Effects of contextual integration on recall of pictures by older adults. *Journal of Gerontology: Psychological Sciences, 45,* 52–57.

Rhodes, S. R. (1993). Age-related differences in work attitudes and behavior: A review and conceptual analysis. *Psychological Bulletin, 93,* 328–367.

Salthouse, T. A. (1984). Effects of age and skill in typing. *Journal of Experimental Psychology: General, 113,* 345–371.

Salthouse, T. A. (1991). *Theoretical perspectives on cognitive aging.* Hillsdale, NJ: Erlbaum.

Salthouse, T. A. (1996). The processing-speed theory of adult age differences in cognition. *Psychological Review, 103,* 403–428.

Salthouse, T. A., Babcock, R. L., Mitchell, D. R., Skovronek, E., & Palmon, R. (1990). Age and experience effects in spatial visualization. *Developmental Psychology, 26,* 128–136.

Schmidt, F. L., Hunter, J. E., & Outerbridge, A. N. (1986). Impact of job experience and ability on job knowledge, work sample performance, and supervisory ratings of job performance. *Journal of Applied Psychology, 71,* 432–439.

Stumpf, S. A., & Rabinowitz, S. (1981). Career stage as a moderator of performance relationships with facets of job satisfaction and role perceptions. *Journal of Vocational Behavior, 18,* 202–218.

Taylor, R. N. (1975). Age and experience as determinants of managerial information processing and decision making performance. *Academy of Management Journal, 18,* 74–81.

Waldman, D. A., & Avolio, B. J. (1986). A meta-analysis of age differences in job performance. *Journal of Applied Psychology, 71,* 33–38.

Yates, J. F., & Patalano, A. L. (in press). Decision making and aging. In D. C. Park, R. W. Morrell, & K. Shifren (Eds.), *Processing of medical information in aging patients: Cognitive and human factors perpectives.* Mahwah, NJ: Erlbaum.

Zacks, R., & Hasher, L. (1997). Cognitive gerontology and attentional inhibition: A reply to Burke and McDowd. *Journal of Gerontology: Psychological Sciences,* 274–285.

Zwahr, M. D. (in press). Cognitive processes and medical decisions. In D. C. Park, R. W. Morrell, & K. Shifren (Eds.), *Processing of medical information in aging patients: Cognitive and human factors perspectives.* Mahwah, NJ: Erlbaum.

Zwahr, M. D., Park, D. C., & Shifren, K. (1998). *The role of age, cognitive abilities, and beliefs in making decisions about estrogen replacement therapy.* Manuscript submitted for publication.

CHAPTER

Roger A. Dixon

The Concept of Gains
in Cognitive Aging

The term "gains" has been used with increasing frequency in the study of psychological aspects of human development, especially life-span human development. Clearly, developmental gains are to be distinguished from developmental "losses." Nevertheless, the meaning and use of the former term, and its relationship to the latter term, have not been fully examined. In this chapter, I focus on the concept of gains as it applies to development throughout life, and especially in late life.

☐ The Idea of Gains

In a traditional dictionary-based sense, a gain is something desired that is won or acquired. A gain constitutes an improvement, an advance, progress, or perhaps even movement towards a valued goal. Gains are not necessarily the product of effort, but they often are, as when one seeks to improve a condition or skill. A loss, on the other hand, reflects a failure to win or acquire, or a failure to preserve or maintain what one has. A loss could be a state of being deprived of something that one previously had or otherwise sought, whether in number (fewer than before) or quality (lower than before). Losses are not typically the product of deliberate effort—i.e., one rarely seeks to lose something that one both has and desires to have—but losses could be the product of failing effort, accident, disease, or progressive decline.

71

Change is a premise of both gains and losses. Change in quantity or quality may be evaluated as (a) a gain if it involves movement from a lower (worse) to a higher (better) state, or (b) a loss if it involves movement from a higher (better) to a lower (worse) state. If there is no change or alteration in the state of a system or process, it is said (colloquially) to be in steady state, a period of maintenance or stability.

A fundamental characteristic of development across the life-span—at multiple levels of analysis, and from birth to death—is that the human organism changes. It becomes different in form, nature, characteristics, and many other respects. The transformations that occur across the life-span are changes that involve periods and varieties of gains, losses, and maintenance. This may be true both in the latter three quarters of the life course (i.e., adulthood) and in the first quarter of life (i.e., childhood). Although the stereotypes of development in childhood and adulthood may be differentially populated by gains and losses, both directions of change may occur in all phases (Baltes, 1987). A simplistic illustration of how gains and losses may be intrinsically related in adulthood may be seen in the observation that as one "gains" in years of age (i.e., becomes older), one "loses" in time left to live (i.e., becomes closer to death).

As adults get older, however, there are losses in more than just time left to live. In fact, with aging, biological (e.g., Medina, 1996), sensory (e.g., Schieber & Baldwin, 1996), and cognitive (e.g., Salthouse, 1991) changes are reasonably and predominantly evaluated as losses. Are there fundamental and meaningful gains that occur with movement through adulthood? Are there changes with aging that can arguably be evaluated as gains? Or does the concept of gains require some modification to accommodate the phenomena of aging? A specific purpose of this chapter is to review the concept of gains as it has been used in scholarship on cognitive changes in adulthood, otherwise known as the field of cognitive aging. An additional purpose is to note empirical and theoretical lacunae in the study of gains and losses. As noted, such gaps may be filled by scholarship derived from several sources, including verbal reports (e.g., on-line, interview, questionnaire) and experimental performance.

☐ Conceptualizing Gains and Losses

That cognitive development in adulthood may not be characterized entirely as losses—and, in fact, could include some manner of gains —has been occasionally noted by psychologists for most of the 20th century. To be sure, the gains of cognitive aging are typically placed in the context of losses. For example, observing age differences in intellectual performance in favor of younger (as compared to older) adults, some early scholars also noted apparent exceptions (e.g., Jones & Conrad, 1933; Pressey, 1919; Sanford, 1902; see Dixon, Kramer, & Baltes, 1985, for review). The exceptions to the "rule" of aging losses have included processes that appeared to be at least generally delayed in the onset of decline, processes that developed with broader bands of individual differences, and processes linked to possible supportive mechanisms. Several recent observers have focused on possible mechanisms for maintenance of cognitive competence and skills and on dynamics between gains and losses (e.g., Baltes, 1987; Baltes & Baltes, 1990; Perlmutter, 1990; Salthouse, 1987, 1990; Uttal & Perlmutter, 1989). Other recent observers have identified processes that are thought to be relatively decoupled from aging decline and, in fact, fundamentally growth-oriented. Such gains are viewed not as exceptions to the rule of losses, but rather as independent of decline, produced as a function of an unfolding (or growing) organism or environment. Overall, intriguing ideas have been issued regarding whether, how, and why gains can appear in cognitive aging.

☐ Complementary Perspectives

This chapter is a companion to the preceding chapter in this volume, by Park, which focuses on basic mechanisms of cognitive aging, and thus more on losses than gains. I emphasize *companion* rather than *contrast*, because although the two chapters have different foci, the theoretical perspectives represented in these chapters are not incommensurable. Indeed, despite some divergence in proximal theoretical and empirical goals, the perspectives represented in the two chapters may be complementary in the study of cognitive aging. Not only do they both attend to issues of gains and losses in cognitive aging—at both a descriptive and an explanatory level—but they share many constraints and global purposes. In addition, both perspectives address the essential tension of cognitive aging, namely, the changing tension or balance between losses and gains across the life-span.

As argued elsewhere (e.g., Dixon & Hertzog, 1996), divergent theoretical perspectives in cognitive aging differ in numerous matters of focus, assumptions, balance, and methods, but they may not so much clash, as competing paradigms might, as complement one another through their differences. Nevertheless, in the field of cognitive aging, alternative perspectives do not often fight over the same territory, as, indeed, informal examinations of the citation patterns of the respective propo-nents have confirmed. The circle of cognitive aging phenomena may be quite large, encompassing a wide variety of (a) issues, concepts, methods, and theories; (b) skills, performances, behaviors, abilities, re-sponses, and beliefs; and (c) observations, directions, interpretations, reasons, and perhaps even causes. It is useful that different sectors of this circle of cognitive aging are in fact being explored. Among these different sectors are phenomena thought to represent aging-related gains and losses.

☐ Treatments of Gains and Losses

There are four principal treatments of the gains-losses issue in cogni-tive aging. Whereas I address the first three issues briefly, the fourth is covered in somewhat more detail. The four treatments, posed as ques-tions, follow.

1. What do scholars say (theoretically, speculatively) about gains and losses in cognitive aging?
2. What do textbook authors teach our students about gains and losses in cognitive aging?
3. What do researchers find when they survey the beliefs of individu-als about gains and losses in cognitive aging?
4. How are gains represented conceptually and empirically in the con-text of losses?

Scholars' Perspectives

As noted earlier, several scholars have constructed theoretical posi-tions that include the concept of gains in cognitive aging. Baltes (1987, 1997) has been a central proponent of the notion that there are in fact gains in cognitive aging. Circumspectly, however, he never fails to note that there are, as well, considerable losses. Overall, life-span de-velopment is portrayed as a complex process reflecting simultaneous transformations of gains, losses, and maintenance. Baltes emphasizes that the gains-losses issue is a life-span issue and, more specifically, that the ratio of gains to losses changes throughout life. Put simply, whereas there are more gains than losses in early life, there are more losses than gains in late life. Perhaps most notable about this portrayal is the idea that there are indeed losses occurring in child development and gains occurring during aging. This constitutes a provocative reformulation of the traditional gains-oriented concept of development. The broader concept of development does not rest, however, on a precise value of the gains:losses ratio at any particular point in the life course or on a precise representation of the shape of the function. Other scholars have produced complementary treatments of the gains-losses issue in cognitive aging (e.g., Perlmutter, 1990; Uttal & Perlmutter, 1989). Similarly, the problem of expanding the concept of development to include both gains and losses has been discussed elsewhere (e.g., Dixon, Lerner, & Hultsch, 1991; Harris, 1957; Lerner, 1984; Wohlwill, 1973).

Textbook Portrayals

How do prominent textbooks on adult development and aging portray the concepts of gains and losses? I informally selected and examined four recently published textbooks in the area. My two principal criteria in selecting these texts were that (a) they be written by one or more active contributors to scholarship in the psychology of adult development, and (b) they be published within the last several years. My perusal was guided by four major concerns:

1. whether and to what extent the gains-losses issue was prominent,
2. the extent to which gains were represented as a feature of cognitive aging,
3. whether the gains as described were related to cognitive loss, and
4. the extent to which prominent theories about aging-related cognitive loss were represented.

Overall, the four textbooks I examined included substantial coverage of aging-related decrements in sensory, health, social role, and cognitive abilities. Specifically, age differences in favor of younger adults were reported for a variety of memory and other cognitive processes. Accompanying the substantial empirical literature on such cognitive losses, however, are well-established and -tested theories regarding the range, ramifications, and causes of these losses (see, e.g., Cerella, 1990; Craik & Jennings, 1992; Light, 1991; Park, this volume; Salthouse, 1991; Zacks & Hasher, 1994). To what extent did the textbooks present this relatively large and influential theoretical literature, as compared to published ideas, empirical results, and theories pertaining to cognitive gains?

In terms of both number of text pages and number of figures or tables, these four textbooks presented far more information pertaining to cognitive gains than to theories of cognitive losses. Indeed, three of the textbooks contained virtually no mention of such prominent theories of cognitive aging as Salthouse's (1991) influential and cogent views on generalized slowing. In contrast, at the theoretical level, the textbooks appeared to focus more on the possible gains of cognitive aging, including postformal operations, dialectical/relativistic thinking, wisdom, creativity, and expertise. Textbooks in the psychology of adult development and aging are identifying and highlighting ideas about gains with aging, but placing such discussion only marginally in the context of theoretical developments regarding cognitive losses. This observation may be more meaningful if one recognizes that the relative size and influence of the literatures pertaining to cognitive gains and losses is decidedly in favor of the latter. Quite possibly, an optimistic perspective regarding cognitive aging was adopted deliberately.

Research on Beliefs About Gains and Losses

What do lay adults believe about gains and losses with aging? Heckhausen and colleagues (e.g., Heckhausen, Dixon, & Baltes, 1989; Heckhausen & Krueger, 1993) have conducted research on beliefs about gains and losses associated with aging, and some of their results pertain to cognitive aging. In a typical procedure, Heckhausen et al. (1989) presented younger and older adults with a series of over 350 adjectives describing a wide range of personality (e.g., skeptical), social (e.g., friendly), and cognitive (e.g., intelligent) characteristics. They used adjectives referring to desirable, undesirable, and neutral characteristics. The participants were asked to rate each adjective for the variable *sensitivity to developmental change* (i.e., does it increase, become stronger, more common; 1 = not at all, 9 = very) and for the variable *desirability* (the desirability of the change; 1 = very undesirable, 9 = very desirable). It is not too much of a speculative leap to view very desirable increases in attributes as gains and very undesirable increases in attributes as losses. Following this, the participants rated the expected *onset age* (age at which the increase starts) and *closing age* (age at which the increase ends) on a scale of adult ages from 20 to 90 years. The overall proportional relationship between gains and losses in adulthood is quite similar to that presented hypothetically by Baltes (1987). That is, the proportion of gains to losses is greater in childhood and much lower in adulthood.

For the purposes of the present chapter, I reexamined the original tables from the Heckhausen et al. (1989) article. In so doing, I conducted a secondary selection of items from the original data. The selection involved the following criteria. The attributes selected were:

• arguably cognitive ones;
• believed to be increasing across adulthood ($M \geq 6$);

- believed to be gains (*M* desirability $\geq$ 6.6) or losses (*M* desirability $\leq$ 3.8);
- considered *aging gains* if they were believed to be gains and have onset ages later than 30 and closing ages no earlier than 70;
- considered *aging gains-to-losses* if they were believed to be gains but have closing ages earlier than 70;
- considered *aging losses* if they were believed to be losses and have onset ages greater than 30 and closing ages no earlier than 70.

It was possible that a category termed *aging losses-to-gains* would have emerged, but it did not.

The results of this informal selection—how these categories are populated—can be easily summarized. The German adults participating in the Heckhausen et al. (1989) study rated as virtually unqualified cognitive gains with aging the following attributes: human knowledge, open-minded, smart, experienced, well-read, reasonable, level-headed, wise, and educated. Cognitive attributes that fit the characteristics of gains-to-losses were: logical, productive, methodical, ready-witted, adap-tive, industrious, and planful. In contrast, cognitive attributes that were believed by the participants to be losses with aging were: moralistic, overcautious, complicated, obstinate, forgetful, headstrong, stubborn, and absent-minded.

In sum, when asked to characterize adult development in terms of a wide range of attributes, the participants produced a pattern of life-course change in the gains:losses ratio that fit the figurative patterns generated by scholars (e.g., Baltes, 1987). Moreover, they identified a set of cognitive attributes that they believed to be desired and to follow trajectories of sustained improvement with aging. These data overlap with recent studies on conceptions of intelligence (e.g., Berg & Sternberg, 1992) and stereotypes of aging (e.g., Hummert, Garstka, Shaner, & Strahm, 1994). For example, in both the Heckhausen et al. (1989) and the Hummert et al. (1994) studies, attributes seen as cognitive gains, such as witty, wise, intelligent, well informed, knowledgeable, and productive (gains-to-losses) emerged under some conditions as stereotypic attributes of older adults. Both studies found that lay persons believed cognitive losses included attributes such as inflexible, slow-thinking, and forgetful.

Summary

According to these brief reviews, the first three treatments of the concept of gains have revealed that many observers—theoretical authors, textbook authors, and lay persons—believe there are reasons to consider the possibility of at least selected gains in cognitive aging. Theoretical scholars have established a conceptual basis for the idea of cognitive gains; textbook authors instruct university students in optimistic tones about the possibilities of cognitive gains with aging; and adult research participants with apparently no special stake in the case identify several processes that might undergo improvement with aging.

It would be unfair to say that scholars have not yet taken up the challenge of conceptually linking aspects of gains and losses in human development (Baltes, 1997). It might be fair to say, however, that thus far the predominant tendency has been to discuss gains and losses separately or in parallel. For example, some authors may comment on the gains and then the losses in the abstract, but not necessarily link the two ideas in theoretical or empirical work. Perhaps there is a disconnection in explanations of cognitive competence and adaptivity (gains or losses) in late adulthood. Whereas there is considerable empirical and theoretical work pertaining to the description and explanation of decline in cognitive abilities with aging, there is very little parallel descriptive and explanatory work pertaining to those cognitive processes that are allegedly maintained or improved with aging. More thorough examination of these linkages should be pursued. Survey researchers, with their skills at interrogating concepts, interpreting questionnaire data, and sampling, could contribute substantially to our understanding about beliefs regarding gains and losses of cognitive aging. Experimental researchers, with their skills at operationalizing constructs in terms of observable performance, could make substantial contributions to charting patterns of change. Perhaps a selective combination of self-report and experimental traditions would prove fruitful.

In the next section, I turn to the fourth major category of scholarship on the treatment of gains and losses. This category includes research on how gains may be conceptualized in the context of losses.

☐ Conceptualizing Gains in the Context of Losses

The fourth major category of treatments is the largest and most complex. This category pertains to both empirical and theoretical work concerning cognitive gains and losses with aging. After examining an extensive literature, I divided it into three main approaches to the issue of cognitive aging gains.

1. *Gains qua Gains*, or the idea that gains emerge and continue despite or independent of the constraints provided by losses. It includes the "never-the-twain-shall-meet" principle, which reflects my infor-

mal observation that researchers who focus on gains qua gains rarely mention the observations or theories of colleagues who focus on cognitive losses, and vice versa.

2. *Gains as Losses of a Lesser Magnitude*, or the idea that some consolation may be taken in cognitive losses that occur (a) later than expected, (b) not universally, (c) at a level less than feared or predicted, (d) at a level that is not debilitating to everyday skills, and so forth.

3. *Gains as a Function of Losses*, or apparent gains that are linked to specific or general losses, that are occasioned by losses, or that compensate for losses.

Each of these subcategories is summarized in turn.

Gains qua Gains

This alternative is perhaps the boldest and most optimistic of the three, in that it represents some aspects of cognitive aging as undergoing continued or renewed growth throughout adulthood. In some instantiations it may derive from a perspective on human development that incorporates the neo-organismic (neo-Piagetian) idea that there is continued growth in thinking or reasoning with advancing age. The growth may even be "structural" or qualitative in nature (see, e.g., Commons, Sinnott, Richards, & Armon, 1989). Examples include research on (a) fifth or postformal "stages" of cognitive development (beyond Piaget's fourth formal operations stage; Sinnott, 1996); (b) dialectical, transactional, relativistic thinking or reasoning (Kramer & Woodruff, 1986); and perhaps (c) wisdom in late life (Baltes & Staudinger, 1993; Sternberg, 1990). Some observers refer to this approach as the "developmental" approach, presumably because a traditional concept of development is employed in which processes that grow are developmental and processes that decline are not. As noted above, however, a broader concept of development includes both growth and decline. If the term "development" is not tantamount to growth, then developmental approaches include all manner of foci of life-span change. Elsewhere, other terms are used to refer to this approach, including organismic, structural, and neo-Piagetian (e.g., Dixon & Hertzog, 1996).

Postformal Operations

A basic research question in postformal operations concerns whether there is a type of rationality that is qualitatively higher than (Piaget's) formal operations (Sinnott, 1996). The stage of formal operations represents a major cognitive advance for those adolescents and young adults who achieve it. Logical, abstract thinking offers many useful problem-solving tools. Some researchers have argued, however, that it is important for mature adults to consider the relativistic, contradictory, and inherently ambiguous nature of some cognitive problems (e.g., Perry, 1968). The use of formal logic and the pursuit of absolute solutions may not be the most adaptive strategy. Abilities or styles of problem solving that are not constrained by formal reasoning (but are probably preceded by it) are referred to as "postformal" operations. Sinnott (1996, p. 362) writes that the "essence of postformal operations" is "Knowing the general-operation rule and letting it filter your reality, consciously choosing the formal operations logical system you'll impose and living it out as 'true'." From this description, postformal operations appear to involve some metacognitive characteristics, including some evaluation and monitoring of when and where to deploy a given analysis or logic.

As Sinnott (1996) acknowledges, however, an important gap in the research base has not yet been closed. Perhaps further specificity regarding the cognitive skills representative of postformal operations will help. For example, Sinnott provides examples of postformal operations that reflect numerous everyday cognitive and social-cognitive skills: "Ability to 'speak' in 'others' languages' or belief systems; better communication; the ability to argue within others' logics; a flexible view of what is possible for a family; . . . awareness of one's own biases and filtered world-views; . . . more creative problem solving; more flexible interpersonal relations" (p. 370) and so forth. A challenge for proponents of this perspective will be to differentiate their view on how these valued skills might develop and be maintained from the views of researchers from other approaches. Theoretically, it may be a challenge for scholars in this area to address the question of whether and how gains in postformal operations can or do develop independently of cognitive, sensory, and neurological losses. Are the mechanisms of cognitive growth in adulthood the same as those promoting cognitive growth in early life? Empirically, it will be important for scholars sharing this perspective to generate more studies testing their provocative and optimistic views of cognitive aging (Sinnott, 1996).

Wisdom

Equally provocative has been the multifaceted research conducted in the past several decades on the development of wisdom with aging. That wisdom may be an aging-related gain can be established by reference to studies on beliefs about aging (e.g., Heckhausen et al., 1989) and common-sense definitions of wisdom (e.g., Berg & Sternberg, 1992;

Sternberg, 1990). That is, wisdom is a positively valued feature of cognition and is often viewed as increasing with age. That it is a gain qua gain can be inferred from a review of the literature which does not typically place it in the context of cognitive losses. Wisdom is dissimilar to postformal operations in two important ways. First, it has an enduring common-sense quality that invokes similar meanings across a broad range of adults. Second, the development of wisdom in adulthood has been a topic of considerable empirical research.

One of the largest research programs devoted to wisdom is that emanating from Baltes and colleagues (see reviews by Baltes & Smith, 1990; Baltes & Staudinger, 1993). Whereas the definition of wisdom in terms of a growing and expert knowledge system pertaining to fundamental issues of life and living is not entirely unlike that for postformal operations (Sinnott, 1996), casting it explicitly in an expertise framework provides a crucial benefit. Knowledge development and the acquisition of expertise in general are well-understood processes (e.g., Ericsson & Charness, 1994). The facts and pertinent mechanisms of the development of expertise are actively researched in a variety of domains. A well-known principle of expertise is that practice and experience in the domain are fundamental premises and mechanisms for further development. Thus, theoretically, given certain assumptions, wisdom as an expertise is established on firm and promising ground.

In the last decade, a growing body of research regarding wisdom and aging has emerged. It is beyond the purposes of this commentary to review this research, but several features deserve to be highlighted. First, the domain of "life pragmatics" has been operationalized in terms of three main exemplars: life planning, life management, and life review. Notably, these domains bear some resemblance to the description of cognitive activities provided by postformal operation researcher Sinnott (1996). Baltes and colleagues, however, have taken this operational definition further in that they have empirically examined each of these areas separately and in a variety of ways (e.g., Baltes & Smith, 1990; Baltes & Staudinger, 1993). Thus, the database from which conclusions are drawn about wisdom as a gain with aging is substantial. More research in this provocative area will shed light on the extent to which one may conclude that wisdom is a process that shows gains across adulthood—whether as a rule or an exception—and what the constraints and supportive conditions are on its development.

Summary

Cognitive aging researchers have not yet established firmly that there are demonstrable gains qua gains through late adulthood. Two examples of research in this area have been mentioned. Research methods have included experiments, interviews, and even small survey and questionnaire studies. The methods and questions of the cognitive psychology of gains could benefit from survey research techniques and resources. Do people believe that there are gains qua gains with cognitive aging? Are wisdom and postformal operations examples of such potential gains? Could selective indicators of gains be developed and included in large-scale surveys? To what extent are there differences in these issues across multiple dimensions of cultural diversity? Researchers in this area would value progress in answering these and other questions.

Gains as Losses of a Lesser Magnitude

Perhaps only a few observers would assert blithely that losing is in any way tantamount to winning, even if one only *just* falls short or does better than expected. But this category is populated by numerous everyday examples. For example, competitors in sports often testify that performing a personal best in a losing effort is nevertheless a victory of sorts. Giving the competition the "old college try," but losing with dignity, can be a consolation to many performers. It can be heartening to find a new way, through innovative strategy or upgraded technology, of performing a leisure or professional skill and thereby managing to meet your own expectations or maintain your own level of performance.

In cognitive aging, this idea is that some consolation may be taken in selected features of certain cognitive losses, such as those that occur later than expected, less universally than expected, and at a level less than feared or predicted, and that seem to be independent of (unrelated to) other abilities or everyday skills and competencies. I have identified numerous examples of this category from the cognitive aging literature, but summarize only selected illustrations here.

Gains as Losses Occurring Later, Less Uniformly, or Less Universally Than Expected

This exemplar is a pivotal one. Given stereotypes of declining cognitive abilities and a vast reservoir of evidence to support these views, it is possible that some consolation may be taken in the evidence that there are some exceptions to the rule. The exceptions need not be of enormous proportions; in fact, evidence pertaining to more-modest-than-expected losses may be theoretically more promising. An excellent example is that provided by Schaie (e.g., 1990, 1994, 1996). In recent reviews of his prodigious Seattle Longitudinal Study, Schaie has presented a figure with data pertaining to maintenance of intellectual abilities across a seven-year interval by four cohorts, namely, those aged 53–60 years, 60–67 years, 67–74 years, and 74–81 years. His analyses suggest that very high proportions of different-age samples maintain one or more intellectual abilities across the seven-year interval. For example, 90% or more of people in all four age groups (including those aged up to 81 years) maintained at least two intellectual abilities. Critics may quibble with Schaie's definition of maintenance and other issues, but the importance of his analysis in the present context is that it illustrates the implicit notion that losses occur in intellectual abilities, but they may not be as great, as uniform, or as universal as some observers would expect. This fact may be viewed, with some optimism, as a gain.

Gains as Losses That Can Be Accommodated

The second illustration is also a prominent one. An excellent example of this phenomenon may be found in the work of Brandtstädter (e.g., Brandtstädter & Greve, 1994; Brandtstädter & Wentura, 1995). The overall effect of losses may be mitigated by processes that serve to compensate through redefinition and redirection. Accommodation and its connection to compensation have been discussed elsewhere (e.g., Bäckman & Dixon, 1992; Dixon & Bäckman, 1995; Salthouse, 1995). Examples of accommodation include:

1. *Reducing one's criterion of success*, such that one may proclaim success in areas of diminished potentiality simply by lowering the standard by which one evaluates performance. Such "bar lowering" occurs regularly in competitive sports, in which there are competitions and records for juniors, seniors, or masters performers. In any activity in which the effects of aging reduce the potential performance, adjusting downward the standard of successful performance may be a form of accommodating to losses.
2. *Adjusting one's goals*, which could include devaluing and disengaging from blocked goals, as well as selecting new and feasible goals. As Brandtstädter and Wentura (1995) note, with declining productive resources in later life, it may not be possible to maintain the highest standards in multiple domains. The task is to manage one's resources efficiently, such that some novel weighted set of goals can be pursued as resources change with age. For example, the accommodating individual may boost or maintain performance in one valued task only if another task requiring a similar constellation of resources is dropped from the set of goals. Rearranging priorities may be an effective means of adjusting to some aspects of aging-related losses.

3. *Constructing palliative meanings* is a form of accommodation by which an individual experiencing losses finds and focuses on selected positive interpretations. Brandtstädter and Wentura (1995) carefully note that it is possible to construct palliative meanings while still being rational and that even some serious losses may be accommodated in this way. As such, it is perhaps most effective in the relief it provides in the experience of losses. Unless linked with another compensatory process, however, it does not directly address, overcome, or cure the deficit.

Gains From Constructing Forgiving Environments

The role that the environment can play in preventing, managing, or compensating for aging-related losses has been reviewed extensively by Charness and Bosman (1995). An early view of how gains can be forged from aging-related losses through efforts at managing the environment was provided by B. F. Skinner (1983). Indeed, Skinner referred to his method of intellectual self-management in old age as providing a "prosthetic environment." Based on his own experience, Skinner emphasized that biological decline (which he characterized colorfully as "decay and rot") is inevitable with aging. Nevertheless, despite inevitable reduction in biological capacities, it is possible to provide prosthetic environments in which older adults' productive behaviors could be reinforced. He notes several examples of managing the environment of older people, such as arranging the environment to contain cues, using collaborators to improve memory performance, influencing the criteria with which others will evaluate one's performance, and avoiding formidable on-line memory tasks through the use of assistive devices and techniques.

Summary

This category, gains as losses of a lesser magnitude, has been a fertile one in recent cognitive aging research. Three examples of subcategories have been briefly summarized. The theme of each is that, although biologically based cognitive losses occur inevitably with aging, some of these losses are not as uniform or universal as expected, or are of a magnitude that can be prevented, postponed, overcome, overlooked, devalued, modified, or otherwise accommodated. As such, losses of this (minor) magnitude can be viewed as gains, in that individuals can continue to perform at an acceptable, successful, if not optimal, level despite decline. Although evidence pertaining to these and other modalities is accumulating, it is not known how extensively such accommodative principles or beliefs are held. Survey researchers could provide an excellent database pertaining to frequency and implications of such approaches to cognitive aging losses.

Gain as a Function of Losses

I now turn to the third approach to the issue of how gains can be conceptualized in the context of losses in cognitive aging. This approach is referred to as "gains as a function of losses." The basic principle is that cognitive losses or deficits are a fundamental and inevitable fact of adult development and aging. Describing and explaining aging-related decrements are major empirical and theoretical goals. Formidable progress in meeting these challenges has been made (e.g., Salthouse, 1991). Nevertheless, some observers have noted an attendant conundrum, namely, that despite the ineluctable and substantial aging-related cognitive losses, there are conditions under which older adults perform in surprisingly effective ways and at notably efficient levels of achievement (e.g., Dixon, 1995; Salthouse, 1990). Therefore, some attention has been directed at questions pertaining to the linkage of losses and gains. Most basic among these questions is whether and how some specific gains could be a function of specific losses.

Research pertaining to this approach exists at several levels of analysis, including those of the brain, psychological skills, and interaction/communication. Although this research naturally exists under different preferences regarding terminology, for my present purpose these niceties will be ignored in favor of focusing on the similarities of the approach and issues. A key term and perspective in this regard is *compensation*. In addition to the forms of compensation described earlier, one that functionally links losses to gains is evident in research in the current perspective. Compensation refers to processes through which a gap between current accessible skills and environmental demands is reduced or closed (Bäckman & Dixon, 1992; Dixon & Bäckman, 1995). The deficit could be due to aging-related decline, injuries to neurological or sensory systems, organic progressive neurological diseases, or congenital deficits. In the present context, relevant compensatory mechanisms include the recruitment and substitution of either new or existing (i.e., latent) skills, resources, or pathways. Thus, in this context the term *gain* refers to the development of new or supplemental means of performing a cognitive task. The gain, however, is a function of a loss because it presumably would not have developed if the deficit had not come into existence, whether through decline or injury. Several examples of research in which gains are assumed to be inextricably linked to losses can be summarized.

Gains as a Function of Losses in the Brain

At the level of the brain, several recent and different examples may be noted. This issue has been summarized in more detail elsewhere (e.g., Dixon & Bäckman, in press). Buckner, Corbetta, Schatz, Raichle, and Petersen (1996) studied the mechanisms through which speech abilities could be maintained following prefrontal damage, such as that occurring as a result of stroke. Predictably, lesions to the left frontal cortex produce speech impairments, such as nonfluent aphasia. After a period of recovery, there are individual differences in the extent of impairment. Buckner et al. (1996) found direct evidence from Positron Emission Tomography (PET) assessment that, at least for one 72-year-old stroke patient, preserved speech and language was apparently due to activation of an area of the brain outside the left prefrontal cortex. That is, the brain apparently developed and activated a new pathway that served a compensatory function. Presumably, this pathway was not available to noninjured individuals. In this sense, therefore, this gain (new pathway for performing a cognitive function) was a function of the loss (lesion to a specific area of the brain). There is a growing body of research showing such gains (i.e., recruitment of alternative sites and pathways in the brain) as a function of losses (e.g., injury, disease).

Behavioral Gains as a Function of Organic Impairment

Cognitive deficits resulting from severe head injuries, organic diseases (e.g., dementia), or aging-related declines in the brain can also be linked with behavioral compensation (Bäckman & Dixon, 1992; Dixon & Bäckman, in press). The losses associated with a brain-related deficit can be counteracted to some extent by a variety of mnemonic strategies, external memory aids, and environmental adaptations (e.g., Wilson, 1995). Wilson and Watson (1996) have proposed a framework for understanding how specific organic memory deficits can be compensated by particular trainable strategies. The focus is on losses associated with brain injury that can be counteracted and managed by behavioral compensation. New techniques for performing old tasks can be generated by the cognitive neurorehabilitation specialist and learned by the injured person. Specific behavioral gains are linked to identifiable neurological losses. The extent of recovery of function—or the extent of gains—is, however, dependent also on several organic characteristics of the injury. For example, more gains may be possible when the injury occurs earlier in life (e.g., before age 30) and when the injury is of lesser (rather than greater) severity. In addition, Wilson and Watson (1996) contend that the extent and duration of gains following organic memory impairment may be associated with the type of rehabilitation program followed.

Gains in Substitutable Skills

The speed with which information is processed declines at a regular rate with human aging (Salthouse, 1991). One implication is that, with aging, skills requiring speeded performance may be executed at slower rates. For skills in which speed of performance is an important criterion of success, such aging-related slowing may have far-reaching detrimental repercussions. For example, transcription typing is a skill in which both speed and accuracy of performance are valued. Task analyses have revealed that among the multiple determinants of this skill are speed-related components such as finger tapping speed and choice reaction time. If performance on these components declines with aging (as it does), then speed of transcription typing should also decline with aging. Interestingly, the molar skill does not necessarily decline with aging. Active, older professional typists who perform accurate transcription typing at a speed comparable to that of younger typists can be identified (e.g., Salthouse, 1984). Moreover, they perform this complex skill at high levels despite losses in speed-related components. Maintenance, despite decline, may be accomplished through gains in substitutable mechanisms, a principal form of compensation (Bäckman & Dixon, 1992; Dixon & Bäckman, 1995; Salthouse, 1987, 1995). As researchers have shown, transcription typists may be using a compensatory mechanism of increased eye–hand span (Bosman, 1993; Salthouse, 1984). That is, the older typist may be processing the to-be-typed text further ahead of the current keystroke than do other skilled typists. One possible inference is that this gain in eye–hand span is a function of the loss of finger speed and reaction time.

Gains In or Via Collaborative Contexts

Recent research in communicative and collaborative mechanisms has focused on their relevance to cognitive deficits, whether as a function of organic injury or aging-related loss. One brief example of each of these is presented.

First, Ahlsén (1991) studied a 47-year-old individual who became aphasic after a sudden illness. The recovery phase was quite long, but after several years the individual began developing "body communication" with semantic loading. That is, the patient, who could not communicate semantic information orally, developed complex gestures to communicate this information visually. Moreover, as verbal expression and communicative patterns returned, the use of body communication declined. The gain was a function of a loss, and as recovery of normal functioning occurred, the new skill declined.

Second, some researchers have recently examined the extent to which older individuals may effectively use collaborators as living external cognitive aids in performing demanding cognitive tasks (e.g., Dixon & Gould, in press; Gould, Trevithick, & Dixon, 1991; Gould, Kurzman, & Dixon, 1994). That is, can individual cognitive deficits be compensated by recruiting alternative pathways not within the individual's brain, but by accessing other brains? Researchers have examined normal older adults (with typical aging-related cognitive declines) as well as adults with organic impairments, such as those associated with Parkinson's Disease. Testing has occurred in both individual and collaborative settings; that is, performance has been measured at both the standard individual level of analysis, as well as at the group level of performance. Measurements have included multiple aspects of cognitive products as well as multiple indicators of collaborative processes (e.g., strategic negotiations). Participants have included unacquainted groups as well as married couples (experienced collaborators). Early results of these studies have shown that experienced older dyads may indeed compensate for individual-level aging-related decline through unique interactive processes (e.g., Dixon, 1996; Gould et al., 1994). In addition, the patterns of collaborative performance are indicative of some degree of benefit as a function of interactive experience (Dixon & Gould, in press). In this example, the losses are typical aging-related cognitive ones. The compensatory gains are not, however, at the individual level of analysis. They are instead at the level of the (human) environment: some older adults may work selectively and strategically with a partner such that the overall level of performance is greater than either partner could achieve and greater than that achieved by numerous comparison groups, including younger and healthy ones (Dixon, 1996). In this sense, then, the gains in recruiting and using other brains may be linked to individual-level losses, or even possibly a function of them.

Summary

This third approach to the issue of cognitive aging gains focuses on how gains may be a function of losses. Several examples of research pertaining to this approach were presented briefly. In all cases, the crucial question of determining precisely that a given gain was in fact a function of a given loss has not been settled. For the present purposes, this is not viewed as a major omission or flaw, for (a) it is extremely difficult to obtain such definitive empirical data, (b) arguments pertaining to the issue are usually based on patterns of results rather than single relationships, and (c) the present goal is to show brief examples of the direction of this research and theory. Nevertheless, it is important to differentiate "gains as a function of losses" from "gains qua gains" and "gains as losses of a lesser magnitude." The former approach is unique in that cognitive losses are taken as targets of analysis, whether at the theoretical or empirical levels. Given a cognitive loss, the question becomes how maintenance of overall performance could be maintained. Typically, such maintenance involves the mechanism of compensatory substitution. Alternative, if not novel, mechanisms are used adaptively to overcome a specific loss.

☐ Conclusion

In this initial analysis of the concept of gains in cognitive aging, I have developed a modest taxonomy representing how this term is used (whether explicitly or implicitly) in the cognitive aging literature. The pertinent literature includes publications in the field, beliefs about aging, and empirical research representing various perspectives. The taxonomy has three major categories: (a) gains qua gains, (b) gains as losses of a lesser magnitude, and (c) gains as a function of losses. These categories may be updated by a variety of research projects, including those for which differential, experimental, clinical, self-report, and survey research procedures are employed. The concept of gains in cognitive aging is a complex one, perhaps more complex than often realized. The phenomena of cognitive aging are actually characterized by multiple determinants, multiple directions, and multiple aspects. This multiplicity is reflected in the variety of cogent and legitimate perspectives and theories on cognitive aging, whether they focus on gains, losses, or both.

☐ Acknowledgments

The author acknowledges grant support from the National Institute on Aging (AG08235) and the Natural Sciences and Engineering Research Council of Canada. I appreciate the helpful comments of David Hultsch and Denise Park on an earlier version of this chapter.

☐ References

Ahlsén, E. (1991). Body communication as compensation for speech in a Wernicke's aphasic: A longitudinal study. *Journal of Communication Disorders, 24,* 1–12.

Bäckman, L., & Dixon, R. A. (1992). Psychological compensation: A theoretical framework. *Psychological Bulletin, 112,* 259–283.

Baltes, P. B. (1987). Theoretical propositions of life-span developmental psychology: On the dynamics between growth and decline. *Developmental Psychology, 23,* 611–626.

Baltes, P. B. (1997). On the incomplete architecture of human ontogeny: Selection, optimization, and compensation as foundation of developmental theory. *American Psychologist, 52,* 366–380.

Baltes, P. B., & Baltes, M. M. (Eds.). (1990). *Successful aging: Perspectives from the behavioral sciences.* New York: Cambridge University Press.

Baltes, P. B., & Smith, J. (1990). Toward a psychology of wisdom and its ontogenesis. In R. J. Sternberg (Ed.), *Wisdom: Its nature, origins and development* (pp. 87–120). Cambridge, England: Cambridge University Press.

Baltes, P. B., & Staudinger, U. M. (1993). The search for a psychology of wisdom. *Current Directions in Psychological Science, 2,* 75–80.

Berg, C. A., & Sternberg, R. J. (1992). Adults' conceptions of intelligence across the adult life span. *Psychology and Aging, 7,* 221–231.

Bosman, E. A. (1993). Age-related differences in the motoric aspects of transcription typing skill. *Psychology and Aging, 8,* 87–102.

Brandtstädter, J., & Greve, W. (1994). The aging self: Stabilizing and protective processes. *Developmental Review, 14,* 52–80.

Brandtstädter, J., & Wentura, D. (1995). Adjustment to shifting possibility frontiers in later life: Complementary adaptive modes. In R. A. Dixon & L. Bäckman (Eds.), *Compensating for psychological deficits and declines: Managing losses and promoting gains* (pp. 83–106). Mahwah, NJ: Erlbaum.

Buckner, R. L., Corbetta, M., Schatz, J., Raichle, M. E., & Petersen, S. E. (1996). Preserved speech abilities and compensation following prefrontal damage. *Proceedings of the National Academy of Sciences, 93,* 1249–1253.

Cerella, J. (1990). Aging and information processing rate. In J. E. Birren & K. W. Schaie (Eds.), *Handbook of the psychology of aging* (pp. 201–221). San Diego, CA: Academic Press.

Charness, N., & Bosman, E. A. (1995). Compensation through environmental modification. In R. A. Dixon & L. Bäckman (Eds.), *Compensating for psychological deficits and declines: Managing losses and promoting gains* (pp. 147–168). Mahwah, NJ: Erlbaum.

Commons, M. L., Sinnott, J. D., Richards, F A., & Armon, C. (Eds.). (1989). *Adult development: Comparisons and applications of developmental models.* New York: Praeger.

Craik, F. I. M., & Jennings, J. M. (1992). Human memory. In F. I. M. Craik & T. A. Salthouse (Eds.), *The handbook of aging and cognition* (pp. 51–110). Hillsdale, NJ: Erlbaum.

Dixon, R. A. (1995). Promoting competence through compensation. In L. Bond, S. Cutler, & A. Grams (Eds.), *Promoting successful and productive aging* (pp. 220–238). Newbury Park, CA: Sage.

Dixon, R. A. (1996). Collaborative memory and aging. In D. J. Herrmann, C. McEvoy, C. Hertzog, P. Hertel, & M. K. Johnson (Eds.), *Basic and applied memory: Theory in context* (pp. 359–383). Mahwah, NJ: Erlbaum.

Dixon, R. A., & Bäckman, L. (1995). Concepts of compensation: Integrated, differentiated and Janus-faced. In R. A. Dixon & L. Bäckman (Eds.), *Compensating for psycho-

logical deficits and declines: Managing losses and promoting gains (pp. 3–19). Mahwah, NJ: Erlbaum.

Dixon, R. A., & Bäckman, L. (in press). Principles of compensation in cognitive neuro-rehabilitation. In D. T. Stuss, G. Winocur, & I. H. Robertson (Eds.), *Cognitive neurorehabilitation: A comprehensive approach.* Cambridge, England: Cambridge University Press.

Dixon, R. A., & Gould, O. N. (in press). Younger and older adults collaborating on retelling everyday stories. *Applied Developmental Science.*

Dixon, R. A., & Hertzog, C. (1996). Theoretical issues in cognition and aging. In F. Blanchard-Fields & T. M. Hess (Eds.), *Perspectives on cognitive change in adulthood and aging* (pp. 25–65). New York: McGraw-Hill.

Dixon, R. A., Kramer, D. A., & Baltes, P. B. (1985). Intelligence: A life-span developmental perspective. In B. B. Wolman (Ed.), *Handbook of intelligence: Theories, measurements, and applications* (pp. 301–350). New York: Wiley.

Dixon, R. A., Lerner, R. M., & Hultsch, D. F. (1991). The concept of development in the study of individual and social change. In P. van Geert & L. P. Mos (Eds.), *Annals of theoretical psychology* (pp. 279–323). New York: Plenum.

Ericsson, K. A., & Charness, N. (1994). Expert performance: Its structure and acquisition. *American Psychologist, 49,* 725–747.

Gould, O. N., Kurzman, D., & Dixon, R. A. (1994). Communication during prose recall conversations by young and old dyads. *Discourse Processes, 17,* 149–165.

Gould, O. N., Trevithick, L., & Dixon, R. A. (1991). Adult age differences in elaborations produced during prose recall. *Psychology and Aging, 6,* 93–99.

Harris, D. B. (Ed.). (1957). *The concept of development.* Minneapolis: University of Minnesota Press.

Heckhausen, J., Dixon, R. A., & Baltes, P. B. (1989). Gains and losses in development throughout adulthood as perceived by different adult age groups. *Developmental Psychology, 25,* 109–121.

Heckhausen, J., & Krueger, J., (1993). Developmental expectations for the self and most other people: Age grading in three functions of social comparison. *Developmental Psychology, 29,* 539–548.

Hummert, M. L., Garstka, T. A., Shaner, J. L., & Strahm, S. (1994). Stereotypes of the elderly held by young, middle-aged, and elderly adults. *Journal of Gerontology: Psychological Sciences, 49,* P40–249.

Jones, H. E., & Conrad, H. S. (1933). The growth and decline of intelligence: A study of a homogeneous group between the ages of ten and sixty. *Genetic Psychology Monographs, 13,* 223–298.

Kramer, D. A., & Woodruff, D. S. (1986). Relativistic and dialectical thought in three adult age-groups. *Human Development, 29,* 280–290.

Lerner, R. M. (1984). *On the nature of human plasticity.* New York: Cambridge University Press.

Light, L. L. (1991). Memory and aging: Four hypotheses in search of data. *Annual Review of Psychology, 42,* 333–376.

Medina, J. J. (1996). *The clock of ages: Why we age, how we age, winding back the clock.* Cambridge, England: Cambridge University Press.

Perlmutter, M. (Ed.). (1990). *Late life potential.* Washington, DC: Gerontological Society of America.

Perry, W. I. (1968). *Forms of intellectual and ethical development in the college years.* New York: Holt, Rinehart, and Winston.

Pressey, S. L. (1919). Are the present psychological scales reliable for adults? *Journal of Abnormal Psychology, 14,* 314–324.

Salthouse, T. A. (1984). Effects of age and skill in typing. *Journal of Experimental Psychology: General, 113,* 345–371.

Salthouse, T. A. (1987). Age, experience, and compensation. In C. Schooler & K. W. Schaie (Eds.), *Cognitive functioning and social structure over the life course* (pp. 142–157). Norwood, NJ: Ablex.

Salthouse, T. A. (1990). Cognitive competence and expertise in aging. In J. E. Birren & K. W. Schaie (Eds.), *Handbook of the psychology of aging* (pp. 310–319). San Diego, CA: Academic Press.

Salthouse, T. A. (1991). *Theoretical perspectives on cognitive aging.* Hillsdale, NJ: Erlbaum.

Salthouse, T. A. (1995). Refining the concept of psychological compensation. In R. A. Dixon & L. Bäckman (Eds.), *Compensating for psychological deficits and declines: Managing losses and promoting gains* (pp. 21–34). Mahwah, NJ: Erlbaum.

Sanford, E. C. (1902). Mental growth and decay. *American Journal of Psychology, 13,* 426–449.

Schaie, K. W. (1990). Intellectual development in adulthood. In J. E. Birren & K. W. Schaie (Eds.), *Handbook of the psychology of aging* (pp. 291–309). San Diego, CA: Academic Press.

Schaie, K. W. (1994). The course of adult intellectual development. *American Psychologist, 49,* 304–313.

Schaie, K. W. (1996). *Intellectual development in adulthood: The Seattle Longitudinal Study.* New York: Cambridge University Press.

Schieber, F., & Baldwin, C. L. (1996). Vision, audition, and aging research. In F. Blanchard-Fields & T. M. Hess (Eds.), *Perspectives on cognitive change in adulthood and aging* (pp. 122–162). New York: McGraw-Hill.

Sinnott, J. (1996). The developmental approach: Postformal thought as adaptive intelligence. In F. Blanchard-Fields & T. M. Hess (Eds.), *Perspectives on cognitive change in adulthood and aging* (pp. 358–383). New York: McGraw-Hill.

Skinner, B. F. (1983). Intellectual self-management in old age. *American Psychologist, 38,* 239–244.

Sternberg, R. J. (Ed.). (1990). *Wisdom: Its nature, origin and development.* Cambridge, England: Cambridge University Press.

Uttal, D. H., & Perlmutter, M. (1989). Toward a broader conceptualization of development: The role of gains and losses across the life span. *Developmental Review, 9,* 101–132.

Wilson, B. A. (1995). Memory rehabilitation: Compensating for memory problems: In R. A. Dixon & L. Bäckman (Eds.), *Compensating for psychological deficits and declines: Managing losses and promoting gains* (pp. 171–190). Mahwah, NJ: Erlbaum.

Wilson, B. A., & Watson, P. C. (1996). A practical framework for understanding compensatory behaviour in people with organic memory impairment. *Memory, 4,* 465–486.

Wohlwill J. F. (1973). *The study of behavioral development.* New York: Academic Press.

Zacks, R. T., & Hasher, L. (1994). Directed ignoring: Inhibitory regulation of working memory. In D. Dagenbach & T. H. Carr (Eds.), *Inhibitory processes in attention, memory, and language* (pp. 241–264). San Diego, CA: Academic Press.

AGE-RELATED CHANGES IN COGNITIVE FUNCTIONING

5

CHAPTER   Fergus I. M. Craik

Memory, Aging, and Survey Measurement

As documented in other chapters of this volume, survey methods are used extensively to assess and measure various aspects of the lives of citizens aged 60 and above. Surveys enable researchers to assess needs, attitudes, and opinions, and to track changes in living habits and in the use of products and services. This information can then be used by government agencies and commercial organizations to frame appropriate policies and to steer business decisions. There are special problems, however, associated with the collection of valid data from older people. As illustrated throughout this book, age-related cognitive changes necessitate the careful interpretation of survey results from elderly respondents; they may have particular difficulties in comprehending questions, especially, perhaps, in telephone interviews; they may be more liable to impose their own assumptions on what is being asked and why; they may have difficulty in holding and integrating the successive parts of long or complex questions, and they may have problems in remembering details of their own habits and actions.

The present chapter addresses these last-mentioned difficulties and problems: those to do with various aspects of memory. Age-related changes in memory are well documented (Craik & Jennings, 1992; Light, 1991, Salthouse 1991). The general consensus is that memory performance does decline in older adults, but also that the amount of loss depends very much on the specific memory task under consideration; performance on some tasks drops considerably in older people, whereas performance on other memory tasks shows little or no decline. It is the memory theorist's job to understand this pattern of differential loss and possible compensation (Dixon & Bäckman, 1995), and the applied researcher's task to show how such age-related changes in memory affect aspects of real-life behavior, including responses to surveys. The bulk of this chapter is devoted to a review of current findings and ideas in the field of memory and aging; each section concludes with the implications of the results for survey measurement in older people.

☐ Types of Memory

Cognitive psychologists typically talk and write about a variety of different memory systems, memory stages, or memory stores. This is a reasonable (and even *necessary*) response to the results of 100 years of laboratory and clinical research showing that performance on some tasks is unaffected by aging, by brain damage, and by adverse environmental conditions, whereas performance on other memory tasks declines catastrophically in the same individuals. To give some classical examples, the patient H.M., who underwent bilateral surgical excision of his hippocampus and surrounding brain areas for the relief of epilepsy, is unable to recollect any personal events experienced since the operation, yet is essentially unimpaired at learning new motor skills and also in the ability to repeat back a series of words or numbers (Milner, Corkin, & Teuber, 1968). The patient K.C. suffered brain damage in a traffic accident; his access to general knowledge of facts and procedures is normal, yet he has *no* access to any personal memory from his entire life. Thus he can give a coherent account of the procedures necessary to change a car tire, yet is unable to recollect any occasion on which he changed a tire, and does not even remember that his brother died in an accident many years ago (Tulving, Hayman, & Macdonald, 1991). In the case of normal aging, older adults (typically aged between 60 and 85 years in the work discussed here) are typically impaired relative to younger control subjects (typically aged 20–30 years) in free recall tasks, in their ability to recall highly specific facts such as names, and in their ability to remember details of where and when events occurred. They are much less impaired, and sometimes superior to their younger counterparts, on other tasks such as word-priming, recognition memory, and knowledge of word meanings (Craik & Jennings, 1992; Salthouse, 1991).

Such findings drive the necessary conclusion that "memory" is not some monolithic entity, but cognitive psychologists unfortunately disagree about how the overall concept should be decomposed. One early scheme suggested a tripartite division into the three successive stages of sensory memory, short-term (or primary) memory, and long-term (or secondary) memory (Atkinson & Shiffrin, 1968; Murdock, 1967).

This classification provides an explanation of why amnesic patients, and to a much lesser degree normal older people, have difficulties in retrieving personal events from hours or days ago, yet can repeat back strings of digits or words at the same level as their younger counterparts (Baddeley & Warrington, 1970; Craik, 1977). That is, their long-term memory is impaired but their short-term memory (in the sense of material "still in mind") is unaffected. An extended and modified version of this tripartite scheme has been suggested by Tulving and his colleagues (e.g., Schacter & Tulving, 1994). They suggest that memory can be divided into five major systems that differ fundamentally from one another. Their five candidates are procedural memory, the perceptual representational system (PRS), primary memory, episodic memory, and semantic memory. Of these five, PRS corresponds roughly to sensory memory, primary memory corresponds to short-term memory, and episodic memory and semantic memory together map onto the former long-term memory. The new system, procedural memory, is responsible for learning associative relations, simple conditioning, and motor and cognitive skills.

One of the main categories of evidence for separate memory systems is the existence of "dissociations" among various tasks that presumably tap the systems differentially. Thus if aging, brain damage, or some other manipulation affects performance on one task, but has no effect on a second task, it is inferred that the tasks are mediated by separate systems. Further convergent evidence from different sources is usually sought before concluding that tasks do indeed tap into different systems (Schacter & Tulving, 1994). This five-system framework provides a good account of such cases as H.M. (impaired episodic memory, intact procedural and primary memories) and K.C. (impaired episodic memory, intact semantic and procedural memories) and normal aging (impaired episodic memory and aspects of semantic memory, intact procedural memory). Although the memory systems viewpoint has its critics (McKoon, Ratcliff, & Dell, 1986), it undoubtedly provides a good descriptive framework within which the main age-related changes in memory may be understood. The following sections provide brief reviews of age-related changes in the different memory systems, and a concluding section draws these findings and conclusions together to point out their implications for the design and interpretation of surveys.

☐ Procedural Memory

The term "procedural memory" is used to cover the learning and retention of a rather wide assortment of motor and cognitive skills, e.g., playing the piano, driving a car, or solving a jigsaw puzzle or a Tower of Hanoi problem, as well as academic skills such as counting, spelling, and reading. These abilities all have a large automatic component associated with them, and typically do not involve the conscious recollection of the initial learning episode. For this reason, procedural memory is often described as involving *implicit* memory processes, in contrast to the *explicit* recollection that is necessarily involved in episodic recall and recognition. It appears to be this bypassing of conscious recollection and conscious decision-making on the one hand, and the heavy involvement of well-learned, automatic mental processes on the other hand, that work together to protect procedural memory skills from the effects of aging and brain damage.

In the cognitive realm, procedural memory is often assessed by means of priming paradigms. For example, reading a word appears to prime the specific perceptual, lexical, and semantic operations involved in the word's analysis, with the result that subsequent analysis of either the same word (e.g., doctor/DOCTOR) or a related word (e.g., doctor/NURSE) is carried out more easily and rapidly. Laver and Burke (1993) carried out a meta-analysis of semantic priming tasks and found that the effect is, if anything, greater in older people. One variant of the priming procedure involves presenting words to study (e.g., "market"), then later giving participants a word-stem completion task in which the first few letters of a word are provided (e.g., "MAR ___") and the task is to complete the word. Light and Singh (1987) tested younger and older people on this task under two instructional conditions; in one condition, subjects were asked to complete each word fragment with the first word that came to mind, and in the other condition they were asked to use the fragments as cues to remember words from the study list. Light and Singh found no age differences in the first (implicit) task; that is, older people were as likely as their younger counterparts to complete MAR___ with "market," as opposed to marble, marriage, etc., but the investigators found that younger participants outperformed older subjects in the explicit cued recall task.

In a second ingenious variant of the priming paradigm developed by Jacoby and Witherspoon (1982), participants are asked to read sentences biasing the less frequent member of a homophone pair (e.g., reign as opposed to rain, hare as opposed to hair). Subjects therefore read a sentence like "the wounded hare limped slowly across the field" and, after a series of similar sentences, were given a spelling test in which they were asked to spell auditorily presented words including the homophones. The finding is that participants are biased to spell the recently encountered variant, and Howard (1988) showed that younger and older subjects did not differ in this respect.

These and other examples show that procedural memory processes are apparently unaffected by aging (see reviews by Craik & Jennings, 1992; Light & La Voie, 1993). Whereas this is generally a positive finding, it can also have negative consequences that are relevant to survey measurement. In a series of recent articles, Jacoby and his colleagues (e.g., Dywan & Jacoby, 1990; Jacoby, 1991; Jennings & Jacoby, 1997) have pointed out that many cognitive tasks involve a mixture of unconscious, implicit processes and consciously mediated, explicit processes. If explicit processes are impaired by aging, but implicit processes are not, then an older person's responses will be more governed by these latter mental operations. Thus Dywan and Jacoby (1990) found that older people were more likely to think that repeated fictitious names were names of real famous people; they misattributed the familiarity associated with repetition to fame in the outside world. Similarly, Jennings and Jacoby (1997) showed that older subjects were more likely than younger subjects to misattribute repetitions of words in a test list to their presentation in a previous study list. These and other examples of false memories experienced more often by older people (see Schacter, Koutstaal & Norman, 1997 for a review) appear to result from the combination of unimpaired procedural (or implicit) memory processes with impaired explicit memory for the episodic context in which the word or other event was originally experienced.

Such false memories can have serious negative consequences for older people in real-life settings. For example, the confusion of imagined or intended actions with real actions, e.g., taking medications or turning off the stove, could be quite dangerous. In the context of surveys, certain responses could be biased or primed by framing questions in a certain way or by the provision of earlier "examples." Results from the cognitive aging literature suggest that these influences would be stronger in older people. Carry-over effects from one section of a survey are also likely to be greater in older respondents. The implication for designers of surveys is that efforts should be made to ensure that age-related differences in responses reflect differences in real behavior, as opposed to differences that are wholly or partially caused by age-related changes in vulnerability to the misleading effects of context and repetition.

☐ PRS and Perceptual Processing

This "system" is clearly a collection of different subsystems dealing with sensory and perceptual information from the different modalities.

Their brain locations are typically those regions associated with the early processing of modality-specific information, and their function is to analyze, integrate, and briefly hold incoming sense data (Tulving & Schacter, 1990). With respect to aging, little direct research has been done on possible age-related changes in PRS functioning (see Craik & Jennings, 1992, for a brief review). Given that procedural memory is essentially intact in older people it seems reasonable to assume that early processing stages, common to implicit and explicit memory, are comparatively unaffected. On the other hand, it is clear that the sensory mechanisms themselves (e.g., vision, hearing, taste, touch, and smell) show marked changes with age, and it is perhaps a more interesting question in the present context to ask how sensory losses affect higher order cognitive processes.

Lindenberger and Baltes (1994) have recently presented some rather dramatic results showing that visual and auditory acuity together accounted for 93% of the age-related variance in intelligence in a large group of older people aged between 70 and 103 years. Intelligence was measured by a battery of 14 cognitive tests, so it seems likely that the result is a valid one. However, it need not be the case that losses in vision and hearing cause losses in intelligence; another possible interpretation is that normal aging is associated with a reduction in a whole variety of physical and mental abilities, and that some "common cause" underlies this generalized reduction in efficient functioning (Lindenberger & Baltes, 1994). That is, to the extent that aging affects a wide range of somatic systems, e.g., the cardiovascular, muscular, respiratory, and central nervous systems, it might be expected that substantial correlations would be found among all functions. Brain function may correlate with muscular strength, for example, although no direct causal mechanism links the two sets of abilities.

Another research line explores the effects of degrading sensory input on cognitive performance in young adults. Spinks, Gilmore, and Thomas (1996) showed that young adults performed like 50-year-olds on Symbol-Digit substitution and on Raven's Advanced Progressive Matrices when visual contrast was degraded to the levels experienced by patients with Alzheimer's disease. Correspondingly, Alzheimer patients' cognitive performance can be improved differentially if the visual contrast of the display is enhanced (Gilmore, Thomas, Klitz, Persanyi, & Tomsak, 1996). In a similar study carried out by Dana Murphy, Bruce Schneider, and myself, memory for recently presented paired associates was greatly reduced in young adults when the auditorily presented stimuli were presented in a background of noise. It is important to note that the young adult subjects perceived the stimuli correctly; nonetheless, the noisy background impaired the ability to lay down adequate memory traces.

Age-related differences in speech comprehension provide another case in which perceptual and cognitive factors interact. This topic is of prime interest to survey researchers who make extensive use of telephone interviews; difficulties in comprehension may result in a different pattern of responses from those obtained in face-to-face interviews. Such potential difficulties may be lessened by the provision of an adequate context, especially the context preceding important information or a crucial question. Wingfield, Alexander, and Cavigelli (1994) explored age differences in identifying spoken words that were presented either in isolation or with varying amounts of preceding and/or subsequent context. The researchers found that younger participants were better able to identify isolated words and made better use of context following the target words. Older and younger subjects were equally able to benefit from preceding context, however. This point was also investigated by Pichora-Fuller, Schneider, and Daneman (1995). Participants listened to short sentences in a range of noisy babble backgrounds, and attempted to identify the final word in each case. The sentences provided a context that was either highly predictive or nonpredictive of the final word; thus both the sensory signal-to-noise ratios and the level of cognitive support were varied in the study. Figure 1A shows typical results from a young adult, an older adult, and an older adult with marked hearing problems (presbycusis). Figure 1B shows the group results in the form of the benefit conferred by the high-context relative to low-context sentences; the figure shows that older and presbycusis subjects benefited more than their younger counterparts from the predictive context, but that higher levels of signal-to-noise ratios were required to reap these benefits.

Other examples of compensation for age-related losses in comprehension by enhancing perceptual or cognitive factors are given by Craik and Anderson (1998) and in chapters in a recent book edited by Dixon and Bäckman (1995). Within the area of survey measurement itself, it is an interesting question as to how changes in the perceptual quality and in the cognitive context affect responses. Older people may be more prone to assume (sometimes wrongly) that they understand what is being asked. Research is needed to explore the possible interactions among age and perceptual and cognitive factors on the validity of responses and the subjective confidence with which these responses are given.

☐ Primary Memory and Working Memory

The general notion of a separate short-term memory system has been well accepted in cognitive psychology since the early 1960s, but

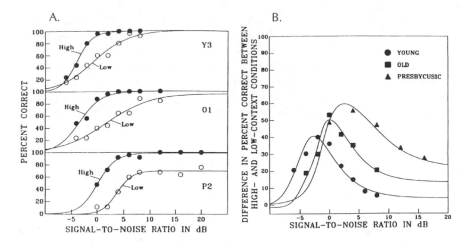

FIGURE 1. (A) Percentage of high-context and low-context words correctly identified as a function of signal-to-noise ratio for three sample subjects, one young adult (Y3), one older adult (O1), and one older presbycusic adult (P2). (B) Mean difference between high context and low context in percentage of correctly identified words as a function of signal-to-noise ratio, for young, old, and presbycusic adults. (Adapted from research given in Pichora-Fuller, Schneider, & Daneman, 1995.)

unfortunately the terminology has been used in a confusing way. Experimental psychologists use the term to refer to a very small fragment of memory, essentially just that information that is still "in mind" after several stimuli have been presented. Good recall of items from the end of a list (the recency effect) is attributed to this special short-term store, for example. However, clinicians tend to use "short-term memory" to refer to memory for recent events over several hours or even days—clearly a very different concept. To clarify matters, Waugh and Norman (1965) suggested the term "primary memory" (PM) to refer to the fragment still in mind, and "secondary memory" for all other information retrieved from memory. PM is thus involved in the recency effect, in span paradigms, in holding telephone numbers in mind, and so on.

The further important concept of working memory (WM) was introduced by Baddeley and Hitch (1974). This notion also refers to information held in mind, but stresses the *functions* of short-term retention, for example, the integration of language and other serially presented stimuli, mental calculations, and reasoning in general. WM is thus a much more dynamic concept than the passive store suggested by PM. But are PM and WM separate systems? I have suggested not (Craik & Rabinowitz, 1984), proposing instead that short-term memory tasks lie on a passive–active continuum, such that passive tasks (e.g., recall of a list of numbers) are relatively pure PM tasks, whereas active tasks (e.g., the Daneman & Carpenter, 1980, reading span task) requiring manipulation, storage, and transformations of held material, are examples of WM tasks.

When age differences are considered, the PM-WM distinction is a useful one in that age-related differences are slight in PM tasks but substantial in WM tasks. Thus, if the task requires immediate repetition of a small amount of material, adult age differences are quite small. If the task requires active manipulation of stored material, however, or requires rapid alternation between storage and processing of further incoming information, then age-related differences are much greater. Examples of tasks with a high PM component include word and digit span (Parkinson, Lindholm, & Inman, 1982), the Brown-Peterson paradigm (Craik, 1977; Inman & Parkinson, 1983), and recall from the recency portion of free recall lists (Delbecq-Derouesne & Beauvois, 1989). Whereas age-related differences are sometimes statistically reliable in such tasks, the general finding is that the differences are small relative to the much larger differences found in secondary memory tasks (see Craik & Jennings, 1992, for a review).

For researchers interested in survey measurement, the comparative absence of an age-related decrement in PM means that older respondents can be relied on to copy down telephone numbers accurately or to transcribe small amounts of information without error from one part of a form to another. However, survey responses may more often tap WM (for example, telephone surveys that involve long complex sentences, or questions with several alternative responses to bear in mind), and here the research data suggest the existence of large age decrements. A number of studies agree that performance on WM tasks declines systematically from early adulthood on (e.g., Craik, Morris, & Gick, 1990; Dobbs & Rule, 1989; Wingfield, Stine, Lahar, & Aberdeen, 1988); there is also some possibility that the age-related decrements increase with increasing task complexity, although here the picture is less clear (Craik, Morris, & Gick, 1990; Salthouse, Mitchell, Skovronek, & Babcock, 1989). There is also debate about the underlying reasons for the age-related decline, with some researchers suggesting a depletion in mental energy or "attentional resources" (Craik & Byrd, 1982) and others arguing for an age-related decline in processing speed (Salthouse, 1991, 1993) or for a decline in the ability to inhibit unwanted information (Hasher & Zacks, 1988; Zacks & Hasher, 1988). Whatever the underlying cause or causes, it is clear that older adults have particular problems in situations where they must hold, manipulate, and integrate moderate amounts of information over short time spans. These difficulties may be exacerbated when the task involves holding some information while simultaneously dealing with further incoming information (Daneman & Carpenter, 1980; Gick, Craik, & Morris, 1988); this may well occur in surveys if a person has to retain a question and initial possible answers while simultaneously evaluating later alternative answers. The bottom line is that designers of surveys should bear these factors in mind when attempting to optimize the validity of information collected from older respondents.

☐ Episodic Memory

When older people complain that their memory "isn't what it used to be" they are usually referring to episodic memory, the ability to recollect specific autobiographical events that have happened comparatively recently. One laboratory analogue that taps this ability is free recall of words, sentences, stories, or pictures. In this paradigm, subjects are presented with a long list of stimuli and then attempt to recall them, without cues or reminders, at a later time (typically anything from 30 seconds to 24 hours after presentation). There is overwhelming evidence that performance on such tests declines with age from the 30s and 40s to the 70s and 80s, and that the age-related decrement in free recall is typically greater than the decrement observed on many other memory tasks, such as PM, procedural memory, and some semantic memory tasks.

Why is episodic memory especially vulnerable to the effects of aging? It seems likely that a number of factors come into play to determine the final outcome. I would like to believe some optimistic accounts that suggest that such age-related declines are all for the best: that a kindly Mother Nature is protecting older memory systems from being overloaded with trivia, for instance. I have difficulty believing such adaptive and compensatory accounts, however. First, the inability to remember details of recent events is often a source of embarrassment and frustration to older people; they would certainly like to remember. Second, the notion of "overloaded memory banks" is quite unlikely given all we know about expertise and memory; this work makes it clear that the more we know about a topic, the easier it is to encode and retrieve further episodic events relevant to that topic (Bransford, Franks, Morris, & Stein, 1979). Thus the metaphor of accrued knowledge as a framework or scaffolding for new events is more apt than the metaphor of a cluttered cupboard. Third, memory is mediated by neural structures in the brain, and the brain is a physical organ like the heart, liver, lungs, and kidneys. These other organs undoubtedly become less efficient with advancing age, and it would be curious indeed if the brain was invulnerable to the effects of aging.

So what actually changes? Cognitive aging researchers have suggested that "attentional resources" decline from midlife to old age, and that such resources are required to fuel the processes necessary to support cognitive performance. It is also necessary to postulate that episodic memory is particularly resource-demanding. Candidates for these "resources" include the availability or utilization of blood glucose, the availability of an adequate blood supply to key areas of the brain, the speed with which mental operations are carried out, and the richness of interconnections among neurons in the central nervous system (Wickens, 1984). The enormous recent upsurge of research in cognitive neuroscience is likely to provide a definitive answer within the next few years. At the behavioral level, one problem associated with episodic memory is that events are often unpredictable and idiosyncratic; we therefore cannot use overlearned schemes and routines to encode and retrieve them. Instead, episodic memory is akin to "fluid intelligence" in that it deals with new information, rather than being able to rely on the accumulated structures of "crystallized intelligence."

One point about age-related differences in episodic memory is that the deficits are often reduced as supportive contextual information is provided, either at encoding (in the form of strategy instructions or the provision of an organized framework into which new events can be placed meaningfully) or at retrieval (in the form of cues, hints, reminders, and reinstatement of the original context). For this effect to appear reliably, it may be necessary to supply cues both at the time of encoding and again at the time of retrieval. For example, Craik, Byrd, and Swanson (1987) gave younger and older subjects lists of unrelated words to learn, either with or without a short descriptive phrase (e.g., a body of water, POND); age differences were smallest when the cues were provided during the learning phase and the retrieval phase. Very much the same result was reported by Shaw and Craik (1989). On the other hand, Park and Shaw (1992) boosted memory performance in an episodic memory task for words by providing the first two, three, or four initial letters of the words at retrieval; these investigators found that younger subjects benefited relatively more from the cues. Finally, Light (1991) concluded from a review of the evidence that the most common finding is that both age groups benefit equally from the provision of such "environmental support." The literature is thus clear on the fact that episodic memory performance can be enhanced in older people by providing supportive contextual material at encoding and retrieval, although the conditions under which older people benefit more, less, or equally relative to younger participants have still to be worked out in detail.

One finding that is generally accepted concerns the greater difficulties experienced by older adults in remembering where and when they experienced an event or learned a fact. Thus a face may "seem very familiar," yet an older person (and indeed many younger people!) may be unable to recollect where and when they saw the face before. In brain-damaged patients this type of failure is referred to as "source amnesia"; the impairment is much less severe in older people, but it may reflect the same inefficiency of frontal lobe functioning in a subclinical form (Craik, Morris, Morris, & Loewen, 1990). Moreover, the degree of source amnesia does seem to increase with age in a normal sample. Using a paradigm devised by Schacter, Harbluk, and McLachlan (1984), McIntyre and Craik (1987) presented made-up facts (e.g., "Bob Hope's father was a fireman") to younger and older participants. One week later, the subjects were given "a general knowledge test" in which they were asked questions like "What was Pablo Picasso's profession?" and "What did Bob Hope's father do for a living?" The participants were also asked to say where and when they had first learned the information, and the researchers found that older people remembered the "new facts" quite well, but forgot that they had learned them during the previous week's session. This age-related forgetting of contextual detail is also seen in the propensity of older people to tell the same anecdote to the same audience a number of times (Koriat, Ben-Zur, & Sheffer, 1988). This failure is probably the result of two age-related inefficiencies: first, the greater likelihood that a given context will evoke a certain observation, question, or story, and second, the reduced likelihood that the older person will remember the previous occasion on which the question was asked or the anecdote told.

It seems possible that the age-related difficulty in remembering context is one manifestation of a more general age-related impairment in dealing with associative information. That is, older people may have special problems in forming and using associative connections among mental events. The need to integrate mental events and the ability to do so is referred to as "binding." Marcia Johnson and her collaborators have recently shown that such binding problems increase with age (Chalfonte & Johnson, 1995), and Naveh-Benjamin (1998) has illustrated the point that older people have particular difficulty when learning and remembering involves associative information.

With regard to survey measurement, the age-related decline in episodic memory means that survey researchers should treat certain classes of responses with caution. For respondents aged 60 and older, questions dealing with specific autobiographical events should ask about large-scale salient events (e.g., "Where did you take your vacation last summer?") rather than about smaller scale details (e.g., "What was the name of the hotel?"). Information relating to the times and places associated with events are particularly difficult for older respondents, so that questions of the type "When did you last buy product X, or use facility Y?" or "Where did you last purchase commodity A or encounter an advertisement for product B?" should be used sparingly and the answers interpreted cautiously. On the other hand, reminders designed to reinstate the general context for a set of questions may be particularly helpful for older people. Paradoxically, contextual information is difficult for older people to recall, yet is often more helpful to them than to their younger counterparts when it is reprovided to assist retrieval (see Schwarz, Chapter 2 for more information about this issue).

☐ Semantic Memory

As used by cognitive psychologists, the term semantic memory refers to our store of factual knowledge, usually dissociated from any episodic recollection of where and when that knowledge was learned. At first it seems that semantic memory in this sense declines little with age. The general knowledge sections of IQ tests are typically answered as well by older as by younger respondents (Salthouse, 1982, 1991); knowledge and use of vocabulary shows very little decline until the late 70s or 80s (Salthouse, 1982); and the age-related declines in the ability to use semantic information are slight or nonexistent (Light, 1992; Light & Burke, 1988). The contrast between the minimal age-related differences in semantic memory performance on the one hand, and the substantial age-related declines in episodic memory performance on the other hand, may be taken as a further proof of the existence of at least two separate memory systems (cf. Tulving, 1983). There are indeed substantial age-related decrements in some aspects of semantic memory functioning, however, and such findings detract from any oversimple formulation. For example, word-finding failures increase with age (Burke, MacKay, Worthley, & Wade, 1991), and one of the most noticeable age-related memory failures is the difficulty that almost all elderly people experience in retrieving names (Cohen & Faulkner, 1986; Maylor, 1990).

It seems possible that it is not the episodic-semantic distinction that determines the presence or absence of age differences in memory, but rather the specificity of the sought-for information. Episodic information is typically quite specific, given that details of the temporal and spatial context are bound up in a satisfactory response, and factual knowledge is often rather general, in that it can be expressed in a variety of different ways. When knowledge is specific, and cannot be rephrased or redescribed in alternative ways (e.g., names), then systematic age-related decrements are found; it remains to be seen whether age-related differences in episodic memory are reduced as the episodic context specified by the question becomes more general.

The fuzzy boundary between episodic and semantic memory is further illustrated by a consideration of work on spatial memory and on remote memory for personal events. Whereas it seems at first that memory for where things occurred and memory for long-ago experiences are both clear cases of episodic memory, a closer examination makes this classification less certain. Remembering where I left a book on a specific occasion is unambiguously "episodic," but memory for where I usually place my keys or park my car shades over into the realm of semantic memory. When it comes to memory for the spatial layout of a building or city, the information in question appears to be rather general and "semantic" in nature. Similarly, memory for remote autobiographical events seems to tap episodic memory, but Cermak (1984) made the interesting point that events from childhood and early adulthood may be told and retold so often that they take on the status of personal or family folklore, often drifting substantially away from the facts of the original event as it actually occurred.

Spatial Memory

However it is classified, memory for spatial information does seem to decline markedly across the life-span, and this result is to be expected in light of the well-established age-related drop in memory for contextual information in general (Spencer & Raz, 1995). Investigations of age differences in spatial memory range from laboratory tasks (e.g., Cherry & Park, 1993; Park, Cherry, Smith, & Lafronza, 1990; Zelinski & Light, 1988) to behavior in real-life settings. In this latter category, Uttl and Graf (1993) tested museum visitors aged 15–74 years on their memory for the spatial layout of museum displays they had recently visited. Participants over 55 showed clear declines in this form of spatial memory. When the task taps well-learned semantic memory, information deficits are still reported. For example, Evans, Brennan, Skorpovich, and Held (1984) asked subjects to recall the buildings from a familiar part of their city and to place the buildings on a schematic map. Older people were poorer than their younger counterparts on both tasks, despite the fact that the older adults were quite familiar with the areas in question. One note of caution here is that there may be a difference between the abstract ability to recall spatial information, and the ability to use familiar spatial cues in real-life navigation. Older people may well be less impaired (or not impaired at all) on the latter class of tasks. If so, such a contrast would fit with the well-established finding of greater age-related declines in explicit than implicit memory (see Craik & Jennings, 1992, for a review).

Remote Memory

The assessment of memories from the remote past presents some interesting methodological challenges. Elderly adults often contrast their "vivid recollection" of things that happened to them as children or as young adults, with their "hazy" memory for things that happened only hours or days before. But the vivid memory from 50 years ago is likely to be of some salient event; it is also likely that the memory has been retrieved and relived many times, rather than being retrieved for the first time after 50 years. These factors of selection and repeated retrieval make it difficult to compare such remote memories with memories of more banal events from recent times. One solution is to use the diary method, in which people record daily events (without review) and are then tested on their memory for these personal events at a later time. The forgetting functions for these real-life events is an exponential multiplied by a power function (Rubin, 1982), but good data from older adults on this paradigm are still needed. In a second method (discussed more fully by Rubin, Chapter 8 in this volume), participants are presented with a single word and are asked to describe a personal memory that is evoked by the word. The evoked memories are then dated as accurately as possible. Rubin, Wetzler, and Nebes (1986) found that the frequency per hour of such generated memories declines steadily from the present to 20 years ago, and that the forgetting functions were similar for subjects in their 20s and those in their 70s. In addition, there is an overrepresented "bump" of memories from the period of 10–30 years of age, suggesting either that this period is particularly rich in salient life events or perhaps that many events around this time have emotional connotations, and are therefore particularly well encoded.

An alternative approach to the study of remote memories is to deal with verifiable public events rather than with personal autobiographical memories. This technique is obviously more objective, but it may fail to capture some aspects of personal memories: the involvement of self, and the emotional interactions of self with others, for example. Nonetheless, studies by Warrington and Sanders (1971) and by Squire (1989) both showed the same general pattern as that reported by Rubin, Wetzler, and Nebes (1986); namely, remembering declined with the remoteness of the event, and the decline was equivalent for younger and older adults.

Truth Effect

A final topic with some implications for survey researchers is the tendency for people to rate repeated statements as being more valid and believable than statements presented only once (Zajonc, 1968). In the literature on marketing, this tendency is known as the truth effect: the perceived validity of an advertisement or a marketing claim increases with repetition (Hasher, Goldstein, & Toppino, 1977). Although little work has been done on this topic with respect to possible age differences, one study by Law, Hawkins, and Craik (1998) showed that the effect is exaggerated in older adults. In the context of survey measurement this could mean that older people may be more susceptible to agreeing with political or marketing statements that are repeated during the course of the survey.

In general, the literature on age-related differences in semantic memory suggests that when surveys deal with recollection of public events, younger and older adults show the same tendency to forget incidents or people as the time interval increases. Older adults typically perform somewhat less well in absolute terms, especially when the sought-for information is very specific, as with names of people and places. Remote personal memories, however sincerely believed, are liable to distortion after repeated reproductions (Bartlett, 1932). Factual information can be primed and made more accessible by recent use, so another caveat for survey researchers concerns the likelihood that people of different ages may have dealt recently with the information in question. Finally, contextual details appear to be particularly vulnerable to the effects of aging.

☐ Conclusions

This brief survey of the literature on aging and memory makes it clear that survey researchers should be aware of a number of results in this area when designing survey instruments or means of administering them. Some effects are predictable and obvious, others less so. In the former category, it should be expected that older people might be less accurate in recalling recent events, especially those involving specific details of time and place. Similarly, common sense should guard against giving long and complex instructions or questions in a telephone interview. In the category of less obvious pitfalls, priming effects may have a greater biasing effect on older respondents; as mentioned previously, the provision of "helpful" examples may bias older respondents in their choice of answers. Reduced perceptual clarity (either reduced visual contrast or a noisy telephone line) may reduce immediate memory for initial alternatives in a multiple-choice format. Both this factor and the decline in WM capacity are likely to bias answers towards the most recent alternative presented. Finally, repetition of information in the context of a survey may result in that information being viewed more favorably (the "mere exposure" effect reported by Zajonc, 1968) or being misattributed to some external source (the "false fame" effect reported by Dywan & Jacoby, 1990).

Safeguards against these sources of bias include such obvious measures as counterbalancing the order of questions or alternative answers, confirming answers by checking with relatives, providing supportive context whenever possible, and reducing the involvement of WM and episodic recall. These measures may not always be practicable, of course, but by being aware of possible sources of bias stemming from age-related memory impairments, survey researchers will at least be able to interpret the responses of older participants with appropriate caution.

☐ Acknowledgments

Preparation of this chapter was facilitated by a grant from the Natural Sciences and Engineering Research Council of Canada. I am grateful also to Denise Park for helpful comments on an earlier version.

☐ References

Atkinson, R. C., & Shiffrin, R. M. (1968). Human memory: A proposed system and its control processes. In K. W. Spence & J. T. Spence (Eds.), *The psychology of learning and motivation* (Vol. 2, pp. 89–195). New York: Academic Press.

Baddeley, A. D., & Hitch, G. J. (1974). Working memory. In G. H. Bower (Ed.), *The psychology of learning and motivation* (Vol. 8, pp. 47–90). New York: Academic Press.

Baddeley, A. D., & Warrington, E. K. (1970). Amnesia and the distinction between long- and short-term memory. *Journal of Verbal Learning and Verbal Behavior, 9,* 176–189.

Bartlett, F. C. (1932). *Remembering: A study in experimental and social psychology.* Cambridge, England: Cambridge University Press.

Bransford, J. D., Franks, J. J., Morris, C. D., & Stein, B. S. (1979). Some general constraints on learning and memory research. In L. S. Cermak & F. I. M. Craik (Eds.), *Levels of processing in human memory* (pp. 331–354). Hillsdale, NJ: Erlbaum.

Burke, D. M., MacKay, D. G., Worthley, J. S., & Wade, E. (1991). On the tip of the tongue: What causes word finding failures in young and older adults? *Journal of Memory and Language, 30,* 542–579.

Cermak, L. A. (1984). The episodic/semantic distinction in amnesia. In N. Butters & L. R. Squire (Eds.), *The neuropsychology of memory* (pp. 55–62). New York: Guilford.

Chalfonte, B. L., & Johnson, M. K. (1995). Feature memory and binding in young and older adults. *Memory and Cognition, 24,* 403–416.

Cherry, K. E., & Park, D. C. (1993). Individual difference and contextual variables influence spatial memory in younger and older adults. *Psychology and Aging, 8,* 517–526.

Cohen, G., & Faulkner, D. (1986). Memory for proper names: Age differences in retrieval. *British Journal of Developmental Psychology, 4,* 187–197.

Craik, F. I. M. (1977). Age differences in human memory. In J. E. Birren & K. W. Schaie (Eds.), *Handbook of the psychology of aging* (pp. 384–420). New York: Van Nostrand Reinhold.

Craik, F. I. M., & Anderson, N. D. (1998). Applying cognitive research problems to aging. In D. Gopher & A. Koriat (Eds.), *Attention and performance* (Vol. 17; in press). Cambridge, MA: MIT Press..

Craik, F. I. M., & Byrd, M. (1982). Aging and cognitive deficits: The role of attentional resources. In F. I. M. Craik & S. Trehub (Eds.), *Aging and cognitive processes* (pp. 191–211). New York: Plenum.

Craik, F. I. M., Byrd, M., & Swanson, J. M. (1987). Patterns of memory loss in three elderly samples. *Psychology and Aging, 2,* 79–86.

Craik, F. I. M., & Jennings, J. M. (1992). Human memory. In F. I. M. Craik & T. A. Salthouse (Eds.), *The handbook of aging and cognition* (pp. 51–110). Hillsdale, NJ: Erlbaum.

Craik, F. I. M., Morris, R. G., & Gick, M. L. (1990). Adult age differences in working memory. In G. Vallar & T. Shallice (Eds.), *Neuropsychological impairments of short-term memory* (pp. 247–267). Cambridge, England: Cambridge University Press.

Craik, F. I. M., Morris, L. W., Morris, R. G., & Loewen, E. R. (1990). Relations between source amnesia and frontal lobe functioning in older adults. *Psychology and Aging, 5,* 148–151.

Craik, F. I. M., & Rabinowitz, J. C. (1984). Age differences in the acquisition and use of verbal information: A tutorial review. In H. Bouma & D. E. Bouwhuis (Eds.), *Attention and performance* (Vol. 10, pp. 471–499). Hillsdale, NJ: Erlbaum.

Daneman, M., & Carpenter, P. A. (1980). Individual differences in working memory and reading. *Journal of Verbal Learning and Verbal Behavior, 19,* 450–466.

Delbecq-Derouesne, J., & Beauvois, M. F. (1989). Memory processes and aging: A defect of automatic rather than controlled processes? *Archives of Gerontology and Geriatrics, 1* (Suppl.), 121–150.

Dixon, R. A., & Bäckman, L. (1995). *Compensating for psychological deficits and declines: Managing losses and promoting gains.* Mahwah, NJ: Erlbaum.

Dobbs, A. R., & Rule, B. G. (1989). Adult age differences in working memory. *Psychology and Aging, 4,* 500–503.

Dywan, J., & Jacoby, L. L. (1990). Effects of aging on source monitoring: Differences in susceptibility to false fame. *Psychology and Aging, 5,* 379–387.

Evans, G. W., Brennan, P. L., Skorpovich, M. A., & Held, D. (1984). Cognitive mapping and elderly adults: Verbal and location memory for urban landmarks. *Journal of Gerontology, 39,* 452–457.

Gick, M. L., Craik, F. I. M., & Morris, R. C. (1988). Task complexity and age differences in working memory. *Memory and Cognition, 16,* 353–361.

Gilmore, G. C., Thomas, C. W., Klitz, T., Persanyi, M. W., & Tomsak, R. (1996). Contrast enhancement eliminates letter identification speed deficits in Alzheimer's disease. *Journals of Clinical Geropsychology, 2,* 307–320.

Hasher, L., Goldstein, D., & Toppino, T. (1977). Frequency and the conference of referential validity. *Journal of Verbal Learning and Verbal Behavior, 16,* 107–112.

Hasher, L., & Zacks, R. T. (1988). Working memory, comprehension, and aging: A review and a new view. In G. H. Bower (Ed.), *The psychology of learning and motivation* (Vol. 2, pp. 193–225). San Diego, CA: Academic Press.

Howard, D. V. (1988). The priming of semantic and episodic memories. In L. L. Light & D. M. Burke (Eds.), *Language, memory, and aging* (pp. 77–100). New York: Cambridge University Press.

Inman, V. W., & Parkinson, S. R. (1983). Differences in Brown-Peterson recall as a function of age and retention interval. *Journal of Gerontology, 38,* 58–64.

Jacoby, L. L. (1991). A process dissociation framework: Separating automatic from intentional uses of memory. *Journal of Memory and Language, 30,* 513–541.

Jacoby, L. L., & Witherspoon, D. (1982). Remembering without awareness. *Canadian Journal of Psychology, 36,* 300–324.

Jennings, J. M., & Jacoby, L. L. (1997). An opposition procedure for detecting age-related deficits in recollection: Telling effects of repetition. *Psychology and Aging, 12,* 352–361.

Koriat, A., Ben-Zur, H., & Sheffer, D. (1988). Telling the same story twice: Output monitoring and age. *Journal of Memory and Language, 27,* 23–39.

Laver, G. D., & Burke, D. M. (1993). Why do semantic priming effects increase in old age? A meta-analysis. *Psychology and Aging, 8,* 34–43.

Law, S., Hawkins, S. A., & Craik, F. I. M. (1998). Repetition-induced belief in the elderly: Rehabilitating age-related memory deficits. *Journal of Consumer Research* (in press).

Light, L. L. (1991). Memory and aging: Four hypotheses in search of data. *Annual Review of Psychology, 42,* 333–376.

Light, L. L. (1992). The organization of memory in old age. In F. I. M. Craik & T. A. Salthouse (Eds.), *The handbook of aging and cognition* (pp. 111–165). Hillsdale, NJ: Erlbaum.

Light, L. L., & Burke, D. M. (1988). Patterns of language and memory in old age. In L. L. Light & D. M. Burke (Eds.), *Language, memory, and aging* (pp. 244–271). New York: Cambridge University Press.

Light, L. L., & LaVoie, D. (1993). Direct and indirect measures of memory in old age. In P. Graf & M. E. J. Masson (Eds.), *Implicit memory: New directions in cognition, development, and neuropsychology* (pp. 207–230). Hillsdale, NJ: Erlbaum.

Light, L. L., & Singh, A. (1987). Implicit and explicit memory in young and older adults. *Journal of Experimental Psychology: Learning, Memory and Cognition, 13,* 531–541.

Lindenberger, U., & Baltes, P. B. (1994). Sensory functioning and intelligence in old age: A strong connection. *Psychology and Aging, 9,* 339–355.

Maylor, E. A. (1990). Age and prospective memory. *Quarterly Journal of Experimental Psychology: Human Experimental Psychology, 42,* 471–493.

McIntyre, J. S., & Craik, F. I. M. (1987). Age differences in memory for item and source information. *Canadian Journal of Psychology, 41,* 175–192.

McKoon, G., Ratcliff, R., & Dell, G. S. (1986). A critical evaluation of the semantic-episodic distinction. *Journal of Experimental Psychology: Learning, Memory, and Cognition, 12,* 295–306.

Milner, B., Corkin, S., & Teuber, H. L. (1968). Further analysis of the hippocampal amnesic syndrome: 14 year follow-up study of H.M. *Neuropsychologia, 6,* 215–234.

Murdock, B. B. (1967). Recent developments in short-term memory. *British Journal of Psychology, 58,* 421–433.

Naveh-Benjamin, M. (1998). Adult-age differences in memory performance: An associative deficit framework. Manuscript submitted for publication.

Park, D. C., Cherry, K. E., Smith, A. D., & Lafronza, V. N. (1990). Effects of distinctive context on memory for objects and their locations in young and elderly adults. *Psychology and Aging, 5,* 250–255.

Park, D. C., & Shaw, R. J. (1992). Effect of environmental support on implicit and explicit memory in younger and older adults. *Psychology and Aging, 7,* 632–642.

Parkinson, S. R., Lindholm, J. M., & Inman, V. W. (1982). An analysis of age differences in immediate recall. *Journal of Gerontology, 37,* 425–431.

Pichora-Fuller, K., Schneider, B., & Daneman, M. (1995). How young and old adults listen to and remember speech in noise. *Journal of Acoustical Society of America, 97,* 593–608.

Rubin, D. C. (1982). On the retention function for autobiographical memory. *Journal of Verbal Learning and Verbal Behavior, 21,* 21–38.

Rubin, D. C., Wetzler, S. E., & Nebes, R. D. (1986). Autobiographical memory across the lifespan. In D. C. Rubin (Ed.), *Autobiographical memory* (pp. 202–221). Cambridge, England: Cambridge University Press.

Salthouse, T. A. (1982). *Adult cognition: An experimental psychology of human aging.* New York: Springer-Verlag.

Salthouse, T. A. (1991). *Theoretical perspectives on cognitive aging.* Hillsdale, NJ: Erlbaum.

Salthouse, T. A. (1993). Speed mediation of adult age differences in cognition. *Developmental Psychology, 29,* 722–738.

Salthouse, T. A., Mitchell, D. R., Skovronek, E., & Babcock, R. L. (1989). Effects of adult age and working memory on reasoning and spatial abilities. *Journal of Experimental Psychology: Learning, Memory, and Cognition, 15,* 507–516.

Schacter, D. L., Harbluk, J. L., & McLachlan, D. (1984). Retrieval without recollection: An experimental analysis of source amnesia. *Journal of Verbal Learning and Verbal Behavior, 23,* 593–611.

Schacter, D. L., Koutstaal, W. E., & Norman, K. A. (1997). False memories and aging. *Trends in Cognitive Sciences, 1,* 229–236.

Schacter, D. L., & Tulving, E. (1994). What are the memory systems of 1994? In D. L. Schacter & E. Tulving (Eds.), *Memory systems 1994* (pp. 1–38). Cambridge, MA: MIT Press.

Shaw, R. J., & Craik, F. I. M. (1989). Age differences in predictions and performance on a cued recall task. *Psychology and Aging, 4,* 131–135.

Spencer, W. D., & Raz, N. (1995). Differential effects of aging on memory for content and context: A meta-analysis. *Psychology and Aging, 10,* 527–539.

Spinks, R., Gilmore, G., & Thomas, C. (1996, April). *Age simulation of a sensory deficit does impair cognitive test performance.* Poster presented at the Cognitive Aging Conference, Atlanta, GA.

Squire, L. R. (1989). On the course of forgetting in very long-term memory. *Journal of Experimental Psychology: Learning, Memory, and Cognition, 15,* 241–245.

Tulving, E. (1983). *Elements of episodic memory.* New York: Oxford University Press.

Tulving, E., Hayman, C. A. G., & Macdonald, C. A. (1991). Long-lasting perceptual priming and semantic learning in amnesia: A case experiment. *Journal of Experimental Psychology: Learning, Memory, and Cognition, 17,* 595–617.

Tulving, E., & Schacter, D. L. (1990). Priming and human memory systems. *Science, 247,* 301–306.

Uttl, B., & Graf, P. (1993). Episodic spatial memory in adulthood. *Psychology and Aging, 8,* 257–273.

Warrington, E. K., & Sanders, H. I. (1971). The fate of old memories. *Quarterly Journal of Experimental Psychology, 23,* 432–442.

Waugh, N. C., & Norman, D. A. (1965). Primary memory. *Psychological Review, 72,* 89–104.

Wickens, C. D. (1984). Processing resources in attention. In R. Parasuraman & D. R. Davies (Eds.), *Varieties of attention* (pp. 63–102). Orlando, FL: Academic Press.

Wingfield, A., Alexander, A. H., & Cavigelli, S. (1994). Does memory constrain utilization of top-down information in spoken word recognition? Evidence from normal aging. *Language and Speech, 37,* 221–235.

Wingfield, A., Stine, E. A., Lahar, C. J., & Aberdeen, J. S. (1988). Does the capacity of working memory change with age? *Experimental Aging Research, 14,* 103–107.

Zacks, R. T., & Hasher, L. (1988). Capacity theory and the processing of inferences. In L. L. Light & D. M. Burke (Eds.), *Language, memory, and aging* (pp. 154–170). New York: Cambridge University Press.

Zajonc, R. B. (1968). Attitudinal effects of mere exposure. *Journal of Personality and Social Psychology, 9,* 1–27.

Zelinski, E. M., & Light, L. L. (1988). Young and older adults' use of context in spatial memory. *Psychology and Aging, 3,* 99–101.

Carolyn Yoon
Cynthia P. May
Lynn Hasher

Aging, Circadian Arousal Patterns, and Cognition

In the past few decades, human chronobiology research has documented rhythms in a variety of biological and physiological functions (e.g., body temperature, blood pressure, metabolic rate, hormonal and digestive secretions) reflecting circadian cycles of approximately 24 hours. Circadian rhythms exhibit pronounced effects on important aspects of everyday life, health, and medical treatment (e.g., Hrushesky, 1989, 1994; Smolensky & D'Alonzo, 1993), as well as on the ability to adapt to shift work (e.g., Monk, 1986; Moore-Ede & McIntosh, 1993). While extensive research addressing general circadian patterns exists, a far smaller literature concerns the extent to which there are individual differences in these patterns and, in turn, differences in performance at different times of day (e.g., Bodenhausen, 1990; Colquhoun, 1971; Folkard, Knauth, Monk, & Rutenfranz, 1976; Folkard, Weaver, & Wildgruber, 1983). This work shows that individual circadian arousal is indeed correlated with performance on a variety of tasks (e.g., efficiency in reacting to stimuli, performing simple arithmetic, engaging in cognitive activity) such that performance peaks at a certain level of circadian arousal, a peak which occurs more or less regularly at a specific point in the day.

Within the field of cognition, awareness of the individual variation in circadian arousal patterns has, until recently, been quite limited. A few studies have demonstrated that this individual difference variable can significantly alter cognitive performance across the day (e.g., Bodenhausen, 1990; Horne, Brass, & Pettitt, 1980; Petros, Beckwith, &

Anderson, 1990). A study by May, Hasher, and Stoltzfus (1993) further found clear age-group differences in circadian arousal patterns, with older adults tending strongly towards a morningness pattern and with college students tending strongly away from this pattern of arousal. They also reported dramatic differences in memory performance across the day (from early morning to late afternoon) for both younger and older adults. However, and of special relevance to the present paper, the patterns of performance differences across the day were quite different for younger and older adults. Herein, we report findings that performance differences across the day are associated with age-related differences in circadian arousal, and that younger adults get better as the day progresses while older adults get worse. This pattern is now known to obtain across a number of tasks, although, as will be seen, there are some very intriguing exceptions as well.

Since survey researchers pose questions to people across the age range, attention to circadian arousal patterns and to their impact on some but not all cognitive processes may help to improve the accuracy and adequacy of responses, particularly by older adults. To the extent that there are individual and group differences in circadian arousal patterns across time of day, errors in survey data may result when the size and direction of response effects are differentially influenced by when a questionnaire is administered and completed. For example, as will be seen, people of all ages have a tendency to produce a strong or highly likely response at nonoptimal times of day and there are many situations in which the most accessible response is not necessarily the correct one. Investigators who rely on questionnaires and surveys to tap memory processes should in particular be alerted to how the variation in circadian arousal may produce systematically biased response data.

We turn now to consider some of the key findings that are of potential relevance to the ability of people, particularly older adults, to answer questions that survey researchers (and others) might ask of them. We begin with the evidence showing age differences in circadian arousal patterns.

☐ Age Differences in Morningness– Eveningness Tendencies

Measure

To assess individual and group differences in circadian patterns, we and others have used the Horne-Ostberg (1976) Morningness-Eveningness Questionnaire, or MEQ. The MEQ is a simple paper-and-pencil test consisting of 19 questions which address such items as sleep-wake habits, subjective assessment of intellectual and physical peak times, and appetite and alertness over the day. Scores on the questionnaire delineate three main types of individuals: morning-types, evening-types, and neither-types. These delineations are validated by a number of findings demonstrating reliable differences between morning- and evening-types on both physiological (e.g., body temperature, heart rate, skin conductance, amplitude of evoked brain potentials; e.g., Adan, 1991; Horne & Ostberg, 1976; Horne, Brass, & Pettitt, 1980; Kerkhof, van der Geest, Korving, & Rietveld, 1981) and psychological measures of behavior (e.g., personality traits, sleep-wake behaviors, perceived alertness; Buela-Casal, Caballo, & Cueto, 1990; Horne & Ostberg, 1976; Mecacci, Zani, Rocchetti, & Lucioli, 1986; Webb & Bonnet, 1978; Wilson, 1990). In addition, the MEQ has high test-retest reliability (e.g., Kerkhof, 1984; Anderson, Petros, Beckwith, Mitchell, & Fritz, 1991), and psychometric tests indicate that it is a valid index of circadian rhythmicity (e.g., Smith, Reilly, & Midkiff, 1989).

Recent work on individual and group differences in morningness-eveningness tendencies indicates a significant shift towards morningness with age (e.g., Adan & Almirall, 1990; Intons-Peterson, Rocchi, West, McLellan, & Hackney, 1998; Kerkhof, 1985; May, Hasher, & Stoltzfus, 1993; Mecacci & Zani, 1983; Vitiello, Smallwood, Avery, & Pascualy, 1986). The shift appears to begin around age 50 (Ishihara, Miyake, Miyasita, & Miyata, 1991), and occurs cross-culturally, as similar patterns have been obtained in Italy (Mecacci et al., 1986), Spain (Adan & Almirall, 1990), England (Wilson, 1990), Japan (Ishihara et al., 1991), Canada (Yoon & Lee, 1998), and the U.S. (May & Hasher, in press). We have now administered the MEQ to over 1,500 college students (aged 18–23) and over 600 older adults (aged 60–75) in different regions of North America and, as can be seen in Figure 1, the norms show clear age differences in the pattern of peak times across the day: roughly 40% of younger adults (all of whom are college students) show eveningness tendencies, with a large proportion of neither-types and less than 10% morning-types. By contrast, less than 3% of older adults show eveningness tendencies, and the majority (~75%) are morning-types. These findings indicate that younger and older adults differ markedly in their circadian peaks over the day, and suggest that for those cognitive functions influenced by circadian arousal patterns, performance of many younger adults will improve across the day, while that of most older adults will deteriorate as the day progresses.

Investigators who utilize surveys, particularly those interested in cognitive aging, thus need to consider how response biases might potentially be introduced when age differences in circadian arousal are not

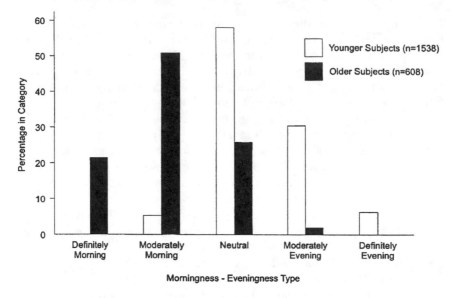

FIGURE 1. Time of day categories for older and younger adults.

accounted for. Biases associated with respondents may act to alter ob-served relations between the independent and dependent variables in ways that either produce relationships when none really exist or cause systematic under- or overestimation of relationships. For example, given that we know that older adults tend to reach their mental peak in the morning while younger adults do so in the evening, surveys assessing cognitive performance that are administered in the evening may serve to exaggerate any true age differences in abilities. (See May et al., 1993, for a more detailed discussion.) Such surveys may also give an in-accurate picture of the values, attitudes, and behaviors of older adults, who may, for example, seem more prejudiced than they actually are (Bodenhausen, 1990). In conducting research that seeks to uncover relationships between age and other variables of interest, investigators, whenever possible, need to guard against such potential sources of response bias.

Differences in Intellectual and Physical Behavior

Accounting for individual differences in circadian arousal in aging studies is critical in situations where intellectual and physical behavior varies across the day in ways that are relevant for those interested in asking questions of others. One set of findings which suggests real differences in behavior across the day comes from a study that addresses media and shopping patterns of older adults, compared with those of younger adults, finding them to be different across time of day (Yoon, 1997). In this study, a questionnaire was administered to younger and older adults regarding when they tend to read newspapers, read magazines, watch television, and go shopping. More than 80% of the older subjects indicated that they read newspapers early in the morning, while only 14% of younger subjects reported doing so early in the morning. Magazines, on the other hand, were read in the afternoon or evening by more than two thirds of both younger and older adults. About half of the older people indicated a clear preference for shopping in the morning or early afternoon, whereas younger people tended to do so in the late afternoon or evening. Older people's distinct preference to shop in the morning is consistent with their tendency to be mentally alert and energetic in the morning. They may reserve those hours to engage in tasks that pose a relatively greater cognitive or physical challenge.

Other studies have found intellectual and physical behavior to vary across age and time of day. One study found that prospective memory involving older adults' medical and appointment adherence was significantly greater in the morning than in the afternoon or evening (Leirer, Tanke, & Morrow, 1994). Another study conducted by Skinner (1985) examined the relationship between grades and time of day when classes are held, among college students. The study involved a simple test comparing mean grades across morning, afternoon, and evening classes and found that grades in morning classes were significantly lower than those in afternoon and evening classes. Although these studies did not collect MEQ-type measures, they suggest real intellectual and behavioral differences across time of day that are quite synchronous with circadian patterns reported elsewhere for these age groups (May et al., 1993; Yoon, 1997). It is conceivable, for example, that differences in intellectual and physical energy will influence the likelihood of participation in studies involving telephone or personal interviews, in ways that might easily bias both the samples obtained and the kinds of answers given.

☐ Changes in Cognitive Performance Across the Day

We have begun to explore the types of cognitive processes that are likely to be affected by the match between an individual's peak circadian arousal period and the time at which testing occurs, an influence referred to as the "synchrony effect" (May et al., 1993). Our goal is to identify those cognitive functions that demonstrate a synchrony effect, as well as those that may be invariant over the day. To this end, our investigations have been guided by an inhibitory framework of attention and memory, positing that successful processing of information depends both on excitatory attentional mechanisms (Allport, 1989; Navon, 1989), which are responsible for the activation of relevant, goal-oriented material, as well as on inhibitory mechanisms, which are responsible for the suppression of irrelevant, off-task information (Allport, 1989; Hasher, Zacks, & May, in press; Navon, 1989). As discussed below, the bulk of data indicates that excitatory processing remains intact across optimal and nonoptimal times, but that inhibitory processing is impaired at individuals' off-peak times. The data are consistent as well in confirming relatively impaired inhibitory processes of older adults. Thus, here we focus on the role of inhibition in information processing, the consequences of inhibitory impairments for cognitive performance, and the implications of such impairments for the administration of surveys.

Inhibition

Inhibitory mechanisms are thought to be critical for three general functions, each of which is directed at controlling the contents of working memory to enable the efficient on-line processing and subsequent successful retrieval of target information (e.g., Hasher et al., in press). First, inhibitory mechanisms prevent irrelevant, off-task information from entering working memory, thus limiting access to purely goal-relevant information. Inhibition also serves to delete or suppress from working memory information that is marginally relevant or that was once relevant but is no longer appropriate for current goals. Taken together, the access and deletion functions act to minimize competition from distracting material during both encoding and retrieval, thus increasing the likelihood that items activated concurrently in working memory are relevant to one another, and that target information will be successfully processed and retrieved. Finally, inhibition operates to restrain strong responses from being emitted before their appropriateness can be evaluated. The restraint function of inhibition thus allows for the appraisal and rejection of dominant responses when they are undesirable, so that a less-probable but more suitable response can be produced.

There are both direct and indirect consequences of diminished inhibition. For example, individuals with impaired inhibitory functioning may be more susceptible to distracting, irrelevant information, whether that distraction is generated from external sources (e.g., speech from a radio or television that has not been turned off during a questionnaire) or internal sources (e.g., distracting thoughts about personal concerns or issues). In addition, the inability to clear away previously relevant but currently inappropriate information may lead to heightened interference for poor inhibitors, resulting in difficulties in acquiring new material, comprehending questions, and retrieving stored memories. Poor inhibitors may also have difficulty disengaging from one line of thought or activity and switching to another, in addition to preventing the production of well-learned responses when those responses are inappropriate.

These direct impairments, produced by deficient inhibitory functioning, may lead to other, indirect cognitive consequences. Since control over working memory also ultimately influences the efficiency of retrieval, diminished inhibition efficiency can further lead to an increased reliance on stereotypes, heuristics, or schemas when making decisions or answering questions, even in situations where detailed, analytical processing is clearly more appropriate (Bodenhausen, 1990; Yoon, 1997). Related to this is the possibility that inefficient inhibitors may be more susceptible to persuasion by weak arguments, particularly if those arguments contain material related to, but inconsequential for, the current topic (Rahhal, Abendroth, & Hasher, 1996; Yoon & Lee, 1998).

Hence, if changes in cognitive functioning at off-peak times do in fact stem from circadian-related deficits in inhibition, then performance at nonoptimal times can be expected to reflect inaccurate assessment of people's opinions and knowledge in question asking situations whenever irrelevant or previously relevant information affects responses, or when strong, prepotent responses must be rejected in favor of subordinate ones. If only inhibitory, but not excitatory, processes vary with arousal, time of testing should not matter whenever tasks simply require access to or production of well-learned material (e.g., vocabulary, simple trivia questions, identification of familiar stimuli), or when strong responses produce correct answers (e.g., word associations, highly practiced motor skills, perceptual priming).

Furthermore, given that surveys are commonly employed to estimate the frequency or amount of certain kinds of behaviors (when records for the relevant population are either nonexistent or difficult to obtain), it is clear that inhibitory functions, as related to variation in levels of circadian arousal, can play a large role in determining the accuracy of respondent reporting. For example, individuals, during their peak times of day, may have relatively greater ability to inhibit irrelevant past events and generate accurate responses, whereas during nonpeak times of day, they may have a tendency to overreport irrelevant events.

In the following sections, we first present direct evidence for on-line (i.e., current) failures of access, deletion, and restraint at off-peak times, and discuss those tasks in which synchrony plays little or no role for either age group. We then present evidence for the subsequent downstream consequences of deficient inhibition at nonoptimal times. In each of the studies to be discussed, younger and older adults were tested at peak and off-peak times of day. All younger adults were evening-types and all older adults were morning-types, as assessed by the MEQ.[1]

Diminished Inhibition at Off-Peak Times

Access Function of Inhibition: Costs of Distraction in Problem Solving

If individuals suffer inhibitory deficits at off-peak times, then distracting information should have a greater effect on their performance relative to participants tested at peak times. To test this prediction, we examined the impact of distraction on younger and older adults' ability to solve word problems at optimal and nonoptimal times of day (May, in press). We used a modified version of the Remote Associates Test (RAT; Mednick, 1962), in which each problem consists of three cue words (e.g., rat, blue, cottage) that are all remotely related to the same target word (e.g., cheese). The participants' task was to identify the target word that connects the three cue words. Of interest was the effect of distractors on individuals' ability to identify the targets. We gauged susceptibility to distraction in two ways: (1) the cost of misleading distraction and (2) the benefit of "leading" distraction.

Previous findings with this task indicate that target identification is impaired on the RAT when misleading distractors are placed next to each of the cue words (e.g., rat [cat], blue [red], cottage [cabin] = cheese; Smith & Blankenship, 1991). The cost of distraction should be greater for participants tested at off-peak relative to peak times, as they may be less able to suppress the irrelevant, misleading information. In addition, we explored the possibility that there may be situations in which the failure to suppress irrelevant information would be beneficial. To do so, we included a small proportion of test items in which the distractors presented with the cue trios were not misleading, but instead were "leading"; that is, they related the cues to the target (e.g., rat [eat], blue [dressing], cottage [diet] = cheese). Any benefits of distraction should be greater at nonoptimal times than at optimal times, when people have more control over distraction.

With all participants instructed to ignore distraction on all trials, we expected that, relative to individuals tested at optimal times, those tested at nonoptimal times would show greater deficits in target identification when misleading distractors were present, and greater benefit when leading distractors were present. The cost of misleading distractors and the benefit of leading distractors were calculated by subtracting the target identification rates for control trials (where no distraction was present) from the rates for misleading and leading trials, respectively. Table 1 shows the impact of distraction on problem solving for younger and older adults tested at peak and off-peak times of day. As expected, synchrony affected performance for both age groups, with those participants tested at off-peak times (i.e., young tested in the morning and old tested in the evening) showing both greater costs of misleading distraction and greater benefits of leading distraction relative to age-mates tested at peak times. In addition, older adults generally showed a larger influence of distraction than younger adults, a finding consistent with an inhibitory-deficit model of aging (Hasher & Zacks, 1988).

With respect to people's ability to answer questions, these data suggest patterns of disruptions (with both costs and benefits), with individuals who are queried at nonoptimal times being particularly vulnerable to distraction when questionnaires are administered in relatively noisy environments (as with mail-in questionnaires, telephone interviews, mall intercept interviews, etc.). If questionnaires are given in "noisy" environments, those irrelevant stimuli can lead to answers that come not from a direct response to the query but rather from a response heavily biased by irrelevant information. To whatever degree

TABLE 1.   EFFECT OF DISTRACTION ON PROBLEM SOLVING FOR YOUNGER AND OLDER ADULTS

Age and Time	Cost	Benefit
Younger adults		
AM (nonpeak)	−11	17
PM (peak)	−2	1
Older adults		
AM (peak)	−10	8
PM (nonpeak)	−18	23

these effects impact on young adults, their impact will be greater on older adults, particularly at their off-peak, evening hours.

Deletion Function of Inhibition: Sustained Activation of No-Longer-Relevant Material

In dynamic experiences, such as conversations, topics and locales change, and these shifts most often require that thought content shift as well. To simulate the need to stop thinking about one topic or idea and to start thinking about another, we assessed individuals' ability to suppress information that was once relevant, but is no longer suitable for current goals. To do this, May and Hasher (in press) used a garden path sentence completion task (Hartman & Hasher, 1991). In the first phase of this task, participants were presented with high-cloze sentence frames that were missing their final words (e.g., "Before you go to bed, turn off the _____"), and were asked to generate an ending for each frame. Once participants generated an ending for a given frame (e.g., "lights" for the present example), a target word appeared, which participants were instructed to remember for a later, unspecified memory test. For half of the sentence frames (filler items), the participant-generated ending appeared; for the remaining sentence frames (critical items), the participant-generated ending was disconfirmed by the presence of a new, less probable but nonetheless plausible ending for the sentence (e.g., "stove"). Thus for critical items, there was an implicit instruction to forget the generated ending (e.g., "lights"), as participants were informed that only the target endings (e.g., "stove") would appear on the subsequent memory test.

Our aim was to determine the accessibility of the target (e.g., "stove") and disconfirmed or no-longer-relevant (e.g., "lights") items from the critical sentence frames for younger and older participants who were tested at peak and off-peak times. On the premise that inhibition acts to delete from working memory items that are no longer relevant for current goals, we expected efficient inhibitors (i.e., younger adults tested at peak times) to have access to target items only; disconfirmed items should be no more accessible than control items as a result of an active suppression operating to delete these items from working memory. By contrast, we expected inefficient inhibitors (i.e., older adults and those tested at asynchronous times) to have access both to target and to disconfirmed items.

To assess these predictions, we used an indirect memory test which enabled a comparison of production rates for target, disconfirmed, and control (i.e., words not presented in Phase 1) items. For this task, participants generated endings to medium-cloze sentence frames (under the guise that they were helping create materials for a new experiment). Three types of frames were included: (a) frames that were moderately predictive of the target endings (e.g., "She remodeled her kitchen and replaced the old _____", for "stove"); (b) frames that were moderately predictive of the disconfirmed endings (e.g., "The baby was fascinated by the bright _____", for "lights"); and (c) frames that were moderately predictive of new, never-seen control endings (e.g., "The kitten slept peacefully on her owner's _____", for "lap"). We calculated priming scores for the target and disconfirmed endings by comparing completion rates for those items to the completion rate for control items[2]; positive priming indicates that the critical items were produced more often than control items, while negative priming indicates that the critical items were produced less often than control items. The priming data can be seen in Figure 2.

Consider first the pattern of priming for younger adults: At peak times, younger adults show reliable priming of target endings and actually show significant, *below-baseline* priming for the disconfirmed endings. These findings suggest that for younger adults at optimal times, the deletion function of inhibition is so efficient that the disconfirmed items

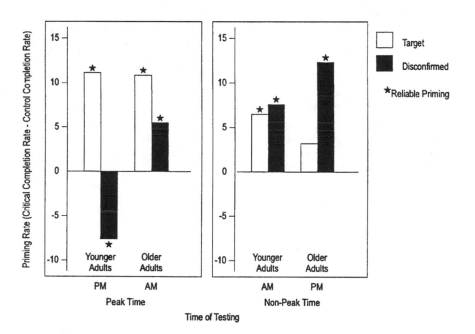

FIGURE 2. Priming for target and disconfirmed items for younger and older adults by time of testing.

are less accessible than items that were never presented. By contrast, younger adults tested at nonoptimal times show positive priming for both target and disconfirmed items, indicating that they are impaired in their ability to delete from working memory no-longer-relevant information at down times of day.

Older adults also demonstrate strong synchrony effects on performance, but their overall pattern of priming is different from that of younger adults due to age-related inhibitory deficits. At their peak time, older adults closely resemble young adults tested at nonoptimal times: They show reliable positive priming for both target and disconfirmed items, suggesting that even at their best time of day, older adults are not efficient at deleting currently irrelevant information from working memory. At nonoptimal times, older adults are severely impaired in suppressing the self-generated but disconfirmed items, so much so that they show marginally enhanced priming for those items relative to older adults tested at peak times, and actually fail to show any priming for experimenter-provided target items. It seems that inhibitory processing for older adults at nonoptimal times is so deficient that they are incapable of abandoning their self-generated, highly probable response, and as a consequence fail to show any priming at all for new target items. The patterns of priming for younger and older adults tested across the day are consistent with the suggestion that inhibitory functioning is diminished at off-peak relative to peak times, resulting in an inability to suppress or delete information that was once relevant, but is no longer appropriate for current goals.

What do these findings mean for the ability of younger and older adults to respond to survey questions? Because the deletion function is less effective for older adults and less effective for each group at nonoptimal times, difficulties can be anticipated whenever a topic shifts in a series of questions. For example, one series of questions might elicit preferences for different types of TV shows, followed by a second series of questions that probe individuals' attitudes towards different types of books. The inability to switch to a new topic may heighten carry-over of responses from the initial topic to a new one, giving unstable or inaccurate responses to the new topic.

Is there a way to increase accurate switching to topic changes? A recent finding suggests that the provision of additional information about the new topic, prior to asking any questions, will help older adults to make the switch that they do not make on their own (see Hasher, Quig, & May, 1997). The findings from this study suggest that when inhibition is deficient, as it is for older adults generally and for anyone tested at nonoptimal times, additional interpretive context is required to enable effective mental shifts to actual changes in context.

Failing to Prevent Strong Responses at Nonoptimal Times: Stop Signal

Inhibitory mechanisms are believed to enable control over behavior by restraining production of strong, dominant, or highly practiced responses, thus enabling the evaluation of and, if necessary, the rejection of those responses if they are deemed inappropriate for the present context. This function of inhibition allows for variation of behavior and, of special interest for question answering, retrieval of nondominating thoughts.

To investigate the possibility that the restraining function of inhibition is impaired at nonoptimal times, we used the stop-signal task (e.g., Logan, 1983, 1985, 1994), in which participants had to withhold a very likely response whenever a stopping cue (which was relatively infrequent) occurred. The ability to prevent a response in the presence of the stopping cue provided a measure of restraint. In this study (May & Hasher, in press), participants were trained to make category judgments (e.g., to say that a chair is a piece of furniture) as quickly as possible. The proportion of stop-signal trials on which participants were successful at stopping their category response is displayed in Figure 3. Synchrony did affect stopping performance, such that both

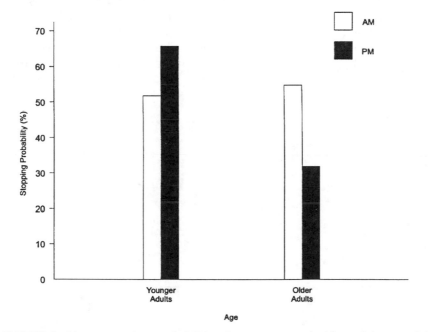

FIGURE 3. Mean stopping probabilities for younger and older adults tested in the morning and in the evening.

age groups were better able to stop when signaled to do so at peak relative to off-peak times. Thus, as with the access and deletion functions of inhibition, the restraint function of inhibition seems to be susceptible to synchrony effects for both younger and older adults. In addition, younger adults were generally better than older adults at withholding responses on stop-signal trials, again supporting an inhibitory-deficit view of aging.

Further evidence that individuals tested at off-peak times have difficulty controlling strong, well-practiced responses comes from a study examining general knowledge (May, Hasher, & Bhatt, 1994). In this study, participants were to answer simple trivia questions as quickly and accurately as possible (e.g., "What hero does Clark Kent become when he changes in a phone booth?"). Included in the list of questions, however, were some "illusion" questions, which, if taken literally, could not be answered (e.g., "How many animals of each kind did Moses take on the Ark?" Note that Noah, not Moses, built the Ark). Participants were warned in advance of the presence of these illusion questions and were instructed not to produce the likely answer (e.g., two), but rather to respond "can't say." Thus participants were asked to suppress the well-learned, highly probable verbal responses to the illusion questions and instead to answer with an alternative response. As illustrated in Figure 4, both younger and older adults showed an effect of synchrony on their ability to prevent strong, probable verbal responses: For illusion questions, participants tested at off-peak times were more likely to generate an inappropriate response (e.g., two) than age-mates tested at peak times.

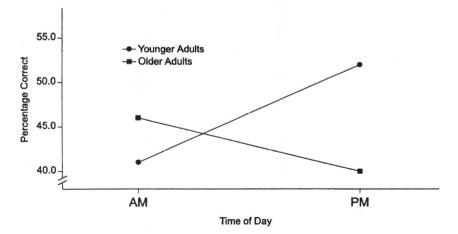

FIGURE 4. Percentage of correct answers on Moses illusion questions for younger and older adults by time of day.

Taken together, these two sets of data suggest that there will be reductions in accuracy in question answering whenever the questions prime a strong response *and* when the respondent is older or is answering at nonoptimal times. Not only can strong responses be based on past knowledge (however inaccurate that might be, e.g., Moses and the Ark) but the responses can also become strong within the context of a series of questions, as when one alternative answer has already been used multiple times or when multiple questions prime similar information.

When Synchrony Does Not Matter

Although the evidence we have reported thus far is consistent with the premise that inhibitory functioning is impaired at individuals' nonoptimal relative to optimal times, several findings also suggest that excitatory functioning does not vary across the day (see Table 2). First, scores on vocabulary tests (taken from several studies) did not change for either younger or older adults across the day, suggesting that retrieval of information from semantic or long-term memory is spared at nonoptimal times. Second, access to well-learned, familiar, or highly practiced responses was consistently preserved at nonoptimal times. We found spared performance on the trivia-type questions, into which illusion statements (e.g., Moses and the Ark) were embedded. Both younger and older adults generated the expected ending for high-cloze sentence frames equally often at optimal and nonoptimal times. In addition, they were as fast and accurate in making category judgments

TABLE 2.   TASKS WITH NO EFFECT ON SYNCHRONY ON AGE

	Younger Adults		Older Adults	
	AM (Nonpeak)	PM (Peak)	AM (Peak)	PM (Nonpeak)
Vocabulary[a] (lap/bowl)	22	23	26	29
Vocabulary[b] (stop signal)	18	17	28	24
Moses trivia[c]	78%	78%	79%	81%
High-cloze rates[d]	89%	89%	88%	87%
Medium-cloze rates	52%	53%	49%	51%
Stop-signal categorization[c]	91%	92%	89%	91%
RAT control completion	36%	32%	33%	32%

Note. [a]ervt v4; max 48; [b]ervt v3; max 36; [c]percentage correct; [d]percentage of sentences completed with expected.

about familiar categories across the day. Finally, no effect of either synchrony or age on target production for control items was obtained for the RAT task in the May (in press) study, a finding which further supports the suggestion that activation processes are not impaired at nonoptimal times.

Thus there are a growing number of findings showing that production of familiar, highly probable, or well-learned responses are not affected by the synchrony between peak circadian periods and testing times. Taken together, these findings are consistent with predictions of an inhibitory framework of synchrony effects that suggest that suppression but not activation processes are affected by circadian arousal.

Indirect Consequences of Diminished Inhibition

In addition to the patterns of impairment and sparing that are directly predicted from an inhibitory framework, there are also indirect or downstream consequences of inhibitory failures that are evident at asynchronous times of day. These deficits may be manifested in a number of ways, including memory impairments, particularly when tasks involve multiple trials, and require the deletion of information from a previous trial in order to remember information only from the current trial. Further-downstream consequences of diminished inhibition at nonpeak times of day include reliance on simple heuristic-based judgments, rather than more careful and effortful evaluations, and increased likelihood of being persuaded by weak arguments. In research utilizing surveys, one can conceive of conditions in which interviewing at peak versus nonpeak times of day might systematically bias the resulting data, not only in the way questions are interpreted by respondents, but in a manner which may be exacerbated by differences in respondent and interviewer characteristics (e.g., gender, race, social status, education level). Evidence of indirect consequences is provided in the sections that follow.

Heightened Susceptibility to Interference

As inhibitory efficiency declines at nonoptimal times of day and with age, span scores should also be reduced at nonoptimal times and for older adults. In memory span tasks, participants are typically given units of information to recall on multiple consecutive trials. Although the type of information tested in span experiments varies greatly from numbers to words to sentences, one common aspect of nearly all span

experiments is that participants first receive small units of information (e.g., one or two words) and progressively advance to larger units
(e.g., six or seven words). Span is determined by the largest unit size
for which participants successfully recall all of the information; thus
those who recall the largest units have the highest span score. Note,
however, that the largest units are also those that involve the greatest
amount of proactive interference, as they are preceded by a number of
trials with very similar information. For those who cannot efficiently
use inhibition to cut off access to previous information, the large units
should be especially problematic, and hence span scores should be
reduced. In addition, since inhibitory efficiency declines at nonoptimal
times, span scores should also be reduced then, relative to at optimal
times.

Recent work by May, Hasher, and Kane (1997) indicates that, indeed,
span tasks do involve proactive interference, and that individuals who
are particularly interference-prone are differentially disadvantaged by
the standard administration of span tasks. To explore the possibility
that synchrony impairs inhibitory functioning, thereby diminishing span
performance, younger and older adults were administered a simple
word span task, in which they read words on a computer screen and
then had to repeat them aloud from memory. The words were presented in sets, beginning with set size 2 and progressing to set size 6.
Each participant completed 3 trials at each set size, and span was calculated as the largest set size at which an individual was correct on 2
of the 3 trials. As can be seen in Figure 5, synchrony did affect span
performance, with both age groups demonstrating higher span scores
at peak relative to off-peak times.

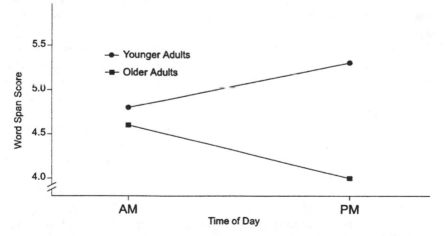

FIGURE 5. Word span scores for younger and older adults by time of day.

Inefficiency at clearing away previously relevant but currently obsolete information thus appears to reduce individuals' ability to store and process information. As a result, older adults and people tested at asynchronous times should have difficulty when questionnaires place heavy demands on working memory (e.g., when they require retrieval of large units of information or when they demand use of a complicated scale), particularly for questions occurring late in a series.

Use of Heuristics

Since research findings seem to suggest that both aging and performance at nonoptimal times can reduce access to details of information that are stored in memory, what is retrieved at nonoptimal times? Along with the evidence we have reviewed suggesting that strong responses are easily accessible, the work of Bodenhausen (1990) suggests that heuristics and schemas, which Alba and Hasher (1983) argued are highly accessible relative to details of complex events, are also highly accessible at nonoptimal times, and so are very likely to be used in evaluation situations. Below, we first discuss findings related to the role of synchrony in people's differential use of heuristics, and then consider further-downstream consequences for persuasion in the following section.

During nonoptimal times of day, individuals appear to rely more on heuristics to process information than they do during optimal times of day. Bodenhausen (1990) found that people used stereotypes in making social judgments at nonoptimal times. Those who reach their mental peak early in the day were more likely to generate stereotypic responses in the afternoon and the evening, while those who reach their peak in the evening exhibited a greater tendency to generate stereotypic responses in the morning.

A study by Yoon (1997) provides further evidence that people rely more on heuristic or schema-based processing rather than detailed processing at nonoptimal times of day, and that this tendency is more pronounced in older than younger adults. In this study, participants were given a recognition task containing target and foil items. Consistent with a pattern of results suggestive of schema-based processing, older people, at their nonoptimal time, had relatively high hit rates and high false alarm rates for foils that were congruent and mildly incongruent (and thus likely to be mistakenly processed as a congruent item), but low false alarm rates for highly incongruent foils. However, at optimal times of day, older adults were as detailed in their processing as younger adults, evidenced by high hit rates and low false alarm rates (see Table 3).

TABLE 3. EFFECTS OF SYNCHRONY AND AGE ON RECOGNITION ACCURACY (YOON, 1997)

Age and Time	Message Items (Hit Rates)	FOILS (False Alarm Rates)		
		Congruent	Incongruent	
			Low	High
Younger adults				
AM (nonpeak)	.81	.20	.06	.02
PM (peak)	.83	.08	.03	.06
Older adults				
AM (peak)	.93	.19	.04	.04
PM (nonpeak)	.77	.43	.37	.09

The results of these two studies suggest the potential importance of considering the role of synchrony when investigating people's use of different types of processing strategies. For example, in social cognition studies involving perceptions of outgroup members' traits and behaviors, individuals are more likely to rely on stereotype-based information, which is often negative, when responding at their nonoptimal compared to optimal time of day. This may, in turn, have implications for identifying important situations in which stereotyped groups may experience systematic disadvantages (e.g., personnel selection, law enforcement).

In addition, the fact that synchrony may influence people's use of heuristic versus more analytic processing impacts on question-asking situations, particularly when investigating age differences. In answering questions that call on relatively detailed and systematic processing of complex information, both younger and older people (but particularly older people), at their nonoptimal times, may be differentially disadvantaged. On the other hand, responses to questions that primarily require individuals to rely on schema-based processing would not be susceptible to synchrony effects and could be safely administered throughout the day.

We further speculate that in designing survey questions, certain formats are more likely to promote schema-based processing, as opposed to more systematic processing. For example, in attempting to formulate the optimal attribute mix for a new product, a methodology such as conjoint analysis may be chosen, where the measures of interest are individuals' trade-offs between various available product features. In such a case, it is crucial that participants not overly focus on any particular attribute (e.g., price) as a proxy for their overall satisfaction with a given bundle of features, a schema-based evaluative behavior more likely at their nonoptimal time of day. Question order may also lead to a distribution of responses that are systematically biased. Imagine a questionnaire in which initial responses involve judgments that commit a respondent to a schema-based or stereotype-based view (e.g., in the U.S., that Asians tend to be good at math). A respondent, once committed to a schema-based view, would likely formulate subsequent responses consistent with that view, a tendency which may be exacerbated during nonoptimal times of day and diminished at optimal times of day. Different conclusions might thus be reached depending on the time of day the questions are asked.

Persuasion

The notion that diminished inhibition efficiency at nonpeak times can lead to an increased reliance on heuristic or schema-based, rather than more analytic, processing, suggests further-downstream consequences for persuasion. The elaboration likelihood model (Petty & Cacioppo, 1986) posits that there can be different routes to persuasion depending on an individual's ability and motivation to process information. In cases where the likelihood of elaboration is high, that is, where ability and motivation to process are high, the attitude change process involves thoughtful scrutiny and detailed processing of persuasive communication (e.g., argument strength). This process is referred to as the "central route" to persuasion. On the other hand, when the individual lacks either the ability or the motivation to process information, a different process of attitude change occurs. This process, referred to as the "peripheral route" to persuasion, involves the use of simple rules-of-thumb, or heuristics, for evaluating the content of a persuasive message (e.g., peripheral cues). We might thus expect people who have neither the ability (e.g., at their nonoptimal time of day) nor the motivation to process incoming messages to be persuaded by cues that are not particularly diagnostic or informative but are nonetheless appealing or relatively effortless to process.

A study by Yoon and Lee (1998) found empirical support for such tendencies. The study examined how synchrony, age, and level of motivation might affect the extent to which people are persuaded by argument strength versus peripheral cues in an advertising setting. Persuasion was assessed by averaging four postmessage attitude ratings. The results suggest that older adults, as well as younger adults, were persuaded by relatively strong arguments (i.e., a "central route"), as opposed to weak arguments, when highly motivated to process advertising messages during their respective peak times (see Table 4A).

TABLE 4A. PERSUASION OF ARGUMENT STRENGTH BY AGE, TIME OF DAY, AND MOTIVATION

Argument Strength	Low Motivation		High Motivation	
	Weak	Strong	Weak	Strong
Younger adults				
AM (nonpeak)	5.7	5.7	3.4	4.8
PM (peak)	5.6	5.8	3.5	5.2
Older adults				
AM (peak)	4.3	6.2	2.3	5.1
PM (nonpeak)	4.5	5.0	3.7	3.3

Note. Average of four postmessage attitude ratings on nine-point scales (1 = negative, 9 = positive).

However, the older adults also seemed to be persuaded by strong arguments even when their motivation to process was low as long as they were exposed to the information during their peak time of day. At the nonpeak time of day, the older adults appeared to be more persuaded via a "peripheral route" (i.e., relevance of the picture to the product featured in the advertisement) under both low- and high-involvement conditions (see Table 4B). These results thus suggest that the ability to process incoming information depending on the time of day, not the level of motivation, is the critical determinant in the persuasibility of older adults. By contrast, younger adults who were highly motivated to process appeared to be persuaded by strong arguments even at their nonoptimal time of day (see Table 4A); they were

TABLE 4B. PERSUASION OF PICTURE RELEVANCE BY AGE, TIME OF DAY, AND MOTIVATION

Picture Relevance	Low Motivation		High Motivation	
	Irrelevant	Relevant	Irrelevant	Relevant
Younger adults				
AM (nonpeak)	5.2	6.3	4.1	3.7
PM (peak)	5.2	6.3	3.8	4.2
Older adults				
AM (peak)	4.8	5.4	3.1	3.4
PM (nonpeak)	4.3	5.7	3.0	4.2

Note. Average of four postmessage attitude ratings on nine-point scales (1 = negative, 9 = positive).

persuaded by relevance of the picture (i.e, the peripheral cue) only when their motivation to process was low (see Table 4B).

This study clearly demonstrates the effects of synchrony and circadian arousal on persuasibility of older adults. Insights gained about how older adults' attitudes are affected by exposure to persuasive communications potentially impact on the issue of questionnaire design. For example, researchers who wish to get an accurate assessment of the strength of an argument relating to a particular topic would need to explicitly account for time of testing, especially if the arguments are complex or responses are to be elicited from older adults.

Previous research involving younger adults has found that the degree to which people will agree with or be persuaded by the substance of an argument may also hinge on the degree to which people are distracted during the presentation of a message. In particular, Petty, Wells, and Brock (1976) demonstrated that weak arguments are particularly persuasive when people are distracted. In a study by Rahhal et al. (1996), the concern was with the degree to which distraction and persuasion effects are heightened at nonoptimal times. They conducted a study in which they created and normed two weak arguments (about abolishing home schooling and police reassignment plans) which were presented in the presence versus absence of distraction to older adults who were tested in the morning or afternoon. The distraction task was extremely simple, and required participants to monitor where an X appeared on a computer screen. While doing this, participants listened to a message, and immediately afterwards, their attitudes towards the message were assessed, using a series of seven-point rating scales. The data (see Figure 6) show clearly that distraction in the morning has

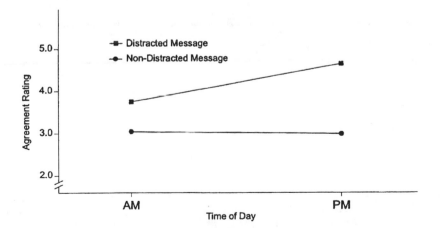

FIGURE 6. Agreement ratings for messages for older adults by time of day.

little impact on attitude scores (how good, wise, favorable, and beneficial the arguments were). But distraction at nonoptimal times has a major impact on older adults, such that the weak arguments were considerably more persuasive in the afternoon.

This study also raises questions about the circumstances under which survey questions are asked. Is there a TV or radio on? Is there someone else in the room while the questioning is occurring? If so, the views of older adults may actually change during the course of an interview if the content of the questions includes any substantive information that might lead to supporting one point of view. Note that it is weak evidence for a particular point that has been found to be compelling under distracting or nonoptimal testing circumstances.

☐ Conclusion

The synchrony between circadian arousal periods really matters for some cognition- and social-cognition-type tasks, but not for others. Moreover, the consequences of synchrony can be greater for older adults than for younger adults given the age-related deficits in inhibition. To the extent that changes in cognitive functioning at off-peak times do in fact stem from circadian-related deficits in inhibition, performance at nonoptimal times reflects deficits such as heightened access to irrelevant information, failures to clear away or suppress information that is no longer useful, and difficulties in restraining or preventing the production of strong, dominant responses that are undesirable or inappropriate. In addition, downstream consequences of diminished inhibition include heightened susceptibility to proactive interference, impaired judgments resulting from retrieval failures, and increased reliance on stereotypes and heuristics.

On the other hand, performance appears to be spared over the day in some instances, such as when tasks simply require access to or production of familiar, well-learned, or practiced material (e.g., vocabulary tests, simple trivia questions), or when strong, dominant responses produce correct answers (e.g., word associations, familiar category judgments).

What are the potential consequences of inefficient inhibition for questionnaire performance? Formats that place particularly heavy memory demands on individuals (e.g., those with complicated scales for responding, or multiple scales that change from section to section, or those that require participants to base current answers on previous ones) may differentially place poor inhibitors at a disadvantage. In those instances, inefficient suppressors may simply shift to strategic, load-reducing strategies, using only parts of a given scale or relying on strong, easily retrieved responses rather than performing the careful, analytical thinking that may be desired by the investigator.

Reliance on strong, familiar, or stereotypic responses may be particularly problematic when trying to assess "temporary" or "momentary" states of individuals or when searching for the possibility of nondominant or unlikely answers. For example, suppose that an investigator is interested in the influence of a spouse's job loss on marital satisfaction. If, in general, a person's marriage is healthy, she may tend to respond "fine," "good," etc. to questions about marriage, despite any temporary decrease in marital satisfaction. A biased set of responses is particularly likely when people are asked such questions at their nonpeak time of day.

Ultimately, researchers may need not only to keep track of when studies are administered but also to instruct study participants as to when during the day they should complete mail-in questionnaires, or to note the time when the questionnaires are completed. As testing time might influence the types of responses likely to be given, the respondents' answers may need to be interpreted in light of that fact. For researchers investigating group differences in cognition and social cognition that involve inhibitory functioning, the time at which questions are asked probably cannot be safely ignored, particularly if the groups of interest differ markedly in age.

☐ Endnotes

1. Unfortunately, the fully-crossed design of Age × Morningness-Eveningness was not possible because so few of the younger adults were morning-types, and virtually none of the older adults was an evening-type.

2. The control items for any given participant had served as presented items for another participant, via a counterbalancing scheme.

☐ Acknowledgments

Much of the research reported in this chapter was supported by National Institute on Aging Grants 12753 and 4306. This research was also supported in part by a grant from the Social Sciences and Humanities Research Council of Canada. We wish to thank the members of the Subject Registry at the Duke University Center for the Study of Aging and Human Development for their participation in many of the reported studies, and to acknowledge Fred Feinberg, Marcus Lee, Chad Massie, and Tammy Rahhal for their help.

☐ References

Adan, A. (1991). Influence of morningness-eveningness preference in the relationship between body temperature and performance: A diurnal study. *Personality and Individual Differences, 12,* 1159–1169.

Adan, A., & Almirall, H. (1990). Adaptation and standardization of a Spanish version of the morningness eveningness questionnaire: Individual differences. *Personality and Individual Differences, 11,* 1123–1130.

Alba, J. W., & Hasher, L. (1983). Is memory schematic? *Psychological Bulletin, 93,* 203–231.

Allport, A. (1989). Visual attention. In M. I. Posner (Ed.), *Foundations of cognitive science* (pp 631–682). Cambridge, MA: MIT Press.

Anderson, M., Petros, T. V., Beckwith, B. E., Mitchell, W. W., & Fritz, S. (1991). Individual differences in the effect of time of day on long-term memory access. *American Journal of Psychology, 104,* 241–255.

Bodenhausen, G. V. (1990). Stereotypes and judgmental heuristics: Evidence of circadian variations in discrimination. *Psychological Science, 1,* 319–322.

Buela-Casal, G., Caballo, V. E., & Cueto, E. (1990). Differences between morning and evening types in performance. *Personality and Individual Differences, 11,* 447–450.

Colquhoun, W. P. (1971). Circadian variations in mental efficiency. In W. P. Colquhoun (Ed.), *Biological rhythms and human performance* (pp. 39–107). London: Academic Press.

Folkard, S., Knauth, P., Monk, T. H., & Rutenfranz, J. (1976). The effect of memory load on the circadian variation in performance efficiency under rapidly rotating shift system. *Ergonomics, 10,* 479–488.

Folkard, S., Weaver, R., & Wildgruber, C. (1983). Multi-oscillatory control of circadian rhythms in human performance. *Nature, 305,* 223–226.

Hartman, M., & Hasher, L. (1991). Aging and suppression: Memory for previously relevant information. *Psychology and Aging, 6,* 587–594.

Hasher, L., Quig, M. B., & May, C. P. (1997). Inhibitory control over no-longer-relevant information: Adult age differences. *Memory & Cognition, 25,* 286–295.

Hasher, L., & Zacks, R. T. (1988). Working memory, comprehension, and aging: A review and new view. In G. H. Bower (Ed.), *The psychology of learning and motivation* (Vol. 22, pp. 193–225). New York: Academic Press.

Hasher, L., Zacks, R. T., & May, C. P. (in press). Inhibitory control, circadian arousal, and age. In D. Gopher & A. Koriat (Eds.), *Attention and performance, XVII, Cognitive regulation of performance: Interaction of theory and application.* Cambridge, MA: MIT Press.

Horne, J., Brass, C., & Pettitt, S. (1980). Circadian performance differences between morning and evening types. *Ergonomics, 23,* 29–36.

Horne, J., & Ostberg, O. (1976). A self-assessment questionnaire to determine morningness-eveningness in human circadian rhythms. *International Journal of Chronobiology, 4,* 97–110.

Hrushesky, W. (1989). Circadian chronotherapy: From animal experiments to human cancer chemotherapy. In B. Lemmer (Ed.), *Chronopharmacology: Cellular and biochemical interactions* (pp. 439–473). New York: Marcel Dekker.

Hrushesky, W. (1994). Timing is everything. *The Sciences, 34(July/Aug.)*, 32–37.

Intons-Peterson, M. J., Rocchi, P., West, T., McLellan, K., & Hackney, A. (1998). Aging, optimal testing times, and negative priming. *Journal of Experimental Psychology: Learning, Memory and Cognition, 24,* 362–376.

Ishihara, K, Miyake, S., Miyasita, A., & Miyata, Y. (1991). Morningness-eveningness preference and sleep habits in Japanese office workers of different ages. *Chronobiologia, 18,* 9–16.

Kerkhof, G. A. (1984). A Dutch-language questionnaire for the selection of morning and evening type individuals. *Nederlands Tijdschrift voor de Psychologie, 39,* 281–294.

Kerkhof, G. A. (1985). Inter-individual differences in the human circadian system: A review. *Biological Psychology, 20,* 83–112.

Kerkhof, G. A., van der Geest, W., Korving, H. J., & Rietveld W. J. (1981). Diurnal differences between morning-type and evening-type subjects in some indices of central and autonomous nervous activity. In A. Reinberg, N. Vieux, & P. Andlauer (Eds.), *Night and shift work: Biological and social aspects* (pp. 457–464). Oxford, England: Pergamon Press.

Leirer, V. O., Tanke, E. D., & Morrow, D. G. (1994). Time of day and naturalistic prospective memory. *Experimental Aging Research, 20,* 127–134.

Logan, G. D. (1983). On the ability to inhibit simple thoughts and actions: 1. Stop signal studies of decision and memory. *Journal of Experimental Psychology: Learning, Memory, and Cognition, 9,* 585–606.

Logan, G. D. (1985). On the ability to inhibit simple thoughts and actions: 2. Stop signal studies of repetition priming. *Journal of Experimental Psychology: Learning, Memory, and Cognition, 11,* 675–691.

Logan, G. D. (1994). On the ability to inhibit thought and action: A users' guide to the stop signal paradigm. In D. Dagenbach and T. Carr (Eds.), *Inhibitory mechanisms in attention, memory, and language* (pp. 189–239). New York: Academic Press.

May, C. P. (in press). Synchrony effects in cognition: The costs and a benefit. *Psychological Bulletin and Review.*

May, C. P., & Hasher, L. (in press). Synchrony effects in inhibitory control over thought and action. *Journal of Experimental Psychology: Human Perception and Performance.*

May, C. P., Hasher, L., & Bhatt, A. (1994, April). *Time of day affects susceptibility to misinformation in younger and older adults.* Presented at the Cognitive Aging Conference, Atlanta, GA.

May, C. P., Hasher, L., & Kane, M. J. (1997). *The role of interference in memory span measures.* Manuscript submitted for publication.

May, C. P., Hasher, L., & Stoltzfus, E. R. (1993). Optimal time of day and the magnitude of age differences in memory. *Psychological Science, 4,* 326–330.

Mecacci, L., & Zani, A. (1983). Morningness-eveningness preferences and sleep-waking diary data of morning and evening types in student and workers samples. *Ergonomics, 26,* 1147–1153.

Mecacci, L., Zani, A., Rocchetti, G., & Lucioli, R. (1986). The relationships between morningness-eveningness, ageing and personality. *Personality and Individual Differences, 7,* 911–913.

Mednick, S. A. (1962). The associative basis of the creative process. *Psychological Review, 69,* 220–232.

Monk, T. H. (1986). Advantages and disadvantages of rapidly rotating shift schedules: A circadian viewpoint. *Human Factors, 28,* 553–557.

Moore-Ede, M., & McIntosh, J. (1993, October 1). Alert at the switch. *Technology Review, 96,* 52–65.

Navon, D. (1989). The importance of being visible: On the role of attention in a mind viewed as an anarchic intelligence system: 1. Basic tenets. *European Journal of Cognitive Psychology, 1,* 191–213.

Petros, T. V., Beckwith, B. E., & Anderson, M. (1990). Individual differences in the effects of time of day and passage difficulty on prose memory in adults. *British Journal of Psychology, 81,* 63–72.

Petty, R. E., & Cacioppo, J. T. (1986). *Communication and persuasion: Central and peripheral routes to persuasion.* New York: Springer-Verlag.

Petty, R. E., Wells, G. L., & Brock, T. L. (1976). Distraction can enhance or reduce yielding to propaganda: Thought disruption versus effort justification. *Journal of Personality and Social Psychology, 34,* 874–884.

Rahhal, T. A., Abendroth, L. J., & Hasher, L. (April, 1996). *Can older adults resist persuasion? The effects of distraction and time of day on attitude change.* Poster presented at the Cognitive Aging Conference, Atlanta, GA.

Skinner, N. F. (1985). University grades and time of day of instruction. *Bulletin of the Psychonomic Society, 23,* 67.

Smith, C. S., Reilly, C., & Midkiff, K. (1989). Evaluation of the circadian rhythm questionnaires with suggestions for an improved measure of morningness. *Journal of Applied Psychology, 74,* 728–738.

Smith, S. M., & Blankenship, S. E. (1991). Incubation and the persistence of fixation in problem solving. *American Journal of Psychology, 104,* 61–87.

Smolensky, M., & D'Alonzo G. (1993). Medical chronobiology: Concepts and applications. *American Review of Respiratory Disease, 147,* S2–S19.

Vitiello, M. V., Smallwood, R. G., Avery, D. H., & Pascualy, R. A. (1986). Circadian temperature rhythms in young adult and aged men. *Neurobiology of Aging, 7,* 97–100.

Webb, W. B., & Bonnet, M. H. (1978). The sleep of 'morning' and 'evening' types. *Biological Psychology, 7,* 29–35.

Wilson, G. D. (1990). Personality, time of day, and arousal. *Personality and Individual Differences, 11,* 153–168.

Yoon, C. (1997). Age differences in consumers' processing strategies: An investigation of moderating influences. *Journal of Consumer Research, 24,* 329–342.

Yoon, C., & Lee, M. (1998). *Age differences in processing of pictorial and verbal information across time of day: Implications for persuasion.* Manuscript submitted for publication.

Zacks, R. T., & Hasher, L. (1994). Directed ignoring: Inhibitory regulation of working memory. In D. Dagenbach and T. Carr (Eds.), *Inhibitory mechanisms in attention, memory, and language* (pp. 241–264). New York: Academic Press.

CHAPTER

John C. Cavanaugh

Metamemory as Social Cognition: Challenges for (and from) Survey Research

Being able to think and reflect on our own cognitions, it can be argued, is what separates humans from other species. Self-reflection, and the personal knowledge that results, form the very foundation of human consciousness (Metcalfe & Shimamura, 1994). We are able to monitor what is perceived, judge what we know or what we need to learn, and to predict the consequences of our actions.

Self-reflection about cognition is referred to as *metacognition* in the psychological literature. Although this term has only been used for about a quarter century, the issue of what people know about their cognition, how they use this knowledge, and why this knowledge is important has been at the core of philosophy for millennia. Indeed, one of the most widely known (and paraphrased) statements in philosophy concerns metacognition—Descartes's famous point *Cogito ergo sum.* Clearly, at least some philosophers believe that metacognition cuts to the very core of the human condition.

The claims involving metacognition in cognitive psychology are much more modest. Indeed, whether people are even capable of meaningful conscious reflection on their thinking is open to debate (e.g., Nisbett & Wilson, 1977). Nevertheless, over the past quarter century increased attention has been focused on metacognition, especially in the domain of memory. This latter area, referred to as *metamemory,* is the oldest and most intensively researched aspect of metacognition.

Because metamemory is the domain most often studied in older adults using survey methods, it is the focus of this chapter.

Although the systematic study of people's knowledge and beliefs about their memory is only a century or so old, awareness of the issue predates recorded history. For example, one can easily imagine that ancient storytellers realized that remembering scripts that took hours (or even days) to recite was a formidable task, which probably led to the use of music as a memory device as well as the creation of classic mnemonic techniques. Indeed, it makes little intuitive sense to argue that the creation of formal memory strategies such as the method of loci would have occurred in the absence of awareness of memory fallibility.

This realization that one's memory is not perfect and that some sort of behavior is necessary to buttress it is one example of the more general notion that people have knowledge about and certain beliefs in reference to memory. Given the label "metamemory" in the early 1970s by John Flavell (1971), memory knowledge and beliefs have moved from a little-researched topic to a significant subject within memory research. Although the definition of metamemory has evolved over the years, in general it refers to knowledge about how we remember, the process of monitoring our memory processing, and the beliefs we hold about memory (Cavanaugh & Perlmutter, 1982; Hertzog & Dixon, 1994).

In this chapter, two major aspects of metamemory research as it pertains to older adults are addressed. First, a brief summary of the major lines of theory and investigation will be presented, focusing mainly on self-report questionnaires assessing memory knowledge and memory self-efficacy as well as their relation to memory performance. Second, key issues from the social cognition literature, along with a framework from viewing metamemory as a type of social cognition, will be presented that focuses on the genesis of individuals' responses to the items. Finally, several specific avenues for future research will be presented from the context of survey and questionnaire research.

This chapter is not intended to be a comprehensive review of the metamemory and aging literature. Several excellent articles and chapters fulfilling this function are available (e.g., Cavanaugh, 1996; Hertzog & Dixon, 1994; West & Berry, 1994). Self-ratings of memory ability have also been routinely used in large survey and interview studies, as described elsewhere in this volume (see especially Chapter 16, by Herzog & Rodgers, and Chapter 14, by O'Rourke, Sudman, Johnson, & Burris). Although not typically included in reviews of the metamemory literature, they nevertheless provide additional evidence regarding what people know and believe about their memory. Thus, the focus here is on identifying key issues in the metamemory literature which are especially relevant for survey methods.

☐ Theory and Research on Metamemory

Although investigations of children's and adults' metamemory have been conducted for roughly a century, a specific focus on older adults' metamemory dates only from the late 1970s and early 1980s. This relatively recent emphasis is due in part to the common stereotype of memory decline and complaint in older adults (Levy & Langer, 1994). At a time when the prevailing world view was inevitable decline, there was little need for theory or research on what older adults knew or believed to be true about memory. However, as it became clear that memory development in late life depends on the type of memory being examined (e.g., working memory, very-long-term memory) and that differences across individuals in memory development are large, metamemory in later life became a potential explanatory variable. These twin notions of intra- and interindividual differences in memory would provide an important conceptual basis for metamemory theory and research.

At roughly the same time, researchers began developing memory questionnaires aimed at assessing what adults knew about memory. This early research (e.g., Herrmann & Neisser, 1978) resulted in the first generation of questionnaires (e.g., the Short Inventory of Memory Experiences). This survey research approach became the major way that systematic developmental research is conducted on age differences in what adults know about their memory and the beliefs they hold about it.

With the joint developments of intra- and interindividual differences and memory questionnaires, the stage was set for the creation of comprehensive survey instruments. Psychometrically sound questionnaires (e.g., Memory Functioning Questionnaire; Metamemory in Adulthood Instrument) appeared in the 1980s, as did early attempts at developing theoretical models. Nearly all subsequent work has been grounded in these early approaches, which has resulted in the creation of metamemory taxonomies.

A Taxonomy of Metamemory

Developing a taxonomy of metamemory turns out to be a bit more difficult than it seems. Part of the complication stems from the inclusion of several different types of processes and information in the definition of metamemory. For example, the inclusion of monitoring aspects implies that metamemory includes feelings-of-knowing (also known as tip-of-the-tongue phenomena), as well as "facts about memory" (e.g., verbatim recall is usually more difficult than gist recall). Although I will briefly discuss feelings-of-knowing, for purposes of this paper I will focus more on the informational aspects.

Hertzog and Dixon (1994) provide a very useful taxonomy of meta-memory using three general categories (see also Cavanaugh & Green, 1990; Cavanaugh & Perlmutter, 1982; Gilewski & Zelinski, 1986; Lovelace, 1990): "(1) declarative knowledge about memory tasks and memory processes—defined as knowledge about both how memory functions and the viability of strategic behaviors for tasks requiring memory processes; (2) memory monitoring—defined as the awareness of the current state of one's memory system; and (3) self-referent beliefs about memory" (p. 229). Memory self-efficacy (Cavanaugh & Green, 1990) is the central construct of memory beliefs, defined as one's sense of mastery or ability to use memory effectively when required.

A multidimensional view of metamemory is critical if one wants to understand what role metamemory plays in remembering (Hertzog & Dixon, 1994) and in how to construct good surveys. As described in more detail later, for example, declarative knowledge, which in this context is often described as facts about memory, is a necessary but not sufficient element in understanding why people select the memory strategies they do; beliefs and other aspects of metamemory also play important determining roles (Cavanaugh & Morton, 1989). Declarative knowledge is important in survey construction because it enables people to understand items and formulate responses.

Theoretical Frameworks

To date, the most thoroughly articulated theoretical framework from an adult developmental perspective concerning metamemory in older adults has been offered by Cavanaugh and colleagues (e.g., Cavanaugh, 1989; Cavanaugh & Morton, 1989). Based on an earlier framework (Cavanaugh, Kramer, Sinnott, Camp, & Markley, 1985), Cavanaugh and colleagues proposed a complex set of reciprocal dynamic interrelationships that denote the influence of cognitive developmental level, personality, situational factors, general knowledge, self-efficacy, effort, memory strategies, and various feedback and evaluation processes.

A critical aspect of the model is that metamemorial self-evaluations are not conducted only on the basis of direct input from content knowledge about memory processes and functions. Rather, the influence of stored content knowledge is mediated through memory beliefs. The importance of this mediation cannot be overemphasized. Cavanaugh and colleagues' framework implies that evaluations of memory ability are not made by simply retrieving and applying objective "memory facts." Instead, evaluations of ability in a given context are constructed by using previously stored information in addition to contemporaneous information processing. For survey research, this means that people's responses to items may be based on the retrieval of previously stored judgments, the construction of responses at the time they are needed, or both (Cavanaugh, Feldman, & Hertzog, 1998).

Most of the adult developmental research on metamemory has focused on the memory beliefs and self-efficacy aspects of Cavanaugh and colleagues' framework. Although the entire framework has not yet been subjected to empirical test, there is, as we will see, a growing body of evidence that at least some of its hypothesized relations have support. It is to this research that we now turn.

Empirical Research on Metamemory

Research on metamemory across adulthood began in part as an outgrowth of research indicating that one reason children do not use efficient memory strategies is that they do not know they should (Flavell, 1971; Cavanaugh & Borkowski, 1980; Schneider & Pressley, 1989). So, for example, some researchers provided older adults with information about the efficacy of various memory strategies. However, this approach was not very successful; for instance, Rabinowitz (1989) demonstrated that additional opportunities and encouragement to use memory strategies is insufficient by itself to produce optimal strategic performance. Specific training to use memory strategies, while somewhat more effective, also does not produce long-term improvement (e.g., Anschutz, Camp, Markley, & Kramer, 1985, 1987).

Early on, though, much metamemory research in gerontology focused on two key questions: What do older people know about their memory? What beliefs about memory do older adults hold?

Memory Beliefs

Most questionnaire research in metamemory has examined memory beliefs. In particular, work has focused on the concept of memory self-efficacy, which is a derivative of Bandura's (1986, 1989) general notion of self-efficacy: the extent to which one believes in his or her ability to mobilize the motivation, cognitive resources, and courses of action necessary to exert control over task demands. Memory self-efficacy can be constructively viewed as hierarchically organized beliefs about the self-as-rememberer ranging from global ("my memory isn't very good") to domain specific ("I can't remember names, but I'm good at faces") to context specific ("I can't remember where I parked in the lot") to local or concurrent ("I can remember this phone number so I don't need to write it down") (Hertzog, Dixon, & Hultsch, 1990). Memory self-efficacy is viewed as a primary (but mediated) influence on performance (Bandura, 1989; Berry & West, 1993; Cavanaugh & Green, 1990) in three ways: (a) on the construction and selection of strategies; (b) on the level of effort or persistence; and (c) on affect-related outcomes of performance. Current adult developmental theories of metamemory postulate that memory self-efficacy, memory abilities, and performance are mutually influential, and that individual differences in each must be taken into account (Cavanaugh & Green, 1990; Hertzog et al., 1990).

To date, researchers have relied mostly on three questionnaires to investigate age differences in memory self-efficacy (see Cavanaugh, 1996, for a discussion of measurement issues): the Metamemory in Adulthood Instrument (MIA), the Memory Failures Questionnaire (MFQ; Gilewski & Zelinski, 1988), and the Memory Self-Efficacy Questionnaire (MSEQ; Berry, West, & Dennehey, 1989). Psychometric research indicates that the MIA subscales of Capacity (measuring perceived ability), Change (measuring perceived change in ability), and Locus (measuring perceived control over memory) converge with the MFQ to identify a factor identified as *memory self-efficacy* (Hertzog, Hultsch, & Dixon, 1989). Several investigations have found age-related differences in memory self-efficacy (e.g., Berry et al., 1989; Cavanaugh & Poon, 1989; Dixon & Hultsch, 1983).

Due to the predicted relationship between self-efficacy and performance, much research has also examined this issue. The data clearly indicate that memory self-efficacy beliefs are often inaccurate, and that memory self-efficacy judgments and performance are typically only moderately correlated (for reviews, see Cavanaugh & Green, 1990; Hertzog & Dixon, 1994; West & Berry, 1994). However, the relation between the two is mediated (e.g., Cavanaugh & Green, 1990) and varies across types of memory tasks (West, Dennehy-Basile, & Norris, 1996) and instructional conditions (Baldi & Berry, 1996). In the former case, self-efficacy beliefs have been shown to predict better verbal memory performance for men (but not for women), and to have no relation with nonverbal memory (Seeman, McAvay, Merrill, Albert, and Rodin, 1996). In the latter case, for example, respondents who complete memory self-efficacy questionnaires in descending order (i.e., from most to least difficult task demands) show higher self-efficacy than those completing the questionnaires in ascending order (Baldi & Berry, 1996).

These data have suggested to some that memory self-efficacy (and memory beliefs in general) must be examined as types of social cognition (Cavanaugh et al., 1998). For example, memory self-efficacy is likely to be influenced by individuals' implicit theories about cognition (Dweck & Leggett, 1988) and how these implicit theories explain memory aging (Hertzog & Dixon, 1994). Similarly, the affect that results from performance (e.g., anxiety, confidence) may be the result of specific levels of self-efficacy (Bandura, 1986, 1989). It is to this integration of metamemory with social cognition we now turn.

☐ Interfaces Between Metamemory and Social Cognition

Despite the fact that metamemory has been viewed as including beliefs about one's memory and aspects of self-efficacy, and that the typical metamemory assessment approach is to ask people to respond to collections of questions about many different aspects of memory, surprisingly little attention has been paid to a number of basic issues such as how people go about responding to metamemory questions (Cavanaugh et al., 1998). The lack of research is especially surprising given the considerable attention that has been given to this and a host of related issues (e.g., the diagnosticity of information, context effects, the role of affect in judgments, etc.) in the social cognition literature (Cavanaugh et al., 1998; Schwarz, 1996).

Fortunately, a few authors have begun making explicit theoretical connections between the metamemory and social cognition literatures (Cavanaugh et al., 1998; Schwarz, 1996). These forays have followed relatively parallel paths, drawing on several central constructs from the social cognition judgment literature and applying them to the case of judgments about one's memory. For purposes of this paper, I will only highlight several of the most important connections; the interested reader is encouraged to read the more extended discussions for a more complete account. Additionally, the reader is reminded that these connections have, for the most part, no empirical data directly addressing the presumptions. Thus, the points of contact are, at this point, purely speculative.

Nevertheless, several aspects of this approach have been applied successfully to other aspects of metamemory, most notably feeling-of-knowing and memory monitoring. For example, several researchers in cognitive psychology have used the notions of accessibility and availability to help explain how monitoring succeeds and fails (e.g., Koriat, 1994; Nelson & Narens, 1990, 1994). Such convergence on similar constructs provides support for the dynamic view of metamemory discussed earlier.

A Theoretical Framework of Metamemory from a Social Cognition Perspective

The social cognition literature has a host of both constructs and data to support them that provides the basis for creating a theoretical framework describing the knowledge and beliefs aspects of metamemory (Cavanaugh et al., 1998). This framework is based on the four core notions of schematicity, accessibility, availability, and diagnosticity, as well as the range of things that influence them (such as context and affect). Cavanaugh et al. (1998) argue that these constructs set the stage for complex, reciprocal interactions among stored self-knowledge about memory, prior judgments about memory, affect, and response constructions triggered by the question being asked. These interactions form the basis for responding to survey items about memory.

To preview a bit, we consider answers to metamemory questions to be based partly on reporting of already-stored information and partly as the result of on-the-spot constructions. Individual differences are apparent in the underlying cognitive structures and the degree to which they are flexible and context dependent (Barsalou, 1987; Kelly, 1955). Coupled with environmental (e.g., task) demands, these structures influence the metamemory judgments people make, which in turn influence subsequent behavior and the cognitive structures themselves (e.g., Cavanaugh & Morton, 1989). Such reciprocity merely acknowledges the reciprocal role of affect, which is both inherent in any existing cognitive structure as well as a result of the judgment process itself. Because the specific assumptions underlying the framework are described in detail in Cavanaugh et al. (1998), the focus here will be on highlighting a few of the more central constructs from social cognition research that have particular importance for survey and questionnaire investigations.

Implications of Social Cognition for Metamemory

The most important implication of a social cognition view of metamemory is that representations of the self concerning memory are actually complex and multifaceted cognitive structures. What one believes at any given moment about oneself as a rememberer, for example, depends in complex ways on how and on which stored judgments about oneself are accessed. Indeed, there is no such thing as permanent cognitive structures about the self (Anderson, 1987; Bargh, 1989; Markus & Wurf, 1987; Feldman & Lynch, 1988). By extension, there is no such thing as a permanent set of self-judgments about memory ability or beliefs. In practical terms, how one views oneself as a rememberer changes over time, an important point to consider (remember?) when trying to interpret the stability of self-judgments.

This implication that the self is a constantly evolving, dynamic process allows for direct connections between metamemory and social cognition research. For example, concepts from the social cognition literature such as schematicity, attributions, self-efficacy, automaticity, and the recall of personal attributes, all of which have been researched extensively, may be brought to bear to understand the nature of metamemory. Of course, such points of contact reveal fundamental (and glaring) gaps in the metamemory literature, as well as fruitful avenues for future survey research.

Schematicity

Referring to traits and other concepts that are highly elaborated components of self-concept or of theories of persons, Markus (1977) used the term schematicity to imply that individuals differ in the concepts they habitually and automatically use to describe themselves and others (Bargh, 1989, 1994), such as "outgoing" or "forgetful." Because these concepts are heavily elaborated and affect-laden (Fiske & Pavelchak, 1986), information processing in their domains is more efficient than is processing in other domains (e.g., responses to these survey items are generated more quickly), and conflicting information is processed more thoroughly (e.g., responses to these survey items take longer to formulate; Kihlstrom & Klein, 1994). In simple terms, people are schematic with respect to a concept (such as "good rememberer") if they rate the concept as highly self-descriptive and highly important; otherwise they are aschematic. In general, schematic concepts are the ones people use when asked to describe themselves.

Schematic concepts are chronically accessible, more elaborated, and likely to have affective loading; aschematic concepts are less likely to have these characteristics. Schematic concepts are used more often for evaluating self and others; aschematic concepts can be used, but only after direct questioning, and are subject to higher levels of context dependence. In short, schematic concepts are much more likely to be invoked when responding to items in a survey. Only with great difficulty and careful design will aschematic concepts be used.

Whether schematicity results in stable metamemory judgments, that is, the degree to which judgments are susceptible to context effects, is open to debate. Cavanaugh et al. (1998) argue that older adults are schematic regarding memory and memory loss (i.e., more likely to refer to memory as "very important" or to describe themselves as "forgetful"), making them much like experts who have long-term or "trait" involvement in a domain (Feldman & Lynch, 1988) or people with well-developed value systems and ideologies (Fischoff, Slovic, & Lichtenstein, 1980). Such memory "experts" would be likely to attend to domain-relevant information automatically, to be capable of accurate analytic and intuitive processing, to organize material in memory around the schematic construct, to process impression-inconsistent information more elaborately, to generate affect automatically, to have context-independent judgment standards and well-developed abstract category representations, and to be less susceptible in general to contextual influences on judgment (Alba & Hutchinson, 1987; Fazio, Sanbonmatsu, Powell, & Kardes, 1986; Feldman & Lindell, 1989; Feldman & Lynch, 1988; Wyer & Srull, 1989). In terms of survey research, this means that questions dealing with memory-related information, for example, would invoke these characteristics more in older adults than younger adults. Of particular importance for metamemory is that influencing such "expert" judgments (e.g., trying to get people to consider additional factors or another viewpoint) would not be easy, as it would require the suppression of automatic responses, which require considerable effort on the respondent's part.

Although none of these implications has been tested directly in the metamemory domain, there are several findings that are consistent with the conclusion that older adults are more schematic with respect to memory decline. For example, Cavanaugh, Grady, and Perlmutter (1983) found that older adults report being more upset at memory failures, even when the personal importance of the to-be-remembered information was rated as low. Cavanaugh (1987) reported high correlations among older adults' self-ratings of memory ability across several domains. Cavanaugh et al. (1983), Cavanaugh and Morton (1988), and Dixon and Hultsch (1983) all reported that older adults claim that having a good memory is important to them, rate themselves as having an adequate memory, yet report more instances of memory failures compared to younger adults. Most attempts at training or modifying memory self-efficacy in older adults has met with modest success at best, with no studies showing strong, long-lasting effects (e.g., see Cavanaugh, 1996, for a review).

Despite suggestive findings, no firm conclusions can be drawn. Schwarz (personal communication, 1996) points out that the assumption of the stability of judgments over time may not be warranted in the area of self-judgments, which at least in college students do not follow the patterns described earlier for older adults. Also, there is some evidence (Knäuper, this volume; Schwarz, this volume) that older adults are more susceptible to response order effects and less affected by item order effects than younger respondents, although this research has not focused on self-ratings of memory ability. It would seem that the only way to find out whether these speculations hold for metamemory is to conduct the appropriate experiments.

Attributional Processes

People ascribe causes to events and behaviors, a point that is routinely incorporated into conceptions of metamemory (e.g., Cavanaugh, 1996). Whether these ascribed causes are logical or not is a function of how the information is framed and how it is processed. Well-known biases in attributional processes exist, caused in part by automatic processing, that is, by the degree to which schematicity holds. In domains in which a person is schematic, information is processed via a chronically accessible causal scenario; in aschematic domains, information is processed via more general structures. For a schematic older adult, this may mean that forgetting an item at the store is due to "getting old"; having one's attention diverted by other events, a potentially plausible explanation, would likely not even be considered. To the extent that a person experiences self-inconsistent task experience (e.g., high rates of success on memory tasks), the individual may eventually differentiate a specific task performance impression from a general memory ability impression on which he or she is schematic (Brewer, 1988; Cavanaugh & Morton, 1988; Cavanaugh, Morton, & Tilse, 1989). In other words, the person may differentiate remembering at the grocery store (which is associated with good performance) and remembering in other stores (which are associated with poor performance). However, in cases of weak or nonexistent general impressions, specific task experience may serve to create or change such impressions due to the incorporation of specific, noncritical features into category representations. This is especially true for topics the person has never thought about before, which may occur when responding to items in a survey.

Automaticity and Awareness

People may not be aware of the many influences on their responses to metamemory questions. This assumption is compatible with Bargh's (1989) concept of conditional automaticity. His framework describes a system in which perceptions of memory events, for example, and judgments about these events are flexible based on past experience and present context, but are experienced phenomenally as states of the world or of the self. People become aware of this process only by consciously attending to variations across situations, and even then probably only with difficulty. Most important, automatic processes cannot be deconstructed through introspection without a great deal of effort, making them very difficult (at best) to describe in response to items on a survey.

Metamemory is no exception. We may "know" a great deal about memory but be essentially unable to introspect and explain how we came to this knowledge (e.g., Nisbett & Wilson, 1977). To the extent that a memory event, such as forgetting to get bread at the grocery store, is categorized automatically, a reasonably accurate estimation of the frequency of such events and a self-judgment on some accessible trait or ability category can be made. If a metamemory question taps this same category, an answer could be directly retrieved and provided as a response. But if the question taps a category not typically used by the person, both specific event memories and existing relevant judgments would be jointly retrieved in order to construct a response, which would be vulnerable to various biasing factors. Understanding how such biasing factors operate is an important avenue for future metamemory research.

Clearly, this aspect of metamemory has major implications for survey construction. Any frequency estimation question is subject to these effects. Without understanding whether the items' and the person's trait categories match, it is nearly impossible to understand the meaning of the responses, especially once they are aggregated across items and respondents.

Recall of Personal Attributes

Responding to metamemory questions requires one to take prior responses into account in creating the present answer, termed the "recall of personal attributes" in the social cognition literature. Ross (1989) proposed that this entails a two-step process: (a) establishing one's present status on the attribute in question; and (b) invoking an implicit theory of stability or change over time on the attribute in order to make a judgment. According to Ross (1989), people view some attributes as relatively more stable than others, and that some normally stable attributes may change under some circumstances that are neither controllable nor positive. Additionally, implicit theories may bias judgments by resulting in underestimation or overestimation of the true change in an attribute, depending on whether the judgment is biased in favor of normative consistency or normative change.

Some data in the metamemory literature are relevant here. Beliefs about memory ability appear to be quite similar, regardless of whether people are rating unspecified age-graded targets or themselves (Ryan, 1992; Ryan & Kwong See, 1993). Cavanaugh and Morton (1988) reported that some older adults expressed strong opinions in favor of normative changes in memory with age, but simultaneously stated that such changes were outside of their control. Additionally, they reported that implicit theories tended to result in inflated ratings of ability earlier in life, a finding verified by McFarland, Ross, and Giltrow (1992), who found that older adults rated themselves as healthier and as having a better memory at age 38 than a group of 38-year-olds rated themselves currently. McDonald-Miszczak, Hertzog, and Hultsch (1995) found that scales measuring self-reported change in memory ability are more influenced by implicit theories of change than by adults' accurate monitoring of actual changes in memory; indeed, they found that actual longitudinal changes were not related strongly to perceived changes. Together, the findings suggest that implicit theories about change and beliefs about current status drive judgments about change that may or may not be accurate reflections of true changes in memory ability. The age differences so often noted in the metamemory questionnaire literature may simply be artifacts of the influence of implicit theories about how aging affects memory. Thus, to gain insight into people's perceptions of change in their memory ability, it is essential to understand their implicit theories about it. Only then will we be able to design appropriate and effective intervention strategies (see also Cavanaugh, 1996).

☐ CONCLUDING POINTS: METAMEMORY, SURVEY RESEARCH, AND SOCIAL COGNITION

As can be surmised from the preceding discussion, adult developmental research on the knowledge and beliefs aspects of metamemory is at a key crossroads. At this point, we know that psychometrically sound questionnaires assessing memory knowledge and beliefs can be constructed, and that under certain circumstances responses to these questionnaires predict memory performance. However, due in part to the focus on creating psychometrically sound questionnaires, and in part to historical biases in adult developmental cognitive research, little effort has been directed toward understanding how people arrive at their responses. In this paper, several core constructs from social cognition have been discussed that may prove useful in understanding these processes. For additional progress to be made, several issues must be examined systematically. Among the most important of these are the following.

- What standards of judgment do people use to make their responses? How do these standards change with different instructional sets? To what extent do memory self-efficacy and attributions about performance vary with standards of judgment? In this context, standards of judgment refer to two separate things: the reference group against which a respondent makes a judgment (e.g., "other people my age," "people older/younger than me") and the level of performance assumed to be typical for this memory situation. Presumably, each type of standard (reference group and performance) could vary independently.
- How accurately do people remember their prior memory performances? What forces shape accuracy? Under what conditions does this represent an episodic memory task (i.e., recall of a specific number of items remembered) versus one in which the respondent uses an estimation strategy?
- What types of memory situations have the most affect-laden outcomes? Which aspects of memory knowledge and beliefs are most influenced by affect?
- Are there systematic age differences in schematicity of memory? If so, does this vary across different memory situations? Does schematicity vary across memory content domains?
- How do implicit theories of memory shape adults' responses? Are implicit theories linked to standards of judgment, schematicity, self-efficacy, and experience of affect?
- Can meaningful patterns of individual differences be identified in how people respond to items in metamemory questionnaires? If so, can such differences be used to better predict performance, maladaptive beliefs, and the like?

Each of these issues can be effectively investigated with carefully designed and conducted survey research. Other chapters in this volume address the various techniques that would be effective; many have already been used extensively in addressing similar issues in the social cognition literature. By adapting these approaches, we will learn a great deal more about the role that metamemory plays in memory performance. For example, Schwarz (this volume) and Knäuper (this volume) describe several conditions under which individuals are susceptible to response scale and question order effects, and how this susceptibility varies with age.

In sum, survey research and metamemory have much to offer each other. By keeping in mind important aspects of how people view memory, better surveys can be constructed that, in turn, will enable better examination of metamemory.

☐ References

Alba, J. W., & Hutchinson, J. W. (1987). Dimensions of consumer expertise. *Journal of Consumer Research, 13,* 411–454.

Anderson, J. R. (1987). Skill acquisition: Compilation of weak-method problem solutions. *Psychological Review, 94,* 192–210.

Anschutz, L., Camp, C. J., Markley, R. P., & Kramer, J. J. (1985). Maintenance and generalization of mnemonics for grocery shopping by older adults. *Experimental Aging Research, 11,* 157–160.

Anschutz, L., Camp, C. J., Markley, R. P., & Kramer, J. J. (1987). Remembering mnemonics: A three-year follow-up on the effects of mnemonic training in elderly adults. *Experimental Aging Research, 13,* 141–143.

Baldi, R. A., & Berry, J. M. (1996). *Memory self-efficacy and memory performance in older adults: Anchoring and choice effects.* Unpublished manuscript, University of Richmond, VA.

Bandura, A. (1986). *Social foundations of thought and action: A social cognitive theory.* Englewood Cliffs, NJ: Prentice-Hall.

Bandura, A. (1989). Regulation of cognitive processes through perceived self-efficacy. *Developmental Psychology, 25,* 729–735.

Bargh, J. A. (1989). Conditional automaticity: Varieties of automatic influence in social perception and cognition. In J. S. Uleman & J. A. Bargh (Eds.), *Unintended thought: Causes and consequences for judgment, emotion, and behavior.* New York: Guilford.

Bargh, J. A. (1994). The four horsemen of automaticity: Awareness, intention, efficiency, and control in social cognition. In R. S. Wyer, Jr. & T. K. Srull (Eds.), *Handbook of social cognition* (2nd ed., Vol. 1, pp. 1–40). Hillsdale, NJ: Erlbaum.

Barsalou, L. W. (1987). The instability of graded structure: Implication for the nature of concepts. In U. Neisser (Ed.), *Concepts and conceptual development: Ecological and intellectual factors in categorization* (pp. 101–140). Cambridge, England: Cambridge University Press.

Berry, J. M., & West, R. L. (1993). Cognitive self-efficacy in relation to personal mastery and goal setting across the life span. *International Journal of Behavioral Development, 16,* 351–379.

Berry, J. M., West, R. L., & Dennehey, D. M. (1989). Reliability and validity of the Memory Self-Efficacy Questionnaire. *Developmental Psychology, 25,* 701–713.

Brewer, M. B. (1988). A dual process model of impression formation. In T. K. Srull & R. S. Wyer (Eds.), *Advances in social cognition* (Vol. 1, pp. 1–32). Hillsdale, NJ: Erlbaum.

Cavanaugh, J. C. (1987). Age differences in adults' self-reports of memory ability. *International Journal of Aging and Human Development, 24,* 271–277.

Cavanaugh, J. C. (1989). The importance of awareness in memory aging. In L. W. Poon, D. C. Rubin, & B. Wilson (Eds.), *Everyday cognition in adulthood and late life* (pp. 416–436). New York: Cambridge University Press.

Cavanaugh, J. C. (1996). Memory self-efficacy as a key to understanding memory change. In F. Blanchard-Fields & T. M. Hess (Eds.), *Perspectives on cognitive changes in adulthood and aging* (pp. 488–507). New York: McGraw Hill.

Cavanaugh, J. C., & Borkowski, J. G. (1980). Searching for metamemory-memory connections: A developmental study. *Developmental Psychology, 16,* 441–453.

Cavanaugh, J. C., Feldman, J. M., & Hertzog, C. (1998). Memory beliefs as social cognition: A reconceptualization of what memory questionnaires assess. *Review of General Psychology, 2,* 48–65.

Cavanaugh, J. C., Grady, J., & Perlmutter, M. (1983). Forgetting and use of memory aids in 20- and 70-year-olds' everyday life. *International Journal of Aging and Human Development, 17,* 113–122.

Cavanaugh, J. C., & Green, E. E. (1990). I believe, therefore I can: Self-efficacy beliefs in memory aging. In E. A. Lovelace (Ed.), *Aging and cognition: Mental processes, self-awareness, and interventions* (pp. 189–230). Amsterdam: North-Holland.

Cavanaugh, J. C., Kramer, D. A., Sinnott, J. D., Camp, C. J., & Markley, R. J. (1985). On missing links and such: Interfaces between cognitive research and everyday problem solving. *Human Development, 28,* 146–168.

Cavanaugh, J. C., & Morton, K. R. (1988). Older adults' attributions about everyday memory. In M. M. Gruneberg & P. Morris, (Eds.), *Practical aspects of memory: Current research and issues* (Vol. 1, pp. 209–214). Chichester, England: Wiley.

Cavanaugh, J. C., & Morton, K. R. (1989). Contextualism, naturalistic inquiry, and the need for new science: A rethinking of everyday memory aging and childhood sexual abuse. In D. A. Kramer & M. Bopp (Eds.), *Transformation in clinical and developmental psychology* (pp. 89–114). New York: Springer-Verlag.

Cavanaugh, J. C., Morton, K. R., & Tilse, C. S. (1989). A self-evaluation framework for understanding everyday memory aging. In J. D. Sinnott (Ed.), *Everyday problem solving: Theory and application* (pp. 266–284). New York: Praeger.

Cavanaugh, J. C., & Perlmutter, M. (1982). Metamemory: A critical examination. *Child Development, 53,* 11–28.

Cavanaugh, J. C., & Poon, L. W. (1989). Metamemorial predictors of memory performance in young and older adult. *Psychology and Aging, 4,* 365–368.

Dixon, R. A., & Hultsch, D. F. (1983). Structure and development of metamemory in adulthood. *Journal of Gerontology, 38,* 682–688.

Dixon, R. A., Hultsch, D. F., & Hertzog, C. (1988). The Metamemory In Adulthood (MIA) questionnaire. *Psychopharmacology Bulletin, 24,* 671–688.

Dweck, C. S., & Leggett, E. L. (1988). A social-cognitive approach to motivation and personality. *Psychological Review, 95,* 256–273.

Fazio, R. H., Sanbonmatsu, D. M., Powell, M. C., & Kardes, F. R. (1986). On the automatic activation of attitudes. *Journal of Personality and Social Psychology, 50,* 229–238.

Feldman, J. M., & Lindell, M. K. (1989). On rationality. In I. Horowitz (Ed.), *Organization and decision theory* (pp. 83–164). Amsterdam: Kluwer-Nijhoff.

Feldman, J. M., & Lynch, J. G., Jr. (1988). Self-generated validity and other effects of measurement on belief, attitude, intention, and behavior. *Journal of Applied Psychology, 73,* 421–435.

Fischoff, B. Slovic, P., & Lichtenstein, S. (1980). Knowing what you want: Measuring labile values. In T. Wallsten (Ed.), *Cognitive processes in choice and decision behavior* (pp. 117–142). Hillsdale, NJ: Erlbaum.

Fiske, S. T., & Pavelchak, M. (1986). Category-based versus piecemeal-based affective responses: Developments in schema-triggered affect. In R. M. Sorrentino & E. T. Higgins (Eds.), *Handbook of motivation and cognition* (pp. 167–203). New York: Guilford.

Flavell, J. H. (1971). First discussant's comments: What is memory development the development of? *Human Development, 14,* 272–278.

Gilewski, M. J., & Zelinski, E. M. (1986). Questionnaire assessment of memory complaints. In L. W. Poon (ed.), *Handbook for clinical memory assessment of older adults* (pp. 93–107). Washington, DC: American Psychological Association.

Gilewski, M. J., & Zelinski, E. M. (1988). Memory Functioning Questionnaire (MFQ). *Psychopharmacology Bulletin, 24,* 665–670.

Herrmann, D. J., & Neisser, U. (1978). An inventory of everyday memory experiences. In M. M. Gruneberg, P. E. Morris, & R. N. Sykes (Eds.), *Practical aspects of memory* (pp. 35–51). New York: Academic Press.

Hertzog, C. (1992). Memory improvement: The possible roles of metamemory. In D. J.

Herrmann, H. Weingartner, A. Searleman, & C. McEvoy (Eds.), *Memory improvement: Implications for memory theory* (pp. 61–78). New York: Springer-Verlag.

Hertzog, C., & Dixon, R. (1994). Metacognitive development in adulthood and old age. In J. Metcalfe & A. P. Shimamura (Eds.), *Metacognition: Knowing about knowing* (pp. 227–251). Cambridge, MA: MIT Press.

Hertzog, C., Dixon, R. A., & Hultsch, D. F. (1990). Metamemory in adulthood: Differentiating knowledge, belief, and behavior. In T. M. Hess (Ed.), *Aging and cognition: Knowledge organization and utilization* (pp. 161–212). Amsterdam: North-Holland.

Hertzog, C., Hultsch, D. F., & Dixon, R. A. (1989). Evidence for the convergent validity of two self-report metamemory questionnaires. *Developmental Psychology, 25*, 687–700.

Kelly, G. A. (1955). *The psychology of personal constructs.* New York: Norton.

Kihlstrom, J. F., & Klein, S. B. (1994). The self as a knowledge structure. In R. S. Wyer, Jr. & T. K. Srull (Eds.), *Handbook of social cognition* (2nd ed., Vol. 1, pp. 153–208). Hillsdale, NJ: Erlbaum.

Koriat, A. (1994). Memory's knowledge of its own knowledge: The accessibility account of the feeling of knowing. In J. Metcalfe & A. P. Shimamura (Eds.), *Metacognition: Knowing about knowing* (pp. 115–135). Cambridge, MA: MIT Press.

Levy, B., & Langer, E. (1994). Aging free from negative stereotypes: Successful memory in China and among the American deaf. *Journal of Personality and Social Psychology, 66*, 989–997.

Lovelace, E. A. (1990). Aging and metacognitions concerning memory function. In E. A. Lovelace (Ed.), *Aging and cognition: Mental processes, self-awareness, and interventions* (pp. 157–188). Amsterdam: North-Holland.

Markus, H. (1977). Self-schemata and processing information about the self. *Journal of Personality and Social Psychology, 35*, 63–78.

Markus, H., & Wurf, E. (1987). The dynamic self-concept: A social-psychological perspective. *Annual Review of Psychology, 38*, 299–337.

McDonald-Miszczak, L., Hertzog, C., & Hultsch, D. F. (1995). Stability and accuracy of metamemory in adulthood and aging: A longitudinal analysis. *Psychology and Aging, 10*, 553–564.

McFarland, C., Ross, M., & Giltrow, M. (1992). Biased recollections in older adults: The role of implicit theories of aging. *Journal of Personality and Social Psychology, 62*, 837–850.

Metcalfe, J., & Shimamura, A. P. (Eds.). (1994). *Metacognition: Knowing about knowing.* Cambridge, MA: MIT Press.

Nelson, T. O., & Narens, L. (1990). Metamemory: A theoretical framework and new findings. In G. Bower (Eds.), *The psychology of learning and motivation* (Vol. 26, pp. 125–141). New York: Academic Press.

Nelson, T. O., & Narens, L. (1994). Why investigate metacognition? In J. Metcalfe & A. P. Shimamura (Eds.), *Metacognition: Knowing about knowing* (pp. 1–25). Cambridge, MA: MIT Press.

Nisbett, R. E., & Wilson, T. D. (1977). Telling more than we can know: Verbal reports on mental processes. *Psychological Review, 84*, 231–259.

Rabinowitz, J. C. (1989). Age deficits in recall under optimal study conditions. *Psychology and Aging, 4*, 378–380.

Ross, M. (1989). Relation of implicit theories to the construction of personal histories. *Psychological Review, 96*, 341–357.

Ryan, E. B. (1992). Beliefs about memory changes across the adult lifespan. *Journal of Gerontology: Psychological Sciences, 47*, P41–P46.

Ryan, E. B., & Kwong See, S. (1993). Age based beliefs about memory changes for self and others across adulthood. *Journal of Gerontology: Psychological Sciences, 48,* P199–P201.

Schneider, W., & Pressley, M. (1989). *Memory development between 2 and 20.* New York: Springer-Verlag.

Schwarz, N. (1996, September). *Metacognition.* Paper presented at the National Institute on Aging Workshop on Social Cognition and Aging, Washington, DC.

Seeman, T., McAvay, G., Merrill, S., Albert, M., & Rodin, J. (1996). Self-efficacy beliefs and change in cognitive performance: MacArthur studies of successful aging. *Psychology and Aging, 11,* 538–551.

West, R. L., & Berry, J. M. (1994). Age declines in memory self-efficacy: General or limited to particular tasks and measures? In J. D. Sinnott (Ed.), *Handbook of adult lifespan learning* (pp. 426–445). New York: Greenwood.

West, R. L., Dennehy-Basile, D., & Norris, M. (1996). Memory self-evaluation: The effects of age and experience. *Aging and Cognition, 3,* 67–83.

Wyer, R. S., Jr., & Srull, T. K. (1986). Human cognition in its social context. *Psychological Review, 93,* 322–359.

CHAPTER David C. Rubin

Autobiographical Memory and Aging: Distributions of Memories Across the Life-Span and Their Implications for Survey Research

Autobiographical memory (Brewer, 1996; Conway, 1990; Conway & Rubin, 1993; Conway, Rubin, Spinnler, & Wagenaar, 1992; Neisser & Fivush, 1994; Rubin, 1986, 1996) and the interaction of autobiographical memory and survey research (Jobe, Tourangeau, & Smith, 1993; Schwarz & Sudman, 1994) have been fruitful areas of study over the last few decades. Because older adults have more life to remember, much of this work has been integrated into the study of cognitive aging. Rather than provide an overview of the field, I will concentrate on one aspect of interest to survey research: how autobiographical memories are distributed over the life-span.

The distribution of autobiographical memories is important for survey research because it indicates from where in the life-span memories are likely to come; that is, it indicates the relative availability of memories as a function of the age of those memories. If a respondent has a question on a survey to answer that depends on specific episodes, it suggests the range of ages of the episodes that the respondent will use. There is a second reason for concentrating on the temporal distribution of memories. It is one topic for which we have a good quantitative description, one that could be used to predict biases in responding.

Two issues need to be mentioned briefly. The first is the accuracy of the memories themselves. The second is the accuracy of the dates. If the autobiographical memories people report from their life are mostly confabulations, or if the dates given bear no direct relation to the actual dates, then the results reported here would be of little use for survey research. Neither condition appears to hold.

The issue of the accuracy of autobiographical memories is one of the most complex and heated in psychology (Brewer, 1996; Robinson, 1996; Schacter, 1996; Winograd & Neisser, 1992). After an extensive review of the philosophical and psychological literature, Brewer (1996, p. 61) comes to the following conclusion: "Recent recollective memories tend to be fairly veridical unless they are influenced by strong schema-based processes. Recollective memories give rise to high confidence in the accuracy of their contents and that confidence can frequently predict objective memory accuracy." Most of the time, people are mostly accurate unless there are biasing factors at work. This summary offers little comfort for individual courtroom cases, but is the best we have, and is less troubling for survey data that are to be aggregated. Depending on the goals of the survey, some of the biasing may not be a problem. People tend to keep their memories consistent with their current views of themselves (Robinson, 1996) and so may distort in ways that are useful for some, but not all purposes.

The question of the accuracy of the dating of memories is easier to discuss because the data are better (Friedman, 1993; Huttenlocher, Hedges, & Prohaska, 1988; Larsen, Thompson, & Hansen, 1996; Thompson, Skowronski, Larsen, & Betz, 1996). It is clear that people do not store the exact dates of most events (Brewer, 1996), but rather construct them using a cyclical time scale of years, seasons or months, and weeks. A person may know an event occurred on a Sunday in June but not know the year. Thus, there are a disproportionate number of events that have dating errors of approximately plus or minus one day, 7 days, 30 days, and 365 days. Nonetheless, the dates people give to events when temporal boundaries are not set are unbiased estimates of when the events actually occurred (Rubin, 1982; Rubin & Baddeley, 1989). There are some exceptions to this generalization (Brown, Rips, & Shevell, 1985; Kemp & Burt, in press), but they are not common.

With these preliminary considerations, we can turn to the distribution of autobiographical memories. The scientific beginnings of the study of autobiographical memory and of their distribution can be traced to Galton (1879; see Crovitz, 1970, and Crovitz & Schiffman, 1974, for an integration into modern cognitive psychology).

Galton (1879) studied his own memories by taking a "leisurely walk along Pall Mall" (p. 151) pausing at approximately 300 objects and using each one to cue a memory. To bring the study into the laboratory, he made a list of words, viewed the words one at a time, recorded the time it took for the word to elicit a memory, recorded a brief response, and noted the age of the memory. His distribution of memories was 39% from "boyhood and youth," 46% from "subsequent manhood," and 15% "quite recent events" (p. 157). This research can be seen as the foundation of two directions in research. The first is the free associations of Freud and Jung. The second is Crovitz and Schiffman's (1974) revival of the technique to study autobiographical memory. Whereas Galton accepted all memories as responses, Crovitz and Schiffman intended that their subjects' responses be episodic memories as defined by Tulving (1972, 1983); that is, memories for events that occurred at one specific time and place.

In order to obtain a temporal distribution, Crovitz and Schiffman (1974) assumed that when a respondent reported that a memory occurred n time-units ago, the implied precision meant that the memory could be distributed evenly over $\pm\frac{1}{2}$ of the time-unit. Thus, a memory that was reported as occurring 24 hours ago was assigned to a bin ranging from 23.5 to 24.5 hours ago, whereas a memory reported as occurring one day ago was assigned to a bin ranging from 12 to 36 hours ago. They plotted these densities at each time marker of English from 1 hour to 17 years ago using the time-units of hours, days, weeks, months, and years. Another technique (Rubin, 1982) asks for exact dates and times, rank-orders these, and forms bins of an odd number of reported memories using the range of each bin to determine the density and the median date of each bin to determine the time ago. The results are the same. A sample distribution (Rubin, 1982, Experiment 2) from 18-year-old undergraduates using the latter technique is shown in Figure 1. Each of the points in the figure is based on the median and range of 85 successively dated memories.

Several points are worthy of note. First, there is a large range of both times and densities—so large that logarithmic scales are used on both axes to allow all the data to be shown. Second, the data closely fit a smooth curve, even though there is no control at learning and little control at recall. Third, the data are close to linear on the log-log paper and thus fit a power function, $\ln(y) = \ln(a) - b \cdot \ln(t)$ or $y = at^{-b}$, with an exponent, b, of about .8. The power function is also a good fit to studies of laboratory learning (Anderson & Schooler, 1991; Rubin, 1982; Rubin & Wenzel, 1996; Wixted & Ebbesen, 1991). In a review of 210 data sets from the literature on human and animal memory, Rubin and Wenzel (1996) found that overall the power function fit as well as any of the 125 two-parameter functions they tested. The power function was clearly superior to the logarithmic and other two-parameter functions only for the autobiographical memory data sets. This difference could be due to

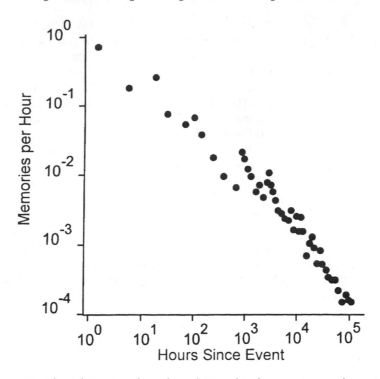

FIGURE 1. The relative number of autobiographical memories per hour reported by undergraduates as a function of the age of those memories. Both axes are logarithmic, so a straight line would be a power function. (Adapted from Rubin, 1982, Figure 2.)

autobiographical memory being different or to the much larger range of recall values present in the autobiographical memory data sets.

If the most recent 10 to 20 years of life of adults ranging in age from 12 to 70 are examined, similar results are obtained (Rubin & Schulkind, 1997b, 1997c; Rubin, Wetzler, & Nebes, 1986). A power function fits a collection of data sets with r^2's all over .95. The slopes vary between .69 and 1.07 across studies from laboratories using different subject populations, stimuli, and methods of aggregating the data, but the slopes did not differ systematically with the average age of the respondents. Thus, for adults of any age it appears that recent memories will be most available, with a monotonically decreasing retention function of the form at^{-b}, with b in the range of .7 to 1.1. The lack of a consistent difference in the slope parameter with the age of the respondent is consistent with the literature on other forms of retention (Giambra & Arenberg, 1993; Hulicka & Weiss, 1965; Rubin & Wenzel, 1996; Wickelgren,

1975). There are differences in learning with age, but once the level of learning is equated, there are at most small differences in the rate of retention with age.

The power function description of autobiographical memory has been shown to hold for individual people and individual cue words and for conditions in which people are asked to provide 50 autobiographical memories from their life without any cue words (Rubin, 1982). Different cues have different effects. For instance, concrete, easy-to-image words, such as fire, house, ship, and tree, which usually have objects as referents, produce older memories (i.e., shallower slopes) than hard-to-image words such as contents, context, memory, and time (Rubin, 1982). This may be one reason that odorants tend to produce old memories (Herz & Cupchik, 1992), though not older than words with the same referent (Rubin, Groth, & Goldsmith, 1984). Odors do, however, produce memories that were less often thought about. Nonetheless, the basic power function is maintained. In summary, there is a robust interpretable, quantitative description of the relative availability of autobiographical memories from the most recent decade or two of life.

We now turn briefly to people's early childhood memories. The retention function is expressed as a function of time ago (i.e., time measured from response). Another component is needed that is expressed as a function of age (i.e., time measured from birth). This is because people tend to recall fewer memories from the first few years of life and no memories from before birth. If the distribution of autobiographical memories of people of different ages are to be described, both a function of time ago, the t in at^{-b}, and a function of time since birth (age − t) is needed. Figure 2 shows distributions of early memories from several sources.

The left panel of Figure 2 shows results from three studies in which undergraduates were asked to provide memories from before the age of 8. For each study the percentage of memories at each year is shown. In the first study, Waldfogel (1948) had 124 undergraduates each spend two 85-minute sessions separated by 35 to 40 days recording experiences up to their 8th birthday. He then tabulated the number of unique, nonrepeated, memories for each person as a function of age. In the second study, Crovitz and Harvey (1979) collected memories of episodes from before age 8 from 17 undergraduates. Each student was instructed to spend 4 hours a week for each of 12 weeks. For these subjects there was a tendency to produce memories from later in the period between 0 and 8 years as the 12 weeks progressed, but this effect is ignored here. In the third study, Crovitz, Harvey, and McKee (1980) had 18 undergraduates spend up to 3 minutes trying to recall an

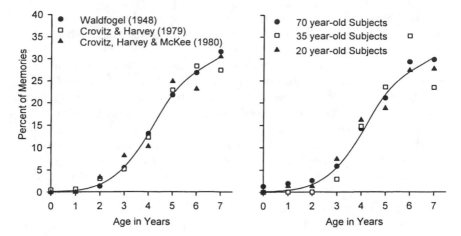

FIGURE 2. The distributions of early childhood memories from several published studies. Percentages of the total number of memories prior to age 8 in each distribution are used so that the plots can be easily compared. The curve fit to the data in both panels is the average distribution of the 8,610 early childhood memories from all studies combined.

autobiographical memory from before age 8 cued by each of 20 nouns. These nouns were drawn from words that described the memories produced in the earlier Crovitz and Harvey study. As can be seen in the left panel, the data are remarkably similar given the differences in procedures, and so one curve is drawn for all three data sets.

The right panel of Figure 2 shows data from Rubin and Schulkind (1997c) for subjects of three different ages: 40 undergraduates who were 20 years old, 20 adults who were 35 years old, and 60 adults who were 70 or 73 years old. The task for these subjects was to produce an autobiographical memory for each of 124 cue words. In contrast, to the left panel just discussed, in the right panel, memories were requested from anywhere in the life-span, not just from the first 8 years; however, only the data from the first 8 years are analyzed here. For each group the number of memories dated as occurring before the 8th birthday was set equal to 100% in the figure. As will be discussed later, some subjects were biased toward earlier memories, and although they did produce more early memories, the shape of their distributions did not differ. Similarly the 20-, 35-, and 70-year-old subjects varied widely in the percentage of the 124 cue words memories that were from before age 8 (6.0, 1.4, and 4.2%, respectively), but the relative distributions from the three age groups are remarkably similar, with the obvious exception that data from groups with more subjects are more regular. The curve fit to the data is the same as that in the left panel. Thus, it appears that, independent of the age of the adult and independent of whether all episodic memories or just those from early childhood are to be retrieved, the same distribution is obtained.

Averaging over all the data shown in Figure 2, by summing the total number of memories produced in each year independent of the study in which the memory was collected, and then dividing by the total number of memories, yields the following percentages for ages 0 through 7: 0.13, 0.38, 1.68, 5.54, 12.96, 21.80, 27.05, and 30.45. This set of values, to which the curves in Figure 2 are fit, provides my best estimate of the relative frequency of childhood memories by age. It is based on a total of 8,610 memories from before age 8.

The discussion so far is sufficient to describe the distribution of autobiographical memories of 20-year-old respondents. However, most of the lives of older adults has not been considered. When the total distribution of older adults is considered, a third component is needed: a *bump*, or increase in memories, from the period after the childhood decline to about age 30. Figure 3 shows a distribution for 70-year-old respondents from several laboratories.

The third component could be termed reminiscence, but the term bump is used to stress the empirical nature of the finding because all

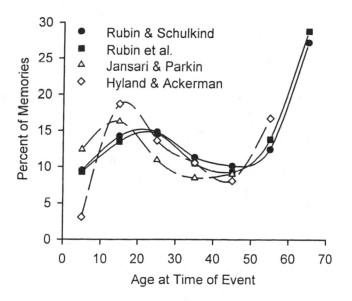

FIGURE 3. The distribution of autobiographical memories over the life-span for older adults from several published studies. The data are normalized so that the area under each curve is approximately the same.

that is implied is that more autobiographical memories are recalled from when a person is between 10 and 30 years old than would be expected from the other two components. The term bump also serves to highlight the lack of a suitable theoretical framework. Reminiscence, while usually lacking the kind of explicit quantitative definition provided here for the bump, has been a topic of great interest in the aging literature (e.g., Butler, 1964; Costa & Kastenbaum, 1967; Havighurst & Glasser, 1972; Romaniuk, 1981). For integrations of studies of the distribution of autobiographical memory with studies of the theoretically richer term reminiscence, see Fitzgerald (1996) and Webster and Cappeliez (1993). Additionally, people with many forms of amnesia often have better memory for older than for more recent events (Butters & Cermak, 1986; Squire, Chace & Slater, 1975; Ribot, 1882), and the description of the bump provides a comparison measure of the extent to which such a pattern occurs in nonclinical populations.

The definition of the bump used here was derived from empirical studies of autobiographical memory that used the cue-word technique. The oldest plot in Figure 3 was taken from Rubin et al. (1986) and is a summary of 1,373 memories of 70 adults sorted into the decades in which the individuals reported that the remembered event had occurred. The subjects, who were about 70 years old, were tested in three different laboratories under slightly different conditions (Fitzgerald & Lawrence, 1984; Franklin & Holding, 1977; Rubin et al., 1986). At the time of data collection, none of the laboratories were expecting a bump, which only appeared on reanalysis of the data in Rubin et al. (1986). In all cases, the subjects were asked to provide an autobiographical memory for each cue word. There were between 20 and 50 cue words per subject. On completing this task, the subjects were asked to date each memory. Roughly half the memories produced by these subjects are not in Figure 3. Memories that occurred within the most recent year of life were not included because doing so would have required extending the vertical axis, making the rest of the curve less visible. Data from 50- and 60-year-olds from the same three and one additional laboratory (Zola-Morgan, Cohen, & Squire, 1983) yielded similar curves. Data from 40-year-olds did not show a clear bump.

The second plot in Figure 3 is a combination of the twenty 70- and twenty 73-year-old subjects from Rubin and Schulkind (1997c) who each provided autobiographical memories to 124 cue words. Again, all memories from the most recent year were eliminated and the area under the curve set to 100%.

The third plot is from Hyland and Ackerman (1988). Subjects were cued with object nouns, activity verbs, and feeling terms from Robinson (1976). Older volunteers showed a clear increase in memories, which peaked in their teens and early 20s. In Figure 3, we plot the data from 12 volunteers with a mean age of 70. Hyland and Ackerman did not exclude recent memories, but report that 47% of the 70-year-old subjects' memories occurred within the subject's most recent decade. In order to make their data comparable with the first two studies, the area under the first six decades of the Hyland and Ackerman data and the Rubin et al. (1986) plot were set equal to each other. Adults in their 60s also showed a clear reminiscence effect. Adults in their 50s showed a possible reminiscence effect, whereas those in their 40s had a nearly equal number of memories from their teens, 20s, and 30s, with 80% of their reports falling in the most recent decade of life. For these adults, as well as the 40-year-old subjects analyzed by Rubin et al. (1986), it is likely that any reminiscence effect was overshadowed by memories for recent events.

Jansari and Parkin (1996) also asked adults to provide autobiographical memories to each of Robinson's (1976) cue words. Half of the subjects were under normal instructions and half had the added requirement that all memories had to be older than 2.5 years. Independent of these instructions, for reasons that are not clear, the data differ slightly from the other data sets in that they have fewer recent memories and more memories from childhood. Nonetheless, if the area under the curves from both of Jansari and Parkin's conditions are equated, the two conditions show patterns similar to each other and to the other data sets. The data for the average of their two conditions for their oldest group, who were between 56 and 60 years old, are plotted in Figure 3, with the area under the curve up to age 50 set equal to that of the Rubin et al. (1986) data set up to age 50.

Thus the bump is a robust and substantial effect. When older adults are asked to provide autobiographical memories from their lives without restrictions to the content or time period, they show a marked increase in memories for events that occurred in adolescence and early adulthood. The only way not to get this result seems to be to ask adults to recall events from individual thirds, quarters, or fifths of their lifespan for 5 or 10 minutes and to then see if some periods have more memories than others (Howes & Katz, 1992; Rabbitt & Winthorpe, 1988).

One question that remains with a method that lets people select whatever memory comes to mind is the role of demand characteristics. The cue-word procedure used is among the most open ended in cognitive psychology, and so exactly what the subject takes the experimental task to be is not clear. The method produces reliable findings, but there are differences in distributions that have no clear cause. Thus, for instance, Jansari and Parkin's (1996) results, which are shown in

Figure 3, have more early memories than other studies. To pursue this issue, a modification, or bias, in the standard instructions was made to favor earlier memories. Instead of asking for *events in a memory experiment,* Rubin and Schulkind (1997c) asked for *memories in an autobiographical memory experiment.* They also changed the content of their one example from a recent event to a childhood event. Figure 4 compares two groups of twenty 73-year-old subjects who, except for the differences just noted, performed the same task with the same 124 cue words. As can be seen, although the bump remains, the effects of such subtle biasing can be substantial. Thus, it appears that slight changes in the framing of a question in a survey of the order just noted, which could bias recalls from early to later periods, could change the autobiographical memories accessed to formulate a response.

Rubin and Schulkind (1997c) measured a host of other properties of autobiographical memories in the hope of distinguishing memories from the bump from memories from other periods. When memories for events from between 10 years old and 30 years old were compared with memories from other periods, there were no differences in reaction time, the properties of the cue words that evoked the memories

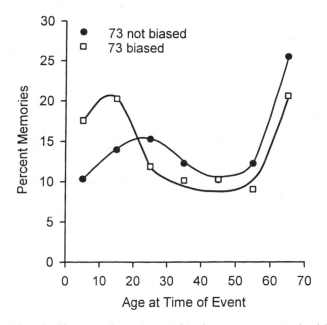

FIGURE 4. The distribution of autobiographical memories over the life-span for older adults, half of whom were biased to have earlier memories. (Adapted from Rubin & Schulkind, 1997c.)

(Rubin & Schulkind, 1997a), and rating scale measures including importance, vividness, emotionality, novelty, and number of times the memory was rehearsed. Because there are no simple obvious measures that distinguish memories in the bump from surrounding memories, it is difficult to know how, why, or even if memories from the bump differ from other memories.

In addition to the studies finding a bump when autobiographical memories were cued by words, several researchers found the bump when older adults were requested to provide either "important" or "vivid" autobiographical memories. Such findings are included here because important memories are more likely to be the basis of answers to some survey questions, whereas the more general word-cued memories are likely to be the basis of others. Instead of cuing each memory with a single word as in the studies just reviewed, Fromholt and Larsen's (1991, 1992) 30 subjects were asked to spend 15 minutes recalling events that had been important in their lives. The volunteers were between the ages of 71 and 89 and had an average of 7 years of education. For their important memories, the bump occurred at the same general place and shape as it did in the studies just reviewed. The change in procedure, however, increased the bump at the expense of memories from the most recent decade of life. In addition, there were slightly more memories in the 10–19-year-old decade than the 20–29-year-old decade. Thus, Fromholt and Larsen demonstrated that, at least for important memories, the bump's existence does not depend on the cuing technique or any details of its procedure and that the request for important memories produces relatively more bump memories. Similar results have been obtained with age-matched adults in the early stages of Alzheimer's dementia and with adults suffering from their first major depression (Fromholt, Larsen, & Larsen, 1995).

Fitzgerald (1988) asked individuals with an average age of almost 70 and an average of 12 years of education to record three "vivid" memories. The plots of the vivid memories correspond more closely to Fromholt and Larsen's (1991, 1992) important memories than to the cue-word studies just reviewed: the bump increased at the expense of recent memories. The bump peaked in the 16–20-year-old five-year period with fewer memories from the two surrounding five-year periods and still fewer from the 2 five-year periods surrounding them. In a later study, Fitzgerald (1996) found that adults between the ages of 31 and 46 produced a clear peak in their distribution of vivid memories between the ages of 16 and 25. Fitzgerald (1996) also demonstrated that younger and older adults both show a clear peak between the ages of 6 and 25 in the distribution of memories that would go into a book about their lives. The inclusion of younger groups demonstrates that the bump for vivid and important memories exists fairly early in life and that the lack of a clear bump in 40-year-old subjects with word-cued memories may be due to the overshadowing by recent memories.

Two additional studies of vivid memories with older adults provide similar results. Benson, Jarvi, Arai, Thielbar, Frye, and McDonald (1992) report on studies in which 10 vivid memories were requested from Japanese and rural Midwestern American subjects. Both groups showed a bump: the Japanese in the 21–30-year-old decade of their lives, the Americans in the 11–20-year-old decade. Cohen and Faulkner (1988) requested 6 vivid memories from adults ranging from 20 to 87. The bump was observed with the following exception. Subjects in the 40–59 and in the 60–87 age ranges recalled the most memories from when they were 0–10 years old.

In general, requests for vivid or important memories produce the bump in older adults, but with a reduction of recent memories compared with the word-cued distribution. Rubin and Schulkind (1997c) had the same forty 70- and 73-year-old subjects perform both tasks producing five important memories and approximately 124 word-cued memories each. The distribution of those subjects, who were not biased toward older memories, is shown in Figure 5. Here memories

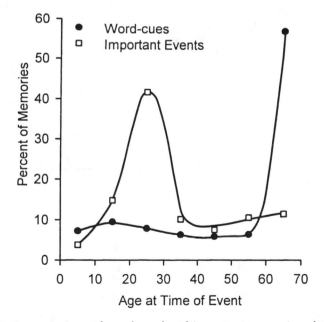

FIGURE 5. A comparison of word-cued and important memories obtained from the same older adults. (Adapted from Rubin & Schulkind, 1997c.)

from the last year are included to allow for a clearer comparison between important and word-cued memories. Consistent with the other studies, the request for important memories produced fewer recent memories. In addition, for the highly educated volunteers, who had an average of 16 years of education, the important memories are reported as falling heavily in the single decade when the subjects were in their twenties. Thus the important memories have a different, narrower, distribution than the word-cued memories. Comparisons with the other distributions of important memories indicate that the location and width of the peak changes with different populations and procedures, with a tendency for groups with less education to have earlier peaks. Nonetheless, the within-group comparison shown in Figure 5 clearly indicates that requests for memories of one kind or another can affect the period of the life-span from which the memories originate. Thus, questions whose answers are based on a different aspect of autobiographical memory may rely on different distributions.

The results reported so far are all from psychological laboratories, though not especially well controlled ones. Similar results appear outside the lab. Figure 6 presents the distribution of episodic and more

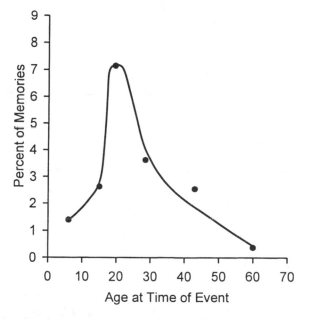

FIGURE 6. The distribution of memories recorded in published autobiographical sketches by famous psychologists. Memories for specific events and those extended over time were combined, weighted by their relative frequency. (Adapted from Mackavey, Malley, & Stewart, 1991, Table 2.)

extended events from the published intellectual autobiographies of famous psychologists (Mackavey, Malley, & Stewart, 1991). The same
bump appears here as in the request for important memories from less
famous subjects.

The bump also appears when one asks for public, as opposed to
private, events. Using telephone surveys, Schuman and his colleagues
have shown that when people are asked for the most important event
or change in the last half-century, they tend to report events or changes
from when they were 10–30 years old (Belli, Schuman, & Jackson, 1997;
Schuman, Akiyama, & Knäuper, 1997; Schuman, Belli, & Bischoping,
1997; Schuman & Rieger, 1992; Schuman, Rieger, & Gaidys, 1994; Schuman
& Scott, 1989). Figure 7 shows the percentage of responses given as the
most important public event of the last 50 years that were either World
War II, John F. Kennedy's assassination, or the Vietnam War as a function of the age of the respondent at the time of the event. In the

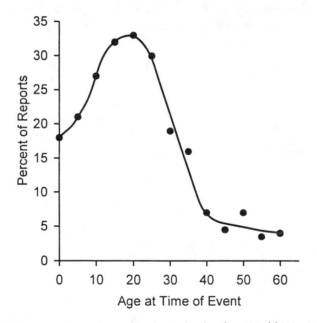

FIGURE 7. The percentage of people who judged either World War II, the assassination of John F. Kennedy, or the Vietnam War to be the most important public
event of the last 50 years as a function of the age of the person at the time of the
event. The values reported are the average percentages of these three events for
each five-year period. For the first periods and the periods over 40 years, the
averages are based on less than three events because there were no respondents
who were of that age at the time of the event. (Adapted from Schuman & Scott,
1989.)

original studies, numerous plots of individual events show the same pattern. The questions and methodology in the work of Schuman and his colleagues are different from the other work reviewed here, but the basic results are the same, indicating that survey and experimental methods lead to the same results. Events judged as important by people are more likely to happen when those people are between 10 and 30 years old. Neisser (1982), in his discussion of flashbulb memories, notes that the recall of one's personal circumstances at the time of an historical event ties one's autobiography to history. Having important personal and public memories peak at the same period of the life-span makes this more likely to occur.

Having dealt at length with the distribution of episodic, autobiographical memories, the relation of such memories to more semantic memories should be considered. There are no studies for such semantic memories, or laboratory studies of any kind, that show the several-order-of-magnitude drop shown in Figure 1, but it will be argued here that for the limited range the data available, such memories follow the same pattern as that already presented. The most well known studies of very-long-term memory for factual material have been done by Bahrick and his colleagues (Bahrick, 1983, 1984; Bahrick, Bahrick, & Wittlinger, 1975). In these studies, there is a rapid drop in memory after initial learning followed by a steady period of little observable drop that lasts a lifetime. Bahrick has described the existence of memories that decline little over decades as *permastore*. Bahrick finds this permastore retention function in many domains, but always in studies in which the material was initially learned early in life, during high school or college, and then tested later at intervals of between a few days and 50 years. If the data in Figure 1 were plotted on a linear scale, they too would drop rapidly and then level off. To show the similarity, some permastore data from Bahrick is plotted in Figure 8 with a power function fit (for more detail on this analysis, see Rubin & Wenzel, 1996). The power function and logarithmic function both fit Bahrick's data, as well as most data collected in the psychological laboratory (Rubin & Wenzel, 1996). If either the logarithmic or power function is used to describe retention, then ratios of time are what is important. The ratio of 3 years to 1 minute is 1,577,880 to 1. By comparison, the ratio of 60 years to 3 years is a meager 20 to 1. Thus, these functions and permastore make very similar predictions about the future loss of any information that still has a moderate level of recall after three years: It will show very little further loss.

Bahrick's studies fit the retention component first discussed in this chapter, but have little to do with the bump. In the data presented here for the bump, the age of the acquisition of the memories varied

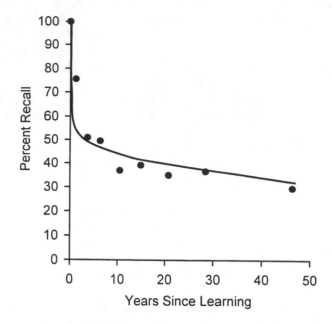

FIGURE 8. Retention data from an aggregation of six free-recall measures of knowledge of campus geography taken from Bahrick (1983). The level of initial learning was set equal to 100%. The curve shown is a power function. (Adapted from Rubin & Wenzel, 1996.)

across the life-span, and the age at recall of the memories was usually held constant. That is, the x-axis was always age at time of learning. The exception are the data reported from Schuman which varied both in age at learning and age at test, but even here the x-axis was age at the time of learning. In contrast, in Bahrick's studies, the age at learning was always fixed and the retention interval could have been labeled in terms of the age of the subject at the time of the test. That is, in the data that produce the bump and in the data that produce perma-store, different variables are confounded with retention interval. In contrast, when we test 70-year-old subjects for factual, semantic material learned at different points in the life-span, the bump is still present.

Rubin, Rahhal, and Poon (1998) constructed multiple-choice questions in a mechanical algorithmic fashion for each year data was available for each of the following five domains: what teams played in the world series, what movie won the academy award, who won the academy award for best actor or actress, what was the most important news event according to the Associated Press, and who lost the presidential election. Thirty older adults were tested in 1984 and 30 other older adults were tested in 1994 to unconfound the particular questions from the subjects' ages at the time of the event queried. All topic areas showed better recall in the bump period than in later years. The combined data for all questions are shown in Figure 9, extending the autobiographical, episodic, free recall results from the studies presented earlier (which had answers that were not checked for correctness) to public, semantic recognition of verifiable responses.

The implications of these distributions for survey research are clear. If the questions respondents are to answer on a survey are based on autobiographical memory, then the database available to them is not uniformly distributed over their life-spans. Rather, the vast majority of memories will come from the recent past. For older adults, there will be a second smaller peak from when they were 10–30 years old. For important or vivid memories, the 10–30 bump can contain more memories than the recent few decades. The answers a respondent gives will be influenced by these distributions to the extent that the available memories differ from those that would have arisen from a more uniform sampling of memory. Because the form of the question can affect the distribution of autobiographical memories obtained by biasing toward older or more recent memories or toward important or more

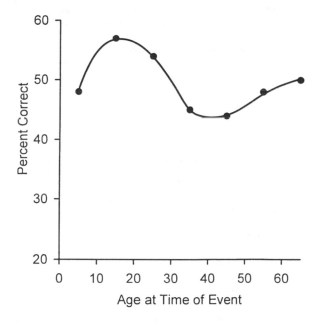

FIGURE 9. The percent of correct answers of older subjects to five-alternative multiple-choice questions as a function of their age at the time of the event questioned. The y-axis begins at 20%, which is chance.

general memories, one cannot be sure exactly what distribution any given survey question would produce without empirical testing. However, the effects discussed here are robust enough that they will certainly play a role.

☐ References

Anderson, J. R., & Schooler, L. J. (1991). Reflections of the environment in memory. *Psychological Science, 2,* 396–408.

Bahrick, H. P. (1983). The cognitive map of a city: Fifty years of learning and memory. In G. H. Bower (Ed.), *The psychology of learning and motivation* (Vol. 17, pp. 125–163). New York: Academic Press.

Bahrick, H. P. (1984). Semantic memory content in permastore: Fifty years of memory for Spanish learned in school. *Journal of Experimental Psychology: General, 113,* 1–27.

Bahrick, H. P., Bahrick, P. O., & Wittlinger, R. P. (1975). Fifty years of memory for names and faces: A cross-sectional approach. *Journal of Experimental Psychology: General, 104,* 54–75.

Belli, R. F., Schuman, H., & Jackson, B. (1997). Autobiographical misremembering: John Dean is not alone. *Applied Cognitive Psychology, 11,* 187–209.

Benson, K. A., Jarvi, S. D., Arai, Y., Thielbar, P. R. S., Frye, K. J., & McDonald, B. L. G. (1992). Socio-historical context and autobiographical memories: Variations in the reminiscence phenomenon. In M. A. Conway, D. C. Rubin, H. Spinnler, & W. Wagenaar (Eds.), *Theoretical perspectives on autobiographical memory* (pp. 313–322). Utrecht, the Netherlands: Kluwer.

Brewer, W. F. (1996). What is recollective memory? In D. C. Rubin (Ed.), *Remembering our past: Studies in autobiographical memory* (pp. 19–66). Cambridge, England: Cambridge University Press.

Brown, N. R., Rips, L. J., & Shevel, S. K. (1986). Public memories and their personal context. In D. C. Rubin (Ed.), *Autobiographical memory* (pp. 137–158). Cambridge, England: Cambridge University Press.

Butler, R. N. (1964). The life review: An interpretation of reminiscence in the aged. In R. Kastenbaum (Ed.), *New thoughts on old age.* New York: Springer-Verlag.

Butters, N., & Cermak, L. S. (1986). A case study of forgetting of autobiographical knowledge: Implications for the study of retrograde amnesia. In D. C. Rubin (Ed.), *Autobiographical memory* (pp. 253–272). Cambridge, England: Cambridge University Press.

Cohen, G., & Faulkner, D. (1988). Life span changes in autobiographical memory. In M. M. Gruenberg, P. E. Morris, & R. N. Sykes (Eds.), *Practical aspects of memory: Current research and issues: Vol. 1. Memory in everyday life* (pp. 277–282). New York: Wiley.

Conway, M. A. (1990). *Autobiographical memory: An introduction.* Milton Keynes, England: Open University Press.

Conway, M. A., & Rubin, D. C. (1993). The structure of autobiographical memory. In A. E. Collins, S. E. Gathercole, M. A. Conway, & P. E. Morris (Eds.), *Theories of memory* (pp. 103–137). Hove, Sussex, England: Erlbaum.

Conway, M. A., Rubin, D. C., Spinnler, H., & Wagenaar, W. A. (Eds.). (1992). *Theoretical perspectives on autobiographical memory* (pp. 495–499). Utrecht, the Netherlands: Kluwer.

Costa, P., & Kastenbaum, R. (1967). Some aspects of memories and ambitions in centenarians. *Journal of Genetic Psychology, 110,* 3–16.

Crovitz, H. F. (1970). *Galton's walk: Methods for the analysis of thinking, intelligence, and creativity.* New York: Harper and Row.

Crovitz, H. F., & Harvey, M. T. (1979). Early childhood amnesia: A quantitative study with implications for the study of retrograde amnesia after brain injury. *Cortex, 15,* 331–335.

Crovitz, H. F., Harvey, M. T., & McKee, D. C. (1980). Selecting retrieval cues for early-childhood amnesia: Implications for the study of shrinking retrograde amnesia. *Cortex, 16,* 305–310.

Crovitz, H. F., & Schiffman, H. (1974). Frequency of episodic memories as a function of their age. *Bulletin of the Psychonomic Society, 4,* 517–518.

Fitzgerald, J. M. (1988). Vivid memories and the reminiscence phenomenon: The role of a self narrative. *Human Development, 31,* 261–273.

Fitzgerald, J. M. (1996). Intersecting meanings of reminiscence in adult development and aging. In D. C. Rubin (Ed.), *Remembering our past: Studies in autobiographical memory* (pp. 360–383). Cambridge, England: Cambridge University Press.

Fitzgerald, J. M., & Lawrence, R. (1984). Autobiographical memory across the life-span. *Journal of Gerontology, 39,* 692–699.

Franklin, H. C., & Holding, D. H. (1977). Personal memories at different ages. *Quarterly Journal of Experimental Psychology, 29,* 527–532.

Friedman, W. J. (1993). Memory for the time of past events. *Psychological Bulletin, 113,* 44–66.

Fromholt, P., & Larsen, S. F. (1991). Autobiographical memory in normal aging and primary degenerative dementia (dementia of the Alzheimer type). *Journal of Gerontology: Psychological Sciences, 46,* 85–91.

Fromholt, P., & Larsen, S. F. (1992). Autobiographical memory and life-history narratives in aging and dementia (Alzheimer type). In M. A. Conway, D. C. Rubin, H. Spinnler, & W. Wagenaar (Eds.), *Theoretical perspectives on autobiographical memory* (pp. 413–426). Utrecht, the Netherlands: Kluwer.

Fromholt, P., Larsen, P. & Larsen, S. F. (1995). Effects of late-onset depression and recovery on autobiographical memory. *Journal of Gerontology: Psychological Sciences, 50,* 74–81.

Galton, F. (1879). Psychometric experiments. *Brain, 2,* 149–162.

Giambra, L. M., & Arenberg, D. (1993). Adult age differences in forgetting sentences. *Psychology and Aging, 8,* 451–462.

Havighurst, R. J., & Glasser, R. (1972). An exploratory study of reminiscence. *Journal of Gerontology, 27,* 245–253.

Herz, R. S., & Cupchik, G. C. (1992). An experimental characterization of odor-evoked memories in humans. *Chemical Senses, 17,* 519–528.

Howes, J. L., & Katz, A. N. (1992). Remote memory: Recalling autobiographical and public events across the lifespan. *Canadian Journal of Psychology, 46,* 92–116.

Hulicka, I. M., & Weiss, R. L. (1965). Age differences in retention as a function of learning. *Journal of Consulting Psychology, 29,* 125–129.

Huttenlocher, J., Hedges, L., & Prohaska, V. (1988). Hierarchical organization in ordered domains: Estimating the dates of events. *Psychological Review, 95,* 471–484.

Hyland, D. T., & Ackerman, A. M. (1988). Reminiscence and autobiographical memory in the study of the personal past. *Journal of Gerontology: Psychological Sciences, 43,* 35–39.

Jansari, A., & Parkin, A. J. (1996). Things that go bump in your life: Explaining the reminiscence bump in autobiographical memory. *Psychology and Aging, 11,* 85–91.

Jobe, J. B., Tourangeau, R., & Smith, A. F. (1993). Contributions of survey research to the understanding of memory. *Applied Cognitive Psychology, 7,* 567–584.

Kemp, S., & Burt, C. D. B. (in press). The force of events: Cross-modality matching the recency of events. *Memory.*

Larsen, S. F., Thompson, C. P., & Hansen, T. (1996). Time in autobiographical memory. In D. C. Rubin (Ed.), *Remembering our past: Studies in autobiographical memory* (pp. 129–156). Cambridge, England: Cambridge University Press.

Mackavey, W. R., Malley, J. E., & Stewart, A. J. (1991). Remembering autobiographically consequential experiences: Content analysis of psychologists' accounts of their lives. *Psychology and Aging, 6,* 50–59.

Neisser, U. (1982). Snapshots or Benchmarks? In U. Neisser (Ed.), *Memory observed: Remembering in natural contexts* (pp. 43–48). San Francisco: Freeman.

Neisser, U. (1988). Commentary on "Vivid memories and the reminiscence phenomenon: The role of a self narrative." *Human Development, 31,* 271–273.

Neisser, U., & Fivush R. (1994). *The remembering self: Construction and accuracy of life narrative.* Cambridge, England: Cambridge University Press.

Rabbitt, P., & Winthorpe, C. (1988). What do old people remember? The Galton paradigm reconsidered. In M. M. Gruenberg, P. E. Morris, & R. N. Sykes (Eds.), *Practical aspects of memory: Current research and issues: Vol. 1. Memory in everyday life* (pp. 301–307). New York: Wiley.

Ribot, T. (1882). *Diseases of memory: An essay in the positive psychology* (W. H. Smith, Trans.). New York: D. Appleton.

Robinson, J. A. (1976). Sampling autobiographical memory. *Cognitive Psychology, 8,* 578–595.

Robinson, J. A. (1996). Perspective, meaning, and remembering. In D. C. Rubin (Ed.), *Remembering our past: Studies in autobiographical memory* (pp. 199–217). Cambridge, England: Cambridge University Press.

Romaniuk, M. (1981). Reminiscence and the second half of life. *Experimental Aging Research, 7,* 315–336.

Rubin, D. C. (1982). On the retention function for autobiographical memory. *Journal of Verbal Learning and Verbal Behavior, 21,* 21–38.

Rubin, D. C. (Ed.). (1986). *Autobiographical memory.* Cambridge, England: Cambridge University Press.

Rubin, D. C. (Ed.). (1996). *Remembering our past: Studies in autobiographical memory.* Cambridge, England: Cambridge University Press.

Rubin, D. C., & Baddeley, A. D. (1989). Telescoping is not time compression: A model of dating autobiographical events. *Memory and Cognition, 17,* 653–661.

Rubin, D. C., Groth, L., & Goldsmith, D. (1984). Olfactory cuing of autobiographical memory. *American Journal of Psychology, 97,* 493–507.

Rubin, D. C., Rahhal, T. A., & Poon, L. W. (1998). Things learned in early adulthood are remembered best. *Memory and Cognition, 26,* 3–19.

Rubin, D. C., & Schulkind, M. D. (1997a). Properties of word cues for autobiographical memory. *Psychological Reports, 81,* 47–50.

Rubin, D. C., & Schulkind, M. D. (1997b). The distribution of autobiographical memories across the lifespan. *Memory and Cognition, 25,* 859–866.

Rubin, D. C., & Schulkind, M. D. (1997c). The distribution of important and word-cued autobiographical memories in 20, 35, and 70 year-old adults. *Psychology and Aging, 12,* 524–535.

Rubin, D. C., & Wenzel, A. E. (1996). One hundred years of forgetting: A quantitative description of retention. *Psychological Review, 103,* 734–760.

Rubin, D. C., Wetzler, S. E., & Nebes, R. D. (1986). Autobiographical memory across the adult lifespan. In D. C. Rubin (Ed.), *Autobiographical memory* (pp. 202–221). Cambridge, England: Cambridge University Press.

Schacter, D. L. (1996). *Searching for memory: The brain, the mind, and the past.* New York: Basic Books.

Schuman, H., Akiyama, H., & Knäuper, B. (1997) *Collective memories of Germans and Japanese about the past half century.* Unpublished manuscript.

Schuman, H., Belli, R. F., & Bischoping, K. (1997). The generational basis of historical knowledge. In J. W. Pennebaker, D. Paez, & Rime (Eds.), *Collective memory of political events: Social psychological perspectives* (pp. 47–77). Hillsdale, NJ: Erlbaum.

Schuman, H., & Rieger, C. (1992). Collective memory and collective memories. In M. A. Conway, D. C. Rubin, H. Spinnler, & W. A. Wagenaar (Eds.), *Theoretical perspectives on autobiographical memory* (pp. 323–336). Utrecht, the Netherlands: Kluwer.

Schuman, H., Rieger, C., & Gaidys, V. (1994). Collective memories in the United States and Lithuania. In N. Schwartz & S. Sudman (Eds.), *Autobiographical memory and the validity of retrospective reports* (pp. 313–333). New York: Springer-Verlag.

Schuman, H., & Scott, J. (1989). Generations and collective memories. *American Sociological Review, 54,* 359–381.

Schwarz, N., & Sudman, S. (1994). *Autobiographical memory and the validity of retrospective reports.* New York: Springer-Verlag.

Squire, L. R., Chace, P. M., & Slater, P. C. (1975). Assessment of memory for remote events. *Psychological Reports, 37,* 223–234.

Thompson, C. P., Skowronski, J. J., Larsen, S. F., & Betz, A. (1996). *Autobiographical memory: Remembering what and remembering when.* Mahwah, NJ: Erlbaum.

Tulving, E. (1972). Episodic and semantic memory. In E. Tulving & W. Donaldson (Eds.), *Organization of memory.* New York: Academic Press.

Tulving, E. (1983). *Elements of episodic memory.* Oxford, England: Oxford University Press.

Waldfogel, S. (1948). The frequency and affective character of childhood memories. *Psychological Monographs: General and Applied, 62*(4), Whole No. 291.

Webster, J. D., & Cappeliez, P. (1993). Reminiscence and autobiographical memory: Complementary contexts for cognitive aging research. *Developmental Review, 13,* 54–91.

Wickelgren, W. A. (1975). Age and storage dynamics in continuous recognition memory. *Developmental Psychology, 11,* 165–169.

Winograd, E., & Neisser, U. (Eds.) (1992). *Affect and accuracy in recall: Studies of "flashbulb" memories.* New York: Cambridge University Press.

Wixted, J. T., & Ebbesen, E. B. (1991). On the form of forgetting. *Psychological Science, 2,* 409–415.

Zola-Morgan, S., Cohen, N. J., & Squire, L. R. (1983). Recall of remote episodic memory in amnesia. *Neuropsychologia, 21,* 487–500.

Timothy A. Salthouse

Pressing Issues in Cognitive Aging

A distinction between two types of cognition has been recognized since at least the 1920s. For example, Foster and Taylor (1920) found that young adults were superior in the construction of sentences containing three specific words and in memory for drawings, whereas older adults had a relative advantage in comprehension of questions, detection of absurdities, and definitions of abstract words. The authors interpreted this pattern in terms of young adults being more adaptable, whereas older adults were postulated to have an advantage when they could benefit from accumulated experience. A comparable classification was made several years later by Jones and Conrad (1933). These researchers found the largest age-related declines on tests that they claimed assessed "native capacity" or "sheer modifiability," and the least age-related declines on tests that they felt were influenced by the "accumulative effects of experience."

Similar distinctions between stable and declining cognitive abilities have subsequently been mentioned by Cattell, Hebb, Welford, Baltes, and many others. A variety of labels have been used to characterize the distinction, such as type A versus type B cognition, fluid versus crystallized intelligence, and cognitive mechanics versus cognitive pragmatics. The fluid-crystallized terminology is probably the most familiar, but I believe the terms *process* and *product* are more descriptive of the intended distinction. That is, by process I refer to the efficiency or effectiveness of processing at the time of assessment. This type of

185

cognition reflects the ability to solve novel problems or to transform and manipulate familiar materials. The term cognitive product refers to the accumulated products of processing carried out in the past, and consequently this type of cognition largely consists of various forms of acquired knowledge.

The two aspects of cognition are not necessarily independent, because all products must be acquired through the operation of processes, and it is also possible that the current level of products influences the efficiency or effectiveness of some processes. It is also important to recognize that these are only two of many possible types of cognition, and that many forms of cognition such as wisdom, judgment, practical intelligence, and social intelligence are not represented in this classification. Nevertheless, process and product aspects should be distinguished if for no other reason than the suspected differential developmental patterns across adulthood.

This distinction between two types of cognition provides the foundation for what I will propose are the six major issues in the field of cognitive aging. The issues are represented in the matrix in Figure 1 and can be characterized as the *what* and *why* of adult age relations on variables reflecting cognitive processes, cognitive products, and the interaction of processes and products. In my opinion these are pressing issues because if they were to be resolved, then enormous progress would have been made toward understanding aging and cognition. Moreover, the issues are relevant to survey research involving adults of different ages because the accuracy of survey responses is almost certainly related to the individual's ability to comprehend what is being asked (i.e., cognitive processes) and to his or her level of relevant knowledge (i.e., cognitive products). I believe we are closer to the answer for some cells in the matrix than for others, but considerable research remains to be done before we can have confidence in any of the conclusions. In the remainder of this chapter I will elaborate on these issues, and report relevant research findings where available.

	Process	Product	Process X Product
What age relation?	??	??	??
Why this age relation?	??	??	??

FIGURE 1. Classification scheme to illustrate the six pressing issues in cognitive aging.

☐ **Process**

I will begin with process aspects of cognition because that has been the focus of the bulk of the research concerned with aging and cognition. Process cognition has been evaluated with many types of experimental and psychometric tests of memory, reasoning, and spatial ability. The assessments are often designed to have minimal influence of prior knowledge, either by the use of highly familiar material, such as digits or common words, or by the use of abstract nonmeaningful material, such as patterns of geometric symbols. Typical tasks used to evaluate efficiency or effectiveness of cognitive processing have involved deliberate recall, abstraction of relations, and transformation of spatial patterns. Process aspects of cognition are likely to be involved when a survey respondent attempts to understand questions posed by the interviewer and to retrieve the relevant information from his or her knowledge system. Other chapters in this volume by Craik; Yoon, May, and Hasher; Kemper and Kemtes; Park; and Wingfield refer to research on the relations of age on specific types of cognitive process measures.

Age–process relations are well documented in the research literature. Perhaps the best way to illustrate them is with results from large samples that include a wide range of ages. Furthermore, because several data sets include measures of both cognitive processes and cognitive products, the age trends for the two types of cognition can be directly compared. We will first consider the relations of age to cognitive process measures.

Figure 2 illustrates data from the 1,322 participants in the 1984 and 1991 cross-sectional samples in Schaic's Seattle Longitudinal Study (Schaie, 1996). Notice that very similar age relations are evident in the composite measures representing inductive reasoning, spatial, perceptual speed, and episodic memory abilities.

Figure 3 illustrates data from over 1,600 adults in the standardization sample for the Woodcock-Johnson (1989/1990) Cognitive Abilities Test for the average of two perceptual speed, reasoning, associative learning, and short-term memory measures in that test battery. Once again there is a nearly monotonic age-related decline in these process measures, with a total magnitude from the youngest to the oldest of at least one total sample standard deviation.

The consistency of the age relations in process measures of cognition across different samples and specific types of tests suggests that we can have considerable confidence in the *what* of age–process relations. That is, at least in cross-sectional samples, it appears that there is an age-related decline of between one and two standard deviations across a range from about 18 to 80 years of age.

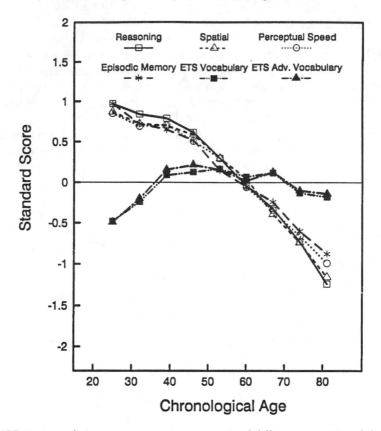

FIGURE 2. Age relations on composite measures of different cognitive abilities in the cross-sectional data from the 1984 and 1991 waves of the Seattle Longitudinal Study (Schaie, 1996).

Unfortunately, relatively little is yet known about the *why* of these negative age–process relations. Many speculations have been proposed, ranging from generation-specific experiences, to changes in working memory, various aspects of attention, or speed of processing, to decreases in the supply of particular types of neurotransmitters, but there is not yet much agreement about the causes of age-related declines in measures of processing efficiency or effectiveness.

However, I do not mean to imply that nothing is known about the relations between age and process measures of cognition because some conclusions about age-process relations are clearly possible. For example, because there is now considerable evidence that age-related differences on various cognitive variables are not independent, I believe that we can conclude that it is unlikely that multiple specific deficits

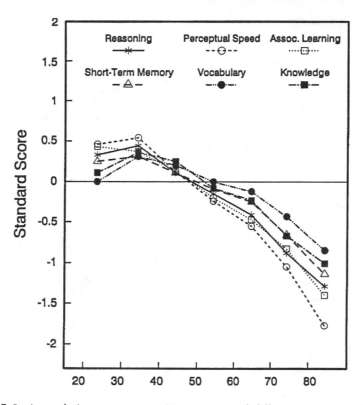

FIGURE 3. Age relations on composite measures of different cognitive abilities from the standardization sample of the Woodcock-Johnson Psychoeducational Test Battery (1989/1990).

are responsible for a very large proportion of the age-related effects on process aspects of cognition. Evidence relevant to this conclusion has been provided by two different types of analytical methods.

One analytical procedure is based on the notion of mediation, and is often represented in the form of models expressed as path diagrams. For example, a number of studies have investigated the plausibility of structural models in which the age-related effects on various measures of cognitive functioning are mediated by age-related reductions in working memory or speed of processing. Figure 4 contains very simple versions of two alternative models of the relations on two variables: one with completely independent age-related effects on the two variables, and the other with shared age-related effects on the variables. Notice that if the age-related effects were independent, as in the top panel of the figure, then there would be no possibility of mediation of age-related

Independent Influences

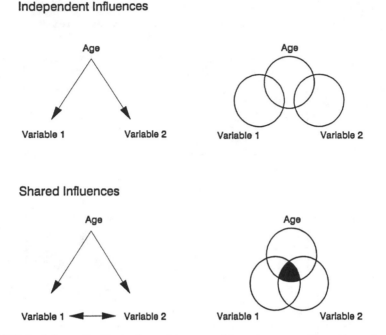

Shared Influences

FIGURE 4. Schematic illustration of two possible outcomes with path analyses of age relations on two different cognitive variables.

effects on one variable through other variables. Over the last 10 years a great deal of research has been conducted with this type of analytical procedure, and almost without exception it has revealed little support for the idea of completely independent age-related influences. In fact, estimates of the amount of shared age-related variance for many combinations of cognitive variables are moderate to large, often exceeding 50% or more of the total age-related variance (e.g., Salthouse, 1994).

A second analytical procedure for investigating the independence of age-related influences in cognition consists of examining the age-related effects in one variable in the context of age effects in other variables. This procedure is sometimes referred to as single common factor analysis and is schematically illustrated in Figure 5. The single common factor analysis procedure is useful for determining the magnitude of the age-related effects on a given variable after controlling for the effects of age on what all variables have in common. It differs from the mediational approach in that there is no commitment to a particular type of variable as being more fundamental or primitive than others, and there is no attempt to specify linkages among variables except in

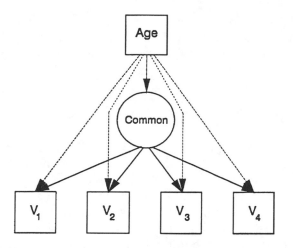

FIGURE 5. Schematic illustration of the single common factor analytical method. Dashed lines represent relations of age to the cognitive variables that are independent of those through the common factor.

terms of the age-related influences on the variables. Although this analytical procedure seems rather simplistic, there are at least two theoretically interesting ways in which differential age relations could occur within this framework. One way in which a variable could have little or no relation to age is if it had a weak or nonexistent loading on the common factor, and a second way is if it had unique relations of age that were independent of the age-related effects through the common factor. The single common factor analytical procedure is just beginning to be explored, but both of the patterns just described have been reported for different variables. Of greatest interest in the present context is that a consistent finding across numerous single common factor analyses is that the independent or unique age-related influences on different cognitive variables, represented in the figure by dotted lines, are almost always few in number and small in magnitude (e.g., Salthouse, 1996; Salthouse, Hancock, Meinz, & Hambrick, 1996; Verhaeghen & Salthouse, 1997). This implies that a large proportion of the age-related influences on different cognitive variables are shared, and are not independent.

Therefore, while there is still no consensus regarding the reasons for age-related declines in process aspects of cognition, some progress has been achieved because we can now be confident that the number of explanations will be much fewer than the number of variables exhibiting age-related declines. It thus seems reasonable to conclude that task-specific interpretations such as inefficient strategies or defective components that are used in a limited set of tasks are unlikely to play a major role in accounting for age–process relations found in many different cognitive variables.

☐ Product

Product aspects of cognition have typically been evaluated with variables reflecting acquired knowledge or other benefits of accumulated experience. For example, tests of vocabulary or knowledge of other types of information have frequently been used to assess product cognition. This type of cognition is clearly relevant to survey research if the questions ask about factual or autobiographical information that is presumed to be within the individual's knowledge base.

Age–product relations are not as consistent as age–process relations. The lack of consistency can be illustrated with data from the same two data sets described earlier. Figure 2 also contains data from two vocabulary tests administered by Schaie to participants in the 1984 and 1991 cross-sectional samples in his study, and it can be seen that the age trend on these measures is largely one of stability. Figure 3 contains the results from a test of vocabulary and a composite measure of knowledge about science, social studies, and humanities from the Woodcock-Johnson standardization data. Note that performance on the knowledge tests of cognitive products in this large and nationally representative sample declines nearly as much as does performance on the perceptual speed, reasoning, associative learning, and short-term memory measures of cognitive processes.

In light of these inconsistent patterns it is reasonable to ask what is responsible for the discrepancies in the age–product relations. Although a definitive answer is not yet possible, I suspect that in representative samples such as the Woodcock-Johnson standardization sample there is frequently a negative relation between age and amount of education, and it seems reasonable to assume that education is typically positively associated with level of knowledge. The relations between age and measures of knowledge may therefore be negative in these representative samples because the average older adult has fewer years of education than the average young adult. In contrast, many cognitive researchers often deliberately try to avoid a confounding of age and amount of education, and consequently in those types of samples, measures of knowledge may either remain stable across adulthood, or possibly even increase with age. However, differential amounts of education are not responsible for all of the variation in the age–product relations because while control of education has been found to eliminate the age-related decline in measures of product cognition in some analyses, the reduction in the magnitude of the relations with age was only about 50% in the Woodcock-Johnson knowledge measures.

Other factors may also be contributing to the variation in the pattern of age–product relations, but because of the inconsistency across samples, no firm conclusions can be reached about the *what* of the relation between age and product measures of cognition at the current time.

Although one might expect an increase with age in knowledge measures, which are presumably based on experience, and more specifically on opportunities for the acquisition of information, we have seen that the results have not confirmed this expectation. Therefore, the principal *why* question with respect to cognitive products is what is responsible for the stability in age–product relations? At least three possible explanations could be postulated to account for the lack of the expected increase with age in measures of knowledge.

One possibility is that there is a decrease in the efficiency of new learning, which together with some losses due to forgetting, might offset or balance the cumulative increases in knowledge such that there is an overall steady state across most of the adult years. This interpretation receives some support from evidence of age-related decreases in the effectiveness of many types of learning, which would presumably reduce the rate of growth of knowledge. A second possible explanation for the absence of age-related increases in measures of knowledge is that there may be limitations in the types of experience one encounters, such that there are early plateaus on the benefits of experience. This interpretation seems plausible because much of the experience in many situations could be redundant, and hence not lead to greater knowledge. In circumstances such as these, only the initial periods of experience may be sufficiently diverse and novel to lead to new knowledge, and therefore much of the experiential advantage of older adults may be "wasted" in the sense that it does not contribute to increments in knowledge.

A third possible interpretation attributes the lack of age-related increases in knowledge measures of product cognition to the manner in which knowledge is typically assessed. That is, in order to have wide applicability, most tests of knowledge are designed to assess relatively general information rather than information specific to particular vocations or avocations. However, it is certainly possible that as people become specialized their interests narrow, and thus their total amount of knowledge could continue to expand, but it might not be detected if it was in a limited domain that was not well represented in tests of general information or vocabulary. Although these hypotheses all seem plausible, they may be difficult to investigate because it is not clear how losses in acquisition efficiency might be calibrated against gains in cumulative products, it is uncertain how diversity of experience could be accurately evaluated, and assessments of different types of specialized knowledge may not be directly comparable. This is not to say that these interpretations are not meaningful and important, but rather that at the present time it does not seem possible to reach any definitive conclusion about the *why* of age–product relations.

☐ Process × Product

The third major aspect of cognition in my proposed classification scheme concerns the joint effects of process and product. More specifically, the focus here is on the *what* and *why* of the relations between the two types of cognition across the period of adulthood. At least two different facets of these issues can be distinguished. The first is how the levels of process and product affect the age relations on one another. And the second is how process and product jointly affect the relations of age on the performance of complex tasks involving both types of cognition. In the context of surveys, these questions may correspond to concerns about: (a) whether a respondent's level of comprehension affects the quality or quantity of information that is reported; (b) whether the amount of knowledge the individual possesses affects his or her ability to understand exactly what is being asked; and (c) whether the combination of comprehension ability and knowledge level affects the accuracy of responses to survey questions.

Two possible outcomes can be specified with respect to the first question, concerned with the relations of the two types of cognition with one another; namely, process and product could have either additive or interactive relations with one another. Additive relations would suggest that there are independent influences of age on cognitive processes and cognitive products, whereas interactions would suggest that the age relations on one aspect of cognition depend on the level of the other aspect of cognition. Perhaps the simplest way in which these possibilities could be examined is in the context of a multiple regression model, in which one tests for the presence of an age × predictor interaction when predicting process scores from age and product variables and when predicting product scores from age and process variables. In order to be meaningful, these types of analyses should be based on relatively large samples in which measures of both process and product aspects of cognition are available. Fortunately the Woodcock-Johnson data set possesses these characteristics.

Regression analyses on the data from the over 1,600 adults in the Woodcock-Johnson standardization sample revealed no interactions of age and product in the prediction of a cognitive process measure (i.e., a composite measure of inductive reasoning, which is considered by the authors of the test battery to be the best measure of fluid or process cognition). Figure 6 illustrates these results with age relations from the top 25%, the middle 50%, and the bottom 25% of the total sample from the distribution of knowledge measures (i.e., vocabulary and a composite of scores from the science, social studies, and humanities tests). Notice that the relations of age to the composite reasoning measure of process cognition were nearly parallel across the three levels of

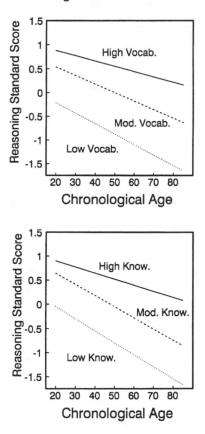

FIGURE 6. Regression lines relating age to composite inductive reasoning performance for the top 25%, middle 50%, and bottom 25% of the distribution of adults on the vocabulary and composite knowledge product measures.

vocabulary performance, and across the three levels of knowledge performance. This implies that although people with higher levels of product cognition also have higher levels of process cognition, the relations between age and measures of process cognition are independent of the level of cognitive products.

In contrast, the interactions of age and process cognition were statistically significant in the prediction of cognitive product measures. Figure 7 illustrates these interactions in the form of the age–product relations for the top 25%, the middle 50%, and the bottom 25% of distribution on the composite inductive reasoning process measure. Notice that with the vocabulary product measure (top panel) there is

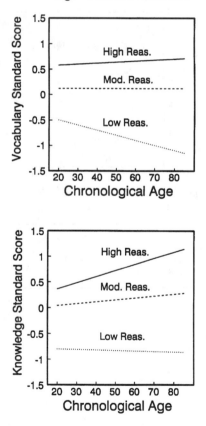

FIGURE 7. Regression lines relating age to cognitive product measures for the top 25%, middle 50%, and bottom 25% of the distribution of adults on the composite inductive reasoning measure.

an age-related decrease only among individuals with low reasoning scores, and with the composite knowledge product measure (bottom panel) there is an age-related increase for adults with high reasoning scores. Although these interactions are potentially quite interesting, they need to be interpreted cautiously because of the small number of individuals in some of the groups. To illustrate, only 22 adults over the age of 60 were in the high-process group, and thus the interaction pattern may be of greater theoretical, than practical, relevance.

The second aspect related to the joint effects of process and product concerns their combined influence on other tasks or activities. That is, the criterion variables in this context are not based on abstract tasks or tests designed to assess process or product forms of cognition, but instead represent more complex activities involving a mixture of processes and products. When both process and product can affect performance, individual differences in performance could be attributable to variations in the level of the predictors, or in the weighting of the predictors. This can be easily conceptualized in terms of a regression equation in which performance is determined by both process and product, i.e., Performance = a(Process) + b(Product). The primary question with respect to aging then becomes whether the weightings of the predictors change with age in addition to their levels, and if so, what is responsible for this change?

This issue is potentially quite interesting because certain patterns within this analytical framework could be interpreted as evidence for the existence of age-related compensation (e.g., Salthouse, 1995). For example, a shift with increased age in the direction of a greater weighting on stable or increasing products and a lesser weighting on declining processes might allow the same, or possibly even increasing, levels of overall performance to be achieved across adulthood despite declines in relevant components.

Some preliminary evidence relevant to this issue is available with very simple criterion tasks such as verbal fluency, with measures of vocabulary serving as the product variable and measures of perceptual speed serving as the process variable (Salthouse, 1993). Two studies in that project revealed that young and old adults had quite different mean levels of the process and product variables, but that the regression coefficients were very similar in the two groups. These results suggest that there may not be age differences in the relative weighting of process and product, but additional research with more complex tasks is needed before much confidence can be placed in this conclusion.

To summarize, although several intriguing possibilities can be specified, relatively little is currently known about either the nature (i.e., the *what*) or the reasons (i.e., the *why*) of the relations between age and the joint effects of process and product. This is unfortunate because it seems likely that most activities outside of the laboratory involve a combination of the two types of cognition, and yet we know very little about how they function together.

☐ Conclusion

In conclusion, I have identified six major, or pressing, issues in aging and cognition. Furthermore, I have suggested that some consensus about the answers was evident for only one of the issues (namely, the decline of process cognition). Nevertheless, I continue to believe that these issues represent the most important questions in the field, and that once answered they will lead to greatly increased understanding about how and why cognitive functioning changes with increasing age. The issues have relevance to survey research because not only can the age relations on process and product aspects of cognition affect the quality of survey responses, but the availability of data from large representative samples such as those typically used in surveys may help contribute to the resolution of the issues.

☐ References

Foster, J. C., & Taylor, G. A. (1920). The applicability of mental tests to persons over fifty years of age. *Journal of Applied Psychology, 4*, 39–58.

Jones, H. E., & Conrad, H. S. (1933). The growth and decline of intelligence: A study of a homogeneous group between the ages of ten and sixty. *Genetic Psychology Monographs, 13*, 223–295.

Salthouse, T. A. (1993). Speed and knowledge as determinants of adult age differences in verbal tasks. *Journal of Gerontology: Psychological Sciences, 48*, P29–P36.

Salthouse, T. A. (1994). How many causes are there of aging-related decrements in cognitive functioning? *Developmental Review, 14*, 413–437.

Salthouse, T. A. (1995). Refining the concept of psychological compensation. In R. A. Dixon & L. Bäckman (Eds.), *Psychological compensation: Managing losses and promoting gains* (pp. 21–34). Hillsdale, NJ: Erlbaum.

Salthouse, T. A. (1996). Constraints on theories of cognitive aging. *Psychonomic Bulletin & Review, 3*, 287–299.

Salthouse, T. A., Hancock, H. E., Meinz, E. J., & Hambrick, D. Z. (1996). Interrelations of age, visual acuity, and cognitive functioning. *Journal of Gerontology: Psychological Sciences, 51B*, P317–P330.

Schaie, K. W. (1996). *Intellectual development in adulthood: The Seattle Longitudinal Study.* New York: Cambridge University Press.

Verhaeghen, P., & Salthouse, T. A. (1997). Meta-analyses of age-cognition relations in adulthood: Estimates of linear and non-linear age effects and structural models. *Psychological Bulletin, 122*, 231–249.

Woodcock, R. W., & Johnson, M. B. (1989/1990). *Woodcock-Johnson Psycho-Educational Battery—Revised.* Allen, TX: DLM.

LANGUAGE COMPREHENSION AND COMMUNICATION

CHAPTER

Arthur Wingfield

Comprehending Spoken Questions: Effects of Cognitive and Sensory Change in Adult Aging

Face-to-face interviews between investigator and respondent have a long history in survey research as a more interactive alternative to written survey presentation. Most notable in the speech domain has been the increasing use of telephone interviews. This raises the important question of how the features of natural speech and the cognitive load required for on-line speech comprehension may affect elderly respondents in survey research. As Knäuper notes in Chapter 17 of this volume, in telephone surveys the respondent is the captive of the speech rate of the telephone interviewer. This is true both in the rate at which questions are read and, when alternatives are used, in the rate at which these are presented. This fact adds the additional dimension of processing speed to the usual issues of comprehending questions in survey research.

Over the past two decades we have learned a great deal about the cognitive load represented by the comprehension of spoken language and the limits imposed both by working memory capacity and by limits in processing speed. As we will show in this chapter, these issues have especially important implications for speech comprehension in the elderly listener.

☐ The Perception of Speech

One of the most salient features of natural speech is the rapid rate at which it arrives. It should first be said that there is no such thing as a "normal" speech rate. Speech rates can run from as slow as 90 words per minute (wpm) for individuals engaged in thoughtful conversation, to rates in excess of 210 wpm for a person attempting to read in a natural manner from a prepared script. On average, however, speech rates in ordinary conversation typically average between 140 and 180 wpm. To put this another way, successful comprehension requires that the words of a sentence be perceptually encoded, their linguistic relations determined, and a coherence (meaning) structure of the message constructed, all with the speech arriving at a rate of 2.3 to 3.0 words per second.

In Figure 1 we enumerate this challenge in terms of four operations, beginning from the acoustic waveform to the comprehension of the message at the discourse level. We refer to this sequence as processing the signal from the bottom up. We will address the other side of this issue, "top-down" processing, later in this section.

At the top of the left side of Figure 1 we show the speech waveform of a speaker who was asked to say in a clear way the phrase "You talk and I'll listen." The speaker said these words into a microphone while a computer digitized the signal and displayed the utterance waveform on the computer screen as shown here. The vertical displacements

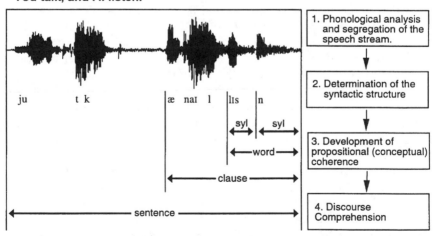

FIGURE 1. Bottom-up processing from the acoustic speech stream.

represent the sound energy, or amplitude, of the speech signal. The larger vertical displacements represent the speech sounds (*phonemes*) that have the most sound energy. These are typically the vowels and the other voiced sounds in the speech stream. (Voiceless phonemes such as the "s" in "whisper" or the "th" in "thin" are typical of the low-energy, high-frequency sounds in English.) A flat area can be seen in the waveform between the words "talk" and "and I'll." This space shows that the speaker paused for a moment between uttering the phrases "You talk" and "and I'll listen." Below the waveform we have indicated in phonetic script the individual speech sounds of the utterance moving along the time base from left to right.

On the right side of the figure we indicate four operations that must be performed, from phonological analysis and segregation of the speech stream, to full discourse comprehension.

1. *Phonological analysis and segregation of the speech stream.* Unlike writing, where words are separated on both sides by visible spaces, in speech words tend to run together without clear separations between words. This is a natural property of the motor dynamics of the speech mechanism, in which it is common for speakers to utter the end of one word as they are already beginning to say the next word. We can see from a careful inspection of the waveform that the words "and" and "I'll" run together without any clear separation. It is also the case that natural speech tends to be surprisingly underarticulated. For example, although a listener will perceptually "hear" a "d" at the end of the word "and," our speaker never actually articulated that sound. This is especially dramatic because our speaker was consciously attempting to speak the utterance especially clearly.

   Cases where areas in the acoustic stream have more than one possible word boundary interpretation are sometimes called *oronyms*, e.g., "stuffy nose" versus "stuff he knows" (Pinker, 1994, p. 160). Subtle acoustic cues may be used to allow one to distinguish the correct perceptual segmentation of "cargo," as in "He saw the car go" versus "He saw the cargo" (Cutler, 1990; Gow & Gordon, 1995). In other cases there may be no acoustic distinction at all. One example is the way most people will utter the sound sequence "better" in fluent speech, whether they are saying the sentence, "I better do my laundry," or the sentence "I bet her five dollars." In such cases, the linguistic context in which the sequence is embedded may be the only source of information for the correct perceptual interpretation (Martin, 1990).

Careful analyses of natural speech utterances show that speakers tend spontaneously to employ a *functional adaptation* in their production. That is, we tend to articulate more clearly words that cannot be easily inferred from context, and to articulate less clearly those that can (Lindblom, Brownlee, Davis, & Moon, 1992). It is important to stress that this dynamic adjustment is not consciously applied by the speaker, any more than listeners are consciously aware of using acoustic and linguistic context in their perceptual operations. Interestingly, even studies of so-called "clear speech," in which speakers purposely attempt to speak especially distinctly, would show far less than perfect intelligibility were it not for the aid of the linguistic context that surrounds the unclear or acoustically ambiguous regions of the speech stream (Cox, Alexander, & Gilmore, 1987; Picheny, Durlach, & Braida, 1986).

2. *Determination of syntactic structure.* As we illustrate in Figure 1, the listener's task includes identification of syllables and words, and also recognition of how these words combine to form linguistic clauses and how these clauses combine to form a sentence. In linguistic terms, the listener must rapidly "parse" the input, or determine the syntactic function of the incoming words.

3. *Development of conceptual coherence.* Determination of the main nouns and verbs in the utterance has as its ultimate goal, of course, the determination of the propositional content, or "ideas," represented in the utterance and how these ideas are semantically related. This is referred to as developing the conceptual coherence of an utterance, both within sentences and across sentences, as context derived from prior utterances and the new information are integrated.

4. *Discourse comprehension.* Although most of psycholinguistics research has focused on understanding perceptual processing at the sentence level, in actual practice the listener's task includes assembling the semantic content of individual sentences in terms of the overall meaning of an utterance across many individual sentences that cross-refer to each other. At the discourse level listeners must not only assemble the full meaning of a message based on the literal content of the utterances but also on inferences from information implied but not actually stated. If we heard as part of a narrative the sentence, "Asking the stranger for the time he ran quickly to make his appointment," we would naturally assume that the stranger had a watch, that the stranger told the person the time, that the questioner was late for the appointment, and so forth. Indeed, when tested, listeners will often falsely remember having heard an item of information that had not been present in the message but that might be reasonably inferred given what had

been heard (cf., Bransford, Barclay, & Franks, 1972; Bransford & Franks, 1971).

Top-Down Versus Bottom-Up Processing

Drawing the directional arrows between the four operations enumerated on the right side of Figure 1 should not imply that comprehension moves in orderly steps from the analysis of the acoustic input to comprehension at the discourse level. Saying that a listener's perception of speech is facilitated by linguistic context already makes clear that lower levels of perception, such as perception at the syllable and word level, can be guided by knowledge derived from the sentence and discourse levels. Listeners can also develop useful expectations about probable word identity from real-world knowledge outside of any information contained in the particular utterance. As in the above example of asking a stranger for the time, speakers (and writers) assume shared knowledge as they organize their productions. The result is common omission of facts or information that can be reasonably inferred.

In the jargon of the literature, we refer to these as "bottom-up/top-down interactions." Bottom-up processing refers to moving from the physical signal of the acoustic input up through words, phrases, and sentences. Top-down processing refers to the use of information already available to a listener that produces context-driven expectations of what is about to be heard.

The fact that speech represents a continuous top-down/bottom-up interaction is one of the reasons why speech can be processed as rapidly as it is. That is, when a listener hears a word in a sentence the listener has two sources of information. One of these is the bottom-up information supplied by the build-up of acoustic information as the uttered word unfolds over time. The second source comes from the top-down information of the sentence context. Because of this latter factor, words can be recognized in fluent speech long before their full acoustic duration has been completed (Grosjean, 1980; Marslen-Wilson, 1987).

An especially dramatic example of the importance of top-down information to speech processing comes from a demonstration offered many years ago by Pollack and Pickett (1963). They performed a simple experiment in which they recorded conversations and then spliced out individual words from the running discourse and presented them to listeners in isolation, without their surrounding context. Not only were these words often totally unrecognizable, but they sometimes barely sounded like words at all. To complete their demonstration, Pollack and Pickett played back the same recordings of the words, but this time re-embedded in their original sentence contexts. The words now sounded crystal clear. Studies such as these have shown that speech perception is heavily context dependent, on both the linguistic and the acoustic contexts that precede a particular word, but also on the context that follows it (Grosjean, 1985; Lieberman, 1963; Pollack & Pickett, 1963; Wingfield, Alexander, & Cavigelli, 1994).

We may thus see that however effortless language comprehension may feel in our everyday experience, the operations that must be performed for effective comprehension are quite complex. Kemper and Kemtes, in this volume, offer an excellent account of processing models that attempt to capture this complexity. A good review can also be found in Gernsbacher (1994).

☐ Speech Comprehension and Working Memory

In reading, the reader can use his or her eye-movements to control the rate of input. The reader can also backtrack to an earlier part of the text if a region in a sentence or a question is confusing or unclear. With a spoken message the rate of speech is controlled by the speaker, and any "looking back" to an earlier part of the message must be done in memory.

Our earlier reference to *functional adaptation* at the level of articulatory clarity and the availability of facilitative context is an example of the natural partnership between speaker and listener. Another example of this partnership can be seen in differences between the characteristics of written and spoken discourse, in which planning constraints on the part of the speaker result in spoken sentences that tend to be shorter and syntactically less complex than their written counterparts. Although this difference in the length and complexity of speakers' natural utterances may be constrained by production limitations in the speaker (e.g., Kemper, Kynette, Rash, Sprott, & O'Brien, 1989), the result is the production of shorter and syntactically simpler sentences that respect the memory and processing constraints of the listener who will have to comprehend the utterance. There are, by the way, many other differences between the way people speak and write, beyond the length and syntactic complexity of the sentences. For example, there are also word frequency differences between spoken and written text. Some of these are quite interesting and unexpected. For example, in writing, the most frequent word is "the," while in spoken telephone conversations it is "I" (Miller, 1951).

One important message from these observations is that texts should be structured differently depending on the intended modality of the presentation. That is, a particular text that seems unremarkable when presented in writing may sound odd if it is used as a script for speaking the same message aloud. At the cognitive level, the longer sentences and more complex syntax that might be reasonable for comprehending written prose could place a greater memory and processing burden on a listener hearing the same text.

Most models of language processing assume that listeners analyze the syntax and semantic content of speech on-line, as the linguistic input is arriving. There are times, however, when processing lags behind, or is conducted at a slower rate than, the actual speech input. In such cases the perceptual system must rely on some form of transient memory system. There are many occasions in natural language processing when this can occur. We have alluded to one of them in our reference to the fact that speech would be far less clear than it is were it not for the support from the surrounding context. In the case of perceptual clarification from context that follows an unclear word, the acoustic form of the ambiguous word must be held in some form of memory representation pending the arrival of additional "downstream" context that will make clear what that word must have been.

Other cases where memory constrains language comprehension are second-pass operations in which we discover that we have misunderstood a sentence as we originally heard it. The most notable of these are so-called "garden path" sentences, such as the sentence "The old man the boats." A sentence like this is confusing because of the tendency on the part of listeners to interpret the word "man" as a noun, as part of the noun phrase, "the old man." This will lead us to expect a verb, but instead we hear another noun phrase ("the boats"). The answer, of course, is that "man" in this sentence is being used as a verb (i.e., "to operate"). The ability to back up and reparse the sentence correctly demands the presence of a memory representation of the original utterance. This will be true whether, as some believe, this representation is in the form of a verbatim trace of the words that had been uttered, or in the form of alternative interpretations below the level of conscious awareness that may later be activated. (Interested readers can find a good discussion of memory requirements and parsing strategies in the resolution of local ambiguities in Abney & Johnson, 1991.)

Although garden path sentences are somewhat extreme, substantial segments of speech input must be held in working memory whenever we have to deal with sentences that have embedded clauses, sentences that have left-branching constructions, or sentences that require the listener to identify the correct referents for several pronouns. Consider the sentence "The man who sold the car to the woman had red hair." In order to know who had red hair we must strip the clause "who sold the car to the woman" from the sentence and hold this clause in working memory while we process for meaning the overall sentence frame in which it is embedded ("The man had red hair"). This example is an interesting one because comprehension of the sentence requires that we not be distracted by the sequence ". . . the woman had red hair." Such a strictly local analysis without access to a mental representation of the full sentence would give us the wrong answer.

In addition to correcting parsing errors and handling complex linguistic structures, a transient memory is also needed to allow temporary holding and integration of phrases and clauses that have already been heard with those that arrive later. This integration is necessary in order to develop full utterance meaning (van Dijk & Kintsch, 1983).

☐ Sensory and Cognitive Change in Adult Aging

As we have tried to show in the above discussion, spoken language comprehension represents a complex process that may strain cognitive resources even for young adults whose memory capabilities and processing speed are presumably at their peak. In the following sections we will examine three factors related to spoken language comprehension in the older listener. These three factors are changes in hearing acuity that can accompany normal aging, changes in the capacity of working memory, and finally, age-related changes in speed with which information can be processed.

Age and Auditory Acuity

Hearing acuity among the elderly shows a wide range of individual differences, and it would be wrong to assume that speaking to an elderly adult automatically demands that one speak especially loudly. Indeed, a very substantial proportion of the noninstitutionalized elderly have no special problem with auditory acuity for speech. Within this background of caution, however, it is certainly the case that large-scale studies have shown that the incidence of clinically significant hearing loss increases across the adult life-span. Depending on the study, estimates of hearing impairment sufficient to affect speech comprehension range between 24% and 30% for noninstitutionalized American adults between the ages of 65 and 74, and between 30% and 48% for those 75 years and older (U.S. Congress, Office of Technology Assessment, 1986). Even those without clinically significant impairment, however, may also have reduced auditory processing efficiency not necessarily detected in standard audiograms (Schneider, Pichora-Fuller, & Kowalchuk, 1994).

The term *presbycusis* literally means "old hearing" and it has two features that are important to this discussion. The first is that the hearing losses associated with age are not uniform across the frequency range. We can see this in Figure 2, in which we have plotted data taken from a large-scale study by the National Center for Health Statistics showing the incidence of hearing loss at various sound frequencies for five different age groups (U.S. Congress, Office of Technology Assessment, 1986, p. 15). The figure is based on the ability of the subjects

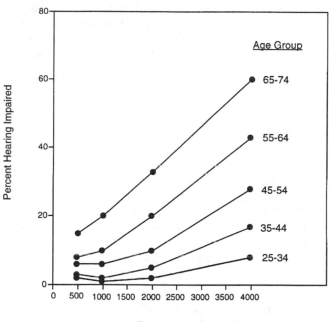

FIGURE 2. The percentage of adults in five age groups showing a hearing impairment for tones presented at various sound frequencies representing the frequency range for speech. These data were taken from a large-scale study conducted by the National Center for Health Statistics (U.S. Congress, Office of Technology Assessment, 1986, p. 15).

to hear tones that varied from 500 to 4000 Hz at an intensity level of 31 dB at least 50% of the time. This range, 500–4000 Hz, was chosen because it includes the general range of speech frequencies (Sekuler & Blake, 1994, p. 335).

The data shown in Figure 2 clearly illustrate that although aging affects hearing at all frequencies, the effect is differentially great at the higher frequencies. This is important for speech, as hearing loss at the higher frequencies will differentially affect the perception of high-frequency and low-energy sounds such as p, k, s, t, sh, ch, and the voiceless th (as in "thin").

Presbycusis, it should be noted, can include more than a high-frequency hearing loss. Not uncommon in elderly hearing is *phonemic regression*, a lack of clarity for complex auditory signals such as speech. In testing, phonemic regression appears in the form of poorer speech discrimination than would be predicted from pure-tone audiometry alone. Especially important to the in-person or telephone survey interviewer are findings that speech perception in elderly adults can be especially vulnerable to the presence of background noise (Dubno, Dirks, & Morgan, 1982; Duquesnoy, 1983; Gordon-Salant, 1987), speaking in a room with poor reverberation characteristics (Gordon-Salant & Fitzgibbons, 1993), and when speech is filtered through bandwidths simulating telephone transmission (Bergman, Blumenfeld, Cascardo, Dash, Levitt, & Margulies, 1976; Bergman, 1980). On the positive side it can be shown that older adults, both presbycusics and older listeners with near-normal hearing, make better use of supporting context than young listeners with normal hearing (e.g., Wingfield, Aberdeen, & Stine, 1991; Wingfield et al., 1994). This is a powerful source of top-down compensation for bottom-up sensory decline. However, on the negative side, it may be that the allocation of processing resources for this top-down support of low-level auditory perception may reduce the resources available for higher level cognitive operations. It has been suggested that this could have a negative age-related impact on interpretive operations as well as on storage and retrieval functions in working memory (Pichora-Fuller, Schneider, & Daneman, 1995).

The issue of sensory decline in cognitive aging has taken on renewed interest with reports that combined visual and auditory acuity account for a large measure of the age-related variance in performance on a range of cognitive tasks (Lindenberger & Baltes, 1994). As Craik points out in Chapter 5 of this volume, this is less likely to be a cause-and-effect relationship than it is a reflection of sensory change co-occurring with other areas of decline. A complicating factor in interpreting such results, of course, is that the accuracy with which sensory thresholds can be measured and defined far exceeds our precision in definition, and hence measurement, of higher level cognitive mediators.

As one considers the common occurrence of auditory declines in aging, one might fear that if elderly adults were to rely too heavily on top-down context in speech processing, they might develop a top-down "style," in which bottom-up information tended to be ignored. In the extreme, this could produce guessing behavior in the elderly listener that would be counterproductive in the long term. Studies we have conducted, however, suggest that this is not so. In one such study we conducted with healthy elderly adults we found that top-down linguistic context rarely overrode clear bottom-up information. In older listeners, as in the young, context was used appropriately to supplement weak sensory input but not to replace it (Wingfield et al., 1991; Wingfield & Stine, 1991).

Age and the Capacity of Working Memory

In the previous section we cited the arguments for the necessity of some form of short-term memory for sentence processing. The memory system most commonly implicated has been referred to as "working memory." Working memory refers to the cognitive system that includes both the ability to temporarily hold the recently received information and a limited-capacity "computation space," in which the materials in memory may be monitored and manipulated (Baddeley, 1986; Just & Carpenter, 1992). The essence of this memory capability is captured in the Daneman and Carpenter (1980) working memory span test. Although the best-known form of the Daneman and Carpenter test is a "reading span" version, because of our present interest in the role of memory in spoken language comprehension, we will focus on the spoken counterpart of the test. (Additional discussions of working memory can be found in the chapters by Craik and Park in this volume.)

In the spoken version of the Daneman and Carpenter test, the subject hears a list of sentences, and then, after all of the sentences have been presented, the subject is required to give from memory the last word in each sentence in the order in which they were presented. To insure that the subject is comprehending the full sentences and not just listening for the final words, a simple expedient is to require the subject to say whether or not each sentence is true or false immediately after it is presented (Wingfield, Stine, Lahar, & Aberdeen, 1988). The number of sentences the subject hears in a set is progressively increased, and the estimate of the span of working memory is taken as the maximum number of sentences that still allow the subject to recall all of the final words. The Daneman and Carpenter span test is thus intended to capture the ability to hold information in memory while simultaneously performing comprehension operations. It is this combination of both holding and manipulation that distinguishes working memory from simple short-term memory storage that would be represented by, for example, verbatim recall of a list of digits or random words.

Figure 3 shows data taken from a study in which younger and older adults were given three span measures, each representing an increase in the mental load associated with the memory task (Wingfield et al., 1988). The older subjects serving in this experiment were healthy, community-dwelling adults with good levels of education and verbal ability. On both of these measures the older subjects were at least equal to the younger subjects in the study who were university undergraduates.

Moving from left to right along the x-axis in the figure, the first point represents the younger and older subjects' mean digit spans, measured as the number of digits they could correctly repeat back immediately after one hearing. Age differences in simple digit span are

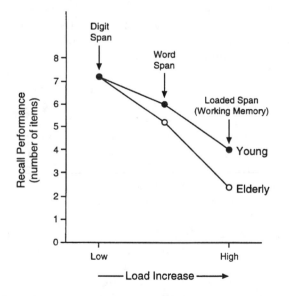

FIGURE 3. Data taken from a study by Wingfield, Stine, Lahar, and Aberdeen (1988), in which young and elderly adults were tested for their ability to recall lists of spoken digits (digit span), lists of words (word span), and the final words of sets of sentences presented for comprehension (loaded span).

typically small if they are present at all (Craik, 1977). Indeed, we can see in this sample that there was no age difference in simple digit span. The next set of points on the graph represent the younger and older subjects' memory spans for lists of random words. Memory spans for words are typically smaller than digit spans (Cavanaugh, 1972), and this was the case here. We can also see that for the word spans there was a small but significant age difference. By far the greater difference, however, appears in the final set of points on the graph. These show the subjects' scores on the spoken version of the Daneman and Carpenter span test referred to above, in which the subjects had to listen to and comprehend the meaning of sets of sentences while holding in memory the last word of each of the sentences in that set. Consistent with the aging literature, this measure, which best taps the capacity of working memory, shows a substantial age difference (Gick, Craik, & Morris, 1988; Light & Anderson, 1985; Tun, Wingfield, & Stine, 1991).

Working Memory, Age, and Language Comprehension

It has been well documented that cognitive resources, whether seen in terms of working memory capacity or the speed with which items can be encoded in working memory, account for a considerable amount of the variance in observed age differences in the recall of spoken (Stine & Wingfield, 1990) and written (Hartley, 1993) text. How does this limited working memory capacity impact on language comprehension and memory for spoken and written language?

The earliest search for this relationship appeared not with contrasts between younger and older adults, but in terms of claims for correlations between individual differences among young adults in comprehension ability and working memory capacity (cf. Daneman & Carpenter, 1980). It was argued that mental operations such as syntactic parsing, integration of propositions, inference, and the assignment of reference, all of which are necessary for text comprehension, varied with individuals' working memory capacity. It was thus a reasonable step to assume that, to the extent that older adults have a smaller working memory capacity than younger adults, one should see significant age differences in linguistic processes that require an especially heavy drain on working memory (Carpenter, Miyaki, & Just, 1994).

Studies in the aging literature would seem to support this suggestion. For example, when older subjects hear short sentences with reasonably simple syntax, their comprehension and recall of speech content is generally quite good. However, as the length and/or syntactic complexity of sentences increases, older people have significantly more difficulty than the young in sentence comprehension (Obler, Fein, Nicholas, & Albert, 1991) and accuracy of recall (Norman, Kemper, Kynette, Cheung, & Anagnopoulos, 1991). These studies would certainly suggest that long sentences, sentences with left-branching constructions, and sentences with double negatives should especially be avoided in text preparation for older and younger adults.

Older subjects can also experience some difficulty when inferential processing and rapid gist extraction is required. This is more likely to be the case when anaphoric distances are especially great, as when a pronoun and its referent are separated by several sentences in a text (Cohen, 1979; Light & Capps, 1986). This is true even for referent trace activation in on-line sentence comprehension (Zurif, Swinney, Prather, Wingfield, & Brownell, 1995). Finally, although older adults make excellent use of linguistic context to aid perception of an indistinct word when the context precedes the word, as well to aid recall (Perry & Wingfield, 1994), memory limitations put older people at a disadvantage when attempting to use linguistic context for retrospective word recognition, as when the identity of a poorly articulated word is not recognized until several words of context are heard after that word (Wingfield et al., 1994).

Findings such as these are usually interpreted as resulting from age-related limitations in working memory capacity as distinct from a loss in linguistic knowledge or vocabulary. Except for cases of neuropathology, neither vocabulary nor procedural knowledge for the use of linguistic rules are thought to diminish with age (Kempler & Zelinski, 1994; Light, 1991; Wingfield & Stine, 1992; see also Kemper & Kemtes in this volume). A good review of working memory and language comprehension, including data from both aphasia and normal aging can be found in Carpenter et al. (1994; see also the review by Daneman & Merikle, 1996).

Data from Tun, Wingfield, and Stine (1991) illustrated the implications of age-related working memory limitations using a dual-task study in which younger and older subjects were tested on their ability to recall the content of spoken passages. Subjects listened to and then recalled prose passages either alone or while having to perform either one of two secondary reaction-time tasks. One of these was a simple task in which the subject needed to monitor a computer screen and press a key when a target letter appeared (e.g., the letter "J"). Alternatively, subjects received a more complex secondary task in which they had to press one key if one letter appeared ("J") and a different key if another letter appeared ("H"). Subjects were told to respond as quickly as possible in their letter detections, but they were also told that attending to and correctly recalling the speech content was their primary task. Following the logic of dual task studies (Kerr, 1973), latencies on the reaction-time task were taken as an index of the processing resources available to the subject after allocation of the necessary resources to the task of remembering the content of the speech passages. The younger subjects, who were college students aged 18–20, and the older subjects, who were healthy community-dwelling adults aged 60–80, were well educated, and both groups had excellent levels of verbal ability as measured by vocabulary test scores. As would be expected, however, there was a significant age difference in working memory spans as measured by the Daneman and Carpenter (1980) span test.

Tun et al. (1991) found that the age differences were small in the simple reaction-time task (responding just to the presence of a single letter), but larger for the choice reaction-time task (responding differentially to a "J" or an "H") . That is, the older subjects had sufficient resource capacity still available after speech processing to conduct the simple reaction-time task as rapidly as the younger subjects, but not the more complex choice reaction-time task.

Evidence that working memory lay at the root of this difference was two-fold. First, Tun et al. (1991) found a significant correlation between subjects' working memory span scores and their choice, but not simple, reaction times. Additional support was offered by comparing a subgroup of high-span older subjects and low-span younger subjects who showed the same scores on the Daneman and Carpenter span test. As might be expected according to the limited-capacity view, the younger and older subjects with similar working memory capacity did not differ significantly on the secondary task performance. Citing this particular study also reminds us of the wide variability in performance levels of individual subjects within the older (and younger) populations. It was indeed possible to find some older subjects whose working memory scores were not far from those of some young adults.

Although "working memory" serves as a descriptive convenience, we should recognize that the term refers less to a tangible construct than it does to the ability to perform well in tasks designed to measure this ability (generally, tasks that require one to do two things at one time, such as both holding and manipulating information in memory). The actual nature of the memory store(s) that support language comprehension still remain a subject of study and some debate. This debate has been especially marked in the neurolinguistics literature in studies of sentence comprehension by brain injured patients whose lesions to certain brain areas leave them with dramatically low span scores on traditional tests of short-term and working memory. From these diminished spans one would expect them to have considerable difficulty with comprehension of sentences that we ordinarily think of as producing heavy demands on memory. Surprisingly, such patients can show good comprehension for sentences with complex relative clause constructions (Caplan & Waters, 1990), and even garden path sentences that require second-pass operations for correct comprehension (Waters & Caplan, 1993).

The data from these patients suggest strongly that the concept of working memory and the way it is measured are clearly only a part of an undoubtedly far more complex representational and processing system for speech comprehension. (A more complete discussion of these issues can be found in Waters & Caplan, 1996, and Wingfield, Waters, & Tun, 1998.)

It is the case that the current literature in cognitive psychology and cognitive aging presents working memory as a functional system with measurable capacity—one that carries, and hence constrains, language comprehension. While the construct continues to have utility, it may be best to think of "working memory" as a place-holder for a memory processing system yet to be fully understood.

Age and Speed of Processing

Slowing is a virtual hallmark of the aging process. We cannot say whether slowing causes inefficient processing or whether inefficient processing slows the system. Whether cause or consequence, we can say that perceptual and response slowing are an almost ubiquitous finding in the aging literature (Salthouse, 1991). Although the issue of slowing is itself a complex one (Fisher & Glaser, 1996), it could be argued that age declines in working memory capacity could arise from an age-related slowing in the rate at which new information can be encoded and stored in memory (Salthouse, 1994).

Given the rapidity of normal speech rates, and hence the rate at which the necessary processing operations must be performed, one might expect "slowed" older people to have special problems with speech comprehension. As we shall see in the following sections, this is certainly the case. We will also see, however, that the problem might be even more severe were it not for the excellent use older listeners routinely make of linguistic context and other top-down sources of information.

Studies of speech-rate effects are typically conducted using computer algorithms that allow one to increase speech rates without disturbing the intonation pattern of the speech or the relative timing patterns of speech-to-silence or vowel durations tied to the linguistic structure of the sentences. The product of this operation is referred to as *time-compressed* speech. The most dramatic effects of age and speech rate are seen when time-compressed word lists are presented without the support of linguistic context. Although both younger and older adults show a decline in recall accuracy with increasing speech rates, such rates of decline can be five times greater for older adults than for younger adults (Konkle, Beasley, & Bess, 1977; Wingfield, Poon, Lombardi, & Lowe, 1985).

Available data suggest that older people's special vulnerability to time-compressed speech is not simply a consequence of age-related differences in hearing acuity. That is, when younger and older adults are matched for hearing acuity (i.e., comparing younger adults with hearing losses that match those of an older group, or comparing normally-hearing young adults with older adults with no audiometric signs of presbycusis), older subjects continue to show a differentially greater vulnerability to time-compressed speech as compared to younger adults (Gordon-Salant & Fitzgibbons, 1993; Konkle et al., 1977; Luterman, Welsh, & Melrose, 1966; Sticht & Gray, 1969).

It is well known that age differences in recall are dramatically reduced by the presence of environmental support such as that offered by subjects' real-world knowledge or supportive context (Craik & Jennings, 1992). It should thus not be surprising that an important factor in speech rate effects and age of the listeners is the role played by linguistic context in helping younger and older adults overcome what otherwise would be very severe effects of overloading perceptual processing rates. Although older subjects continue to show differentially greater difficulty with rapid speech than the young, age effects are significantly reduced when words are presented in a sentence context (Wingfield et al., 1985).

Studies we and others have conducted have shown that older listeners make especially good use of the prosodic pattern of normal speech to help comprehension at all times, but especially when listening conditions are difficult (Cohen & Faulkner, 1986; Stine & Wingfield, 1987; Wingfield, Lahar, & Stine, 1989). (*Prosody* is a generic term that includes the intonation pattern, or pitch contour of speech. Prosody also includes word stress and variations in speech timing, such as the pauses that sometimes follow the ends of major linguistic elements or the lengthening of final vowels in words that precede clause boundaries.) It should be noted that although older people can be shown to benefit from effective use of stress and other prosodic features to aid in speech comprehension (e.g., Cohen & Faulkner, 1986), exaggerated stress and intonation that crosses over the line to patronizing "elderspeak" will risk demeaning and hence alienating older listeners (see Kemper & Kemtes in this volume).

An important corollary to older listeners' effective use of normal prosody to aid speech comprehension is the finding that older listeners' comprehension is especially disturbed when speech is delivered with an anomalous or unusual prosodic pattern (e.g., Wingfield, Wayland, & Stine, 1992). This finding serves to caution that potential age effects should be taken into account when using concatenated speech in automated telephone menus where normal prosody is absent or poorly simulated.

To get a sense of how older (and younger) listeners may get overloaded by receiving too much information too fast, we had younger and older subjects listen to and recall sentences that contained the same number of words (16 to 18 words) but that varied in the number of propositions, or idea units, they contained (4, 6, 8, or 10 propositions). We also presented the speech at three different speech rates: a fast-normal rate of 200 wpm, and then time-compressed to two very rapid rates of 300 and 400 wpm (Stine, Wingfield, & Poon, 1986). This allowed us to measure speech rate not simply in terms of words or syllables per second, but in terms of the number of propositions delivered per unit time. This way of measuring input rate illustrates how one can increase speech processing load either by increasing the propositional (informational) density of the speech, or by increasing the speech rate, or both.

Figure 4 is taken from Wingfield and Stine (1992), in which we plotted subjects' recall for the content of spoken sentences as a function of speech input rate expressed as propositions per second. The values shown on the abscissa are thus a compound product of the number of propositions contained in the sentences and the presentation rate of these sentences. The top curve in Figure 4 shows a best-fit linear function for the percentage of propositions recalled from the speech and the speech presentation rate for a group of university undergraduates ("young" subjects). Figure 4 also shows data for two groups of healthy elderly adults with good levels of education and vocabulary scores. The lowest curve shows data for a group of older adults matched with the young for years of formal education and scores on a standard vocabulary test ("matched elderly"). We can clearly see by comparing the young adults and this matched elderly group that the elderly subjects had poorer recall performance than the young group regardless of speech rate. It can also be seen, however, that the difference is smaller at the slower presentation rates (e.g., .78 propositions per second) than at the faster rates (e.g., 3.91 propositions per second). That is, the matched elderly's recall curve has a steeper slope than that of

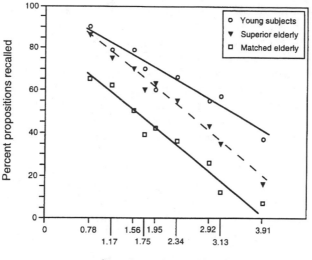

FIGURE 4. Mean percentage of propositions recalled as a function of speech input rate measured as propositions per second. Data are shown for a group of young subjects and a group of elderly subjects who were matched for years of education and vocabulary scores (the upper and lower solid lines). The middle (dashed) line shows performance for a group of elderly subjects who were superior to the young and matched elderly group in years of education and vocabulary scores. (From Figure 7.1 of Wingfield & Stine, 1992, p. 107.)

the young subjects. This was confirmed in an analysis of variance by a significant age-by-speech rate interaction for these two groups along with main effects of age and of speech rate.

Of special note is a second group of elderly subjects represented by the middle broken line in Figure 4. This curve represents the performance of the second group of elderly adults. These subjects were of the same age as the first elderly group. They differed in that they had especially high verbal scores and levels of education that exceeded those of the young subjects and the matched elderly group. This group is labeled in Figure 4 as "superior elderly." The fact that the performance curve for this group comes closer to that of the young subjects is interesting, but it should not be surprising in view of the general finding that age differences in recall performance tend to be smaller for elderly subjects with especially good levels of education and verbal ability (Hultsch & Dixon, 1990). Indeed, at the slowest rate of .78 propositions per second (a 4-proposition sentence heard at 200 wpm) there was virtually no age difference at all. These data correspond well with the view that older adults with high vocabulary scores show a smaller decline in memory performance with advancing age than those with lower scores (West, Crook, & Barron, 1992; Zelinski & Gilewski, 1988).

In spite of this difference in overall performance levels between the two elderly groups, however, the two elderly groups showed exactly the same rates of decline in recall performance with increasing input rates. That is, education and verbal ability may affect the overall level of recall performance (as measured by the y-intercepts of the performance curves), but not processing speed (as measured by the slopes of the lines).

These speech-rate data demonstrate an age-sensitive vulnerability to cognitive overload from too much presented too rapidly. This overload problem may contribute to recency effects reflected in elderly adults' greater tendency than the young to endorse the final alternatives offered in multiple-choice selections in telephone surveys (see Knäuper in this volume).

☐ Does Slowing Speech Help?

If older subjects' comprehension is especially vulnerable to rapid speech, one is bound to ask whether slowing the speech input will help. The answer to this question is "yes," but only if the slowing is done in a principled way. For example, Schmitt and McCrosky (1981) slowed speech by resampling the speech signal and uniformly increasing the durations of all of the speech elements—words, syllables and silent periods—by proportionally equal amounts. Their results were mixed: although slowing the speech helped older adults' comprehension (Schmitt & McCrosky, 1981), slowing the speech by too much appeared to risk making the comprehension worse (Schmitt, 1983). The studies by Schmitt and colleagues also supply an important caution about taking subjects' own impressions at face value. That is, there were instances in which older subjects said that they preferred the speech with slower rates and that they felt they were easier to comprehend. However, when the results were tabulated, these subjects had not actually scored better for comprehension with the slower speech (Schmitt & Carroll, 1985; Schmitt & Moore, 1989).

This mixed evidence for the value of slowing might appear to run counter to reports in the literature (Cohen, 1979) and to the intuition of investigators and their older subjects that slower speech rates yield better comprehension than rapid speech rates (Obler et al., 1991). The reason for these apparently mixed findings is that how the speech is slowed is as important as how much the speech is slowed. We can illustrate this point with some unpublished data from our own laboratory in which we time-compressed speech from an original speaking rate of 165 wpm to a very rapid speech rate of 300 wpm. This was done by digitizing the speech and reiteratively removing small unnoticed segments of the speech signal equally across speech and silent intervals so as to reproduce the speech in 55% of its original playing time without disturbing the overall prosodic pattern. The subjects' task was simply to listen to the speech passage and when it was finished to recall as much of the information from the passage as possible.

Our goal in this study was to determine whether subjects' performance for time-compressed speech would be improved if we inserted silent periods at positions in the speech passages that corresponded to natural linguistic constituents, such as after major clauses and between sentences. Studies with young adults would certainly suggest that this would be so (Overmann, 1971; see also Aaronson, Markowitz, & Shapiro, 1971). We had, however, two specific interests. The first was to determine whether older listeners would benefit from time-restoration in the same manner as younger adults, and the second was to determine the effects of where time was restored.

The data from this experiment are shown in Figure 5. The left panel shows results for a group of young adults who were university students, and the right panel shows results for a group of community-

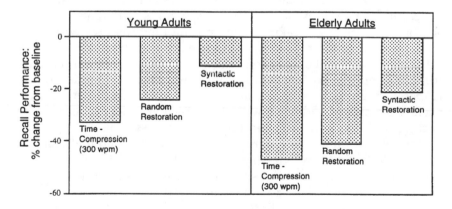

CONDITION

FIGURE 5. Percent reduction in recall performance for time-compressed speech heard at 300 wpm relative to a noncompressed original rate of 165 wpm, and when processing time was restored at random points or at syntactically salient points in the speech message. Data for young adults are shown in the left panel and data for a comparable group of elderly adults are shown in the right panel.

dwelling elderly adults with vocabulary scores and years of formal education completed equal to or superior to the young subjects. Our goal was to insure that any age differences obtained would not be attributable to the elderly group being at a disadvantage in terms of general verbal ability.

The first bar on the left in each of the two panels represents a difference score between the number of propositions subjects were able to recall from the narrative passages presented at 165 wpm and the number they were able to recall when comparable passages were presented time-compressed to 300 wpm. We can see that both the young and elderly subjects' recall accuracy declined. We can also see that the elderly subjects showed a differentially greater proportional decline than that of the young subjects as measured against each groups' own performance baselines for the normal speech rate. This is a finding that would be expected from prior literature on age and speech-rate effects previously cited (e.g., Gordon-Salant & Fitzgibbons, 1993; Konkle et al., 1977; Wingfield et al., 1985).

We used two schemes for time restoration. In one case, which we called *syntactic restoration,* we restored available processing time by using a speech-editing computer program to insert silent periods at the ends of clauses and sentences. We distributed this time proportionally according to the length of a segment such that we paused proportionally longer following sentence boundaries than clause boundaries. Overall, however, the total time restored was equivalent to the loss of processing time represented by the playing-time differences between the original passage speaking-time and the time-compressed version. In the second restoration scheme, referred to as *random restoration,* we introduced pauses of exactly the same durations as in the syntactic restoration condition except that the pauses were inserted randomly with respect to linguistic content. (A number of passages were presented under each of the above conditions, with the particular passages heard under each condition varied and counterbalanced across subjects.)

Our data are shown in Figure 5, where it can be seen that restoring time at syntactic boundaries (syntactic restoration) brought both age groups closer to their normal speech-rate baselines than restoring the same amount of time at random points relative to the linguistic content. We can also observe, however, that time-restoration at syntactic points brought the young subjects closer to their baselines than was the case for the elderly subjects. In fact, when we conducted a follow-up study in which we increased the pause durations at syntactic points equivalent to restoring 125% of lost time, the young subjects returned completely to their baseline levels for noncompressed speech. The elderly, although getting closer to their baseline performance, did not fully recover to that point. Our emphasis on higher level slowing should thus not discount the complex nature of aging effects in auditory processing that could interact negatively with time-compressed speech at lower levels as well (cf. Schneider et al., 1994). The consequences of such age-related changes in lower level processing will be bound to place limits on recovery no matter how much processing time is made available to the listener.

We introduced these data to make two points. The first is that slowing speech is of benefit to older listeners as well as to the young, but that *where* processing time is supplied is as important as how much time is supplied. The second point is that rapid speech can result in a processing overload for older subjects for which even insertion of lengthy pauses at periodic intervals may not be a complete antidote. For these reasons, presentation rate and the manner of presentation should be considered important factors when designing speech materials for communication with older listeners.

☐ Summary: Five Principles of Age and Spoken Language Comprehension

Our goal in this chapter was to review recent research pertaining to the comprehension of spoken language by healthy older adults. In the course of this review we have addressed several known areas of age-related decline. These included declines in auditory acuity, the capacity of working memory, and the rate at which speech input can be processed. In this concluding section we wish to draw from these data to highlight five important principles relating to adult aging and spoken language comprehension.

1. Adult aging is often accompanied by declines in auditory acuity that may especially affect sensory processing for speech. Except in cases of neuropathology, however, linguistic knowledge remains preserved in older adulthood. This combination of areas of loss and preservation leads to a spontaneous use by older adults of top-down information drawn from linguistic context to supplement the impoverished bottom-up signal. This top-down/bottom-up interaction also characterizes natural language processing by younger adults under difficult listening conditions.
2. Slower processing rates and greater susceptibility to working memory overload emphasizes the importance of designing speech materials that will not overly stress the processing system. Unlike reading, where one can backtrack on the printed page to re-read a sentence

that was unclear in meaning, in speech perception any such "look back" must be done in memory. In this regard one should thus avoid the use of language structures that place a heavy burden on memory capacity. These would include very long sentences, sentences whose comprehension requires memory for referents that occurred far previously in the passage, and sentences with especially high propositional density or complex syntax.

3. The presence of normal prosody (intonation, timing, stress) has been shown to help older listeners by aiding in the rapid detection of the linguistic structure and the semantic focus of a question or statement. It is important, however, to avoid an exaggerated prosody that crosses the line into patronizing "elderspeak." Abnormal prosody can occur with automated telephone systems using synthesized or concatenated natural speech. Research has shown that while anomalous prosody can interfere with speech comprehension for both younger and older adults, it can be especially damaging to the older adults.

4. It is important to avoid simple principals, such as "slower is better." We have shown that offering older adults additional time to process rapid speech input by pausing at periodic intervals is helpful. We have also seen, however, that where one pauses in a speech message is as important as how long one pauses. Pausing for a beat or two at the ends of sentences, clauses, and other main thought units in a spoken presentation will facilitate understanding and retention for what has been heard.

5. Although one can form certain generalities regarding sensory and cognitive change in adult aging, individual differences in these regards can be very wide. Thus, for example, many older adults retain good hearing acuity for speech and relatively good capacity in tests of working memory. As such, one cannot design speech materials adapted to "the elderly." One can, however, design materials that respect processing limitations for adult listeners regardless of age. These principles may take on more importance for some individuals than others, but they will be important to all.

☐ Acknowledgments

The author's research is supported by NIH Grant R37 AG04517 from the National Institute on Aging. The author also gratefully acknowledges support from the W. M. Keck Foundation. Christine Koh, Kristen Prentice, Debra Titone, and Patricia Tun are thanked for their help and valuable input in the preparation of this chapter.

☐ References

Aaronson, D., Markowitz, M., & Shapiro, H. (1971). Perception and immediate recall of normal and compressed auditory sequences. *Perception and Psychophysics, 9*, 338–344.

Abney, S. P., & Johnson, M. (1991). Memory requirements and local ambiguities of parsing strategies. *Journal of Psycholinguistic Research, 20*, 233–250.

Baddeley, A. D. (1986). *Working memory*. Oxford, England: Oxford University Press.

Bergman, M. (1980). *Aging and the perception of speech*. Baltimore: University Park Press.

Bergman, M., Blumenfeld, V. G., Cascardo, D., Dash, B., Levitt, H., & Margulies, M. K. (1976). Age-related decrements in hearing for speech. *Journal of Gerontology, 31*, 533–538.

Bransford, J. D., Barclay, J. R., & Franks, J. J. (1972). Sentence memory: A constructive versus interpretive approach. *Cognitive Psychology, 3*, 193–209.

Bransford, J. D., & Franks, J. J. (1971). The abstraction of linguistic ideas. *Cognitive Psychology, 2*, 331–350.

Caplan, D., & Waters, G. S. (1990). Short-term memory and language comprehension: A critical review of the neuropsychological literature. In G. Vallar & T. Shallice (Eds.), *Neuropsychological impairments of short-term memory* (pp. 337–389). Cambridge, England: Cambridge University Press.

Carpenter, P. A., Miyaki, A., & Just, M. A. (1994). Working memory constraints in comprehension: Evidence from individual differences, aphasia, and aging. In M. Gernsbacher (Ed.), *Handbook of psycholinguistics* (pp. 1075–1122). San Diego, CA: Academic Press.

Cavanaugh, J. P. (1972). Relation between the immediate memory span and the memory search rate. *Psychological Review, 79*, 525–530.

Cohen, G. (1979). Language comprehension in old age. *Cognitive Psychology, 11*, 412–429.

Cohen, G., & Faulkner, D. (1986). Does "elderspeak" work? The effect of intonation and stress on comprehension and recall of spoken discourse in old age. *Language and Communication, 6*, 91–98.

Cox, R. M., Alexander, G. C., & Gilmore, C. (1987). Intelligibility of average talkers in typical listening environments. *Journal of the Acoustical Society of America, 81*, 1598–1608.

Craik, F. I. M. (1977). Age differences in human memory. In J. E. Birren & K. W. Schaie (Eds.), *Handbook of the psychology of aging* (pp. 384–420). New York: Van Nostrand Reinhold.

Craik, F. I. M., & Jennings, J. M. (1992). Human memory. In F. I. M. Craik and T. A. Salthouse (Eds.), *The handbook of aging and cognition* (pp. 51–110). Hillsdale, NJ: Erlbaum.

Cutler, A. (1990). Exploiting prosodic probabilities in speech segmentation. In G. Altmann (Ed.), *Cognitive models of speech processing: Psycholinguistic and computational perspectives* (pp. 105–121). Cambridge, MA: MIT Press.

Daneman, M., & Carpenter, P. A. (1980). Individual differences in working memory and reading. *Journal of Verbal Learning and Verbal Behavior, 19*, 450–466.

Daneman, M., & Merikle, P. M. (1996). Working memory and language comprehension: A meta-analysis. *Psychonomic Bulletin and Review, 3*, 422–433.

Dubno, J. R., Dirks, D. D., & Morgan, D. E. (1982). Effects of mild hearing loss and age on speech recognition in noise. *Journal of the Acoustical Society of America, 172*, 34–35.

Duquesnoy, A. J. (1983). The intelligibility of sentences in quiet and noise in aged listeners. *Journal of the Acoustical Society of America, 74*, 1136–1144.

Fisher, D. L., & Glaser, R. A. (1996). Molar and latent models of cognitive slowing:

Implications for aging, dementia, depression, development, and intelligence. *Psychonomic Bulletin and Review, 3,* 458–480.

Gernsbacher, M. A. (Ed.). (1994). *Handbook of psycholinguistics.* San Diego, CA: Academic Press.

Gick, M. L., Craik, F. I. M., & Morris, R. G. (1988). Task complexity and age differences in working memory. *Memory and Cognition, 16,* 353–361.

Gordon-Salant, S. (1987). Age-related differences in speech recognition performance as a function of test format and paradigm. *Ear and Hearing, 8,* 270–276.

Gordon-Salant, S., & Fitzgibbons, P. J. (1993). Temporal factors and speech recognition performance in young and elderly listeners. *Journal of Speech and Hearing Research, 36,* 1276–1285.

Gow, D. W., & Gordon, P. C. (1995). Lexical and prelexical influences on word segmentation: Evidence from priming. *Journal of Experimental Psychology: Human Perception and Performance, 21,* 344–359.

Grosjean, F. (1980). Spoken word recognition processes and the gating paradigm. *Perception and Psychophysics, 38,* 299–310.

Grosjean, F. (1985). The recognition of words after their acoustic offset: Evidence and implications. *Perception and Psychophysics, 38,* 299–310.

Hartley, J. (1993). Aging and prose memory: Tests of the resource-deficit hypothesis. *Psychology and Aging, 8,* 538–551.

Hultsch , D., & Dixon, R. A. (1990). Learning and memory in aging. In J. E. Birren & K. W. Schaie (Eds.), *Handbook of the psychology of aging* (3rd ed., pp. 258–274). New York: Academic Press.

Just, M. A., & Carpenter, P. A. (1992). A capacity theory of comprehension: Individual differences in working memory. *Psychological Review, 99,* 122–149.

Kemper, S., Kynette, D., Rash, S., Sprott, R., & O'Brien, K. (1989). Life-span changes to adults' language: Effects of memory and genre. *Applied Psycholinguistics, 10,* 49–66.

Kempler, D., & Zelinski, E. M. (1994). Language in dementia and normal aging. In F. A. Huppert, C. Brayne, & D. W. O'Connor (Eds.), *Dementia and normal aging* (pp. 331–365). New York: Cambridge University Press.

Kerr, B. (1973). Processing demands during mental operations. *Memory and Cognition, 1,* 401–412.

Konkle, D. F., Beasley, D. S., & Bess, F. H. (1977). Intelligibility of time-altered speech in relation to chronological aging. *Journal of Speech and Hearing Research, 20,* 108–115.

Lieberman, P. (1963). Some effects of semantic and grammatical context on the production and perception of speech. *Language and Speech, 6,* 172–187.

Light, L. L. (1991). Memory and aging: Four hypotheses in search of data. *Annual Review of Psychology, 42,* 333–376.

Light, L. L., & Anderson, P. A. (1985). Working memory capacity, age, and memory for discourse. *Journal of Gerontology, 40,* 737–747.

Light, L. L., & Capps, J. L. (1986). Comprehension of pronouns in young and older adults. *Developmental Psychology, 22,* 580–585.

Lindblom, B., Brownlee, S., Davis, B., & Moon, S. J. (1992). Speech transforms. *Speech Communication, 11,* 357–368.

Lindenberger, U., & Baltes, P. B. (1994). Sensory functioning and intelligence in old age: A strong connection. *Psychology and Aging, 9,* 339–355.

Luterman, D. M., Welsh, O. L., & Melrose, J. (1966). Responses of aged males to time-altered speech. *Journal of Speech and Hearing Research, 9,* 226–230.

Marslen-Wilson, W. D. (1987). Functional parallelism in spoken word recognition. *Cognition, 25,* 71–102.

Martin, R. C. (1990). Neuropsychological evidence on the role of short-term memory in sentence processing. In G. Vallar & T. Shallice (Eds.), *Neuropsychological impair-*

ments of short-term memory (pp. 390–427). Cambridge, England: Cambridge University Press.

Miller, G. A. (1951). *Language and communication.* New York: McGraw-Hill.

Norman, S., Kemper, S., Kynette, D., Cheung, H., & Anagnopoulos, C. (1991). Syntactic complexity and adults' running memory span. *Journal of Gerontology: Psychological Sciences, 46,* P346–P351.

Obler, L. K., Fein, D., Nicholas, M., & Albert, M. L. (1991). Auditory comprehension and aging: Decline in syntactic processing. *Applied Psycholinguistics, 12,* 433–452.

Overmann, R. A. (1971). Processing time as a variable in the comprehension of time-compressed speech. In E. Foulke (Ed.), *Proceedings of the 2nd Louisville Conference on Rate and/or Frequency-Controlled Speech* (pp. 103–118). Louisville, KY: University of Louisville.

Perry, A. R., & Wingfield, A. (1994). Contexual encoding by young and elderly adults as revealed by cued and free recall. *Aging and Cognition, 1,* 120–139.

Picheny, M. A., Durlach, N. I., & Braida, L. D. (1986). Speaking clearly for the hard of hearing II: Acoustic characteristics of clear and conversational speech. *Journal of Speech and Hearing Research, 29,* 434–446.

Pichora-Fuller, M. K., Schneider, B. A., & Daneman, M. (1995). How young and old adults listen to and remember speech in noise. *Journal of the Acoustical Society of America, 97,* 593–607.

Pinker, S. (1994). *The language instinct.* New York: William Morrow.

Pollack, I., & Pickett, J. M. (1963). The intelligibility of excerpts from conversation. *Language and Speech, 6,* 165–171.

Salthouse, T. A. (1991). *Theoretical perspectives on cognitive aging.* Hillsdale, NJ: Erlbaum.

Salthouse, T. A. (1994). The aging of working memory. *Neuropsychology, 8,* 535–543.

Schmitt, J. F. (1983). The effects of time compression and time expansion on passage comprehension by elderly listeners. *Journal of Speech and Hearing Research, 26,* 373–377.

Schmitt, J. F., & Carroll, M. R. (1985). Older listeners' ability to comprehend speaker-generated rate alteration of passages. *Journal of Speech and Hearing Research, 28,* 309–312.

Schmitt, J. F., & McCrosky, R. L. (1981). Sentence comprehension in elderly listeners: The factor of rate. *Journal of Gerontology, 36,* 441–445.

Schmitt, J. F., & Moore, J. R. (1989). Natural alteration of speaking rate: The effect on passage comprehension by listeners over 75 years of age. *Journal of Speech and Hearing Research, 32,* 445–450.

Schneider, B. A., Pichora-Fuller, M. K., & Kowalchuk, D. (1994). Gap detection and the precedence effect in young and old adults. *Journal of the Acoustical Society of America, 95,* 980–991.

Sekuler, R., & Blake, R. (1994). *Perception* (3rd ed.). New York: McGraw-Hill.

Sticht, T. G., & Gray, B. B. (1969). The intelligibility of time compressed speech as a function of age and hearing loss. *Journal of Speech and Hearing Research, 12,* 443–448.

Stine, E. A. L., & Wingfield, A. (1987). Process and strategy in memory for speech among younger and older adults. *Psychology and Aging, 2,* 272–279.

Stine, E. A. L., & Wingfield, A. (1990). How much do working memory deficits contribute to age differences in discourse memory? *European Journal of Cognitive Psychology, 2,* 289–304.

Stine, E. A. L., Wingfield, A., & Poon, L. W. (1986). How much and how fast: Rapid processing of spoken language in later adulthood. *Psychology and Aging, 1,* 303–311.

Tun, P. A., Wingfield, A., & Stine, E. A. L. (1991). Speech-processing capacity in younger and older adults: A dual-task study. *Psychology and Aging, 6,* 3–9.

U.S. Congress, Office of Technology Assessment (1986, May). *Hearing impairment and elderly people—A background paper* (OTA-BP-BA-30). Washington, DC: U.S. Government Printing Office.

van Dijk, T. A., & Kintsch, W. (1983). *Strategies of discourse comprehension.* New York: Academic Press.

Waters, G. S., & Caplan, D. (1993, October). *Comprehension of garden path structures in a patient with an impairment of short-term memory.* Poster presented at the Academy of Aphasia Meeting, Tucson, AZ.

Waters, G. S., & Caplan, D. (1996). The capacity theory of sentence comprehension: Critique of Just and Carpenter (1992). *Psychological Review, 103,* 761–772.

West, R. L., Crook, T. H., & Barron, K. L. (1992). Everyday memory performance across the lifespan: Effects of age and noncognitive individual differences. *Psychology and Aging, 7,* 72–82.

Wingfield, A., Aberdeen, J. S., & Stine, E. A. L. (1991). Word onset gating and linguistic context in spoken word recognition by young and elderly adults. *Journal of Gerontology: Psychological Sciences, 46,* P127–P129.

Wingfield, A., Alexander, A. H., & Cavigelli, S. (1994). Does memory constrain utilization of top-down information in spoken word recognition? Evidence from normal aging. *Language and Speech, 37,* 221–235.

Wingfield, A., Lahar, C. J., & Stine, E. A. L. (1989). Age and decision strategies in running memory for speech. *Journal of Gerontology: Psychological Sciences, 44,* P106–P113.

Wingfield, A., Poon, L. W., Lombardi, L., & Lowe, D. (1985). Speed of processing in normal aging: Effects of speech rate, linguistic structure, and processing time. *Journal of Gerontology, 40,* 579–585.

Wingfield, A., & Stine, E. A. L. (1991). Expert systems in nature: Spoken language processing and adult aging. In J. D. Sinnott & J. C. Cavanaugh (Eds.), *Bridging paradigms: Positive development in adulthood and cognitive aging* (pp. 237–258). New York: Praeger.

Wingfield, A., & Stine, E. A. L. (1992). Age differences in perceptual processing and memory for spoken language. In R. L. West & J. D. Sinnott (Eds.), *Everyday memory and aging: Current research and methodology* (pp. 101–123). New York: Springer-Verlag.

Wingfield, A., Stine, E. A. L., Lahar, C. J., & Aberdeen, J. S. (1988). Does the capacity of working memory change with age? *Experimental Aging Research, 14,* 103–107.

Wingfield, A., Waters, G. S., & Tun, P. A. (1998). Does working memory work in language comprehension?: Evidence from behavioral neuroscience. In N. Raz (Ed.), *The other side of the error term: Aging and development as model systems in cognitive neuroscience.* Amsterdam: Elsevier.

Wingfield, A., Wayland, S. C., & Stine, E. A. L. (1992). Adult age differences in the use of prosody for syntactic parsing and recall of spoken sentences. *Journal of Gerontology: Psychological Sciences, 47,* P350–P356.

Zelinski, E. M., & Gilewski, M. J. (1988). Memory for prose and aging: A meta-analysis. In M. L. Howe, & C. J. Brainerd (Eds.), *Cognitive development in adulthood* (pp. 133–158). New York: Springer-Verlag.

Zurif, E. B., Swinney, D., Prather, P., Wingfield, A., & Brownell, H. (1995). The allocation of memory resources during sentence comprehension: Evidence from the elderly. *Journal of Psycholinguistic Research, 24,* 165–182.

Susan Kemper
Karen Kemtes

Aging and Message Production and Comprehension

Message production begins with the formulation of a message and includes steps of discourse planning, lexical selection, and syntactic encoding prior to the final step of phonological production. Message comprehension begins with a text, presented aurally or visually, and ends with the recovery of a representation of that text as ideas or propositions. Errors, reflecting attentional lapses, processing limitations, and execution problems, can arise at any stage of production or comprehension. Normative aging processes, arising from general slowing of cognitive processes (Salthouse, 1992), reductions of working memory capacity (Light, 1991), or a breakdown of inhibitory processes (Hasher & Zacks, 1988), may exacerbate production or comprehension problems.

This chapter examines what is currently known about how normal aging affects message production and comprehension and examines how aging affects messages addressed to older adults. It must be noted at the outset that research on aging and message production has, like the study of production processes in general, lagged behind studies of message comprehension and memory because of the difficulties inherent in experimentally manipulating production processes. This chapter focuses on discourse production and comprehension since the effects of aging on syntactic and lexical encoding and processing have been recently reviewed (Kemper, 1992; Kemper & Hummert, 1997). It also reviews what is know about how Alzheimer's disease affects older adults' message production and comprehension. The chapter concludes with a dilemma raised by research in this field.

☐ Changes in Message Production by Older Adults

Discourse encompasses a variety of communication skills, ranging from opening and closing conversations, maintaining and shifting topics, and telling stories, to establishing and modifying personal relationships, conveying individual and group identity, gaining and avoiding compliance, and being polite, saving face, or giving offense. To date, little research has examined older adults' discourse skills.

There is some evidence that discourse skills increase with age: older adults create elaborate narrative structures that include hierarchically elaborated episodes with beginnings describing initiating events and motivating states, developments detailing the protagonists' goals and actions, and endings summarizing the outcomes of the protagonists' efforts; evaluative codas are often attached to older adults' narratives which assess the contemporary significance of these stories (Kemper & Anagnopoulos, 1997; Kemper, 1990; Kemper, Rash, Kynette, & Norman, 1990; Pratt, Boyes, Robins, & Manchester, 1989; Pratt & Robins, 1991). Narrative stories told by older adults are evaluated more positively, preferred by listeners, and are more memorable than those told by young adults (Kemper & Anagnopoulos, 1997; Kemper et al., 1990; Pratt et al., 1989; Pratt & Robins, 1991).

Other discourse skills appear to be vulnerable to aging. Older adults often have difficulty with referential communication tasks. In one such referential communication task, Hupet, Chantraine, and Nef (1993) tracked how dyads of young and older adults formulated mutually acceptable labels for abstract drawings. The older adults benefited less from repetition of the task than the young adults; whereas the young adults added new information to previously used descriptions, the older adults tended to supply totally new labels. The older adults' problems with this task may have resulted from forgetting of the old labels from trial to trial or from their inability to inhibit irrelevant thoughts or associations, including the new descriptions.

In a series of studies, Kemper and her colleagues (Kemper, Othick, Gerhing, Gubarchuk, & Billington, in press; Kemper, Othick, Warren, Gubarchuk, & Gerhing, 1996; Kemper, Vandeputte, Rice, Cheung, & Gubarchuk, 1995) have compared young-young, old-old, and young-old dyads on a referential communication task involving giving map directions. Whereas young adults spontaneously adopt a simplified speech style when addressing older adults versus age-equivalent peers, older adults do not appear to code-switch. This may be due to a number of factors, including: (a) Older adults may not be sensitive to the same situational cues that elicit code-switching from the young adults; (b) Older adults may not be able to vary their grammatical complexity or semantic content while simultaneously executing the complex task; (c) Older speakers may have "optimized" their speech to peers as a result of extensive practice at communicating with other older adults and adults experiencing communicative problems; hence, shifting to a nonoptimal speech style when addressing younger adults would not be an appropriate strategy; (d) Older adults may be unwilling to shift to a simplified speech style when they are addressing peers since this form of speech may resemble patronizing talk (Ryan, Hummert, & Boich, 1995) or secondary baby talk (Caporael, 1981).

The discourse of young and older adults differs in other ways. For instance, dyads of older adults mix talk about the past along with talk about the present to achieve a shared sense of meaning and personal worth which is lacking in the discourse of young adults (Boden & Bielby, 1986). In addition, conversations with older adults are often marked by "painful self-disclosures" of bereavement, ill-health, immobility, and assorted personal and family problems (Coupland, Coupland, & Giles, 1991). Painful self-disclosures may serve several different goals for communicators (Coupland, Coupland, & Grainger, 1991; Shaner, 1996), for example, maintaining face by contrasting personal strengths and competencies with past problems and limitations, and coping with personal losses and difficulties. Yet, painful self-disclosures also maintain and reinforce negative age stereotypes about the elderly as weak and disabled (Shaner, 1996). Consequently, such self-disclosures can suppress conversational interactions and limit the quality of intergenerational communication (Nussbaum, Hummert, Williams, & Harwood, 1996).

Intergenerational communication may also be limited by other attributes of older adults' speech. Giles and Williams (1994) have observed that young people often feel patronized by older adults who may adopt a "not-listening," "disapproving," or "overprotecting" style when interacting with young adults. Age disclosure on the part of the older partner, also noted by Coupland, Coupland, and Grainger (1991), may, like painful self-disclosures, lead to unsatisfactory intergenerational interactions by emphasizing the differences between older and young partners. Collins and Gould (1994) note, however, that younger and older women appear to conform to the same norms regarding disclosures of negative and intimate life events and suggest that intergenerational communication may not conform to the stereotype that older adults dominate conversations with negative stories about the past.

A final discourse style often presumed to accompany aging is verbosity, or repetitious, prolonged, off-target speech. However, recent research (Arbuckle & Gold, 1993; Arbuckle, Gold, & Andres, 1986; Gold, Andres, Arbuckle, & Schwartzman, 1988; Gold & Arbuckle, 1992; Gold, Arbuckle, & Andres, 1994) has suggested that verbosity is not a general characteristic of older adults but is an extreme form of talkativeness that results from intellectual decline associated with frontal lobe impairments (see Arbuckle & Gold, 1993, for a review of these issues). Frontal lobe impairments disrupt inhibitory processes and lead to preservative behaviors on other tasks. Verbosity can be characterized as involving a loss of the ability to inhibit competing responses; hence, an age-related loss of frontal lobe function may lead to increased verbosity among older adults. Verbosity, like talk of the past, painful self-disclosures, and age disclosures, may disrupt social interactions and lead to a loss of interpersonal contact and social support. Unlike the other discourse practices of older adults, however, verbosity appears to reflect changes in message production processes that lie at the juncture between normal and pathological aging.

☐ Changes in Message Comprehension by Older Adults

Discourse comprehension involves several steps, from decoding the auditory or visual stimulus to constructing a syntactic, semantic, and discourse representation of the message. The following sections review some of the recent research on studies of older adults' discourse comprehension which have tended to focus separately on issues of auditory-based discourse and text-based discourse.

Auditory-Based Discourse

Stine and Wingfield (1990) note that there is an apparent paradox of language processing in older adults. Older adults have difficulty with some effortful processes, such as semantic encoding, and are slower in many cognitive tasks, but normal older adults have relatively few difficulties understanding everyday discourse. Wingfield and colleagues have focused on empirical investigations of how the semantic, syntactic, and prosodic structure of speech influence adults' discourse comprehension. Stine, Wingfield, and Poon (1986), for example, tested whether increased propositional density of text and increased presentation rates disrupt older adults' recall of auditorily presented text. Stine et al. (1986) found that older adults were not differentially influenced by the high propositionally dense text, though recall performance was poorer for speeded text presentation. In a related study, Wingfield and Stine (1986) found that older adults, like young, segment auditory-based prose at syntactic boundaries and that recall performance did not decline as the rate of presentation increased. Stine and Wingfield (1988) found that while there are minimal quantitative age differences in the recall of propositionally dense speech, there are significant qualitative differences for older relative to younger adults.

Older adults' comprehension of everyday information, such as television newscasts, remains well preserved. Stine, Wingfield, and Myers (1990) examined younger and older adults' recall of information from a television newscast which was presented in auditory format, auditory supplemented with a written transcript, or the original auditory and visual recording. Although the written transcript and visual presentation aided younger adults' recall of the information, older adults did not benefit.

The research on discourse comprehension suggests that older adults' language performance does not show an inevitable decline under normal discourse conditions. Older adults' comprehension is compromised when the structure of the discourse is complex and when it is presented at very rapid rates.

Text-Based Discourse

The studies of older adults' text and prose processing have largely shown that text level characteristics, such as propositional content and syntactic complexity or whether the prose is narrative or expository greatly influence older adults' text comprehension. For example, Zelinksi, Light, and Gilewski (1984) have found that older and younger adults recalled qualitatively similar features of the expository text, although older adults recalled less information than younger adults. In a study on younger and older adults' processing of narrative and expository texts, Tun (1989) found that recall was better for narrative than expository texts. Further, younger adults recalled more of the text than older adults irrespective of text type.

The syntactic and semantic content of prose also influences older adults' comprehension. Though overall recall of propositionally dense text may be unimpaired, older adults tend to recall fewer main ideas relative to younger adults (Stine & Wingfield, 1988). Light and Capps (1986) found that older adults had more difficulty than younger adults identifying pronominal referents as text processing load increased. Researchers have also documented deficits in older adults' ability to generate inferences from text (Cohen, 1979; Zacks, Hasher, Doren, Hamm, & Attig, 1987; but see Zelinski, 1988).

Recent research on text comprehension in aging has focused on the text- and reader-level variables that influence processing as it takes place or on-line. Hartley, Stojack, Mushaney, Kiku-Annon, and Lee (1994) compared younger and older adults' recall of prose that was presented in experimenter- and self-paced presentation tasks. They found that older adults recalled less than young adults as the time available for processing increased. At the text level, Stine (1990) found that younger and older adults allocated word-by-word reading times similarly for word-level and more global phrase-level features of the text. Younger adults allocated additional reading time to the ends of phrases, clauses, and sentences, whereas older adults paused at clause boundaries only. A related study by Stine, Cheung, and Henderson (1995) extended this earlier research by showing that specific word-, phrase-, sentence-, and discourse-level features of text influenced older adults' word-by-word reading times and explicit recall of narrative texts such that overall, older adults tended to allocate less reading time to processing new concepts. Stine-Morrow, Loveless, and Soederberg (1996) demonstrated that younger and older adults' on-line reading times were qualitatively similar in that both age groups allocated more reading time to text sectors with complex syntax, new concepts, and longer words. However, older adults did allocate less reading time, relative to young adults, to new concepts.

☐ Changes in Message Production and Comprehension Due to Alzheimer's Disease

Communication problems are often the first symptoms of a progressive dementia such as Alzheimer's dementia, and communication problems frequently are noted by spouses and other family members (Bayles & Tomoeda, 1991; Orange, 1991; Rau, 1991). Clinical markers of the onset of Alzheimer's disease are difficult to distinguish from nonclinical age-related lapses of attention or memory, "benign senescent forgetfulness" or "nonpathological age-associated memory impairments" (Huppert,

1994; Kral, 1962). Distinguishing "normative" age-related changes to message production from "nonnormative" or pathological changes may be important for the early diagnosis, hence possible treatment, of Alzheimer's disease and related disorders.

Many of the impairments to discourse which have been observed in adults with Alzheimer's dementia may stem from their gross word-finding problems, whereas other problems may stem from attentional deficits and cognitive confusions. The heavy use of deixtic terms such as "this" and "that," the loss of specific reference and loss of cohesion, the prevalence of vague terms and "empty speech," a loss of detail, an increase in repetition and redundancy, and confusing shifts in topic and focus have all been noted as characteristic of the speech of adults with Alzheimer's dementia (Bayles, Boone, Tomoeda, Slauson, & Kaszniak, 1989; Bayles & Kaszniak, 1987; Garcia & Joanette, 1994; Hier, Hagenlocker, & Shindler, 1985; Hutchinson & Jensen, 1980; Nicholas, Obler, Albert, & Helm-Esterbrooks, 1985; Ripich & Terrell, 1988; Ripich, Terrell, & Spinelli, 1983; Ulatowska, Allard, & Donnell, 1988; Ulatowska & Chapman, 1991).

Other discourse-level communication problems have also been linked to Alzheimer's dementia. Whereas healthy older adults follow a story grammar in telling personal narratives, relating setting information, complications, the protagonist's actions, and a resolution, the spontaneous narratives of adults with Alzheimer's dementia characteristically supply only setting information (Ulatowska et al., 1988; Ulatowska & Chapman, 1991) unless they are prompted by their conversational partner (Kemper, Lyons, & Anagnopoulos, 1995). The ability to use or follow a familiar script, or a series of temporally and causally linked events such as eating in a restaurant, going to a movie, or holding a wedding, is also impaired by Alzheimer's dementia (Grafman, Thompson, Weingartner, Martinez, Lawlor, & Sunderland, 1991; Harrold, Anderson, Clancy, & Kempler, 1990), as are spontaneous turn-taking, topic initiation, topic maintenance, topic shifting, conversational repairs, and speech acts, such as requesting, asserting, clarifying, and questioning (Bayles & Kaszniak, 1987).

Some aspects of metalinguistic abilities appear to be preserved in individuals with Alzheimer's dementia. Saunders (1996) has noted that humor, reflecting metalinguistic awareness of cognitive problems, is often used by patients undergoing a neurological examination. Self-deprecatory remarks, making fun of memory lapses, and humorous remarks are often used by patients when they are unable to respond to the clinician's examination questions. A breakdown of self-awareness and metalinguistic skills may contribute to the discourse problems of adults with Alzheimer's dementia; Hamilton (1994a, 1994b) has suggested that the progression of Alzheimer's dementia is indicated by an erosion of metalinguistic skills marked by declines in requests for clarification, references to memory problems, and self-evaluation of skills and abilities. By carefully tracing communication breakdowns during a series of conversations spanning 4½ years between herself and Elsie, a woman with Alzheimer's dementia, Hamilton was able to elucidate four stages to the deterioration of communication.

Stage 1. Elsie was an active participant in the conversations, but one who was bothered by word-finding problems as well as memory lapses; she was aware of her communication problems and attempted to deal with them through excuses, circumlocutions, and other metalinguistic comments. Turn-taking, joking, and speech formalisms were preserved.

Stage 2. Elsie remained an active participant in the conversations, but her awareness of and responses to her memory lapses and word-finding problems had disappeared. Perseverations and excessive repetitions had begun to appear.

Stage 3. Elsie's participation in the conversation was markedly reduced; perseverations were common; formulaic language, e.g., "ready-made" conversational routines, predominated; and neologisms frequently occurred. Politeness markers, expressions of appreciation, and joking routines had disappeared from Elsie's conversation.

Stage 4. Elsie had become a passive participant; lexical language was lost, replaced by a limited repertoire of nonverbal responses, e.g., uhhuh, mhn, mm Hm, mmm, hmm? Elsie was able to draw upon this repertoire to request repetitions and clarifications, take a turn during the conversation, and indicate her interest in her surroundings.

As others have noted, end-stage Alzheimer's dementia is often characterized by mutism, inappropriate nonverbal vocalizations, and, frequently, failures to respond to others (Lamar, Obler, Knoefel, & Albert, 1994).

☐ Changes in Message Production to Older Adults

A special speech register, sometimes termed "elderspeak," has been described as an accommodation to communicating with older adults; elderspeak may be evoked by negative stereotypes of older adults as well as their actual communicative needs and, hence, elderspeak is addressed to healthy older adults as well as those who are or are presumed to be cognitively impaired (Caporael, 1981; Caporael & Culbertson, 1986; Caporael, Lukaszewski, & Culbertson, 1983; Kemper, 1994; Ryan,

Giles, Bartolucci, & Henwood, 1986; Ryan, Bourhis, & Knops, 1991). Elderspeak has been characterized as involving a simplified speech register with exaggerated pitch and intonation, simplified grammar, limited vocabulary, and slow rate of delivery. It appears to be a robust phenomenon that occurs in a wide range of settings involving older adults such as craft classes, legal seminars, and congregate meals as well as in nursing homes for demented and nondemented older adults (Kemper, 1994), although it is most often associated with nursing homes and other health care facilities (Ashburn & Gordon, 1981; Gibb & O'Brien, 1990; Gubrium, 1975; Lanceley, 1985; Ryan, Hummert, & Boich, 1995). Many of the characteristics of elderspeak, such as its slow rate, exaggerated prosody, and simplified syntax and vocabulary, resemble the characteristics of other speech registers such as those directed at young children, foreigners, and household pets (Warren & McCloskey, 1997). Elderspeak is assumed to have these special characteristics because it enhances or facilitates communication with older adults.

Kemper and her collaborators (Kemper, Vandeputte, Rice, Cheung, & Gubarchuk, 1995; Kemper et al., 1996) have begun to examine this claim. They have shown that young adults spontaneously adopt a simplified speech register when addressing older listeners during a referential communication task. The referential communication task used in these studies required the listener to reproduce a route drawn on a map, following directions given by the speaker. Dyads of young-young, older-older, and young-older adults alternated as speakers and listeners. Older adults showed little variation in their speech style whether they were addressing young or older listeners. Young adults, however, adopted a simplified speech style when instructing older listeners; the simplified style not only provided more information in terms of words, utterances, instructions, and location checks on the listener's progress but it also "packaged" this information differently. The young adults paused more often, used shorter sentences, used few complex syntactic constructions, and reduced the informational content of individual utterances by lowering propositional density, a measure of how much information is packed in an utterance. These speech adjustments appeared to benefit the older listeners, who were able to reproduce the maps more accurately than when they were paired with older speakers.

The young adults' use of elderspeak may have been triggered by beliefs about the communicative competence of older adults or by actual communicative problems of their older partners, as signaled by their older partners' behavior during the referential communication task. Older listeners frequently interrupted speakers to repeat the speakers' instructions, request clarification, or express confusion or difficulty with the task. These interruptions may have cued the young adults to simplify their speech. In order to investigate this possibility, Kemper et al. (1996) replicated the study with one major change: listeners were prohibited from interrupting the speaker to request clarification or express confusion. In the second study, young adults again spontaneously adopted a simplified speech register when addressing older listeners during the referential communication task. This speech register resembled other forms of elderspeak in that it was marked by reductions in speaking rate, sentence length, the use of complex syntactic constructions, and propositional density, and by increases in words, utterances, instructions, and repetitions. The young adults' use of elderspeak in the second study was not cued by the actual behavior of the older listeners during the task, since listeners were prohibited from interrupting the speakers. Rather, the young speakers were drawing upon a set of stereotypes of the communicative problems of older adults in order to modify their speech.

In both Kemper, Vandeputte, Rice, Cheung, and Gubarchuk (1995) and Kemper et al. (1996), the young adults' use of elderspeak improved the performance of the older adults on the referential communication task; older listeners performed more accurately when paired with young speakers than when paired with other older adults. The young speakers' decrease in sentence length, grammatical complexity, and propositional density, and their increase in words, utterances, instructions, repetitions, and location checks were associated with lower error scores by the older listeners. Working memory limitations appear to impair the older adults' performance on the referential communication tasks, and it is likely that the young adults' speech accommodations reduced working memory demands because they provided more information and packaged that information into shorter and simpler utterances (Kemper, 1992; Kemper, Anagnopoulos, Lyons, & Heberlein, 1994).

It is important to note that in these studies, the young adults' use of elderspeak was not without cost. Although the older adults did better on the referential communication task when paired with young partners, they reported more expressive and receptive communication problems. The older adults' self-reported communication problems with young partners were associated with shorter sentences, slower speaking rate, higher pitch, greater pitch range, and more speaker repetitions. These stylistic factors appear to trigger older adults' perceptions of themselves as communicatively impaired, leading to increased self-report of expressive and receptive problems. The older adults' self-reported expressive and receptive problems were not associated with the young adults' grammatical complexity or other semantic content and repetitions.

Elderspeak is also modified by practice and task familiarity; when Kemper et al. (in press) gave young adults extended practice on the same referential communication task with older partners, the young adults adopted further simplifications to their speech including further shortening their sentences, further increasing their production of sentence fragments, and shifting to a very slow speaking rate. This "streamlined" form of elderspeak appeared to result from an assessment of the communicative needs of their older partners; when partnered with other young adults, extended practice leads young adults to shift to shorter, more fragmented speech, but speech that was also very terse, highly repetitious, and delivered at a very fast rate.

The use of elderspeak in these studies did enhance the performance of the older adults, but the older adults reported experiencing more expressive and receptive communication problems when they were paired with young partners who used elderspeak. The use of elderspeak appeared to trigger older adults' perceptions of themselves as communicatively impaired and led to increased self-report of expressive and receptive problems by the older adults (Kemper, Vandeputte, Rice, Cheung, & Gubarchuk, 1995; Kemper et al., 1996). The streamlined version of elderspeak which resulted from extended practice had an even more deleterious effect on the older adults' self-assessment of their communicative competence (Kemper et al., in press) than the spontaneous, unpracticed form. These findings lend further support to the "communicative predicament of aging" model of Ryan et al. (1986) (see below). In this case, the "communicative predicament of aging" is that elderspeak led to a decrease in the older adults' self-ratings of communicative competence yet it also improved their performance on the referential communication tasks.

☐ Conclusions

Only through systematic research will it be possible to show which elderspeak or other discourse modifications will help older adults, especially those with Alzheimer's dementia, and which will hurt. There is a danger that the inappropriate use of such elderspeak modifications may impair communication with older adults. Harwood, Giles, and Ryan (1995) argue that the use of elderspeak as well as other age-based behavioral modifications contributes to development of an "old" identity, reinforcing negative stereotypes of older adults and lowering older adults' self-esteem. Following Ryan et al. (1986), they further argue that a downward spiral can result such that elderspeak contributes to the social isolation and cognitive decline of older adults, triggering further speech simplifications. Ryan et al. (1986) term this the "communicative predicament of aging." The predicament is that elderspeak can lead to a negative spiral of perceived and actual communicative impairments, but the failure to use appropriate speech accommodations for older adults may also lead to social isolation and cognitive decline. Other observational studies, as well as simulation studies using scripted interactions, have noted that elderspeak conveys a sense of disrespect towards its recipients, limits their conversational interactions, and implies that they are cognitively impaired (Edwards & Noller, 1993; Gubrium, 1975; Ryan et al., 1991; Ryan, Hamilton, & Kwong See, 1994; Ryan, MacLean, & Orange, 1994). O'Conner and Rigby (1996), following Ryan et al. (1991), suggest that older adults, especially those in nursing homes, adapt to situational demands by becoming more accepting of elderspeak.

The psychosocial consequences of the use of elderspeak are assumed to be offset by its positive benefits for enhancing communication with older adults. Although there is little empirical support for this assumption, caregivers and service providers commonly justify their use of elderspeak by claiming that it helps older adults' comprehension, especially that of older adults with dementia. One way to avoid the communicative predicament of aging would be to adopt appropriate speech modifications: to modulate the use and form of elderspeak based on the actual communicative needs of one's conversational partners rather than stereotypic assumptions about the cognitive impairments of older adults (Orange, Ryan, Meredith, & MacLean, 1995; Ryan, Meredith, MacLean, & Orange, 1995). The available descriptive and observational studies of elderspeak do not evaluate whether young adults can or will tune their speech to the actual communicative needs of older adults. The studies by Kemper and her collaborators (1995, 1996, and in press) suggest that young adults simplify their speech as a result of extended practice with a task and on the basis of stereotypic assumptions about older adults' communicative needs rather than on the basis of actual behavioral cues and the performance of older adults. It may be necessary to disentangle those parameters of elderspeak which actually benefit older adults' performance from those that trigger older adults' negative self-assessments.

☐ Acknowledgments

Preparation of this chapter was supported by grants AG09952 and AG00226 from the National Institute on Aging.

☐ References

Arbuckle, T., & Gold, D. P. (1993). Aging, inhibition, and verbosity. *Journal of Gerontology: Psychological Sciences, 48*, P225–P232.

Arbuckle, T. Y., Gold, D., & Andres, D. (1986). Cognitive functioning of older people in relation to social and personality variables. *Psychology and Aging, 1*, 55–62.

Ashburn, G., & Gordon, A. (1981). Features of a simplified register in speech to elderly conversationalists. *International Journal of Psycholinguistics, 7*, 31–43.

Bayles, K., Boone, D. R., Tomoeda, C., Slauson, T., & Kaszniak, A. W. (1989). Differentiating Alzheimer's patients from the normal elderly and stroke patients with aphasia. *Journal of Speech and Hearing Disorders, 54*, 74–87.

Bayles, K. A., & Kaszniak, A. W. (1987). *Communication and cognition in normal aging and dementia.* Boston: College-Hill.

Bayles, K. A., & Tomoeda, C. K. (1991). Caregiver report of prevalence and appearance order of linguistic symptoms in Alzheimer's patients. *The Gerontologist, 31*, 210–216.

Boden, D., & Bielby, D. D. (1986). The way it was: Topical organization in elderly conversation. *Language and Communication, 6*, 73–89.

Caporael, L. (1981). The paralanguage of caregiving: Baby talk to the institutionalized aged. *Journal of Personality and Social Psychology, 40*, 876–884.

Caporael, L. R., & Culbertson, G. H. (1986). Verbal response modes of baby talk and other speech at institutions for the aged. *Language and Communication, 6*, 99–112.

Caporael, L. R., Lukaszewski, M. P., & Culbertson, G. H. (1983). Secondary babytalk: Judgments of institutionalized elderly and their caregivers. *Journal of Personality and Social Psychology, 44*, 746–754.

Cohen, G. (1979). Language comprehension in old age. *Cognitive Psychology, 11*, 412–429.

Collins, C. L., & Gould, O. N. (1994). Getting to know you: How own age and other's age relate to self-disclosure. *International Journal of Aging and Human Development, 39*, 55–66.

Coupland, J., Coupland, N., & Giles, H. (1991). My life in your hands: Processes of intergenerational self-disclosure. In N. Coupland, J. Coupland, & H. Giles (Eds.), *Language, society, and the elderly* (pp. 75–108). Oxford, England: Basil Blackwell

Coupland, J., Coupland, N., & Grainger, K. (1991). Intergenerational discourse: Contextual versions of ageing and elderliness. *Ageing and Society, II*, 189–208.

Edwards, H., & Noller, P. (1993). Perceptions of overaccommodations used by nurses in communication with the elderly. *Journal of Language and Social Psychology, 1*, 207–223.

Garcia, L. J., & Joanette, Y. (1994). Conversational topic-shifting analysis in dementia. In R. L. Bloom, L. K. Obler, S. de Santi, & J. S. Ehrlich (Eds.), *Discourse analysis and applications: Studies of adult clinical populations* (pp. 161–184). Hillsdale, NJ: Erlbaum.

Gibb, H., & O'Brien, B. (1990). Jokes and reassurances are not enough: Ways in which nurses related through conversation with elderly clients. *Journal of Advanced Nursing, 15*, 1389–1401.

Giles, H., & Williams, A. (1994). Patronizing the young: Forms and evaluations. *International Journal of Aging and Human Development, 39*, 33–54.

Gold, D., Andres, D., Arbuckle, T., & Schwartzman, A. (1988). Measurement and correlates of verbosity in elderly people. *Journal of Gerontology: Psychological Sciences, 43*, 27–33.

Gold, D. P., & Arbuckle, T. Y. (1992). Interactions between personality and cognition and their implications for theories of aging. In E. A. Lovelace (Ed.), *Aging and cognition: Mental processes, self-awareness, and interventions* (pp. 351–377). Amsterdam: North Holland.

Gold, D. P., Arbuckle, T. Y., & Andres, D. (1994). Verbosity in older adults. In M. L. Hummert, J. M. Wiemann, & J. F. Nussbaum (Eds.), *Interpersonal communication in older adulthood: Interdisciplinary theory and research* (pp. 107–129). Thousand Oaks, CA: Sage.

Grafman, J., Thompson, K., Weingartner, H., Martinez, R., Lawlor, B. A., & Sunderland, T. (1991). Script generation as an indicator of knowledge representation in patients with Alzheimer's disease. *Brain and Language, 40,* 344–358.

Gubrium, J. F. (1975). *Living and dying at Murray Manor.* New York: St. Martin's.

Hamilton, H. (1994a). *Conversations with an Alzheimer's patient.* Cambridge, England: Cambridge University Press.

Hamilton, H. (1994b). Requests for clarification as evidence of pragmatic comprehension difficulty: The case of Alzheimer's disease. In R. L. Bloom, L. K. Obler, S. de Santi, & J. S. Ehrlich (Eds.), *Discourse analysis and applications: Studies in adult clinical populations* (pp. 185–200). Hillsdale, NJ: Erlbaum.

Harrold, R. M., Anderson, E. S., Clancy, P., & Kempler, D. (1990). Script knowledge deficits in Alzheimer's disease. *Journal of Clinical and Experimental Neuropsychology, 12,* 397.

Hartley, J. T., Stojack, C. C., Mushaney, T. J., Kiku-Annon, T. A., & Lee (1994). Reading speed and prose memory in older and younger adults. *Psychology and Aging, 9,* 216–223.

Harwood, J., Giles, H., & Ryan, E. B. (1995). Aging, communication, and intergroup theory: Social identity and intergenerational communication. In J. Nussbaum & J. Coupland (Eds.), *Handbook of communication and aging* (pp. 133–159). Hillsdale, NJ: Erlbaum.

Hasher, L., & Zacks, R. T. (1988). Working memory, comprehension, and aging: A review and a new view. In G. H. Bower (Ed.), *The psychology of learning and motivation* (Vol. 22, pp. 193–226). New York: Academic.

Hier, D. B., Hagenlocker, D., & Shindler, A. G. (1985). Language disintegration in dementia: Effects of etiology and severity. *Brain and Language, 25,* 117–133.

Hupet, M., Chantraine, Y., & Nef, F. (1993). References in conversation between young and old normal adults. *Psychology and Aging, 8,* 339–346.

Hutchinson, J. M., & Jensen, M. (1980). A pragmatic evaluation of discourse communication in normal elderly and senile elderly in a nursing home. In L. K. Obler & M. L. Albert (Eds.), *Language and communication in the elderly* (pp. 59–73). Lexington, KY: D. C. Heath.

Kemper, S. (1990). Adults' diaries: Changes made to written narratives across the lifespan. *Discourse Processes, 13,* 207–223.

Kemper, S. (1992). Language and aging. In F. I. M. Craik & T. A. Salthouse (Eds.), *Handbook of aging and cognition* (pp. 213–270). Hillsdale, NJ: Erlbaum.

Kemper, S. (1994). "Elderspeak:" Speech accommodations to older adults. *Aging and Cognition, 1,* 17–28.

Kemper, S., & Anagnopoulos, C. (1997). Linguistic creativity in older adults. In C. Adams-Price (Eds.), *Creativity and aging: Theoretical and empirical perspectives* (pp. 289–310). New York: Springer Publishing.

Kemper, S., Anagnopoulos, C., Lyons, K., & Heberlein, W. (1994). Speech accommodations to dementia. *Journal of Gerontology: Psychological Sciences, 49,* P223–P230.

Kemper, S., & Hummert, M. L. (1997). New directions in research on aging and message production. In J. O. Greene (Ed.), *Message production: Advances in communication theory* (pp. 127–150). Mahwah, NJ: Erlbaum.

Kemper, S., Lyons, K., & Anagnopoulos, C. (1995). Joint story-telling by Alzheimer's patients and their spouses. *Discourse Processes, 20,* 205–217.

Kemper, S., Othick, M., Gerhing, H., Gubarchuk, J., & Billington, C. (in press). Practicing speech accommodations to older adults. *Applied Psycholinguistics.*

Kemper, S., Othick, M., Warren, J., Gubarchuk, J., & Gerhing, H. (1996). Facilitating older adults' performance on a referential communication task through speech accommodations. *Aging, Neuropsychology, and Cognition, 3,* 37–55.

Kemper, S., Rash, S. R., Kynette, D., & Norman, S. (1990). Telling stories: The structure of adults' narratives. *European Journal of Cognitive Psychology, 2,* 205–228.

Kemper, S., Vandeputte, D., Rice, K., Cheung, H., & Gubarchuk, J. (1995). Speech adjustments to aging during a referential communication task. *Journal of Language and Social Psychology, 14,* 40–59.

Lamar, M. A. C., Obler, L. K., Knoefel, J. E., & Albert, M. L. (1994). Communication patterns in end-stage Alzheimer's disease: Pragmatic analyses. In R. L. Bloom, L. K. Obler, S. de Santi, & J. S. Ehrlich (Eds.), *Discourse analysis and applications: Studies in adult clinical populations* (pp. 216–236). Hillsdale, NJ: Erlbaum.

Lanceley, A. (1985). Use of controlling language in the rehabilitation of the elderly. *Journal of Advanced Nursing, 10,* 125–135.

Light, L. (1991). Memory and aging: Four hypotheses in search of data. *Annual Review of Psychology, 42,* 333–377.

Light, L., & Capps, J. L. (1986). Comprehension of pronouns in younger and older adults. *Developmental Psychology, 22,* 580–585.

Nicholas, M., Obler, L. K., Albert, M. L., & Helm-Esterbrooks, N. (1985). Empty speech in Alzheimer's disease and fluent aphasia. *Journal of Speech and Hearing Research, 28,* 405–410.

Nussbaum, J. F., Hummert, M. L., Williams, A., & Harwood, J. (1996). Communication and older adults. In B. R. Burleson (Ed.), *Communication yearbook 19* (pp. 1–47). Newbury Park, CA: Sage.

O'Conner, B. P., & Rigby, H. (1996). Perceptions of baby talk, frequency of receiving baby talk, and self-esteem among community and nursing home residents. *Psychology and Aging, 11,* 147–154.

Orange, J. B. (1991). Perspectives of family members regarding communication changes. In R. Lubinski (Ed.), *Dementia and communication* (pp. 168–187). Philadelphia: Decker.

Orange, J. B., Ryan, E. B., Meredith, S. D., & MacLean, M. J. (1995). Application of the communication enhancement model for long-term care residents with Alzheimer's disease. *Topics in Language Disorders, 15,* 20–35.

Pratt, M. W., Boyes, C., Robins, S., & Manchester, J. (1989). Telling tales: Aging, working memory, and the narrative cohesion of storytellers. *Developmental Psychology, 25,* 628–635.

Pratt, M. W., & Robins, S. L. (1991). That's the way it was: Age differences in the structure and quality of adults' personal narratives. *Discourse Processes, 14,* 73–85.

Rau, M. T. (1991). Impact on families. In R. Lubinski (Ed.), *Dementia and communication* (pp. 152–167). Philadelphia: Decker.

Ripich, D. N., & Terrell, B. Y. (1988). Patterns of discourse cohesion and coherence in Alzheimer's disease. *Journal of Speech and Hearing Disorders, 53,* 8–15.

Ripich, D. N., Terrell, B. Y., & Spinelli, F. (1983). Discourse cohesion in senile dementia of the Alzheimer type. In R. H. Brookshire (Ed.), *Clinical aphasiology conference proceedings* (pp. 316–321). Minneapolis, MN: BRK Publishers.

Ryan, E. B., Bourhis, R. Y., & Knops, U. (1991). Evaluative perceptions of patronizing speech addressed to elders. *Psychology and Aging, 6,* 442–450.

Ryan, E. B., Giles, H., Bartolucci, G., & Henwood, K. (1986). Psycholinguistic and social psychological components of communication by and with the elderly. *Language and Communication, 6,* 1–24.

Ryan, E. B., Hamilton, J. M., & Kwong See, S. (1994). Younger and older adult listeners' evaluations of baby talk addressed to institutionalized elders. *International Journal of Aging and Human Development, 39,* 21–32.

Ryan, E. B., Hummert, M. L., & Boich, L. H. (1995). Communication predicaments of aging: Patronizing behavior toward older adults. *Journal of Language and Social Psychology, 14,* 144–166.

Ryan, E. B., MacLean, M., & Orange, J. B. (1994). Inappropriate accommodation in communication to elders: Inferences about nonverbal correlates. *International Journal of Aging and Human Development, 39,* 273–291.

Ryan, E. B., Meredith, S. D., MacLean, M. J., & Orange, J. B. (1995). Changing the way we talk with elders: Promotion health using the communication enhancement model. *International Journal of Aging and Human Development, 41,* 89–107.

Salthouse, T. A. (1992). *Mechanisms of aging–cognition relations in adulthood.* Hillsdale, NJ: Erlbaum.

Shaner, J. L. (1996). *Painful self-disclosures of older adults: Judgments of perceived motivations and discloser characteristics.* Unpublished doctoral dissertation, Department of Communication Studies, University of Kansas, Lawrence, KS.

Stine, E. A. L. (1990). On-line processing of written text by younger and older adults. *Psychology and Aging, 5,* 68–78.

Stine, E. A. L., & Wingfield, A. (1988). Memorability functions as an indicator of qualitative age differences in text recall. *Psychology and Aging, 3,* 179–183.

Stine, E. A. L., & Wingfield, A. (1990). The assessment of qualitative age differences in discourse processing. In T. M. Hess (Ed.), *Aging and cognition: Knowledge organization and utilization* (pp. 33–91). North-Holland: Elsevier.

Stine, E. A. L., Wingfield, A., & Myers, S. D. (1990). Age differences in processing information from television news: The effects of bisensory augmentation. *Journals of Gerontology, 45,* P1–P8.

Stine, E. A. L., Wingfield, A., & Poon, L. W. (1986). How much and how fast: Rapid processing of spoken language in later adulthood. *Psychology and Aging, 1,* 303–311.

Stine-Morrow, E. A. L., Loveless, M. K., & Soederberg, L. M. (1996). Resource allocation in on-line reading by younger and older adults. *Psychology and Aging, 11,* 475–486.

Tun, P. A. (1989). Age differences in processing expository and narrative text. *Journal of Gerontology: Psychological Sciences, 44,* P9–P15.

Ulatowska, H. K., Allard, L., & Donnell, A. (1988). Discourse performance in subjects with dementia of the Alzheimer type. In H. Whitaker (Ed.), *Neuropsychological studies of nonfocal brain damage* (pp. 108–131). New York: Springer-Verlag.

Ulatowska, H. K., & Chapman, S. B. (1991). Discourse studies. In R. Lubinski (Ed.), *Dementia and communication* (pp. 115–132). Philadelphia: Decker.

Warren, A., & McCloskey, L. A. (1997). Language in social contexts. In J. Berko Gleason (Ed.), *The development of language* (4th ed., pp. 210–258). Boston: Allyn and Bacon.

Zacks, R. T., Hasher, L., Doren, B., Hamm, F., & Attig, M. S. (1987). Encoding and memory of explicit and implicit information. *Journal of Gerontology, 42,* 418–422.

Zelinski, E. (1988). Integrating information from discourse: Do older adults show deficits? In L. Light & D. M. Burke (Eds.), *Language, memory, and aging* (pp. 133–160). New York: Cambridge University Press.

Zelinski, E. M., Light, L. L., & Gilewski, M. J. (1984). Adult age differences in memory for prose: The question of sensitivity to passage structure. *Developmental Psychology, 20,* 1181–1192.

CHAPTER 12

Sheree T. Kwong See
Ellen Bouchard Ryan

Intergenerational Communication: The Survey Interview as a Social Exchange

Although the purposes for conducting interviews are many (e.g., interviewing potential employees, medical interviews, cognitive testing, and community surveys of older adults), all situations have in common an interviewer and a respondent engaging in a social exchange. Appropriately, in one of the first comprehensive accounts of the interviewing process, Bingham and Moore (1924) referred to the interview as a "conversation with a purpose."

In the survey interview the purpose is to gain information. The roles of the interviewer and respondent are prescribed. The interviewer is seeking information, and the role of the respondent is to provide this information. In the simplest conceptualization of the process, the interviewer asks a question, the intent of the question is interpreted by the respondent as the interviewer intended, and then the respondent provides a full and unconditional answer (interviewer → respondent → interview product). A well-designed interview and a properly trained interviewer can result in a close approximation to this outcome. Indeed, full expositions and recommendations for conducting good interviews are available (e.g., Cannell & Kahn, 1968; and Groves & Kahn, 1979 for telephone interviews).

In the last few decades, however, a wealth of methodological research applying concepts from cognitive and social psychology has supported a more complex framework for thinking about interviewing.

245

It is widely acknowledged that a number of factors can influence the collection of complete and valid data in the interview context. This chapter addresses some of those factors and has four parts. In the first section, we present a framework for understanding the interactive forces influencing the interview process. After expounding on the elements of the framework we use it to focus on unique considerations when the interviewer is young and the respondent is old. Statistics on the age of interviewers from a survey by the British Market Research Society indicate that a good percentage of interviewers (approximately 60%) are under 45 years of age. A U.S. estimate is comparably high (47%; statistics reported in Morton-Williams, 1993). Therefore, intergenerational communication in surveys is common.

Understanding the special considerations involved in intergenerational survey interviews will require familiarity with the literature on beliefs about and attitudes toward aging. In the second section, we briefly review this literature. In the third section, we review the literature which suggests that beliefs and attitudes influence the behavior of young and old adults, an important element of the framework. After each section we link the literature back to the framework. The chapter concludes by pointing out areas in need of future research which follow from viewing the survey interview of older adults in terms of intergenerational communication.

☐ The Interview as a Social Exchange: A Framework

A critical review of methodological studies of factors influencing the interview process led Kahn and Cannell (1957; Cannell & Kahn, 1968) to conceptualize the interview as a complex social process. Adopting an interpersonal focus, the *interview product* results not from a one-way flow of information initiated by the interviewer, but rather from the joint and dynamic interchange between the interviewer and respondent. The individual life histories and individual differences that the interviewer and respondent bring to the exchange, as well as the transaction created by the interview process itself, are important mediators of the interview product. The multiple forces interacting in the interview context are shown in Figure 1. This framework is adapted from a model proposed by Cannell and Kahn (1968). The framework also incorporates ideas from a multiple influences model of language performance in late life by Ryan, Kwong See, Meneer, and Trovato (1992).

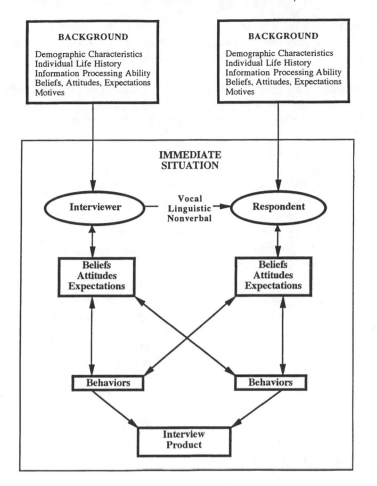

FIGURE 1. Framework of the interactive forces influencing the interview process.

Starting at the top of the framework, the interviewer and respondent each bring their backgrounds into the interview context. One's background is a product of demographic characteristics such as age, gender, ethnic status, and social class. If not directly apparent, these background variables can be inferred from a number of behaviors such as language style, dress, work role, leisure activities, or the decor of one's home. Individual life history reflects one's experiences living in one or more cultural systems. Individual differences in information processing refer to cognitive mechanics necessary to process social and verbal information in the interview context. These mechanics include memory, attention, speed of processing, and cognitive strategies. Beliefs, attitudes (emotional postures about one's beliefs), and expectations reflect knowledge acquired from one's culture, customs, and life experiences. Note that in this chapter, we use the terms beliefs and attitudes interchangeably. Although there may be no affect associated with particular beliefs, our discussion is facilitated by the assumption that beliefs about growth and enhancement in aging are associated with positive attitudes, and beliefs about age-related decline are associated with negative attitudes.

Motives refer to the impetus for conducting the interview (e.g., likes talking to people, so became an interviewer) or agreeing to the interview (e.g., altruistic motives or for payment), and motives dictate how one will conduct oneself during an interview (e.g., acting in a way to present oneself in a positive light). Interactively, these background variables shape the formation, delivery, and reception of interview questions in the immediate situation.

The communicated message itself is the integration of three elements. The linguistic message is considered the core message and is composed of the sound system (i.e., phonology and intonation), grammatical structure (i.e., combinations of verbal sounds into words, combinations of words into sentences and longer discourse), and the meaning system (i.e., knowledge of the meanings of words and sentences). Supplementing the linguistic message are vocal components (such as voice quality, modifications in pitch, loudness, or inserted silences) and nonverbal components (such as gestures, facial expression, and interpersonal distance). The dynamics of the interview situation are shown by the crossing arrows in the framework. As can be seen, the interviewer and respondent both bring acquired beliefs and expectations into the immediate situation. These beliefs influence the delivery of the linguistic message. For example, believing that the respondent will be sensitive to the interview questions may lead an interviewer to ask the questions differently than when not believing this to be true. In reaction to the message and overall social interaction, the respondent may have beliefs and attitudes about the self and/or the interviewer confirmed and then behave in accordance with these beliefs and expectations during the interview. These behaviors, both verbal and nonverbal, can then reinforce beliefs, attitudes, and expectations of the interviewer about the respondent in a feedback loop. The final interview product reflects the dynamic and interactive influences of all these forces. In the survey literature, the influences of background variables are investigated as sources of bias or variance in measurement. Considerable attention has been paid to the role of cognitive factors as mediators of question comprehension (Tanur,

1992). Moreover, a number of studies have shown that respondent behaviors are affected by interviewer characteristics such as race (e.g., Anderson, Silver, & Abramson, 1988) and gender (e.g., Groves & Fultz, 1985). With a few exceptions, relatively little attention has been paid to the impact of chronological age as an influence in the interview context.

Other chapters in this volume summarize the literature on age differences in cognitive information processing and highlight the impact on the reception and comprehension of survey questions (the linguistic message in our framework). The focus of this chapter will be to discuss the biasing effects of the beliefs and attitudes about aging that the interviewer and respondent bring into the survey interview context. In order to understand the dynamics involved in intergenerational communication, we need to address two questions: (a) What are beliefs and attitudes about aging that young interviewers and old respondents bring into the interview context? (b) What is the evidence that these beliefs influence behavior? A review of the aging attitude literature addressing these questions follows.

☐ Beliefs and Attitudes About Aging and Old Age

The study of beliefs about and attitudes toward aging has been a focal point of research in the psychology of aging for many years (see Crockett & Hummert, 1987; Green, 1981; Hummert, Shaner, & Garstka, 1995; Kogan, 1979, for reviews). Some of the first studies on the topic were survey and questionnaire studies. Tuckman and Lorge (1953), for example, presented a series of statements about old people (e.g., they are forgetful, they are helpless) to young participants and asked them to indicate their belief in each statement with a yes or no response. The overall pattern of results suggested that the young participants looked upon old age as a time characterized by failing mental and physical health, loneliness, and economic insecurity. Moreover, not only did young adults view aging negatively, but older adults held negative stereotypes (combinations of beliefs) as well (Tuckman & Lorge, 1954). Butler (1969) coined the term "ageism" to refer to negative attitudes about aging and discriminatory actions that would presumably accompany these negative attitudes. But are the aged targets of widespread negative stereotyping?

Most of the survey and questionnaire studies presented negative statements about old people. As a result, respondents did not have the opportunity to express positive beliefs and attitudes. The design of the questionnaires, therefore, may have made it appear that people were prejudiced against old people (Botwinick, 1984). Studies which have used different techniques for assessing beliefs and attitudes continue to uncover negative age stereotypes but also suggest a more complicated conclusion than early questionnaire studies. These techniques can generally be categorized as direct and indirect assessments of attitudes (Dovidio & Fazio, 1992).

In direct assessments, the general procedure is to have participants think about the social category of "old" and to make conscious assessments based on one's beliefs about this category. There are several different approaches for measuring beliefs. One approach has been to adapt standardized tests and to have respondents estimate performance of different target ages.

In an examination of beliefs about aging memory, Ryan (1992) used the Short Inventory of Memory Experiences (Herrmann & Neisser, 1978). Respondents first completed the inventory of memory in eight domains of everyday life for themselves as a benchmark. In counterbalanced order, they then completed the questionnaire with a typical 25-year-old and a typical 70-year-old in mind. Ryan found that young adults ($M = 36$ years) had more positive expectations for the memory of persons aged 25 years than for those aged 70 years. A second experiment used a between-subjects design to determine whether the target age differences would be replicated. In addition, the anticipated slope of decline across the adult life-span was examined more specifically with four target ages (25, 45, 65, and 85 years). Beliefs about the memory of 25-year-olds were significantly more positive than for 45- and 65-year-olds, which were correspondingly higher than for 85-year-olds. The latter pattern of results has also been found for two self-efficacy factors of the Dixon and Hultsch (1983) Metamemory in Adulthood scale (Ryan & Kwong See, 1993).

Using the same approach but looking instead at intelligence, Hendrick, Gekoski, and Knox (1991) asked young adults to estimate the performance of one of four target age groups on the Schaie-Thurstone Adult Mental Abilities Test (STAMAT). On all five STAMAT scales (Recognition Vocabulary, Letter Series, Word Fluency, Number Addition, and Figure Rotation), the young adults expected older women targets (ages 64 and 84 years) to perform less well than younger women targets (ages 24 and 44 years). Using the Wechsler Adult Intelligence Scale and different target ages (21 or 71 years of age), Hendrick, Knox, Gekoski, and Dyne (1988) also found estimates in favor of younger targets on subtests related to memory and psychomotor speed (Digit Symbol and Digit Span). However, the old targets were rated more favorably on a subtest that assessed practical judgment and acquired knowledge.

Ryan, Kwong See, Meneer, and Trovato (1992) examined age-based beliefs about conversational skills using the Language in Adulthood (LIA) questionnaire. The format of the LIA involves the presentation of a series of statements about an individual's receptive and expressive language skills (e.g., "I often lose track of who said what in a group conversation" and "I find it hard to speak when pressed for time," respectively). Respondents indicate agreement to the statements using 7-point likert scales. In the study, young adults (M = 26 years) and older adults (M = 73 years) completed the LIA for themselves and then in terms of the typical 25-year-old or the typical 75-year-old. As predicted based on cognitive research on age differences in language (Kemper, 1992; Kemper and Kemtes, this volume), the younger respondents reported fewer problems with receptive and expressive aspects of conversational language performance than their older counterparts. In terms of social perceptions, both respondent groups expected individuals aged 25 to experience fewer problems with receptive and expressive language than individuals aged 75, except for two specially selected items where the ratings predictably favored those aged 75 (telling enjoyable stories and sincerity in talking).

Another direct approach has been to use trait sorting and generation tasks (e.g., Hummert, 1990; Hummert, Garstka, Shaner, & Strahm, 1994; Schmidt & Boland, 1986). Consistent with the emerging pattern of the latter two studies reviewed, these studies have not found one pervasive negative stereotype of old age. Instead, trait-sorting studies support the conclusion that there are multiple stereotypes of aging. Hummert (1990), for example, had young adults sort traits into groups with reference to either an old or a young target. Overall, there was little overlap between stereotypes of the young versus old target groups, indicating the perception of distinct age categories. Giving labels to clusters of traits to capture the stereotype, Hummert found that there are negative stereotypes of older adults (e.g., Severely Impaired, Recluse, Despondent) but also some positive ones as well (e.g., Perfect Grandparent, which encompasses traits such as kind, wise, and knowledgeable). This pattern of results was also found when young (20-year-olds), middle-aged (age range 30s–50s) and elderly (age range 60s–80s) were asked to do the trait sorting (Hummert et al., 1994). Judging by the number of stereotypes produced in the sorting, it also appeared that the elderly respondents had the most diverse beliefs about aging, followed by the middle-aged, and then the young adults. Of the three groups of respondents, elderly adults and middle-aged adults attribute more positive traits to aging.

Collectively, studies using direct assessments are consistent. However, the interpretation of the results is also limited because it can be argued that the age manipulation is transparent and the methodology subject to demand characteristics. That is, raters make their response in line with age stereotypes because they know what the stereotypes should be, even though they may not actually believe the stereotypes. The interpretation of direct assessment studies would be more convincing if it could be shown that positive and negative stereotypes of aging are internalized by young and old adults. This evidence comes from indirect assessments of aging attitudes.

Devine (1989) has argued that prejudice has automatic and controlled components. In her theoretical model, stereotypes are automatically activated when encountering a member, or a symbolic equivalent, of a stereotyped group. Prejudice is moderated by controlled inhibition of the automatically activated stereotype. Procedures which are used to examine effects of automatic stereotype activation can also provide evidence that young and old adults have internalized positive and negative stereotypes of old people.

Perdue and Gurtman (1990) used a subliminal priming paradigm to assess ageist attitudes. In their study, college undergraduates were briefly shown the words "young" and "old." The primes were then masked immediately with positive and negative adjectives. The task was to decide if the adjective had a positive or negative connotation. The priming effects clearly provided evidence that young adults have negative beliefs about the social category old. Responses to negative traits were faster after being subliminally primed by the word old. Conversely, the respondents made faster decisions about positive traits after subliminal exposure to the young prime word than to the old prime word.

Levy (1996) used a similar procedure to examine young and old adults' implicit stereotypes about aging. Participants were told that flashes would appear above or below a bullseye on a computer screen. Their task was to identify the location of the flash. Unknown to them, the flashes were words that were meant to prime either senile (e.g., decline, incompetent) or wise (e.g., wise, insightful) stereotypes of aging. First, young and old adults were slower to indicate the location of the flash following prime words than neutral words. The latter is predicted by the assumption that reaction time should be greater when primes activate existing stereotypes. With respect to positive and negative stereotypes, it was also found that reaction time to identify the location of wisdom-related prime words for both young and old adults was slower than for the senile-related prime words. Levy interpreted the latter as evidence that the wisdom-related stereotype was a less dominant image of aging and that the longer time reflects the time taken to switch from the more dominant senility image.

Summary and Links to Framework

Together, the studies which have assessed attitudes directly and indirectly provide evidence for negative beliefs about aging. Young adults believe that aging is associated with decline in intelligence, memory, and language. As the early survey studies in the 1950s found, people tend to believe that old age is a time characterized by loneliness and mental decline. Moreover, these findings using direct measures do not appear to simply be demand-awareness effects. Evidence from indirect assessments indicate that negative beliefs exist below awareness in young adults and old adults and that these stereotypes are activated by old age cues. The studies reviewed in this section have cued the old age stereotype by having participants think about old age as a category, giving traits associated with the category, or providing chronological age as the activating cue. Other studies have shown that other old age cues such as voice and physiognomic cues also trigger negative stereotypes (Giles, Coupland, Williams, & Nussbaum, 1992; Hummert, 1994; Ryan & Capadano, 1978).

This review, however, also makes clear that stereotypes about old age are not all negative. There are expectations for stability or enhancement in domains in which life experience and accumulated knowledge are important. That is, older adults are expected to have greater practical knowledge, to be wise, to tell good stories. In sum, people hold multiple stereotypes of the elderly, some negative and some positive. The assessment of beliefs and attitudes about aging have revealed a more complex story than early studies would have suggested. Whether older adults are evaluated more negatively seems to be highly dependent on the dimension of assessment (Kite & Johnson, 1988). When young and older adults are compared on measures related to competency (e.g., memory), evaluations tend to be more negative. When young and old are compared on personality traits (e.g., kindness, sincerity), ratings are less negative and may be more favorable.

Referring back to our framework, this review suggests that interviewers and respondents bring into the interview both positive and negative beliefs and expectations for performance. The nature of the interview will dictate whether positive or negative beliefs will be most influential. For example, if the interview is about significant life events and uses an open-ended format, the young interviewer and old respondent may enter the context with positive expectations. If the interview involves the administration of a cognitive status questionnaire, participants may enter the interview with trepidation.

A significant feature of the framework is the supposition that beliefs and attitudes about aging influence the behaviors of both the interviewer and respondent. In the next section we review the evidence that age-based beliefs influence behavior. Given the salience of memory and language in the interview context (Tanur, 1992), we limit our review to studies in these domains.

☐ Patronizing Communication and Age-Biased Interpretations of Behavior

Thus far in our discussion of beliefs about aging, it might seem that having organized sets of beliefs is completely negative. This is not necessarily so. In fact, many beliefs are true and reflect our cumulative experiences. A number of aspects of cognition, such as memory, do show decline in aging (see Craik, this volume). Some older people are wise (e.g., Smith & Baltes, 1990) and tell good stories (e.g., Pratt & Robins, 1991). Beliefs are good in that they can serve as guides to how we should behave or how others are likely to behave in social situations. The problem with beliefs, however, is that they are often perceived to be more universal than they really are (i.e., all older people have poor memory). The automatic activation of old age stereotypes when encountering an old person can lead to behaviors which may not be appropriate for the particular situation. It is the overaccommodation in line with negative stereotypes and underaccommodation to an individual older recipient's needs which is thought to give rise to the patronizing communication sometimes used by partners conversing with older adults (Ryan, Hummert, & Boich, 1995).

Patronizing communication has both verbal and nonverbal features (see Ryan, Hummert, et al., 1995, for a review). The key verbal characteristics are vocabulary and grammar simplification, redundancy, and restriction of topics (e.g., always talking about the past with older adults). Characteristic vocal characteristics are high pitch, exaggerated intonation, and slowed rate of speech. Nonverbal cues which accompany the verbal message include such behaviors as rolling one's eyes, patting on the head, and talking with one's hands on one's hips. Surveys of community-dwelling seniors indicates that many have had experience with this communication style (Ryan, Giles, Bartolucci, & Henwood, 1986). Laboratory studies which have paired young and old participants in a communication task report that the young adults spontaneously adopt this speech style (e.g., Kemper, Vandeputte, Rice, Cheung, & Gubarchuk, 1995).

Kemper and Kemtes (this volume) discuss in detail the cognitive information processing impact of patronizing communication on language

comprehension by older adults. In this chapter the focus is on perceptions of the speech style and the social impact for communication. Illus-
trating the distinction, in the Kemper et al. (1995) study pairing young
and old participants, the simplified speech style adopted by the young
communicators enhanced older adults' comprehension in the communication task. However, despite the benefit, the older adults reported
more expressive and receptive problems when interacting with the young
adults. Perhaps, as suggested by Ryan et al. (1986), the young adults'
speech adjustments may have conveyed a lack of respect to the older
listeners and contributed to feelings of lowered self-esteem.

While the motivation for using patronizing communication may be
to convey nurturance, the message is nonetheless perceived as disrespectful (Ryan, Hamilton, & Kwong See, 1994). Community-dwelling
older adults indicate dissatisfaction with patronizing communication
(e.g., Ryan & Cole, 1990). Studies of perceptions of patronizing speech
indicate that perceivers also find this speech style less than desirable.
For example, Ryan, Bourhis, and Knops (1991) and Ryan et al. (1994)
had respondents read or listen to transcripts of intergenerational conversations. The younger partner delivered a message either in normal
adult speech or in a patronizing register. With respect to perceptions,
adult respondents rated the users of patronizing register to be less
respectful and recipients to be more frustrated and less satisfied with
the interaction.

The negativity associated with patronizing communication has potential implications for both partners engaging in the exchange (Ryan
et al., 1986). For older recipients, being addressed in this way reinforces implicit self-stereotypes about age (e.g., I must be losing it if
everyone speaks to me this way), which leads to losses in self-esteem
and feelings of control, and may even lead to avoidance of social interaction altogether. Moreover, older adults begin to behave in accordance with old age stereotypes. Baltes and colleagues have documented
the shaping of age-stereotyped behaviors of residents by nursing staff
in an institutional setting (e.g., Baltes, Wahl, & Reichert, 1991). For
young communicators, observation of stereotypical behaviors exhibited by the older adults feeds back negatively and reinforces negative
stereotypes (e.g., this person must be losing it if they are getting so
upset for nothing). Several studies have shown that young adult raters
do indeed interpret the behaviors of older targets in accordance with
negative age stereotypes, which is the basis of the negative feedback
loop.

Ryan and Laurie (1990) assessed young adults' reactions to male speakers
who were either young (in their 20s) or old (in their 70s). Participants
responded to three messages from different speakers who were from

the same age category (young or old). In counterbalanced order, the young or old speakers were heard giving effective messages which allowed listeners to follow the instructions accurately and confidently, ineffective ambiguous messages, and noisy messages in which there was background interference caused by a faulty tape recording. Overall, the older speakers were rated as less competent than young speakers. Two other findings show age-biased interpretation of behavior. First, young listeners did not rate an old effective speaker any higher than his less effective peer even though they did make this differentiation for young speakers. Second, the speaker attracting the least favorable evaluation was the old speaker whose message was presented on a noisy tape, a condition for which the experimenter explicitly took the blame. Thus, the communication behaviors were interpreted differently for older and younger speakers, to the distinct disadvantage of the older speaker. Older speakers were not given credit for successful (effective) performance and were blamed more for being associated with a negative situation out of their control.

Similar age bias has been shown in the memory domain. Erber, Szuchman, and Rothberg (1990) had respondents read scenarios in which everyday memory failures were described (e.g., forgetting a telephone number). Critically, the same memory failures made by young and older adults were evaluated differently. The memory failures of older targets were judged as indicating greater mental difficulty than the identical failures of young targets. Bieman-Copland and Ryan (1998) have shown that both young and old perceivers evaluate memory successes and failures in a more favorable light for young targets than for old targets.

Together these studies show not only that young adults have negative views of aging but that negative views influence their behavior (patronizing speech and age-biased interpretations). Evidence linking negative self-stereotyping to the behavioral performance of older adults is scant. However, a cross-cultural study by Levy and Langer (1994) suggests a link between negative beliefs and memory decline in old age. Reasoning that older Deaf Americans and the mainland Chinese culture would be less exposed to negative stereotypes of aging, they compared the memory performance of these two groups to older Hearing Americans. As predicted, the older Deaf Americans and Chinese performed significantly better on a number of different memory tests. Further measures taken in the Levy (1996) study referred to previously in the second section of this chapter strengthens the conclusion from the latter correlational study.

To quickly reiterate the procedure used in the Levy (1996) study, participants were subliminally presented words that were meant to prime either senile or wise stereotypes of aging. Importantly for our discussion, activation of the positive stereotype tended to improve memory performance, memory self-efficacy, and older adults' views of aging. Activation of the negative stereotype had the opposite effect on the three measures. This compelling pattern was not found for younger adults, indicating that senility and wisdom were not relevant self-stereotypes for the young adults, whereas they were for the old. Nicely, this study shows that activation of old age stereotypes influences the performance of older adults for whom these stereotypes are internalized as self-relevant.

Summary and Links to the Framework

In the second section of this chapter, we concluded that young and old adults bring both positive and negative beliefs about aging into the interview context. In this section we reviewed evidence that these beliefs influence the behavior of both young and old. We focused on the impact of negative beliefs, but with some extrapolation one can see how positive beliefs might be similarly influential. For young adults, negative expectations for the competency of older adults led to verbal and nonverbal modifications in communication (patronizing communication) and age-biased interpretations of behavior. For old adults we reviewed evidence that activation of negative beliefs can lead to decrements in performance. That is, the behaviors of old adults begin to align with negative stereotypes. To understand the dynamics of intergenerational communication, we made use of a negative feedback model introduced by Ryan et al. (1986).

Linking these ideas back to the framework, there appears to be good support for the view that beliefs about aging need to be considered as important mediators of the interview product. In our reasoning, age-biased modifications in the formulation and delivery of the linguistic message impact on the reception of that message by the respondent. Patronizing communication can serve as a cue to age for the elderly respondent. This cue can then prime self-relevant negative stereotypes, which influences the behavior of the older respondent. Given Levy's compelling study on the impact of negative stereotypes on memory performance, one can readily see the impact in cognitive screening surveys.

The behaviors exhibited by the older respondent (e.g., poorer memory performance or unwillingness to exert effort) confirmed beliefs held by the interviewer, which led to the modifications in the delivery of the linguistic message in the first place. In the end, the result of the negative feedback loop is the contextual aging of the older respondent. The interview product reflects the interviewing of the expected old person.

☐ The Survey Interview as a Social Exchange: Future Directions

In this chapter we presented a framework for understanding the interactive forces which influence the interview product. We used the framework to organize discussion of the unique considerations when the interview involves intergenerational communication (i.e., the interviewer is young and the respondent is old). We focused on the role of beliefs and expectations as mediators of the final interview product.

To build our argument that beliefs and attitudes are important considerations, we necessarily turned to studies examining attitudes outside of the survey interview context. The impact of age as a source of bias has not been a focus point of research in the survey literature. The few studies suggest that this neglect needs to change. Groves and Magilavy (1986) examined correlates of interviewer effects, defined as the tendency for answers provided by the respondent and recorded by the interviewer to vary, across nine different telephone survey studies. Their findings looking at correlates associated with the respondent are most telling. What they found was that gender and education of respondent were uncorrelated with interviewer effects, but age of the respondent was correlated. Elderly respondents were found to exhibit larger susceptibility to interviewer effects than young respondents. Similarly, Belli, Weiss, and Lepkoswki (this volume) report on the occurrence of interviewer tailoring during the surveying of elderly participants. These results suggest that interviewers may have the tendency to adapt questions or to fail to adequately probe when the respondent is old.

Our claim is that age-based beliefs are influential in the interview context. However, it can be argued that we are overestimating the influence of beliefs in the survey context because interviewers undergo extensive training to deliver questions in a standard and consistent manner. Our discussion is not meant to ignore the impact of training. In fact, future study could be directed at assessing the impact of training on elderly survey data quality. Rather, our discussion suggests that training and standardization may not eliminate all age bias. Moreover, the discussion gives direction as to what topics should be covered in training.

To the extent that old age stereotypes are activated automatically

(Devine, 1989; Perdue & Gurtman, 1990), training should be directed at consciously controlled inhibition of old age stereotypes. The first step is sensitizing interviewers to their beliefs and attitudes toward aging and how these beliefs might lead them to behave toward and interpret the responses of older respondents differently. Although it may seem obvious that interviewers would naturally glean this understanding from training, a casual review of textbooks on interviewing techniques reveals a lack of sensitivity to this issue even on the part of the trainers. Either no recommendations for interviewing older people are made or recommendations like the follow are given:

> Interviewers need to be aware that the subject matter of a survey can sometimes be distressing to elderly or disabled respondents, especially if the interview touches on family members, bereavement or loneliness. A sympathetic ear and patience to allow the respondent to digress . . . is usually all that is required. . . . Because many respondents are pleased to have contact with someone and are not pressurized for time, elderly people in particular may be prone to digress. (Morton-Williams, 1993, pp. 192–193)

The latter highlights a point we made earlier. The motivation behind adopting a patronizing communication style may be to convey caring and nurturance. However, the end result is likely to be perceived as disrespectful and may lead to loss of self-esteem on the part of the older respondent. As suggested by a model for enhancing intergenerational communication in the health care context (Ryan, Meredith, MacLean, & Orange, 1995), to gain compliance and rapport with the older respondent, the best strategy is to become attuned to the individual needs of the particular respondent and to accommodate communication appropriately.

Our discussion also suggests that special consideration be given to the role of age bias in telephone interviews. To compensate for slower speeds of language processing and hearing loss (see Wingfield, this volume), older adults have been found to rely more on visual cues which accompany speech (e.g., lip movements; Thompson, 1995). Interviews on the telephone are devoid of visual cues. Might expectations for decline in hearing (Ryan et al., 1994), combined with older respondents' greater difficulty on the telephone, exaggerate the effects of age bias in the interview context?

In conclusion, the framework offers a useful guide for thinking about the dynamics involved in intergenerational survey interviews and is useful in directing future research in this area. In this chapter we highlight a need for research on the role of age-based beliefs and attitudes as a source of response and measurement bias.

☐ Acknowledgments

Preparation of this manuscript was supported by grants from the Social Sciences and Humanities Research Council of Canada.

☐ References

Anderson, B. A, Silver, B. D., & Abramson, P. R. (1988). The effects of the race of the interviewer on race-related attitudes of black respondents in SRC/CPS National Election Studies. *Public Opinion Quarterly, 52,* 289–324.

Baltes, M. M., Wahl, H.-W., & Reichert, M. (1991). Successful aging in long-term care institutions. *Annual Review of Gerontology and Geriatrics, 11,* 311–338.

Bieman-Copland, S., & Ryan, E. B. (1998). Age-biased interpretation of memory successes and failures in adulthood. *Journal of Gerontology: Psychological Sciences, 53B,* 105–111.

Bingham, W. V. D., & Moore, B. V. (1924). *How to interview.* New York: Harper and Row.

Botwinick, J. (1984). *Aging and behavior* (3rd ed.). New York: Springer-Verlag.

Butler, R. N. (1969). Age-ism: Another form of bigotry. *The Gerontologist, 9,* 243–246.

Cannell, C. F., & Kahn, R. L. (1968). Interviewing. In G. Lindzey & E. Aronson (Eds.), *The handbook of social psychology* (2nd ed., Vol. 2, pp. 526–595). Reading, MA: Addison-Wesley.

Crockett, W. H., & Hummert, M. L. (1987). Perceptions of aging and the elderly. In K. W. Schaie & C. Eisdorfer (Eds.), *Annual review of gerontology and geriatrics* (Vol. 7, pp. 217–241). New York: Springer-Verlag.

Devine, P. G. (1989). Stereotypes and prejudice: Their automatic and controlled components. *Journal of Personality and Social Psychology, 56,* 5–18.

Dixon, R. A., & Hultsch, D. F. (1983). Structure and development of metamemory in adulthood. *Journal of Gerontology, 38,* 682–688.

Dovidio, J. F., & Fazio, R. H. (1992). New technologies for the direct and indirect assessment of attitudes. In J. M. Tanur (Ed.), *Questions about questions* (pp. 204–237). New York: Russell Sage Foundation.

Erber, J. T., Szuchman, L. T., & Rothberg, S. T. (1990). Everyday memory failure: Age differences in appraisal and attribution. *Psychology and Aging, 5,* 236–241.

Giles, H., Coupland, N., Williams, A., & Nussbaum, J. (1992). Intergenerational talk and communication with older people. *International Journal of Aging and Human Development, 34,* 271–298.

Green, S. K. (1981). Attitudes and perceptions about the elderly: Current and future perspectives. *International Journal of Aging and Human Development, 13,* 99–119.

Groves, R. M., & Fultz, N. (1985). Gender effects among telephone interviewers in a survey of economic attitudes. *Sociological Methods and Research, 14,* 31–52.

Groves, R. M., & Kahn, R. L. (1979). *Surveys by telephone.* New York: Academic Press.

Groves, R. M., & Magilavy, L. J. (1986). Measuring and explaining interviewer effects in centralized telephone surveys. *Public Opinion Quarterly, 50,* 251–266.

Hendrick, J. J., Gekoski, W. L., & Knox, V. J. (1991). Accuracy of young adults' perceptions of cognitive ability across adulthood. *Canadian Journal on Aging, 10,* 165–176.

Hendrick, J. J., Knox, V. J., Gekoski, W. L., & Dyne, K. J. (1988). Perceived cognitive ability of young and old targets. *Canadian Journal on Aging, 7,* 192–203.

Herrmann, D. J., & Neisser, U. (1978). An inventory of everyday memory experiences.

In M. M. Gruneberg, P. E. Morris, & R. N. Sykes (Eds.), *Practical aspects of memory* (pp. 35–51). New York: Academic Press.

Hummert, M. L. (1990). Multiple stereotypes of elderly and young adults: A comparison of structure and evaluations. *Psychology and Aging, 5,* 182–193.

Hummert, M. L. (1994). Physiognomic cues to age and the activation of stereotypes of the elderly in interaction. *International Journal of Aging and Human Development, 39,* 5–19.

Hummert, M. L., Garstka, T. A., Shaner, J. L., & Strahm, S. (1994). Stereotypes of the elderly held by young, middle-aged, and elderly adults. *Journals of Gerontology, 49,* P240–P249.

Hummert, M. L., Shaner, J. L., & Garstka, T. A. (1995). Cognitive processes affecting communication with older adults: The case for stereotypes, attitudes, and beliefs about communication. In J. F. Nussbaum & J. Coupland (Eds.), *Handbook of communication and aging research* (pp. 105–131). Mahwah, NJ: Erlbaum.

Kahn, R. L., & Cannell, C. F. (1957). *The dynamics of interviewing.* New York: Wiley.

Kemper, S. (1992). Language and aging. In F. I. M. Craik & T. A. Salthouse (Eds.), *The handbook of aging and cognition* (pp. 213–270). Hillsdale, NJ: Erlbaum.

Kemper, S., Vandeputte, D., Rice, K., Cheung, H., & Gubarchuk, J. (1995). Speech adjustments to aging during a referential communication task. *Journal of Language and Social Psychology, 14,* 40–59.

Kite, M. E., & Johnson, B. T. (1988). Attitudes toward older and younger adults: A meta-analysis. *Psychology and Aging, 3,* 233–244.

Kogan, N. (1979). Beliefs, attitudes, and stereotypes about old people. *Research on Aging, 1,* 11–36.

Levy, B. (1996). Improving memory in old age through implicit self-stereotyping. *Journal of Personality and Social Psychology, 71,* 1092–1107.

Levy, B., & Langer, E. (1994). Aging free from negative stereotypes: Successful memory in China and among the American deaf. *Journal of Personality and Social Psychology, 66,* 989–998.

Morton-Williams, J. (1993). *Interviewer approaches.* Aldershot, England: Dartmouth.

Perdue, C., & Gurtman, M. (1990). Evidence for the automaticity of ageism. *Journal of Experimental Social Psychology, 26,* 199–216.

Pratt, M. W., & Robins, S. L. (1991). That's the way it was: Age differences in the structure and quality of adults' personal narratives. *Discourse Processes, 14,* 73–85.

Ryan, E. B. (1992). Beliefs about memory changes across the adult life span. *Journal of Gerontology: Psychological Sciences, 47,* P41–P46.

Ryan, E. B., Bourhis, R. Y., & Knops, U. (1991). Evaluative perceptions of patronizing speech addressed to elders. *Psychology and Aging, 6,* 442–450.

Ryan, E., & Capadano, H. L. (1978). Age perceptions and evaluative reactions toward adult speakers. *Journal of Gerontology, 33,* 98–102.

Ryan, E. B., & Cole, R. (1990). Evaluative perceptions of interpersonal communication with elders. In H. Giles, N. Coupland, & J. Wiemann (Eds.), *Communication, health, and the elderly* (pp. 172–190). Manchester, England: Manchester University Press.

Ryan, E. B., Giles, H., Bartolucci, G., & Henwood, K. (1986). Psycholinguistic and social psychological components of communication by and with the elderly. *Language and Communication, 6,* 1–24.

Ryan, E. B., Hamilton, J. M., & Kwong See, S. (1994). Patronizing the old: How do younger and older adults respond to baby talk in the nursing home? *International Journal of Aging and Human Development, 39,* 21–32.

Ryan, E. B., Hummert, M. L., & Boich, L. H. (1995). Communication predicaments of aging: Patronizing behavior toward older adults. *Journal of Language and Social Psychology, 14,* 144–166.

Ryan, E. B., & Kwong See, S. (1993). Age-based beliefs about memory changes for self and others across adulthood. *Journal of Gerontology: Psychological Sciences, 48,* P199–P201.

Ryan, E. B., Kwong See, S., Meneer, W. B., & Trovato, D. (1992). Age-based perceptions of language performance among younger and older adults. *Communication Research, 19,* 423–443.

Ryan, E. B., & Laurie, S. (1990). Evaluations of older and younger adult speakers: Influence of communication effectiveness and noise. *Psychology and Aging, 5,* 514–519.

Ryan, E. B., Meredith, S. D., MacLean, M. J., & Orange, J. B. (1995). Changing the way we talk with elders: Promoting health using the Communication Enhancement Model. *International Journal of Aging and Human Development, 41,* 87–105.

Schmidt, D. F., & Boland, S. M. (1986). The structure of impressions of older adults: Evidence for multiple stereotypes. *Psychology and Aging, 1,* 255–260.

Smith, J., & Baltes, P. B. (1990). Wisdom-related knowledge: Age/cohort differences in response to life-planning problems. *Developmental Psychology, 26,* 494–505.

Tanur, J. M. (Ed.). (1992). *Questions about questions.* New York: Russell Sage Foundation.

Thompson, L. A. (1995). Encoding and memory for visible speech and gestures: A comparison between young and older adults. *Psychology and Aging, 10,* 215–228.

Tuckman, J., & Lorge, I. (1953). Attitudes toward old people. *The Journal of Social Psychology, 37,* 249–260.

Tuckman, J., & Lorge, I. (1954). Old people's appraisal of adjustment over the life-span. *Journal of Personality, 22,* 417–422.

SURVEYING OLDER
RESPONDENTS

13

CHAPTER

Susan Schechter
Paul Beatty
Gordon B. Willis

Asking Survey Respondents About Health Status: Judgment and Response Issues

Measurement of subjective phenomena has long been of interest to survey researchers (Turner & Martin, 1984). Although health surveys tend to focus on measuring objective phenomena, use of subjective quality of life measures has grown considerably in recent years (Erickson, Wilson, & Shannon, 1995; Patrick & Erickson, 1993). Questions about health status have become an important component of health surveillance and are generally held as valid indicators of service needs and intervention outcomes (Hennessy, Moriarty, Zack, Scherr, & Brackbill, 1994). Furthermore, self-assessed health status has proved to be a more powerful predictor of mortality and morbidity than many objective measures of health (Idler, 1992). This power, along with the simplicity of administering these questions, makes them potentially quite valuable to researchers.

Increasingly, health surveys ask respondents to report on subjective experiences such as pain, anxiety, depression, and low energy levels, as well as overall assessments of their physical and mental health. These kinds of survey questions can increase our understanding of important health factors such as medical conditions, limitations with daily activities, and states of mental health. Over the last several years, research has been conducted to identify potential problems with these questions and to establish their methodological and conceptual integrity. This chapter addresses how respondents answer these questions, with an emphasis on the problems that respondents may have in providing a response that conforms with question format. Results from cognitive laboratory interviews and a field experiment are presented, and their implications are discussed.

☐ Difficulties in Measuring Health-Related Quality of Life

The federal initiative known as Healthy People 2000 sets forth objectives with targets for improving health in the United States. These objectives include prevention of disease, disability, and premature death, and also enhancement of quality of life (Department of Health and Human Services, 1991). Specifying quality of life represents a unique effort on the part of national policy makers to formally recognize this concept as an important component of health. In health promotion and disease prevention activities, quality of life is often interpreted as a key indicator of one's overall health status. However, establishing valid and reliable measures of these sorts of subjective health reports is challenging.

In 1993, new measures of health-related quality of life were introduced into the Centers for Disease Control and Prevention's Behavioral Risk Factors Surveillance System (BRFSS), which uses telephone surveys to monitor health risk behaviors among adults (Centers for Disease Control and Prevention, 1995). Figure 1 contains the BRFSS quality of life questions investigated for this study.

The self-perceived health status item (Question 1) has been commonly used for some time in health and economic surveys. The other six questions in Figure 1 are newer and less common. They ask for a numerical report of a subjective experience: respondents must specify the number of days they have experienced a given health status. Response error to these sorts of survey questions can result if the respondent has difficulty interpreting either what the question is really asking or what a satisfactory response will be. Generally, the response format (in this case, number of days) gives clues to respondents about the meaning of the question, what sort of information is being requested, and how to formulate an answer (Schwarz & Hippler, 1991). Thus, the response format must correspond logically to the question. An incompatibility between the way respondents conceptualize their answer and the format they must use to express it may lead to re-

1. **Self-perceived health status**
   Would you say that in general your health is:
   a. Excellent
   b. Very good
   c. Good
   d. Fair, or
   e. Poor?

2. **Not-good physical health days**
   Now thinking about your physical health, which includes physical illness and injury, for how many days during the past 30 days was your physical health not good?
   _____ days

3. **Not-good mental health days**
   Now thinking about your mental health, which includes stress, depression, and problems with emotions, for how many days during the past 30 days was your mental health not good?
   _____ days

4. **Pain days**
   During the past 30 days, for about how many days did pain make it hard for you to do your usual activities, such as self-care, work, or recreation?
   _____ days

5. **Depression days**
   During the past 30 days, for about how many days have you felt sad, blue, or depressed?
   _____ days

6. **Stress days**
   During the past 30 days, for about how many days have you felt worried, tense, or anxious?
   _____ days

7. **Vitality days**
   During the past 30 days, for about how many days have you felt very healthy and full of energy?
   _____days

FIGURE 1. Quality of life measures.

sponse difficulties and confusion about what qualifies as an adequate response (Beatty, Herrmann, Puskar, & Kerwin, in press; Schechter & Herrmann, 1997; Sudman, Bradburn, & Schwarz, 1996; Willis, 1996). Further confounding these potential difficulties are issues unique to surveying older respondents, as well as issues inherent in administering surveys by telephone.

Incompatibility Between Question Meaning and Explicit Response Format

Based on prior research and our own experience in laboratory testing of questionnaires, we hypothesized that some survey respondents will have difficulty providing quantitative reports of their subjective health. In particular, we wondered whether questions that measure "number of days in the past 30 days" use an appropriate response format, especially for older respondents. Some past research has suggested that older respondents report factual information (e.g., whether they voted, amount of taxes paid, and so forth) as accurately as younger respondents (Rodgers & Herzog, 1987). The present survey questions, however, deal with subjective evaluations of health. We cannot determine the validity of such subjective responses, but can determine how well responses conform to the specified response format, which we call the precision of the response.

Subjective health evaluations are likely to be more complicated for older respondents due to increased physical limitations, impairments, or illnesses. Furthermore, some of these conditions are chronic and may not easily be described as occurring or not occurring for a given number of discrete days. For example, it would be reasonable to think that a respondent suffering from debilitating arthritis might report their health status in a more general descriptive form (e.g., "my arthritis has been much better lately") rather than provide a numerical report. Jobe, Keller, and Smith (1996) found that older respondents often provide narrative answers and are less likely to respond within the format specified by the question. They suggested that older respondents may have trouble translating frequency information recalled from memory into required survey response categories.

Another factor we thought might cause difficulty was the use of the phrase "not good" to describe physical and mental health status. This wording implies that health is typically "good" and recall is only required for those days that are exceptions. Increased health and memory problems associated with aging could make older respondents less able or willing to express these exceptions numerically.

Issues Regarding Response Strategies

Beyond the general issue of whether respondents typically give numeric responses, we were interested in the cognitive strategies used to answer these questions. Herrmann (1994) reviewed several experiments and found that it is difficult to predict which strategy respondents will use for retrospective reports (e.g., for frequency-based reports, using estimation or enumeration of specific episodes). If this is the case, it is especially unclear what strategy a respondent will use to answer a question when the response format does not seem to be naturally applicable to the topic. For this investigation, therefore, we questioned whether respondents would count number of days, estimate, or use some other strategy that would result in a numeric response (see Blair & Burton, 1987; Sudman et al., 1996). Of further concern was the possible identification of strategies that would lead respondents to give a response that seemed to comply with the format, but which would not constitute a codeable answer (e.g., a descriptive phrase such as "Not too many days" or a range of numbers such as "Five to 10 days").

☐ Cognitive Laboratory Interviews

Cognitive interviewing is a form of intensive interviewing in which volunteer subjects explain the basis of their responses to survey questions. The method is especially useful for the detection of problems or issues inherent in survey questions that are covert and normally not revealed through a field-based question-asking and -answering process (Forsyth & Lessler, 1991; Royston, 1989; Willis, Royston, & Bercini, 1991). In order to investigate issues related to question interpretation, strategies used by respondents, and adequacy of response scales, we conducted cognitive interviews with 48 subjects (note that we use the term "subject" to refer to a participant in a cognitive interview, and "respondent" to refer to a participant in a field survey). Eighteen subjects were 70 years of age or older; 30 subjects were under 70 years of age. All subjects were recruited through flyers, newspaper advertisements, or through direct contact with a senior citizen group.

Interviews were conducted in three rounds over a 15-month period. The rounds varied primarily by interview protocol and mode of interview administration. The first round consisted of 18 interviews, which were conducted face-to-face in a cognitive laboratory, using an interviewing protocol with suggested probes following each survey question. For example, after the question ". . . for how many days during the past 30 days was your physical health not good?" the scripted probes included "How did you decide on that number of days? Did you have any difficulty deciding whether days were 'good' or 'not good'?" Interviewers were encouraged to use these probes, but allowed to add probes to pursue unexpected issues that arose in interviews (for further discussion of cognitive interviewing techniques, see Bercini, 1992; DeMaio & Rothgeb, 1996; Forsyth & Lessler, 1991; Willis, 1994;

Willis et al., 1991). In this first round, 7 of the 18 subjects were 70 years of age or older.

In a second round consisting of 20 face-to-face interviews, interviewers replaced the cognitive probing with an in-depth debriefing after the interview, to minimize interruptions and simulate actual field conditions more closely (see Beatty, Schechter, & Whitaker, 1996, for further description of the differences in interviewing procedures between the first and second rounds). Probing was limited in order to assess how precisely subjects would answer the questions. Only 2 of the 18 subjects in the second round were 70 years of age or older. A third round of 10 interviews relied on a similar interview protocol, but these interviews were conducted over the telephone. One subject was 69 years old and the remaining 9 were 70 years of age or older.

Difficulties in Answering Health Status Questions

Combined results from the three rounds of interviews revealed that close to 40% of subjects rated their health as excellent or very good, another 36% said good, 17% said fair, and 9% said poor. The distribution was comparable to results in larger telephone surveys such as the BRFSS; the percentage of "excellent" and "very good" responses was slightly lower, and the percentage of "poor" responses was slightly higher than in BRFSS data (see Siegel, 1994, for a discussion of 1993 BRFSS health status data), which was probably attributable to our small sample size. Subjects generally reported that their ratings were based on the absence or presence of medical conditions, although some mentioned health-related behaviors or changes in physical abilities. To a lesser degree, subjects referred to the opinion of doctors or compared themselves to others in their age group. There was no noticeable difference between older (70 years of age or older) and younger subjects with respect to the ease of answering the general health status question or the ability to discuss the bases for the answer. As expected, older subjects were more likely to mention declining health, impairments, and serious medical conditions as the reason for their rating. They also tended to compare themselves to other older people or to mention the opinions of peers.

A fair number of subjects, both young and old, had difficulty providing responses to the other quality of life questions that asked for reports of number of days. In particular, the question about not-good physical health days had the highest number of responses indicating problems or confusion. Those who reported a number often indicated that they estimated or guessed to comply with the survey demand.

Dominant response strategies did not seem to reflect the recall of discrete episodes from memory. Some subjects apparently interpreted the response format as a scale from 0 to 30 and selected a representative estimate, rather than reporting a discrete number of days. Other subjects gave answers that implied zero but were not numeric (e.g., ". . . my physical health is good, I don't remember in 30 days seeing any doctors."). A few subjects rejected the premise of the question and never gave a number, even when probed (e.g., "I can't answer that"), while others gave a number only after probing that specifically asked for a numeric response. To illustrate difficulties among the older subjects, Figure 2 contains selected responses to the physical health status question, and Figure 3 contains selected responses to the mental health status question.

Precision of Responses

In an effort to measure the extent of these response difficulties, we developed codes for the precision of responses. Precision in this study refers to how well the response conformed to the answer format, not

---

Now thinking about your physical health, which includes physical illness and injury, for how many days during the past 30 days was your physical health not good?

Subject 1: *A day to me is some good and some bad . . . everyday with me has a high and a low.*

Subject 4: *Well, by "not good" what do you mean? Like last night my arthritis bothered me an awful lot and I couldn't sleep all night long. Aside from that it's fairly good because I've been able to go out and participate in activities.*

Subject 5: *During the past 30 days? Well, I've been dizzy but outside of that it's been fair. I was able to go out.*

Subject 6: *Well, I had a pain in my chest a week ago Friday . . . and I called emergency and then I went to my private doctor.*

Interviewer: So, how many days during the past 30 days was your physical health not good?

Subject 6: *Well, it's a hard question to answer. Because actually it was just like a knowledge of my health that was lacking. Actually, I wasn't any sicker than I am now, but I just didn't know what was going on.*

FIGURE 2. Responses to question about days physical health was not good.

Now thinking about your mental health, which includes stress, depression, and problems with emotions, for how many days during the past 30 days was your mental health not good?

Subject 2: *Not good? My mental health has always been good.*

Interviewer: So would you say zero?

Subject: *No, not necessarily, because I do get stressful sometimes.*

Interviewer: So if you had to come up with a number of days. . .

Subject: *I'd pick overall, 3 to 5 days.*

Subject 7: *I don't know . . . I don't have any trouble that way.*

Subject 10: *I have a teenager living with me so we have little discussions. I mean nothing big. . . . Do you mean being depressed?*

Subject 15: *Mental health? I find myself frustrated by my memory loss. . . . I can't do what I was able to do because of the emphysema.*

Interviewer: Do you think you could pick a number of days that your mental health was not good?

Subject: *No . . . my mental health is an extension of being able to operate and to know where I'm going and what I'm doing.*

FIGURE 3. Responses to question about days mental health was not good.

the validity or accuracy of the response per se (subjective judgments cannot be externally validated). After the first round of 18 cognitive interviews, audiotape recordings of 17 interviews were transcribed (one interview was not transcribed due to inaudible taping). For each question on the transcript, we reviewed the question and answer exchanges and selected the first answer that we thought would have been acceptable to a survey interviewer as the response. If the subject gave no responses of that quality, we identified for coding purposes the subject's "best" answer. Responses were rated on a 4-point precision scale by two coders who worked independently and later reconciled any differences in coding (see Beatty et al., 1996, for details on the coding procedures; Beatty, Schechter, & Whitaker, in press, for discussion of variation in cognitive interviewer probing behavior).

In the analysis that follows, we collapsed the four precision codes into a dichotomy of precise and imprecise. Answers were coded as precise if a numerical response between 0 and 30 was given, or a narrative response was given which required only minimal interpretation, confirmation, or probing to arrive at a number. For example, a response of "I feel that way every day" was coded as precise because there was further evidence in the transcript that the subject meant 30 days. Ranges of 3 days or less were also coded as precise (e.g., "1 to 3 days"), as we found that subjects who initially responded with small ranges were typically willing to select one number if probed to do so. Answers were coded as imprecise if they failed to conform to the survey requirement; that is, if a number could not be entered as the answer to the question or a number was only provided after extensive probing not typically done in a field survey. For example, the answer "At least five days, maybe more" was imprecise because even after probing, the subject did not select a number or provide a small range of acceptable numbers. Other respondents did not provide any quantitative response. Answers such as "I can't put it in terms of days" indicated that the respondent rejected the basic premise of the question. Table 1 shows the comparison of precision for older and younger subjects interviewed in the first round. Using Fisher's Exact Test, the

TABLE 1. PRECISION OF REPORTING FOR QUALITY OF LIFE QUESTIONS, BY AGE

During the past 30 days, how many days have you had/felt	Under 70 yrs ($n = 10$)[a]		70 yrs+ ($n = 7$)[b]	
	Precise	Imprecise	Precise	Imprecise
Not-good physical health	100.0 (10)	0.0 (0)	28.6 (2)	71.4* (5)
Not-good mental health	90.0 (9)	10.0 (1)	71.4 (5)	28.6 (2)
Pain	90.0 (9)	10.0 (1)	57.1 (4)	42.9 (3)
Depression	50.0 (5)	50.0 (5)	57.1 (4)	42.9 (3)
Stress	80.0 (8)	20.0 (2)	71.4 (5)	28.6 (2)
Vitality	80.0 (8)	20.0 (2)	28.6 (2)	71.4* (5)

[a]Subjects under 70 ranged from 21 to 63 years of age (mean age 34, median age 25); 5 were male, 5 were female.
[b]Subjects over 70 ranged from 71 to 94 years of age (mean age 80, median age 83); 4 were male, 3 were female.
*$p < .05$.

differences in precision by age group were significant ($p <. 05$) for the not-good physical health and vitality questions.

Differences in response precision were found even among this small sample of subjects. For example, when reporting not-good physical health days, none of the younger subjects gave imprecise answers, compared to 71% of the older subjects' answers. A similar pattern emerged with answers to the vitality question (days feeling healthy and full of energy): 20% of the younger subjects gave imprecise answers, compared to 71% of the older subjects' responses. In other instances (e.g., questions about stress and depression), imprecision was found for both age groups. Notably, at least 2 of the 7 older subjects gave imprecise answers for each question.

A subsequent round of 20 interviews was conducted in response to concerns that the informal style of cognitive interviewing and intensive probing may have been responsible for the imprecise responses. For this second round, subjects were not recruited according to age criteria in order to focus strictly on effects of the interviewing protocol. Rather than use cognitive interviewing techniques, interviewers were instructed to use traditional field interviewing probes (see Fowler & Mangione, 1990) only if needed in order to obtain quantitative responses. Interviewers then conducted a debriefing immediately following the interview, during which the subjects were asked to retrospectively report on the basis for their answers.

With minimal interviewer probing, subjects gave precise responses for nearly all questions in this round. However, in the debriefings, subjects expressed doubts about the quality of their responses and talked of frustrations with the response format. Although these subjects were younger and therefore probably had fewer health problems to consider, they still reported concerns and issues with the questions.

The third and final round consisted of 10 interviews conducted by telephone with subjects aged 69 or older. Responses were not coded for precision or imprecision because the interviewing procedures differed significantly from previous rounds. Nevertheless, the interviews provided additional impressionistic evidence that largely supported earlier conclusions. Altogether, our results suggested that older people were particularly challenged by the response format.

Specifically, in this third round, we found it more common for subjects to express confusion about the response format than about the meaning of the question itself. Reviews of the transcripts revealed a high prevalence of narrative responses. With persistence, interviewers were sometimes able to obtain precise responses, but the subjects tended to explain somewhat complicated answers, rather than provide straightforward, numeric responses. For example, one subject's answer to the question ". . . how many days have you felt sad, blue or depressed?" was "Sometimes I felt sad, don't know about blue or depressed. I guess three times a week because I couldn't go to the gym. But I don't know about the number." In another example with a subject who consistently failed to give numeric responses, an interviewer probed with "Are questions that ask for number of days hard to answer?" and the subject replied "Well, 30 days doesn't mean anything, it depends upon who and what context. . . . I can't see anything that 30 days or 60 days means. It depends upon the circumstances."

☐ Field Study

In addition to the cognitive interviewing study, data from a field experiment offered the opportunity to examine on a larger scale the initial findings of the laboratory interviews (see Beatty, Willis, Schechter, 1997, and Willis & Schechter, 1997, for further discussion of validation of laboratory studies through field experiments). Although field studies do not provide a direct means for the study of cognitive processes, as do cognitive interviewing studies, the response distributions obtained often contain relevant clues, and they allow a test of predictions made on the basis of experiences from the cognitive interviews. The general health status item, the question on not-good physical days, and that on not-good mental health days (Questions 1–3 in Figure 1) were embedded in a 1,000-case random-digit-dial telephone omnibus survey of the U.S. household population, which we label the "field study." A total of 866 respondents were under 70, and 98 were 70 or older (age was unknown for 36).

A main comparison of interest involved responses to the not-good physical health and not-good mental health days questions, especially as mean values might differ with age. Table 2 shows that days of not-good physical health increased significantly with age ($p < .003$ by a

TABLE 2. FIELD STUDY: AVERAGE NUMBER OF NOT-GOOD DAYS IN PAST 30 BY AGE

Age Group	(*n*)	Physical Health	Mental Health
18–44	545	3.1 (6.7)	5.3 (8.5)
45–69	314	4.8 (9.5)	5.3 (9.4)
70+	90	6.0 (11.0)	2.7 (7.2)

Notes. Numbers in parentheses are standard deviations. Data are weighted by several demographic variables, including age.

regression analysis including age as an independent factor and number of days as a dependent variable). Days of not-good mental health decreased with age ($p < .0001$); older respondents rated their mental health as higher than other age groups. There was evidence for age-related trends in health status as measured by number-of-day questions, and that these trends were in opposite directions for physical and mental health.

Since nonresponse and "don't know" responses are sometimes thought of as one type of index of question difficulty (Beatty et al., in press; Knauper, Belli, Herzog, & Hill, 1995; Knauper, Belli, Hill, & Herzog, 1997), item nonresponse was also analyzed to determine if, as predicted based on the cognitive interviewing results, the questions posed response problems for older respondents. Although missing data levels in general were low for this survey, older respondents failed to provide responses significantly more often than younger respondents for both the physical and mental health status questions. As Table 3 shows, nonresponse occurred less than 1% of the time for these items in the younger group, but was considerably higher (7% to 8%) for the older group ($p < .001$, using Fisher's Exact Test). It is relevant to note that higher nonresponse among older people was not a general phenomenon in this survey. For example, 100% of older respondents answered the self-perceived health status question.

☐ Discussion

Several complex factors may be involved in the cognitive processing of subjective questions on health, and these factors may pose special difficulties for older respondents. Based on the results of the cognitive

---

TABLE 3. MISSING REPORTS OF NUMBER OF NOT-GOOD DAYS IN THE PAST 30 BY AGE

Question/Age	Total	Missing Reports*
Physical health		
18–69	866	6 (0.7%)
70+	98	8 (8.2%)
Mental health		
18–69	866	6 (0.7%)
70+	98	7 (7.1%)

Notes. For this analysis, data are unweighted (raw) counts.
*$p < .001$.

interviews and field study conducted to investigate these processes, we discuss each of these major factors below.

Perceptions of Subjective Health Experiences

This investigation first questioned whether perceptions of key health status are generally shared between survey designers and respondents. In the cognitive interviews, subjects tended to respond quickly to the self-perceived health status question and articulated the basis for their answers. Older respondents seem similar to their younger counterparts in patterns and bases for answering self-perceived health status, as reported by other authors as well (Groves, Fultz, & Martin, 1992; Idler, 1992; Schechter, 1993). However, in examining responses to the more cognitively demanding number-of-days questions, both the cognitive interviews and the field test revealed difficulties in answering the questions and found differences between the age groups. These differences may reflect actual differences in health, or differences in health perceptions across age, or both.

Disentangling these variables was beyond the scope of this study, but future research could surely examine this. For example, it would be helpful to explore whether days of not-good mental health decrease with age due to actual improved mental health or to perceptions of the nature of mental health between age groups. Second, it would be worthwhile to explore further the conceptual differences between use of the terms not-good versus good health.

Response Strategies Used

Beyond the issue of comprehension of key concepts, we examined the cognitive strategies used by respondents to answer questions with number-of-days formats. From the cognitive interviewing results, some subjects seemed to search memory and count in order to provide a numeric response. However, the frequency of imprecise answers suggests the possibility that a nontrivial proportion of subjects may have adopted an alternative strategy despite the implied requirement to retrieve and count days. Those giving responses like "The whole time" or even "No, never" may have simply reported their impression of their health over the recent past, without giving serious thought to either the 30-day reference period or the number-of-days format. More directly, there were subjects who acknowledged to the interviewer that they did not (or in a few cases, would not) put effort into recalling the actual number of days for a particular health status. Some subjects verbalized use of a heuristic to respond (e.g., "I'll give a wild guess and say 6 days"). Others were not quite so clear in their response strategy but appeared to give a quick guess, representative of a typical month. Thus, a fair number of subjects may have bypassed the cognitive effort required in answering the given question by resorting to narratives or guessing. The finding that older subjects gave less precise answers than younger respondents suggests that older people may be more likely to use alternative cognitive strategies (although another explanation is discussed below).

Effectiveness of Response Format

The last issue considered involved the questions' effectiveness in producing an answer in terms of number of days. Every cognitive interviewer for the project agreed that subjects had pervasive difficulties doing so, especially among older subjects or those with serious medical conditions or limitations.

Item nonresponse has been used as a conservative measure of question problems (Knauper et al., 1995) and is sometimes thought of as providing a "best-case" indicator of how well questions are working. Telephone interviewers in the field study used standard survey probes when necessary in order to obtain a codeable response. Interestingly, for the questions on days of not-good physical and mental health, there was roughly 10 times as much item nonresponse among older respondents as among younger ones. This is of concern especially if one assumes that among those who did answer the question, (a) some older respondents failed to answer initially but gave a response that the interviewer interpreted, recoded, and keyed as a number, and (b) some older respondents may have given a numeric response based on a guess, merely to satisfy the interviewer's request for a number. Although interviewer-based probing can be relied on to "steer the respondent" and to avoid missing data, several studies suggest that interviewer errors increase when questions require extensive probing (Fowler & Mangione, 1990; Mangione, Fowler, & Louis, 1992). Further studies should focus on the administration of the questions and the resolution of problems to explore the nature of probing taking place.

The finding that some subjects may not answer in the question format suggests an additional issue for consideration: Did subjects have difficulties associated with the 30-day reference period itself rather than the format of the question? A review of studies by Sudman and Bradburn (1982), Sudman et al. (1996), and others suggests that the

30-day reference period selected by the questionnaire designers was probably an acceptable choice; that is, according to general questionnaire design principles, the question was designed properly and should work as intended. It is unlikely that subjects could not recall events in the 30-day reference period (as, in fact, some subjects in the cognitive interviews seemed to confirm). Rather, the key issue appears to be that important aspects of physical and mental health may not be discrete events that can be expressed easily in terms of days.

Finally, it is worthwhile to revisit the evidence that older respondents tended to be less likely to produce a precise answer to the not-good health days questions. Failure of older people to follow the demands of the question does not necessarily imply some general failing on their part related to cognitive processing, or even the use, on their part, of fundamentally different cognitive strategies. In particular, ease or difficulty of formulating a response may depend on the complexity of the pattern of health status that represents the person's life (chronicity, periodicity, and so on). Because older people are more likely to have complex health patterns, it may be that their difficulty derives not from cognitive processes associated with aging, but rather with measurement problems inherent in assessing quality of life for this age group. This notion is supported by the fact that the older subjects did not demonstrate the same magnitude of problems with the other health-related survey question administered to them (i.e., the general self-perceived health status question). This hypothesis could be tested by determining whether younger respondents with multiple, complex health conditions similarly exhibit difficulty in answering number-of-days questions.

Implications for Field Surveys

The debate between the need to formalize and standardize question administration and the reality that survey respondents encounter difficulty answering particular questions would benefit by focusing on issues such as those found in this investigation. Researchers in recent years have been inclined to suggest that the design of questions and selection of response format should not be viewed in a strict quantitative sense, but better conceptualized as part of an ongoing conversation between the researcher and the respondent (Beatty, 1995; Groves, 1989; Schaeffer & Maynard, 1996; Suchman & Jordan, 1990; Sudman et al., 1996; Schober, in press). In designing survey questions, the response format establishes a minimum standard of acceptable answers. Fowler (1984) clarifies that respondents and researchers must share the same perceptions of what constitutes an adequate answer. Certainly, one would not argue that a question asking "How many days . . .?" fails to clearly communicate to the respondent that a number is sought. However, such communication is of no help if the use of a precise number does not match the respondent's representation of the critical concept.

Another view of our results would be that the number-of-days questions do in fact work well and should be retained, but only in the context of certain forms of data analysis. In particular, since it appears that respondents sometimes have difficulty producing a quantitative response based on enumeration, perhaps responses to these questions might be used as an index of recent health, rather than as a precise measure. Rather than serving as point estimates, then, these should be used as correlate measures in analytic studies that attempt to relate such measures to other theoretically meaningful measures of health status and functioning, or simply as a comparative measure by which to assess group differences. More generally, a cognitive study of this type might help survey methodologists develop guidance about how particular measures should and should not be used by secondary analysts, especially with respect to the degree of specificity inherent in statistical estimates.

☐ Conclusion

Questionnaire designers typically focus on developing questions that will work for the average survey respondent. In this study, a simple response format was used to solicit a numeric response from the respondent. It is unclear to what degree respondents selected the strategy of recalling number of days and counting or estimating to provide an answer. However, our findings revealed that for some individuals, the response format was inconsistent with the question topic, and even a relatively simple format such as number of days was not easily used. Older people seemed to have unique difficulties complying with the response format. Perhaps some quality-of-life questions may be generally complex for respondents with multiple or extensive health problems. Overall, issues regarding cognitive burden and associated response error become more important when interviewing older respondents.

Finally, we point out that despite indications that the number-of-days questions are sometimes problematic, this study was not designed to test the validity of these questions. Overall, we do not argue that these questions are without credibility or value, on an aggregate basis. Rather, our focus has been to investigate particular problems that some people may have in answering them, to examine the response processes they use when attempting to arrive at an acceptable answer, and to perhaps indicate limitations in the uses of such data. In particular, because these questions seem to be particularly difficult for older people, researchers and policy makers need to be aware of these issues when both developing and analyzing survey instruments that target older respondents.

☐ Acknowledgments

The authors are grateful to Matthew Zack, David Moriarty, Ronald Wilson, and Norbert Schwarz for helpful comments on an earlier draft of this manuscript. In addition, many thanks to Karen Whitaker for helping in the coding and analysis of cognitive interview transcripts. The opinions expressed herein are the authors' and do not necessarily represent the official views or positions of the National Center for Health Statistics.

☐ References

Beatty, P. (1995). Understanding the standardized/non-standardized interviewing controversy. *Journal of Official Statistics, 11,* 147–160.

Beatty, P., Herrmann, D., Puskar, C., & Kerwin, J. (in press). Don't know responses in surveys: Is what I know what you want to know, and do I want you to know it? *Memory.*

Beatty, P., Schechter, S., & Whitaker, K. (1996). Evaluating subjective health questions: Cognitive and methodological investigations. *1996 Proceedings of the section on survey research methods.* Alexandria, VA: American Statistical Association, 956–961.

Beatty, P., Schechter, S., & Whitaker, K. (in press). Variation in cognitive interviewer behavior—Extent and consequences. *1997 Proceedings of the section on survey research methods.* Alexandria, VA: American Statistical Association.

Beatty, P., Willis, G., & Schechter, S. (1997). *Evaluating the generalizability of cognitive interview findings.* Statistical policy working paper 26: Seminar on statistical methodology in the public service. Washington, DC: Statistical Policy Office, Office of Management and Budget, 353–362.

Bercini, D. (1992). Pretesting questionnaires in the laboratory: An alternative approach. *Journal of Exposure Analysis and Environmental Epidemiology, 2,* 241–248.

Blair, E., & Burton, S. (1987). Cognitive processes used by survey respondents to answer behavioral frequency questions. *Journal of Consumer Research, 14,* 280–288.

Centers for Disease Control and Prevention (1995). Health-related quality-of-life measures—United States, 1993. *Morbidity and Mortality Weekly Report, 44,* 195–200.

DeMaio, T., & Rothgeb, J. (1996). Cognitive interviewing techniques: In the lab and in the field. In N. Schwarz & and S. Sudman (Eds.), *Answering questions: Methodology for determining cognitive and communicative processes in survey research* (pp. 176–196). San Francisco: Jossey-Bass.

Department of Health and Human Services (1991). *Healthy people 2000: National health promotion and disease prevention objectives* (DHHS Pub. No. PHS91-50212). Washington, DC: U.S. Government Printing Office.

Erickson, P., Wilson, R., & Shannon, I. (1995). Years of healthy life: Charting improvements in the nation's health. In J. Dimsdale & A. Baum (Eds.), *Quality of life in behavioral medicine research* (pp. 43–56). Mahwah, NJ: Erlbaum.

Forsyth, B., & Lessler, J. (1991). Cognitive laboratory methods: A taxonomy. In P. Biemer, R. Groves, L. Lyberg, N. Mathiowetz, & S. Sudman (Eds.), *Measurement errors in surveys* (pp. 393–418). New York: Wiley.

Fowler, F. (1984). *Survey research methods*. Newbury Park, CA: Sage.

Fowler F., & Mangione, T. (1990). *Standardized survey interviewing: Minimizing interviewer-related error*. Newbury Park, CA: Sage.

Groves, R. (1989). *Survey errors and survey costs*. New York: Wiley.

Groves, R., Fultz, N., & Martin, E. (1992). Direct questioning about comprehension in a survey setting. In J. Tanur (Ed.), *Questions about questions* (pp. 49–61). New York: Sage.

Hennessy, C., Moriarty, D., Zack, M., Scherr, P., & Brackbill, R. (1994). Measuring health-related quality of life for public health surveillance. *Public Health Reports, 109*, 665–672.

Herrmann, D. (1994). The validity of retrospective reports as a function of directness of retrieval processes. In N. Schwarz & S. Sudman (Eds.), *Autobiographical memory and the validity of retrospective reports* (pp. 21–37). New York: Springer-Verlag.

Idler, E. (1992). Self-assessed health and mortality: A review of studies. In S. Maes, H. Leventhal, & M. Johnston (Eds.), *International review of health psychology* (pp. 33–54). New York: Wiley.

Jobe, J., Keller, D., & Smith, A. (1996). Cognitive techniques in interviewing older people. In N. Schwarz & S. Sudman (Eds.), *Answering questions: Methodology for determining cognitive and communicative processes in survey research* (pp. 197–219). San Francisco: Jossey-Bass.

Knauper, B., Belli, R., Herzog, R., & Hill, D. (1995, May). *The quality of survey data as affected by question difficulty and respondents' cognitive capacity*. Paper presented at the 50th Conference of the American Association for Public Opinion Research, Fort Lauderdale, FL.

Knauper, B., Belli, R., Hill, D., & Herzog, R. (1997). Question difficulty and respondent's cognitive ability: The effect on data quality. *Journal of Official Statistics, 13*, 181–199.

Mangione, T., Fowler, F., & Louis, T. (1992). Question characteristics and interviewer effects. *Journal of Official Statistics, 8*, 293–307.

Patrick, D., & Erickson, P. (1993). *Health status and health policy: Quality of life in health care evaluation and resource allocation*. New York: Oxford University Press.

Rodgers, W., & Herzog, R. (1987). Interviewing older adults: The accuracy of factual information. *Journal of Gerontology, 42*, 387–394.

Royston, P. (1989). Using intensive interviews to evaluate questions. In F. J. Fowler, Jr. (Ed.), *Health survey research methods* (pp. 3–7). (DHHS Publication No. PHS 89-3447). Washington, DC: U.S. Government Printing Office.

Schaeffer, N., & Maynard, D. (1996). From paradigm to prototype and back again: Interactive aspects of cognitive processing in standardized survey interviews. In N. Schwarz & S. Sudman (Eds.), *Answering questions: Methodology for determining cognitive and communicative processes in survey research* (pp. 65–88). San Francisco: Jossey-Bass.

Schechter, S. (1993). *Investigation into the cognitive processes of answering self-assessed health status questions*. Working Paper Series No. 2. Hyattsville, MD: National Center for Health Statistics.

Schechter, S., & Herrmann, D. (1997). Proper use of self report questions in effective measurement of health outcomes. *Evaluation and the Health Professions, 20,* 28–46.

Schober, M. (in press). Making sense of questions: An interactional approach. In M. Sirken, D. Herrmann, S. Schechter, N. Schwarz, J. Tanur, & R. Tourangeau (Eds.), *Cognition and survey research.* New York: Wiley.

Schwarz, S., & Hippler, H. (1991). Response alternatives: The impact of their choice and presentation order. In P. Biemer, R. Groves, L. Lyberg, N. Mathiowetz, & S. Sudman (Eds.), *Measurement errors in surveys* (pp. 41–56). New York: Wiley.

Siegel, P. (1994). Self-reported health status: Public health surveillance and small-area analysis. In S. Schechter (Ed.), *Proceedings of the 1993 NCHS conference on the cognitive aspects of self-reported health status.* Working Paper Series No. 10. Hyattsville, MD: National Center for Health Statistics.

Suchman, L., & Jordan, B. (1990). Interactional troubles in face-to-face surveys interviews. *Journal of the American Statistical Association, 85,* 232–241.

Sudman, S., & Bradburn, N. (1982). *Asking questions.* San Francisco: Jossey-Bass.

Sudman , S., Bradburn, N., & Schwarz, N. (1996). *Thinking about answers: The application of cognitive processes to survey methodology.* San Francisco: Jossey-Bass.

Turner, C., & Martin, E. (1984). *Surveying subjective phenomena.* New York: Sage.

Willis, G. (1994). *Cognitive interviewing and questionnaire design: A training manual.* Working Paper Series No. 7. Hyattsville, MD: National Center for Health Statistics.

Willis, G. (1996). The use of strategic processes by survey respondents. In D. Herrmann, C. McEnvoy, C. Hertzog, P. Hertel, & M. Johnson (Eds.), *Basic and applied memory research: Practical applications* (Vol. 2, pp. 153–165). Mahwah, NJ: Erlbaum.

Willis, G., Royston, P., & Bercini, D. (1991). The use of verbal report methods in the development and testing of survey questionnaires. *Applied Cognitive Psychology, 5,* 251–267.

Willis, G., & Schechter, S. (1997). Evaluation of cognitive interviewing techniques: Do the results generalize to the field? *Bulletin de Méthodologie Sociologique, 55,* 40–66.

Diane O'Rourke
Seymour Sudman
Timothy Johnson
Jane Burris

CHAPTER

Cognitive Testing of Cognitive Functioning Questions

Over the last decade, there has been an increased interest in using survey techniques to measure the cognitive functioning of older, noninstitutionalized persons. Simultaneously, there has been rapid growth in understanding the cognitive processes used by respondents of all ages to answer survey questions and how these processes affect the quality of survey responses. In this chapter, we discuss why the quality of the responses of older respondents may differ cognitively from those of younger ones. We present some data from a sample of older adults to illustrate how cognitive processes affect survey measures of cognitive functioning and how cognitive interviews may be used to understand these effects.

The use of cognitive techniques in survey research began in the late 1970s, when government and academic researchers gathered to discuss the feasibility of applying, integrating, and testing previous cognitive research using survey methodology (Jobe & Mingay, 1991). The information processing view of cognitive psychology led survey researchers to see the respondent as a response system that underwent multiple processes when answering a question (Jobe & Mingay, 1991; Sudman, Bradburn, & Schwarz, 1996). Although several cognitive models of the survey response process currently exist (Jobe & Herrmann, 1994), it is generally understood that there are four basic stages involved in responding to survey questions: (a) question interpretation, (b) memory retrieval, (c) judgment formation, and (d) response editing (Strack & Martin, 1987; Tourangeau, Salter, D'Andrade, & Bradburn, 1984).

The merger of cognitive science and survey research yielded benefits for both disciplines. The primary benefit for survey research was the use of cognitive interviewing techniques and laboratory collaboration between the two disciplines, while cognitive researchers benefited from the use of longitudinal surveys and the opportunity to test the memory of everyday occurrences in natural settings (Jobe & Mingay, 1991).

The methods for determining the cognitive processes used by respondents include cognitive interviewing, interactional analysis, and a range of other methods such as sorting, response latency, and expert judgment (Schwarz & Sudman, 1996). Cognitive interviewing has been described as "one of the most successful areas of applied memory research" (Bekerian & Dennett, 1993, p. 275). A cognitive interview differs from a typical interview in that, in addition to obtaining answers to the questions, more is found out about how the respondent is answering and/or how the method of data collection is working. Verbal protocols, both concurrent and retrospective, focus groups, confidence ratings, paraphrasing, and memory cues are a few examples of cognitive interviewing techniques used by survey researchers (Jobe & Mingay, 1989; Sudman et al., 1996).

A cognitive interview in which verbal protocols are used is referred to as a think-aloud or talk-aloud interview. Verbal protocols were first developed by Ericsson and Simon (1980, 1993). The think-aloud interview may integrate other cognitive techniques, such as probes and paraphrasing, to elicit richer information from respondents. Retrospective protocols are one of the primary cognitive techniques used to assess a respondent's understanding of a word, phrase, or sentence, while concurrent protocols simply record the respondent's think-aloud interview. Think-alouds are also used to identify the respondents' retrieval strategies and judgment formation.

Because people live to older ages and more older people live alone rather than with children and other relatives, it is increasingly important to be able to assess cognitive functioning of older people as part of survey research. The work of Herzog and her colleagues on cognitive functioning and older people (Herzog & Schaie, 1988; Herzog & Rodgers, 1989; Herzog & Wallace, 1995; Rodgers & Herzog, 1992) has been especially important, and other significant contributions have been made by Albert (1994); Brandt, Spencer, and Folstein (1988); Fillenbaum, George, and Blazer (1988); Fillenbaum, Hughes, Heyman, George, and Blazer (1988); Hermann (1983); Holzer, Tischler, Leaf, and Myers (1984); Hultsch, Hammer, and Small (1993); Jobe, Keller, and Smith (1995); Jorm and Jacomb (1989); Larrabee and Levin (1986); Launer, Dinkgreve, Jonker,

Hooijer, and Lindeboom (1993); Nesselroade, Pedersen, McClearn, Plomin, and Bergeman (1988); and Scherr et al. (1988). However, to date, no one has used cognitive methods to test cognitive functioning questions with older respondents.

Essentially, three types of questions have been used to test memory and cognitive functioning in older people. First are subjective questions, such as "How would you rate your memory at the present time? Would you say it is excellent, very good, good, fair, or poor?" Questions such as these draw on the respondent's self-perception and require a subjective appraisal of their cognitive abilities. Subjective questions, whether global or specific, compel respondents to use judgmental strategies that may induce the construction of a specific target for comparison (Schwarz, Wanke, & Bless, 1994). The Metamemory Questionnaire (Zelinski, Gilewski, & Thompson, 1980) and the Memory Functioning Questionnaire (Gilewski, Zelinski, & Schaie, 1990) are two examples of instruments used to explore everyday memory problems encountered by older people. Items on these questionnaires address specific problems such as remembering names, appointments, and what people tell you. Although cognitive problems with self-perception questions are well recognized, these subjective questions are moderately correlated with performance on memory tasks, as well as with other variables such as general health and depression.

A second type of question consists of self-reports of current and past behaviors. The well-known Instrumental Activities of Daily Living (IADL) Scale (Lawton & Brody, 1969) is often used to assess the ability of older persons to perform tasks, such as shopping and housekeeping, as well as their medication-taking habits and their ability to handle finances. An individual's self-reports may also be used as indicators of short-term memory and for inferences about cognitive abilities and memory. Questions about a respondent's educational and work history may be used to test long-term memory.

A third type of cognitive assessment question attempts to test memory more directly. Respondents are asked to perform actual cognitive tasks, such as remembering a series of words, performing arithmetic tasks, reporting the current date, and recalling who is the current president of the United States (Herzog & Wallace, 1995).

☐ Older Respondents and Cognitive Processes

As is pointed out in several other chapters in this book, as we age there is a decline in short-term memory and total energy level. These two factors, either singly or jointly, affect the various stages in responding to survey questions.

Question Interpretation

For short, simple questions, there is no reason to expect that any respondents would have difficulties or that there would be differences between older and younger respondents. However, as questions become longer or more complex, older respondents are more likely than younger ones to have difficulty in remembering the entire question and would be more likely to forget some parts of the question and thus to misunderstand it.

If a question is ambiguous to some respondents, then they will use information from previous questions to help them disambiguate the meaning. This is one of the reasons why context effects (the effects of question placement in relation to other questions) are often observed (Sudman et al., 1996, Chap. 3). For older respondents, these context effects may be lower than for younger respondents because older respondents are less likely to remember the previous questions (see Knäuper, Chapter 17 in this volume).

Memory Retrieval

There is little evidence to suggest that there are differences in long-term memory between younger and older respondents, but as the memory retrieval becomes more difficult and requires greater effort, older respondents may abort their search for information sooner than younger respondents. This disparity is especially true for questions asking about lifetime behavior. In general, then, older respondents retrieve less information than younger ones when answering a question.

Judgment Formation

Because of differences in short-term memory and energy, older respondents are likely to use less information and less effort in forming their judgments about both attitudes and behavior. For questions about frequent behaviors, all respondents reduce their efforts by estimating rather than counting, but older respondents are even more likely to estimate than younger ones (Sudman et al., 1996, Chap. 9).

Response Editing

For close-ended questions, the final task faced by respondents is to select the answer category that best matches their judgments. There is substantial evidence that the order in which responses are presented has an effect on respondents (Sudman et al., 1996, Chap. 6). To the extent that short-term memory plays a role, one would expect different order effects for older versus younger respondents. Thus, greater order effects for older respondents would be expected on orally administered questionnaires for which the respondent must remember all the answers than on self-administered questionnaires in which all the answer categories are visible.

☐ Cognitive Interview Methods for Older Respondents

In conjunction with the National Center for Health Statistics (NCHS), the Survey Research Laboratory (SRL; University of Illinois at Chicago) used cognitive interviews to discover how older respondents answered questions about cognitive functioning and the problems they had with specific questions. Primarily, this research related to the first two phases of the survey process, that is, how respondents understood questions and how they retrieved information to answer these questions.

Because no one type of question can cover all aspects of memory and cognition, we used various sampling methods. We started with a focus group of nine respondents, all over the age of 70, at a senior citizens' social center in Champaign, Illinois. We then conducted face-to-face cognitive interviews with 13 persons who responded to announcements that we had posted at senior citizen apartment complexes. As the final step, we conducted 49 telephone cognitive interviews, 39 in Champaign-Urbana conducted by SRL staff, and 10 in the Washington, DC metro area conducted by NCHS staff. The Washington metro interviews were conducted with people who had responded to a flyer passed out at a meeting at their senior citizen housing unit. They were not paid an incentive. In Champaign-Urbana we identified several senior citizen housing complexes and, using a city directory, were able to identify the telephone numbers of persons living in those complexes. We called those numbers, screened for eligibility, and interviewed those who agreed to cooperate. In addition, some volunteers from those complexes called in response to flyers we had left at those locations. Champaign-Urbana respondents were paid $10 to participate.

Our experience suggests that the sampling method we used in Champaign-

Urbana is an excellent way of getting a sample of older persons for cognitive interviewing. We obtained a broad age range, and willingness to cooperate was good, increased by our offer to pay an incentive. Refusals seemed unrelated to the topic of the study, but were the same ones that are generally given by refusers: lack of time or interest. (The telephone interviews were conducted in the two weeks before Christmas. We were amused by the refusals of two 100-year-olds, both of whom said they were too busy, one due to holiday shopping and bridge club!)

The methods we used yielded samples of adults who were generally functioning at a relatively high or at least satisfactory cognitive level (like those typically interviewed for surveys). The problems they faced were those typically found among older people: poor vision and hearing and mobility difficulties. In our limited sample, about a quarter of our respondents wore hearing aids, and over 40% claimed that hearing was a problem, although we had no difficulty in completing our interviews.

Although this sample was not random, it had residential, educational, and income diversity. Most of the face-to-face interviews were conducted in private residences. While all of the telephone interviews in Champaign-Urbana were conducted with residents of senior citizen housing complexes, the economic circumstances of the residents varied dramatically. One apartment complex is publicly subsidized for low-income older people and disabled persons. Several others are private apartment complexes for those with middle incomes. Another is an upper-income, staged-care complex that included medium- to high-priced condominiums. As is typical of the older population, most of the respondents were female (74%). Education ranged from none to Ph.D., with the median being a high school diploma. Age ranged from 67 to 96 (including 6 people in their 90s), with a median age of 80.

Because we were testing the questions, they were asked as they originally had been drafted. But after the respondent had answered, structured probe questions were asked that assisted us in determining whether or not changes to the proposed question were needed. Once the proposed question had been asked, the interviewer was free to ask additional, unstructured probes as necessary. If the respondent said something that seemed unclear or that might lead to interesting methodological information, the interviewer was free to query in any way.

☐ Examples of Cognitive Testing of Cognitive Functioning Questions

Although the questionnaire used to conduct the cognitive interviews contained over 50 questions, many with subparts, only a small subset that exemplifies the cognitive testing of cognitive functioning questions is discussed in this section. The questions we tested on self-reports of current and past behaviors yielded no interesting results, and thus are excluded from the discussion.

Subjective Memory Appraisals

Respondents were asked a global memory status question using the same format as a typical global health status question: "How would you rate your memory at the present time? Would you say it is excellent, very good, good, fair, or poor?" Aside from the standard problem that different respondents calibrate their rating scales differently (e.g., what is "fair"), the key problem of this question was that respondents used different standards of comparison. We attempted to determine the standards of comparison they used by first asking an open-ended probe ("Why do you think that it's [rating given]?") and then, if necessary, a closed-ended question ("Did you compare your memory to that of other people your age, to younger people, to how good your memory used to be, or did you do something else?"). One fourth of the sample compared their memory to that of others their age, one third compared it to what it used to be, and the remaining third did not use explicit comparisons. Most of these respondents said something like "I don't have any problems with memory, so I'd rate myself as very good or good."

We would expect that respondents who compare themselves to others will generally rate themselves higher than those who compare their current memory to their prior memory, and that is the case in this small sample (see Table 1). Interestingly, in our sample the respondents who didn't use explicit comparisons seem distributed in about the same way as those who compared themselves to others, as opposed to those who compared their current memory to their prior

TABLE 1.   RATING OF MEMORY BY METHOD USED (IN PERCENTAGES)

Rating	Compared to Others	Compared to Prior	Absolute Memory
Excellent	6	0	13
Very good	38	17	33
Good	44	50	38
Fair	6	22	8
Poor	6	11	8
Total	100	100	100
n	16	18	24

memory. Our recommendation for improving understanding of this question is to make it more explicit by stating the comparison we would like respondents to make: "Compared to other people your age, how would you rate your memory?"

As a follow-up to the global memory question, we asked: "How would you rate your memory for remembering the names of people you meet? Would you say it is [same answer categories]?" and "How would you rate your memory for remembering something you have just been told or heard on TV, [same answer categories]?" Respondents gave significantly lower ratings to their ability to remember names or something they had just been told or heard on TV than they did in response to the general memory question, as may be seen in Table 2. These questions caused no cognitive problems because they are more specific, although the "names" question is still more specific than the "been told or heard on TV" question; 13% of respondents on this latter question said that their memory depended on how interested they were in what they had heard. An open-ended question asking what respondents found hard to remember confirmed these results. Remembering names was mentioned as something hard to remember by almost one third (32%) of the respondents.

It is not surprising that response to the global question on overall memory is correlated .54 ($p < .001$) with memory for names, and .68 ($p < .001$) with memory for something just told or heard on TV; the correlation between names and something just told or heard on TV is .45 ($p < .001$). Using all three items combined increases the reliability of the subjective measure of memory.

As an additional subjective memory appraisal, we asked respondents: "Compared with one year ago, would you say your memory is better

TABLE 2. RATING OF MEMORY OVERALL AND BY SPECIFIC TYPE (IN PERCENTAGES)

Rating	Overall	Names	Something Just Told or Heard on TV
Excellent	7	3	5
Very good	30	10	23
Good	44	32	36
Fair	11	28	20
Poor	8	27	3
Depends	0	0	13
Total	100	100	100
n	61	60	53

now, about the same, or worse now than it was then?" After their answer, they were asked: "Why do you think that?" Then they were asked a similar question but "compared to 10 years ago." Because the vast majority (76%) of the respondents rated their memory the same as it was one year ago, it is clearly better to ask about 10 years ago, a time frame long enough to show change. (Fully 60% reported that their memory was worse now.) The correlation between these two questions was .41. These two memory comparison questions were also correlated with the three memory ratings questions discussed above. The intercorrelations ranged from .31 to .56.

Cognitive Tasks

One standard measure of cognitive functioning is to ask a respondent to listen to and then recall several words aloud. We tested the following question: "Now I'm going to read you a set of eight words and ask you to recall as many as you can. We have purposely made the list long so that it will be difficult for anyone to recall all the words. Most people recall just a few. Please listen carefully as I read the set of words. When I finish, I will ask you to recall aloud as many of the words as you can, in any order. Do you have any questions? [Wait for answer.] The words are: army, bird, car, dog, lake, plant, ticket, and winter. Now please tell me the words you can recall."

The range of words recalled was wide (0 to 7), with a mean and median of 4. Column 2 of Table 3 shows the percentage of the sample

TABLE 3.   RATING OF RECALL FOR WORD MEMORY QUESTION*

Word	Percentage Remembering	
	Initial Query	End-of-Interview Query
Army	76.4	34.5
Bird	56.4	27.3
Car	27.3	18.2
Dog	65.5	43.6
Lake	41.8	29.1
Plant	43.6	16.4
Ticket	41.8	12.7
Winter	50.9	23.6
Mean recalled	4.0	2.0
Median recalled	4.0	2.0

*$n = 56$.

remembering each of the words the first time they were asked. There is, as expected, an order effect, with the first two words on the list and the last word remembered better than the words in-between. The interesting exception is the word "dog," which is the fourth word on the list, but is remembered by almost as many people as the first word. Many people also recalled words that were not one of the eight. Several people recalled "cat," which could be a misrecall of "car," but is probably due to an association with "dog." One 83-year-old woman, who may have grown up on a farm, recalled "bird" (her only correct recall) as well as "hogs," "chicken," and "cows." One coding consideration is how to treat the recall of words that sound alike. One 72-year old man recalled "picket." Clearly he misheard the word "ticket." Should respondents be penalized for memory if they have a hearing problem or if the person who interviews them is not very articulate?

After respondents had recalled as many words as they could remember, we asked "How did you go about trying to remember the words?" Some respondents said they tried to remember the first letter of each word, made easier because the words were in alphabetical order. Several respondents used word associations (e.g., he was in the "army"). The respondents' use of these memory aids indicate that level of recall may be related to the order of the words and the specific words used. Abstract words may be harder to recall.

Toward the end of the interview (30 questions later), respondents were asked to recall any of the eight words that they could still remember. Again the range was wide (0 to 6) but the median and mean were two words lower (both 2.0, respectively) than for initial recall. The percentage of respondents remembering specific words toward the end of the interview is shown in column 3 of Table 3. The greatest drop is for the word "army," which was the first word on the list. The correlation between scores for the initial and end-of-interview word list recall was .63 ($p < .001$). It is clear that the same short-term memory is being tested both times. Asking the word list twice increases the reliability of the measure.

Respondents generally found the word memory tests to be interesting and clearly related to memory. More than 80% thought that the questions were a good way to test memory. Almost half (43%) of the respondents thought that some of the questions in the interview were hard, and the eight-word recall was mentioned by 64% of those respondents as being hard, which topped the list of hard questions. In addition, 29% of the respondents found these questions interesting, and they topped the list of interesting questions. As one respondent said: "I learned something about myself. My memory isn't as good as I think."

When asking this question over the telephone, the interviewer must explain to the respondent before reading the words that it is essential that he/she not write anything down, for this invalidates the test. We purposely did not do this, so as not to corrupt the question as it was given to us. However, after we asked the respondents to recall the eight words, we asked if they had written anything down. In our sample, 6 of the 49 telephone respondents indicated that they had written down some of the words or letters to help them remember. (The data for these respondents were removed from the analysis for this question.) Of course, others could have too but did not want to admit it. Absent instructions to the contrary, this will naturally occur.

Another cognitive word test went as follows: "Now I am going to spell a word forward and I want you to spell it backwards. The word is 'world,' spelled W-O-R-L-D. Please spell 'world' backwards." This question showed reasonable variability. While the majority (56%) spelled world backwards correctly on the first try, approximately 10% stumbled before getting it right (e.g., "D-L-O-R, no, R-O-W"). Another 8% erred on the first try, but immediately corrected themselves. Over one quarter (26%) of the respondents spelled the word backwards incorrectly. The most frequent error was "D-L-O-R-W." Some respondents spelled the word aloud forward before spelling the word backwards, as if to better visualize it. The cognitive testing did not find any problems with asking a question of this type.

Another way to test cognitive functioning is to ask numerical questions. One such question that was tested went as follows: "For this next question, please try to count backwards as quickly as you can from the number I will give you. Please start with 86." (The interviewer was instructed to let the respondent count for 10 seconds.) Most (77%) of the respondents could do this well. Another 15% did fairly well but missed a number along the way, and another 2% could complete the task after further instructions. However, almost 7% of the respondents could not complete this task. They either did not comprehend what was being asked of them or could not count backwards from 86. One 79-year-old woman first said "86, 87." When read the original question again, she said "6, 5, 4, 3."

In the original version, if the respondent was unable to complete the task, interviewer instructions said "Allow the respondent to try again if (he/she) wishes to do so." We found that this was not adequate clarification for respondents with real problems. We ultimately added the following probe for respondents who could not complete the task: "We want you to count backwards. For example, starting with 90, you would say 90, 89, 88, 87, 86. Now *you* start with 86 and count backwards as quickly as possible." Even then some respondents could not do so, but for several the added instructions made a difference.

While the interviewers tried to stop respondents after approximately 10 seconds, it became clear that time was not a major issue; they would either go backwards correctly, possibly skipping one number along the way, or were not able to do so. Using how far backwards respondents get as a cognitive variable is problematic for two reasons. First, although the question asks the respondent to count backwards as quickly as possible, some people simply speak more slowly and deliberately than others, adding an additional factor to their math skills and cognitive abilities. Second, some respondents were slow in starting. For example, they would pause before starting (probably recalling the task in their mind), or would reiterate the task aloud (e.g., "okay, count backwards from 86"). While over two thirds (72%) of the respondents thought this question was a good way to test memory, it did not seem to discriminate well among noncognitively impaired adults. If this question is used, it is imperative that the 10-second time period begin only when the respondent begins to count.

Another numerical cognitive test question asked respondents to do subtractions in their head: "Now let's try some subtraction of numbers. 100 minus 7 equals what? (ANSWER) And 7 from that equals what? (ANSWER) And 7 from that equals?" (continuing for 5 subtractions). This question is a problem for a great many people; however, it is unclear how much of the problem is due to cognitive capability and how much is due to the perhaps poor quality of decades-old math education.

While almost one third (30%) of the respondents were able to complete the task accurately (i.e., starting with 100, subtract 7 five times and come up with the correct answers), many more could not do so. Some people did the first substraction correctly and then could not continue; others erred further along. About 76% of the respondents correctly subtracted 3 or 4 times out of 5. The remaining quarter got fewer than three right.

As a probe question, we asked: "Do you think this is a good way to test memory or not?" Many respondents did not think so, because for some it represented a task they had never mastered in the first place. Some respondents mentioned that they "never had been good at math." Many of these people were probably cognitively capable of doing those subtractions if they were under less pressure and/or if they could do them with a paper and pencil.

Our interviewing also brought up an important consideration for the coding and analysis of these data: how to score correct and incorrect answers. On the one hand, there is only one correct answer to each subtraction, if all preceding ones are done correctly. However, about half (49%) of the respondents made an error in one subtraction and then continued to subtract 7 correctly, although they were now subtracting from a number different from ours. For example, 100 minus 7 equals 93, minus 7 equals 86. One respondent subtracted 7 from 93 and came up with 87 (wrong), but then subtracted 7 from that and got 80 (a correct subtraction of 7). It would not be meaningful to code all subsequent responses as wrong, if the respondent got back on track. Cognitively, he/she was fulfilling the task. Also, should later errors be counted as much as early errors? Our conclusion is that these questions are less satisfactory for testing memory and cognitive functioning than are the word list questions.

☐ Recommendations for Measuring Cognitive Functioning in Surveys

Based on the results of the focus group and the cognitive interviews and our evaluation of the meaning of these results, we can make some preliminary recommendations for researchers attempting to measure memory and cognitive functions of older respondents via surveys. (We define older respondents as those who are are not living in nursing homes, who are not obviously cognitively impaired, and who are able to respond for themselves.)

We begin with some general observations.

1. Target respondents will generally be willing to participate in interviews that measure their cognitive functioning. Most respondents will find such a survey highly salient, interesting, and enjoyable. For an interview of half an hour or less, there is no indication that fatigue will be a problem.
2. Obtaining information about disabilities (e.g., vision, hearing, and mobility problems) and illnesses and medications is important, so as not to attribute cognitive difficulties to a respondent when the difficulties are really physical.
3. When testing cognitive functioning and memory, for reasons of both reliability and validity, ask questions of various types (e.g., subjective memory appraisals, current behaviors, and short-term memory tests). Any single question or type of question may be confounded by measurement problems, social desirability issues, and physical problems.

Regarding *subjective memory appraisal items*:

4. The single best subjective question to ask is "Compared to other people your age, how would you rate your memory at the present

time. Would you say it is excellent, very good, good, fair, or poor?" This wording gets all respondents comparing themselves to others their age. Other questions asking about subjective memory ratings for specific items, such as names or something just told or heard on TV, produce lower ratings but ratings that are correlated with overall memory and thus add to the reliability of the subjective measure.

5. Ask respondents also to compare their memories now to what they were in the past. If the previous year is used, only 20% of respondents report worse memory, compared to 60% if 10 years earlier is used as the comparison point.

6. The moderate positive intercorrelations among the five subjective questions examined suggests they and similar items might be usefully combined into a reliable measure of subjective memory appraisal. In our small sample, for example, these five questions were combined to produce a Cronbach's alpha of .80.

For *memory test items*:

7. Of all the memory test questions, the one asking respondents to remember the eight words was most successful in all respects, although the actual selection of words may need some modification to ensure that the words are clear to as many respondents as possible when spoken over the telephone. One way to ensure that the stimulus (speed, clarity) is identical for all respondents would be to record the words with a single speaker and then to play the recording to the respondent on the phone.

8. Although asking this series of words twice adds time to the instrument, the additional burden to respondents seemed negligible and asking twice does increase the reliability of the measure. The correlation between scores on the two sets is .64.

9. Asking respondents to spell "world" backwards also seems an effective way of testing cognitive functioning if one resolves how to score respondents who erred on their first try but immediately corrected themselves.

10. Generally, the numerical questions did not work as well with our respondents as did the word questions. The question asking respondents to count backwards is difficult to administer in its present form because it requires the interviewer to time the respondent for 10 seconds while having to listen carefully. It will also be difficult to code because it is not clear how to handle slips of a single number or different rates of speech. It might be useful to dichotomize the approximately 10% of respondents who cannot understand at all what is to be done or cannot do it at all from those

who understand but who answer more slowly or make minimal mistakes.

11. The subtraction question is highly problematic because it confounds basic subtraction skills with memory. Many respondents just are not used to do doing mental arithmetic, and the social pressure of the interview may add to their anxiety. Also, it is not at all clear how this question should be coded.

12. Like most other survey questions, those used to test cognitive functioning can benefit from being tested through cognitive interviewing. Conducting an interview exactly the way it will be done ultimately, a standard pretest, cannot identify all or even most of the problems that may be present. The cognitive interviewing process uses the participants as testers as well as respondents. Once the problems are identified, changes in wording and process can be made to better ensure that the results of the cognitive testing are reliable and valid.

13. If at all possible, we believe that cross-cultural evaluations of these items are necessary. Potential cross-cultural variability in the interpretation of subjective memory appraisal questions, in particular, should be investigated.

14. Cognitive functioning items also should be assessed for use with older respondents found in nursing homes and other nonindependent living arrangements, as it remains unclear from our work how applicable these items would be in these settings. This additional work will contribute to the continued development of cognitive functioning measures.

☐ Acknowledgments

This study was funded by a Professional Services Contract from the National Center for Health Statistics. We wish to thank Susan Schechter and Karen Whitaker of NCHS for conducting additional interviews for this study.

☐ References

Albert, M. (1994). Brief assessments of cognitive function in the elderly. *Annual Review of Gerontology and Geriatrics, 14,* 93–106.

Bekerian, D. A., & Dennett, J. L. (1993). The cognitive interview technique: Reviving the issues. *Applied Cognitive Psychology, 7,* 275–297.

Brandt, J., Spencer, M., & Folstein, M. (1988). The telephone interview for cognitive status. *Neuropsychiatry, Neuropsychology, and Behavioral Neurology, 1,* 111–117.

Ericsson, K. A., & Simon, H. A. (1980). Verbal reports as data. *Psychological Review, 8,* 215–251.

Ericsson, K. A., & Simon, H. A. (1993). *Protocol analysis: Verbal reports as data.* Cambridge, MA: MIT Press.

Fillenbaum, G. G., George, L. K., & Blazer, D.G. (1988). Scoring nonresponse on the Mini-Mental State Examination. *Psychological Medicine, 18,* 1021–1025.

Fillenbaum, G. G., Hughes, D. C., Heyman, A., George, L. K., & Blazer, D.G. (1988). Relationship of health and demographic characteristics to Mini-Mental State Examination score among community residents. *Psychological Medicine, 18,* 719–726.

Gilewski, M. J., Zelinski, E. M., & Schaie, K. W. (1990). The memory functioning questionnaire for assessment of memory complaints in adulthood and old age. *Psychology and Aging, 4,* 482–490.

Hermann, D. J. (1983). Questionnaires about memory. In J. E. Harris & P. E. Morris (Eds.), *Everyday memory: Actions and absent-mindedness* (pp. 133–151). London: Academic Press.

Herzog, A. R., & Rodgers, W. L., (1989). Age differences in memory performance and memory ratings as measured in a sample survey. *Psychology and Aging, 4,* 173–182.

Herzog, A. R., & Schaie, K. W. (1988). Stability and change in adult intelligence: 2. Simultaneous analysis of longitudinal means and covariance structures. *Psychology and Aging, 3,* 122–130.

Herzog, A. R., & Wallace, R. B. (1995). *Measures of cognitive functioning in the AHEAD survey.* Working paper, Institute for Social Research, University of Michigan, Ann Arbor.

Holzer, C. E., III, Tischler, G. L., Leaf, P. J., & Myers. J. K. (1984). An epidemiologic assessment of cognitive impairment in a community population. *Research in Community and Mental Health, 4,* 3–32.

Hultsch, D. F., Hammer, M., & Small, B. J. (1993). Age differences in cognitive performance in later life: Relationships to self-reported health and activity life style. *Journal of Gerontology: Psychological Sciences, 48,* P1–P11.

Jobe, J. B., & Herrmann, D. (1994). *Comparison of models of survey cognition and models of memory.* Paper presented at the Third Practical Aspects of Memory Conference, College Park, MD.

Jobe, J. B., Keller, D. M., & Smith, (1995). Cognitive techniques in interviewing older people. In N. Schwarz & S. Sudman (Eds.), *Answering questions: Methodology for determining cognitive and communicative processes in survey research* (pp. 197–219). San Francisco: Jossey-Bass.

Jobe, J. B., & Mingay, D. J. (1989). Cognitive research improves questionnaires. *American Journal of Public Health, 79,* 1053–1055.

Jobe, J. B., & Mingay, D. J. (1991). Cognition and survey measurement: History and overview. *Applied Cognitive Psychology, 5,* 175–192.

Jorm, A., & Jacomb, P. (1989). The Information Questionnaire on Cognitive Decline in the Elderly (IQCODE): Sociodemographic correlates, reliability, validity and some norms. *Psychological Medicine, 19,* 1015–1022.

Larrabee, G. J., & Levin, H. S. (1986). Memory self-ratings and objective test performance in a normal elderly sample. *Journal of Clinical and Experimental Neuropsychology, 8,* 275–284.

Launer, L. J., Dinkgreve, M. A. H. M., Jonker, C., Hooijer, C., & Lindeboom, J. (1993). Are age and education independent correlates of the Mini-Mental State Exam performance of community-dwelling elderly? *Journal of Gerontology: Psychological Sciences, 48,* P271–P277.

Lawton, M. P., & Brody, E. M. (1969). Assessment of older people: Self-maintaining and instrumental activities of daily living. *Gerontologist, 9,* 1979–1986.

Nesselroade, J. R., Pedersen, N. L., McClearn, G. E., Plomin, R., & Bergeman, C. S. (1988). Factorial and criterion validates of telephone-assessed cognitive ability measures. *Research on Aging, 10,* 220–234.

Rodgers, W. L., & Herzog, A. R. (1992). Collecting data about the oldest old: Problems and procedures. In R. M. Suzman, D. P. Willis, & K. G. Manton (Eds.), *The oldest old* (pp. 135–156). New York: Oxford University Press.

Scherr, P. A., Albert, M. S., Funkenstein, H. H., Cook, N. R., Hennekens, C. H., Branch, L. G., White, L. R., Taylor, J. O., & Evans, D. A. (1988). Correlates of cognitive function in an elderly community population. *American Journal of Epidemiology, 128,* 1084–1101.

Schwarz, N., & Sudman, S. (Eds.). (1996). *Answering questions: Methodology for determining cognitive and communicative processes in survey research.* San Francisco: Jossey-Bass.

Schwarz, N., Wanke, M., & Bless, H. (1994). Subjective assessment and evaluations of change: Some lessons from social cognition research. *European Review of Social Psychology, 5,* 181–210.

Strack, F., & Martin, L. L. (1987). Thinking, judging, and communicating: A process account of context effects in attitude surveys. In H.-J. Hippler, N. Schwarz, & S. Sudman (Eds.), *Social information processing and survey methodology* (pp. 123–148). New York: Springler-Verlag.

Sudman, S., Bradburn, N. M., & Schwarz, N. (1996). *Thinking about answers: The application of cognitive processes to survey methodology.* San Francisco: Jossey-Bass.

Tourangeau, R., Salter, W., D'Andrade, R., & Bradburn, N. (1984). Cognitive sciences and survey methods. In T. B. Jabine, M. L. Straf, J. M. Tanur, & R. Tourangeau (Eds.), *Cognitive aspects of survey methodology: Building a bridge between disciplines* (pp. 35–43). Washington, DC: National Academy Press.

Zelinski, E. M., Gilewski, M. J., & Thompson, L. W. (1980). Do laboratory tests relate to self-assessment of memory ability in the young and old? In L. W. Poon, J. L. Fozard, L. S. Cermak, D. Arenberg, & L. W. Thompson (Eds.), *New directions in memory and aging: Proceedings of the George A. Talland Memorial Conference* (pp. 519–544). Hillsdale, NJ: Erlbaum.

15

CHAPTER

Robert F. Belli
Paul S. Weiss
James M. Lepkowski

Dynamics of Survey Interviewing and the Quality of Survey Reports: Age Comparisons

One of the most important considerations for any survey data collection is the quality of survey reports, and how these reports depend on the cognitive processes that respondents employ while answering survey questions (Sudman, Bradburn, & Schwarz, 1996). Given the evidence that aging affects language and memory processing (Craik & Jennings, 1992; Kemper & Kemtes, this volume), determining the respective roles of age and cognitive processes upon the quality of survey reports deserves focused attention. This chapter will explore one piece of this domain by examining the associations among age of respondent, the characteristics of the verbal exchanges between interviewers and respondents, and the quality of survey retrospective reports on hospitalizations and physician office visits. Of particular interest is whether there is any evidence that interviewer tailoring affects the quality of retrospective reports differentially for older and younger respondents.

Research has consistently demonstrated impairments suffered by older subjects in their long-term memory abilities when tested in laboratory settings (Craik & Jennings, 1992), and there is some evidence that older persons have difficulties in remembering details from their autobiographical pasts (Borrini, Dall'Ora, Della Sala, Marinelli, & Spinnler, 1989; Holland & Rabbitt, 1990). However, although retrospective reporting errors are consistently observed among all age groups in surveys (Belli

& Lepkowski, 1996; Cannell, Fisher, & Bakker, 1965; Herzog & Rodgers, 1989), age-related effects in the accuracy of retrospective reports have been inconsistently found. Older people at times do not show any performance decrements in their retrospective reporting in comparison to younger respondents, such as reports on past voting behavior and being hospitalized (Herzog & Dielman, 1985; Herzog & Rodgers, 1989). At other times, older persons have been found to be less accurate in their retrospective reports. Cannell et al. (1965) found a trend of poorer reporting of hospitalizations among older respondents, and a meta-analysis by Sudman and Bradburn (1974), on the reporting of expenditures, financial and medical histories, and past voting behavior, did demonstrate a significant increase in underreporting with age. Thus, although there is some degree of evidence of age-related deficits in the retrospective reports of older respondents in surveys, the inconsistency of findings suggest that in comparison to controlled laboratory settings, survey settings are either masking the memory deficits that the aged are experiencing, or promoting the abilities of older respondents to remember their pasts.

Since surveys do not present to-be-remembered material in controlled settings that can directly account for memory differences between young and old, a number of factors other than improving the memory performance of older people can contribute to similar rates of retrospective reporting accuracy between older and younger respondents. Factors that are most clearly seen as possibilities are those associated with the nature of the to-be-remembered information. For example, the reporting of voting behavior is notorious for leading to overreporting, which may be due more to social desirability factors than to memory processes (Presser, 1990; but also see Belli, Traugott, Young, Traugott, McGonagle, & Rosenstone, 1998, for a memory-based explanation of overreporting), and social desirability concerns may be less pronounced among older people. As another example that involves the salience of the to-be-remembered information, hospitalizations may be encoded more thoroughly by older than younger respondents as their occurrence is likely to signal life-threatening events more often among older persons.

Surveys may also introduce environmental or contextual supports that especially aid the memory processes of older respondents (Craik & Jennings, 1992). One possibility is that older respondents may be more motivated while answering survey questions and be better able to deal with the tedious nature of the survey process, because, in comparison to younger respondents, they may feel less pressed for time and may actually find greater enjoyment in the opportunity for social interaction. Another possibility, the target of the present chapter, is that environmental support may arise from interviewers tailoring their techniques to meet the perceived cognitive or social challenges posed by older respondents.

Although survey interviewing is most usually conducted using techniques of standardization (Beatty, 1995), in which the interview is scripted in advance and interviewers, for example, are required to read questions exactly as written, even when following standardized maxims there is considerable latitude in the kinds of verbal behaviors that interviewers will employ. A great deal of latitude emerges in standardized interviewing as interviewers are expected to repeat questions in whole or in part, or to probe respondents nondirectively, whenever they recognize that respondents are not fully comprehending what is being asked. Moreover, despite the maxims of standardized interviewing techniques, it is widely recognized that interviewers do violate them (Oksenberg, Cannell, & Kalton, 1991; Schaeffer & Maynard, 1996; Suchman & Jordan, 1990). Ostensibly to assist respondents (among other reasons), interviewers at times will ask questions that are discrepant to the questions as written by the survey researchers, and they will at times probe respondents in ways that will bias the responses that are provided.

Importantly, given the latitude that interviewers display in their interviewing technique, there is evidence of the differential interviewing techniques for older respondents in comparison to younger ones. Moles (1987) found evidence for interviewer tailoring in that interviewers more often repeated question stems and response options to older than younger respondents, and they also reminded older respondents more often to examine their respondent booklets, apparently in response to the greater difficulty that they perceived among their older respondents toward understanding and evaluating the survey questions that they had asked. Herzog and Rodgers (this volume) note the presence of interviewer tailoring by the greater repetition of nouns in a cognitive functioning test for older than younger respondents. Evidence for interviewer tailoring also arises in the work of Groves and Magilavy (1986), who found in analyses of nine telephone surveys that there was more interviewer-associated variance in survey reports for older than younger respondents. This finding of greater interviewer effects for older respondents suggests that interviewer tailoring may be having influences on the data quality of some older respondents, but not others.

Stereotypes of aging may play a role in interviewer tailoring toward the aged. Kwong See and Ryan (this volume) note that young adults believe aging is accompanied by declines in intelligence, memory, and language use. Moreover, such beliefs correspond to patronizing communication patterns with older people (see also Kemper & Kemtes, this volume). However, patronizing communication may have both positive and negative consequences. For example, Kemper, Vandeputte, Rice, Cheung, & Gubarchuk (1995) did find, in a problem solving task involving dyads, that young subjects adopted a simplified and patronizing speech style when paired with older subjects. Although the older subjects reported that they had experienced more receptive and expressive problems when paired with young subjects, the speech adjustments made by the younger subjects toward their older partners, which included providing more information to older listeners, did improve the older subjects' performances. Similarly, interviewers may be adjusting their verbal styles in their exchanges with older respondents, which can compensate for deficits that would otherwise arise when remembering past events. Regarding this issue, there is evidence that interviewer alterations from exact question reading does not harm and may actually improve the accuracy of respondent reports about their health visits to physicians (Belli & Lepkowski, 1996; Dykema, Lepkowski, & Blixt, 1997).

To illustrate the potential role of interviewer tailoring on the quality of retrospective reports, consider an exchange between a professional interviewer and a 75-year-old female respondent from a health survey (depicted in Table 1) conducted by the Survey Research Center at the University of Michigan. The question objectives are concerned with gaining a frequency report on the number of physician office visits that occurred in the past 6 months. As written, the question reads, "How many times have you seen or talked to a medical doctor or assistant about your own health at a *doctor's office* or *at an HMO* since December, 1, 1992?" As can be seen, the interviewer said a number of phrases that deviated from standardized question wording. The year of the reference period was not mentioned, and the interviewer introduced the notions that the respondent should not consider times in which a physician ("him") was seen in the hospital, but only times when a physician was seen in "his office." Following the question reading is a very lively exchange in which an office visit report for the respondent's "blood pressure and sugar" was determined to have occurred before the reference period, in which the interviewer then encourages the respondent to think of particular kinds of physicians ("back doctor or your foot doctor"), and which finalizes with the interviewer leading the respondent to think of the time after she had gotten "out of the hospital," apparently "since April." There can be no doubt that in this exchange the interviewer was tailoring her interviewing in an attempt to assist the respondent's long-term memory recall.

TABLE 1.

I: How many times have you seen or talked to a medical doctor or assistant about your own health at a doctor's office or at an HMO since December the first? Don't count the times you saw him when you were in the hospital. How many times have you gone to his office or to his. . . .

R: Well, I went to the doctor's office to see about my, oh, my blood pressure and sugar.

I: Alright, how often do you go to see him?

R: Well I got to make an appointment now because I haven't been there in about, oh, about six months or more.

I: Oh, it's been a good while! So, have you been to see your back doctor or your foot doctor, other than when . . .

R: I don't, I don't have a straight back doctor, and I have to go to a specialist for my leg.

I: Alright now, have you seen any doctors since you got out of the hospital?

R: Uh-huh. Yeah.

I: Alright, how many times have you gone to the doctor since April?

R: Oh, I've gone twice.

I: Twice? Thank you.

However, whether the interviewer's verbal behavior in this exchange was more harmful or more beneficial toward this older respondent's accuracy of report is an open question. This exchange reveals a great deal of "common ground" that had been developed in prior question-answer exchanges (Clark & Schober, 1992). The omission of the year could potentially lead to confusion on the respondent's part as to what is the exact reference period, yet such confusion would likely be attenuated since preceding questions asking about visits to doctors in emergency rooms and urgent care centers used the exact same reference period. In addition to the emergency room and urgent care questions, an even earlier question asked about overnight stays in the hospital. There can be no doubt that these earlier exchanges had encouraged the interviewer to introduce statements telling the respondent to not count the times in which the doctor had been seen in the hospital or those that involved visits to certain specialists, and to focus attention on the time period after April. In this latter case, the interviewer may have been correct in her assumption that such tailoring of the respondent's focus of retrieval would assist in gaining an accurate report. One the other hand, such tailoring may have been misguided. The directive character of the interviewer's probing may have biased the respondent away from remembering relevant office visits. Additionally, older respondents have been shown to have greater difficulty than younger ones in remembering earlier questions (Herzog & Rodgers, 1989; Knäuper, this volume), and thus the interviewer may have been making an incorrect assumption about this respondent having remembered her answers to previous questions.

This exchange raises a couple of key issues. The first is whether the type of interviewer tailoring that is revealed in this exchange occurs more frequently with older than younger respondents. To examine this first issue, we will report on *behavior coding* measures (Fowler, 1992; Fowler & Cannell, 1996; Oksenberg et al., 1991), which are measures derived from the coding of taped interviews that examine various aspects of the verbal behavior of interviewers and respondents. More specifically, interviewers are coded on whether they ask questions as written or make significant changes from the script in their question reading, and on whether they probe and provide feedback in a nondirective or directive manner. Respondents are coded on whether they have overt problems in understanding questions and on whether their responses meet question objectives. In analyses that associate behavior codes with age, we do find that, in general, there is greater interviewer tailoring, as evidenced by a greater number of question reading changes and higher levels of probing, with older than younger respondents. In addition, older respondents reveal greater difficulties in understanding questions, and they more often provide inadequate responses, in comparison to younger ones.

The second key issue is whether interviewer tailoring affects the quality of survey retrospective reporting differentially for older and younger respondents. In this chapter, we seek to discover whether age modifies the associations between behavior codes and the response accuracy of reported health events, as would be revealed by an interaction between age and behavior coding measures as predictors of response accuracy. Indeed, analyses reveal interactions between age and some of the behavior codes, which indicate that the dynamics of verbal exchange differentially predict response accuracy for older and younger respondents. However, there is no clear evidence of the efficacy of interviewer tailoring among older respondents.

☐ Method

Survey

A total of 2,006 members of an HMO in the Detroit metropolitan area responded in a face-to-face standardized survey about health and health care utilization (66.6% response rate). Probability sampling techniques were used to select respondents within the HMO, with oversampling of individuals between the ages of 14 and 17 years, those older than 65 years, and persons who were African American. Interviews were conducted during the period of April to August, 1993, and each lasted approximately one hour. Questions on the survey included number of hospital stays, number of visits to health care providers, health insurance coverage, health expenditures, and the presence of medical conditions. Nearly all interviews were, with respondent permission, audiotape recorded. In addition, respondents were asked if research staff could obtain medical records data from their HMO. A total of 1,834 respondents gave permission to both requests.

Behavior Coding

Through stratified random sampling controlling for respondent age, gender, and race, a sample of 455 taped interviews were selected and behavior coded. The age distribution of those respondents whose tapes were behavior coded included 53 persons (12%) between 14 and 17 years, 29 (6%) between 18 and 24 years, 66 (15%) between 25 and 34 years, 88 (19%) between 35 and 44 years, 57 (13%) between 55 and 64 years, and 69 (15%) who were 65 years or older at the time of the interview. Six behavior coders with interviewing experience as well as experience monitoring interviewer performance or behavior coding were given coding training commensurate with their experience. All coders participated in group training sessions involving the coding of selected interview passages and thorough follow-up discussion of a subset of independently coded interviews.

The behavior coding scheme is depicted in Table 2. Each question-answer exchange between interviewer and respondent was assessed for the presence or absence of each of the codes listed in Table 2. As can be seen, the codes are grouped according to major aspects of the questioning process, which includes interviewer question asking, respondent answering, interviewer probing, and interviewer feedback. Assignment of only one of the interviewer question-asking codes was

TABLE 2. BEHAVIOR CODES

Interviewer question-asking codes

Q-E   Exact: Reads exactly as written or makes insignificant changes.
Q-S   Significant changes: Makes wording changes that can affect written question meaning.
Q-O   Other changes: Verifies, states, or suggests an answer; reads nonapplicable question; skips applicable question.

Respondent answering codes

R-I   Interruption: Interrupts question with an answer.
R-C   Clarification: Expresses uncertainty, requests question repetition, or seeks clarification.
R-Q   Qualified response: qualifies answer with phrases such as "about," "I guess," "maybe," etc.
R-U   Uncodable/inadequate response: Response does not meet question objectives.
R-DK   Expressions of "don't know" that occur before a final codable response is given.

Interviewer probing codes

P-A   Adequate probing: Probing is non-directive and sufficient.
P-I   Inadequate probing: At least one probe is directive, or under- or overprobes.

Interviewer feedback codes

F-AS   Acceptable short: Neutral and appropriate short phrase (1–3 words) such as "Thank you."
F-AL   Acceptable long: Neutral and appropriate longer phrase such as "Thanks. That's useful information for our study."
F-US   Unacceptable short: Offers short phrase that may indicate approval for the content of the response.
F-UL   Unacceptable long: Offers longer phrase that may indicate approval for the content of the response.
F-UR   Unacceptable reward: Approval for a "don't know" response, refusal, digression, interruption, or inadequate final answer.

---

mandatory per every exchange; only one of the interviewer probing codes could be assigned per exchange, but no assignment of this type of code was also permitted if no probing had occurred (and if, in the judgment of the coder, probing wasn't necessary).

Following the coding scheme, the exchange depicted in Table 1 would be assigned codes Q-S for the significant change in question asking from the script, R-U for the respondent providing a number of comments that do not provide an answer to the number of times physicians were seen, P-I for the directive probes focusing the respondent's attention to the period after her hospital stay, and F-AS for the "thank you" offered by the interviewer after the response of "twice" was obtained.

☐ Results and Discussion

Two sets of models were applied to the data to examine the relationships among age, behavior code assignments, and the accuracy of responses. The first set concentrated on broadly defined measures of behavior codes, while the second set was more focused in examining a more specific assignment of behavior codes.

First Set: Broad Measures

Age and Behavior Coding

Our initial interest was in whether there existed a relationship between age of respondent and the verbal behavior of interviewers and respondents over a broad set of questions. Behavior coding was conducted on the major portion of the survey involving questions on health care utilization, access to health care, health expenditures, injuries, and chronic conditions. Due to skip patterns, respondents were asked an unequal number of questions. Therefore, we computed for each behavior in Table 2 the proportion of all questions asked for which the behavior occurred.

Two regression models were estimated: (a) behavior code assignments (for each code separately) regressed on a linear term for age, and (b) behavior regressed on linear age and the square of age, as a quadratic term. Although our expectations were limited to discovering a linear trend in which there would be higher levels of interviewer tailoring for older respondents, we included the analysis of quadratic models to assess the possibility of curvilinear age effects.

The results of these models are presented in Table 3, which presents the coefficients and their p-values (for terms that were significant at $\alpha = .10$) for the linear term in the first model and the quadratic term in the second model. We also conducted the same models with the addition of including the level of respondent education as a control variable, which did not affect the pattern of results for respondent age, and thus are not reported. One clear trend in the linear terms is that all

TABLE 3.   ASSOCIATIONS OF BEHAVIOR CODE ASSIGNMENTS WITH AGE: FIRST SET

Code	Linear Age		Quadratic Age	
	β	p	β	p
Q-E	−0.05	ns	−0.01	=.03
Q-S	0.05	=.10	0.004	<.01
Q-O	0.02	<.001	0.001	<.001
R-I	0.05	<.001	0.002	=.08
R-C	0.06	<.001	0.001	=.02
R-Q	−0.003	ns	0.001	=.03
R-U	0.10	<.001	0.003	<.001
R-DK	0.05	<.001	0.002	<.01
P-A	0.03	<.01	0.002	<.01
P-I	0.07	<.001	0.004	<.001
F-AS	−0.06	ns	0.004	<.05
F-AL	0.01	=.05	0.000	ns
F-US	0.01	=.09	0.000	ns
F-UL	0.002	ns	0.000	ns
F-UR	0.02	<.001	0.000	ns

of the significant associations indicate that the assignment of behavior codes occurs more often during the verbal exchanges that include older respondents. Many of these behaviors are suggestive of interviewer tailoring, including some that are discrepant from the ideals of standardized interviewing techniques, such as significant question reading changes (Q-S), inadequate probing (P-I), and unacceptable reward (F-UR). Some of the significant associations involve behaviors, such as adequate probing (P-A) and acceptable long feedback (F-AL) that, although consistent with the ideals of standardized interviewing, are also suggestive of a greater degree of tailoring. Among significant associations involving quadratic terms, all except exact question reading (Q-E) show a pattern in which the behaviors occur more frequently in exchanges involving younger or older respondents than middle-aged respondents. For exact question reading, the exchanges of middle-aged respondents received this assignment most often.

Figures 1, 2, and 3 depict the predicted values of significant question reading changes (Q-S), expressions for clarification (R-C), and expressions of "don't know" (R-DK) as a function of age for the linear and quadratic equations. These particular behaviors are selected for illustration at this point as they emerge in the interaction effects reported

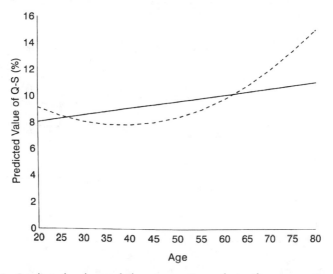

FIGURE 1. Predicted values of the proportion of significant question wording changes (Q-S) as a function of age depicting the linear regression curve (solid line) from the model for that regressed Q-S on a linear term for age (solid line), and depicting the quadratic regression curve (dashed line) in a model that regressed Q-S on both linear age and the square of age: broad measures.

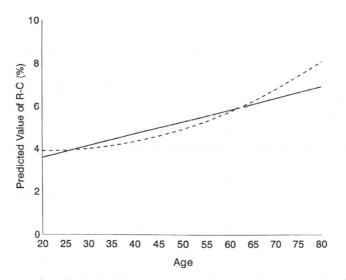

FIGURE 2. Predicted values of the proportion of respondent expressions for clarification (R-C) as a function of age depicting the linear regression curve (solid line) from the model for that regressed R-C on a linear term for age (solid line), and depicting the quadratic regression curve (dashed line) in a model that regressed R-C on both linear age and the square of age: broad measures.

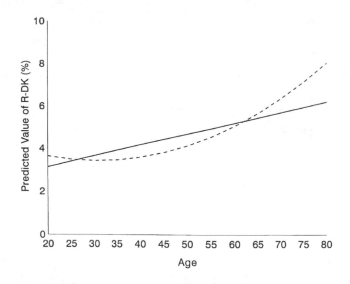

FIGURE 3. Predicted values of the proportion of respondent expressions of "don't know" (R-DK) as a function of age depicting the linear regression curve (solid line) from the model for that regressed R-DK on a linear term for age (solid line), and depicting the quadratic regression curve (dashed line) in a model that regressed R-DK on both linear age and the square of age: broad measures.

below. The predicted values for the behaviors approximately double from the lowest to highest respondent ages, particularly for quadratic models. Age of respondent is strongly related to the nature of the verbal interaction with interviewers.

Overall, these data are consistent with the hypothesized interviewer tailoring for older respondents, although there is an unexpected finding that interviewer tailoring was pronounced for younger respondents as well. Interviewers are more likely to deviate from standardized question reading with both younger and older respondents, with older respondents receiving a higher proportion of changed question reading than younger respondents. Apparently, interviewers are tailoring their verbal behaviors to meet what they perceive as the different demands of respondents who vary in ages. Younger and particularly older respondents also show more difficulty with handling the demands of the survey than do middle-aged respondents, since they are more likely to have problems understanding survey questions and more likely to provide inadequate responses. Probing tends to occur when the respondent seeks clarification or provides a response that is less than adequate. Interviewers probe more often for younger and older respondents, with both optimal and less-than-optimal probing (from the standpoint of standardized interviewing ideals) for these groups. Optimal and less-than-optimal feedback is also elevated for older respondents. All of these findings support the notion of interviewer tailoring behavior to the age of the respondent. That is, significant question reading changes, adequate and inadequate probing, and acceptable and unacceptable feedback, tend to occur more often with older (as well as younger) respondents. Such tailoring may help to overcome respondent problems, may contribute to increasing respondent problems, or may be caused by them.

Accuracy

Next, within the first set of models, we sought to examine how age and behavior code assignments may interact in predicting the accuracy of responses. Accuracy of response was determined by considering the data to four reports on the survey. The first report was about hospital stays, which involved two survey questions: (1) a yes/no response to "Since (CURRENT MONTH) 1st, 1992, have you been a patient in a hospital *overnight*?"; and (2) given a "yes" response to this first question, "How many different times did you stay in any hospital overnight or longer since (CURRENT MONTH) 1st, 1992?" The reported number of hospital stays was determined as either the value reported in (2) or zero if the answer to the first question was "no." In a few instances where respondents gave a range even after interviewer probing (e.g., 1–3 times), the midpoint of the range was used.

The second, third, and fourth reports all concerned number of health care visits, but the reference period varied from one report to the other. The second report used a long reference period where respondents were randomly assigned to one of two reference periods, *6 months* or *12 months*. Data on number of visits were collected in a series of questions about health care visits to hospital emergency rooms, urgent care centers, doctor's offices, and any other health care facility. Following this series, the interviewer summed the number of reported visits and asked "I see that the total number of visits you had to medical doctors or assistants during the past (reference period: 6 or 12) months is (TOTAL). Is this number correct?" If the respondent answered "No," the interviewer read a scripted probe to determine the exact number of visits. For the purposes of this analysis, if the respondent confirmed the interviewer's summed number of visits, that sum was used as the survey report. If the respondent answered "No" to the confirming question, the respondent's final answer to the scripted probe was used as the survey response.

The third and fourth reports involved shorter reference periods of four and two weeks, respectively. If there were no health visits reported to the long reference period question, respondents were coded as having zero visits to both the 4- and 2-week reference period questions. If there was one or more health care visits reported to the long reference period question, respondents were asked, "Including visits to hospital emergency rooms, urgent care centers, doctor's offices or HMO's, and to other places that you already told me about, (was this visit/how many of these visits were) during the past 4 weeks shown on this calendar?" Answers of "no" or "none" resulted in zero reports for both the 4- and 2-week reference periods; otherwise the reported value was entered. Additionally, any nonzero response to the 4-week reference period was followed with "(Was this visit/ How many of these visits were) during the past two weeks shown on this calendar?", with responses entered for the 2-week reports.

For all these measures, the absolute value of the difference between the survey report and the medical record was computed. These absolute values were standardized for each of the four reports. The standardized values for each respondent were then summed and the sum restandardized to yield an overall or global measure of accuracy across the four reports. Interpreting discrepancies between reports and records as an indication of accuracy must be done with caution, however. The medical records are known to be incomplete by failing to capture visits made to facilities outside of the HMO (Jay, Belli, and Lepkowski, 1994). One sequence of questions involved detailed queries concerning the last visit to a medical care provider, including where care was received. Approximately 16% of respondents reported having a last visit to a medical facility which was outside the HMO. Although the level to which respondents reported out-of-system visits is not known, we assume that they are present and would lead respondents to report visits that would not appear in the medical records. Thus, our global measure of accuracy should not be considered as completely valid. Nevertheless, the measure does capture some degree of report accuracy and it is adequate for our purposes.

In associating the global accuracy measure with age, two regression models were estimated, one with linear and a second with linear and quadratic terms for age. Neither term was significantly associated with accuracy, although the linear term did suggest a trend in which older respondents were less accurate than younger ones ($b = 0.004$, $p = .13$). Since the model with only the linear term was a better fit of the data than the one which included the quadratic term, subsequent analyses testing age by behavior code interactions used only the linear age term in the model.

Given the evidence of interviewer tailoring reported previously, the question arises whether interviewer tailoring for older respondents improves the accuracy of survey reports. If so, we would expect to see interactions between age and behavior codes in predicting the accuracy of response. For example, the presence of significant question reading changes (Q-S) indicates that interviewers are tailoring their verbal behavior to meet the perceived demands of respondents. If such tailoring was of benefit, and benefited older respondents more than younger respondents, we would expect to see a statistically significant age by Q-S interaction, such that for older respondents a high level of significant question reading changes is associated with greater accuracy, whereas for younger respondents more frequent significant question reading changes may not show any appreciable association with accuracy.

We constructed separate models for each of the behaviors which had shown significant linear or quadratic age terms in the models presented earlier associating age with the behavior codes. In the present models, the accuracy measure was regressed on age of respondent, the proportion of question exchanges in which behavior codes were assigned, and the interaction of age and behavior codes. Three behaviors had significant interactions with age, significant question reading changes (Q-S , $b = 0.0004$, $p = .06$), respondent expressions for clarification (R-C, $b = 0.0014$, $p = .02$), and expressions of "don't know" (R-DK, $b = 0.0014$, $p < .01$). Figures 4, 5, and 6 depict these interaction effects by fixing the level of behavior code assignments at around the 20th and 80th percentiles, and by providing the regression lines in predicting accuracy (higher standard absolute differences indicate greater inaccuracy) as a function of respondent age. The patterns of these three interactions consistently show that high levels of behavior are associated with lower accuracy for older respondents, but higher accuracy for younger respondents.

These results show a dynamic relationship between the verbal exchanges that occur with respondents of different ages and the accuracy of responses. Somewhat surprisingly, the directions of the interactions are opposite those expected if interviewer tailoring was of special benefit to older respondents. In fact, they are more consistent with an interpretation that younger respondents benefit more from interviewer tailoring. However, there are considerations that preclude any firm conclusions regarding the role of interviewer tailoring in these results. Since the data are observational and use global measures of behavior codes and accuracy which are not directly tied each other, the causal relationships underlying these effects cannot be directly inferred. It may be the case that what is driving effects on accuracy are the characteristics of the respondents in the survey process, rather than any

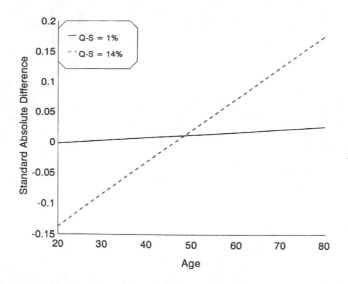

FIGURE 4. Predicted values of the global measure of accuracy (standard absolute difference) as a function of age by fixing the levels of significant question wording changes (Q-S) at 1% and 14%. Higher levels of difference indicate greater inaccuracy: broad measures.

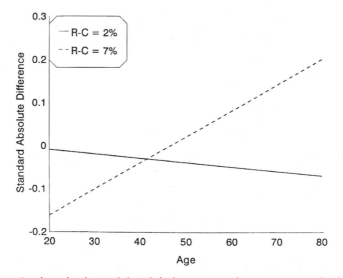

FIGURE 5. Predicted values of the global measure of accuracy (standard absolute difference) as a function of age by fixing the levels of respondent expressions for clarification (R-C) at 2% and 7%. Higher levels of difference indicate greater inaccuracy: broad measures.

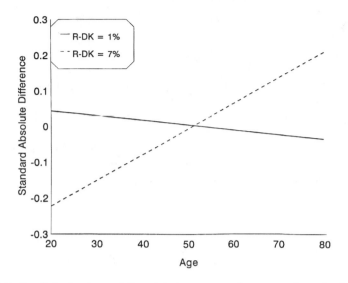

FIGURE 6. Predicted values of the global measure of accuracy (standard absolute difference) as a function of age by fixing the levels of respondent expressions of "don't know" (R-DK) at 1% and 7%. Higher levels of difference indicate greater inaccuracy: broad measures.

interviewer verbal behaviors. Consider that respondent verbal behaviors, such as respondent expressions for clarification (R-C) and expressions of "don't know" (R-DK), show the same interaction patterns as significant question reading changes (Q-S). One possible explanation is that respondents who seek clarification or express uncertainty by saying "don't know" encourage a more dynamic verbal interaction with interviewers. In turn, interviewers tend to engage in more, but ineffectual, discrepant question-asking behaviors in subsequent questions. Older respondents who engage in these behaviors more frequently are generally having more difficulty with the survey process, which is reflected in poorer levels of accuracy. For younger respondents though, those who engage more frequently in these behaviors may be expressing a greater degree of thoughtfulness in the survey process, which eventually is reflected in higher levels of accuracy. Although this is one possible explanation, the important point is that these patterns of interactions can be explained without any need to appeal to interviewer tailoring as a factor.

Of course, these data do not rule out the possibility that interviewer tailoring is affecting the quality of survey responses. Perhaps when faced with respondents who are experiencing difficulty with the survey process, interviewer tailoring is especially effective with younger respondents, but may actually exacerbate the difficulties of older respondents. Or, the tailoring may be effective with both groups, but older respondents experiencing difficulties would perform even more poorly without the tailoring.

These findings convey a first approximation regarding age differences associated with the nature of the verbal exchanges between interviewers and respondents and the quality of response. More focused analyses may provide another picture of these interrelationships where only the behaviors observed during the sequence of questions asking about hospital stays and office visits are considered. Unlike the broad behavior measures, these focused measures of verbal behavior allow an examination of those verbal exchanges that are in direct connection to the quality of report.

Second Set: Focused Measures

The survey questions dealing with hospital stays and office visits were asked adjacent to each other, encompassing a localized sequence during the interview. Thus, examining the behavior code assignments in this relevant sequence of questions is logically appealing, as these exchanges form a continuous whole. For the focused analyses, measures of behavior code assignments are the proportion of questions asked during the hospital stays and office visit sequence where each behavior occurred, for each interviewer-respondent dyad.

Age and Behavior Coding

As previously, two regression models were estimated: regressing behavior (for each code separately) on a linear term for age, and behavior on a linear and a quadratic term for age. The results are presented in Table 4. As with the broad measures, including the education of respondents as a control variable did not affect the pattern of results for respondent age, and thus the results of these models are not reported. In general, the significant associations that do emerge reflect the patterns observed in the broad measures, with behaviors occurring more frequently for older respondents. There are, however, fewer behaviors for which the quadratic terms were found to be significant. Thus, when examining behavior codes focusing only on those questions that are directly tied to the recall of the number of hospital stays and office visits, verbal behaviors are heightened predominantly for older respondents, whereas, as reported previously, analyses on the broad measures that included the behaviors from the other survey questions led

**TABLE 4. ASSOCIATIONS OF BEHAVIOR CODE
ASSIGNMENTS WITH AGE: SECOND SET**

Code	Linear Age		Quadratic Age	
	β	p	β	p
Q-E	−0.09	ns	−0.005	ns
Q-S	0.09	=.09	0.002	ns
Q-O	0.02	<.01	0.000	ns
R-I	0.04	=.07	−0.001	ns
R-C	0.06	=.02	−0.001	ns
R-Q	−0.02	ns	0.001	ns
R-U	0.15	<.01	0.004	<.01
R-DK	0.10	<.001	0.001	ns
P-A	0.08	<.001	0.001	ns
P-I	0.09	<.001	0.003	=.02
F-AS	−0.01	ns	0.001	ns
F-AL	0.01	ns	0.000	ns
F-US	0.03	<.05	0.000	ns
F-UL	−0.01	ns	0.001	<.05
F-UR	0.03	<.01	0.000	ns

to elevated behavior code assignments among the younger respondents as well.

Accuracy

Following the logic for the broad measures, we constructed separate models for each of the behavior codes which had significant linear or quadratic age terms in the models associating age with behavior. The accuracy measure was regressed on age of respondent, the focused behavior measure, and the interaction of age and the behavior. Only the age by R-DK (expressions of "don't know") interaction was significant, $b = 0.0009$, $p < .02$. Figure 7 depicts this interaction effect where the level of R-DK was fixed at around the 20th and 80th percentiles. The pattern of this interaction is nearly identical with the age by R-DK interaction observed with the broad measure.

Tests for interaction effects with the focused measures provided no indication that interviewer tailoring improves the quality of reports specifically with older respondents. Question reading, probing, and feedback were elevated among older respondents, yet none had significant interactions with age. As these specific behavior code assignments

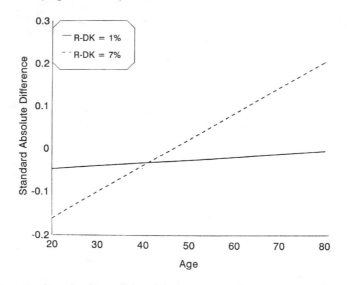

FIGURE 7. Predicted values of the global measure of accuracy (standard absolute difference) as a function of age by fixing the levels of respondent expressions of "don't know" (R-DK) at 1% and 7%. Higher levels of difference indicate greater inaccuracy: specific measures.

are directly tied to those exchanges that consisted of the targeted behavioral frequency reports, there is greater certainty that these behaviors are reflecting processes that would most directly affect the accuracy of reports, more than the broad behavior measures reported previously. The lack of significant interactions, particularly with age and significant question reading changes (Q-S), brings into question the importance of the age and Q-S interaction found with the broad measures. Indeed, although results cannot rule out the possibility that older persons are receiving benefits from interviewer tailoring, there is no compelling evidence that interviewer tailoring benefits the accuracy of responses.

☐ Conclusions

The standardized survey interview presents a unique social situation that confronts survey participants by requiring them to engage in novel patterns of communication (Clark & Schober, 1992). The manner in which interviewers deal with respondents in assisting their understanding of the survey interview and its objectives, including the accurate reporting of past events, can affect data quality. Our specific aim in this research was to determine whether interviewer tailoring may be offsetting deficits that would otherwise arise in the retrospective reports of older respondents. The present results do show that older respondents are more likely to engage in verbal comments such as interruptions, expressions of uncertainty, and uncodable responses. Such verbalizations in the survey context may be analogous to behaviors from other contexts where the speech of older persons is marked by the tendency to engage in verbose speech that is off-target to the task as well as difficulty switching to relevant speech registers (Arbuckle & Gold, 1993; Kemper & Kemtes, this volume; Gold, Andres, Arbuckle, & Schwartzman, 1988). Moreover, the present results also show that interviewers are more likely to engage in verbal behaviors that are discrepant from the ideals of standardized interviewing with older respondents, perhaps as attempts to tailor their communication to meet the perceived challenges that they face.

Such tailoring may be the survey equivalent of patronizing speech or *elderspeak*, which has been demonstrated to improve the problem solving of older subjects in the laboratory (Kemper & Kemtes, this volume; Kemper et al., 1995; Kwong See & Ryan, this volume; Ryan, Giles, Bartolucci, & Henwood, 1986). However, although our results do point to evidence of interviewer tailoring among the aged, there is no compelling evidence of its efficacy.

Failure to find efficacy for interviewer tailoring in the present study does not rule out the possibility that effective tailoring that assists older respondents in answering survey questions is ongoing. The behavior coding measures, designed originally to monitor interviewer performance and to examine those survey questions that pose the greatest difficulties for respondents to answer (Fowler, 1992; Fowler & Cannell, 1996; Oksenberg et al., 1991), may not be particularly sensitive to detecting the kinds of interviewer tailoring that may be of assistance to respondents. For example, significant question reading changes (Q-S) occur in any situation in which the meaning of the question is altered from the script. Thus, significant question reading changes may involve both improvements and decrements to intended question meanings, and a more refined coding scheme to capture whether the question reading was beneficial or not may yet find benefits to tailoring.

Other coding refinements could include examining the motivational characteristics of the interview (Kahn & Cannell, 1957; Kwong See & Ryan, this volume) and the digressive comments offered both by interviewers and respondents that are not directly tied to achieving question objectives (cf. Arbuckle & Gold, 1993; Gold et al., 1988). Ongoing work in our laboratory is developing coding schemes in both areas. As part of this work, Belli and Chardoul (1997) found that older respondents were more likely to make digressions than younger ones, and that interviewers were more likely to make digressive comments toward older respondents. Older respondents were particularly noteworthy for the extent of their storytelling. This work provides insight into age differences in those communication patterns that are used to set the stage for the survey interview. Our hope is that additional research along these lines will extend the findings presented in this chapter and provide a richer understanding of the associations among age-related differences in communication patterns and the quality of survey reports.

☐ References

Arbuckle, T. Y., & Gold, D. P. (1993). Aging, inhibition, and verbosity. *Journal of Gerontology: Psychological Sciences, 48*(5), 225–232.

Beatty, P. (1995). Understanding the standardized/non-standardized interviewing controversy. *Journal of Official Statistics, 11*, 147–160.

Belli, R. F., & Chardoul, S. A. (1997, May). *The digressions of survey actors in a face-to-face health interview.* Paper presented at the annual conference of the American Association for Public Opinion Research, Norfolk, VA.

Belli, R. F., & Lepkowski, J. M. (1996). Behavior of survey actors and the accuracy of response. *Health Survey Research Methods: Conference Proceedings* (pp. 69–74). DHHS Publication No. PHS 96-1013). Hyattsville, MD: U.S. Department of Health and Human Services.

Belli, R. F., Traugott, M. W., Young, M., Traugott, S., McGonagle, K., & Rosenstone, S. (1998, May). *Reducing vote overreporting in surveys through reducing source memory confusions.* Paper presented at the annual conference of the American Association for Public Opinion Research, St Louis, MO.

Borrini, G., Dall'Ora, P., Della Sala, S., Marinelli, L., & Spinnler, H. (1989). Autobiographical memory. Sensitivity to age and education of a standardized enquiry. *Psychological Medicine, 19*, 215–224.

Cannell, C. F., Fisher, G., & Bakker, T. (1965). Reporting of hospitalization in the health interview survey. *Vital and Health Statistics* (Series 2, No. 6, PHS Publication No. 1000). Washington, DC: U.S. Government Printing Office.

Clark, H. H., & Schober, M. F. (1992). Asking questions and influencing answers. In J. Tanur (Ed.), *Questions about questions: Inquiries into the cognitive bases of surveys* (pp. 15–48). New York: Russell Sage.

Craik, F. I. M., & Jennings, J. M. (1992). Human memory. In F. I. M. Craik and T. A. Salthouse (Eds.), *The handbook of aging and cognition* (pp. 51–110). Hillsdale, NJ: Erlbaum.

Dykema, J., Lepkowski, J. M., & Blixt, S. (1997). The effect of interviewer and respondent behavior on data quality: Analysis of interaction coding in a validation study. In L. Lyberg, P. Biemer, M. Collins, E. de Leeuw, C. Dippo, N. Schwarz, and D. Trewin (Eds.), *Survey measurement and process quality* (pp. 287–310). New York: Wiley.

Fowler, F. J. (1992). How unclear terms affect survey data. *Public Opinion Quarterly, 56*, 218–231.

Fowler, F. J., & Cannell, C. F. (1996). Using behavioral coding to identify cognitive problems with survey questions. In N. Schwarz & S. Sudman (Eds.), *Answering questions: Methodology for determining cognitive and communicative processes in survey research* (pp. 15–36). San Francisco: Jossey-Bass.

Gold, D., Andres, D., Arbuckle, T., & Schwartzman, A. (1988). Measurement and correlates of verbosity in elderly people. *Journal of Gerontology: Psychological Sciences, 43*(2), P27–P33.

Groves, R. M., & Magilavy, L. J. (1986). Measuring and explaining interviewer effects in centralized telephone surveys. *Public Opinion Quarterly, 50,* 251–266.

Herzog, A. R., & Dielman, L. (1985). Age differences in response accuracy for factual survey questions. *Journal of Gerontology, 40,* 350–357.

Herzog, A. R., & Rodgers, W. L. (1989). Age differences in memory performance and memory ratings as measured in a sample survey. *Psychology and Aging, 4,* 173–182.

Holland, C. A., & Rabbitt, P. M. A. (1990). Autobiographical and text recall in the elderly: An investigation of a processing resource deficit. *The Quarterly Journal of Experimental Psychology, 42A*(3), 441–470.

Jay, G. M., Belli, R. F., & Lepkowski, J. M. (1994). Quality of last doctor visit reports: A comparison of medical record and survey data. *1994 Proceedings of the section on survey research methods.* Alexandria, VA: American Statistical Association, 362–372.

Kahn, R. L., & Cannell, C. F. (1957). *The dynamics of interviewing.* New York: Wiley.

Kemper, S., Vandeputte, D., Rice, K., Cheung, H., & Gubarchuk, J. (1995). Speech adjustments to aging during a referential communication task. *Journal of Language and Social Psychology, 14,* 40–59.

Moles, E. (1987). *Perceptions of the interview process.* Unpublished manuscript. Institute for Social Research and Institute of Gerontology, The University of Michigan, Ann Arbor.

Oksenberg, L., Cannell, C. F., & Kalton, G. (1991). New strategies for pretesting survey questions. *Journal of Official Statistics, 7*(3), 349–365.

Presser, S. (1990). Can changes in context reduce vote overreporting in surveys? *Public Opinion Quarterly, 54,* 586–593.

Ryan, E. B., Giles, H., Bartolucci, G., & Henwood, K. (1986). Psycholinguistic and social psychological components of communication by and with the elderly. *Language and Communication, 6,* 1–24.

Schaeffer, N. C., & Maynard, D. W. (1996). From paradigm to prototype and back again: Interactive aspects of cognitive processing in standardized survey interviews. In N. Schwarz & S. Sudman (Eds.), *Answering questions: Methodology for determining cognitive and communicative processes in survey research* (pp. 37–64). San Francisco: Jossey-Bass.

Suchman, L., & Jordan, B. (1990). Interactional troubles in face-to-face interviews. *Journal of the American Statistical Association, 85,* 232–241.

Sudman, S., & Bradburn, N. M. (1974). *Response effects in surveys.* Chicago, IL: Aldine.

Sudman, S., Bradburn, N. M., & Schwarz, N. (1996). *Thinking about answers: The application of cognitive processes to survey methodology.* San Francisco: Jossey-Bass.

16

CHAPTER

A. Regula Herzog
Willard L. Rodgers

Cognitive Performance Measures in Survey Research on Older Adults

A great deal has been learned in recent years about age-related cognitive performance and underlying processes, much of it through laboratory and clinical research. More recently, measures of cognitive performance have been included in several large-scale sample surveys. There appear to be at least two major reasons for the inclusion of cognitive performance measures in surveys. First, descriptive information about cognitive functioning and its natural course in the older population as well as the predictors and consequences of cognitive functioning are still needed because experimental and clinical investigations are not well suited to providing representative population estimates. For example, findings are inconsistent about whether crystallized intelligence or knowledge declines with age, an inconsistency that might possibly reflect the use of nonprobability samples in experimental cognition research (Salthouse, 1997). Or, information is sparse on how cognitive impairment and decline impacts on the daily functioning of older people, on their need for formal health care and informal assistance, and on their economic resources. These are all areas where survey research can make unique contributions.

Second, many researchers are suspicious of the quality of survey data obtained from older respondents. Measures of cognitive performance are included in surveys by these researchers in order to study the relationship between data quality and cognitive functioning and to potentially exclude from the analysis respondents who measure low on cognitive functioning or to adjust the analysis for their level of cognitive functioning.

Survey research methodology differs from that used in laboratory and clinical research. A typical survey is characterized by (a) a large sample that represents the population of interest, (b) standardized methodologies that are often self-report measures but may include tests and clinical examinations if these can be adapted to the survey context, and (c) multivariate analytical procedures that are designed to address the correlational nature of these studies (Rossi, Wright, & Anderson, 1983). Ideally, surveys are also (d) longitudinal, a design feature that provides additional power to dealing with the correlational nature of these studies (Cook & Campbell, 1979). While these characteristics present strengths of the survey method for representative assessment of cognitive performance, they also present challenges that are typically not encountered in the well-controlled environment of the laboratory or even the clinic. Logistically, the measure of cognition must be brief and appropriate for lay interviewers to administer in the less controlled home environment. Ideally, the measure also should be suitable for use either over the telephone or face-to-face and not be sensitive to such mode differences. Nevertheless, a comprehensive and broadly differentiating measure that yields little missing data and permits repeated administrations over time is typically desired for descriptive and explanatory purposes.

In several recent surveys we have included measures of cognitive functioning and have wrestled with some of the challenges described above. In this paper we summarize some of our efforts and present preliminary findings. Specifically, we will discuss:

1. a cognitive battery designed for the nationwide Asset and Health Dynamics Among the Oldest Old (AHEAD) survey that demonstrates the feasibility of measuring cognitive performance in a survey;
2. methodological issues encountered when administering cognitive preformance tests; and
3. substantive findings that suggest the construct validity of the cognitive measures.

☐ A Cognitive Performance Battery

The cognitive performance measures in AHEAD include an immediate and a delayed 10-noun free recall test to measure memory; a Serials 7s test to measure working memory; a timed counting-backward test to measure speed of processing; naming of date, president, and vice-president to measure orientation; and two definitions plus an abbreviated Wechsler Adult Intelligence Scale-Revised (WAIS-R) vocabulary test to measure knowledge or premorbid intelligence. Most of these cognitive measures were adapted from the Telephone Interview for Cognitive Status (TICS) by Brandt, Spencer, and Folstein (1988).

These cognitive measures represent a range of difficulty levels; some of the naming tasks are the easiest, the recall and the Serial 7s tasks are the most difficult. An exploratory factor analysis revealed two factors: a memory factor on which the two recall tests have high loadings, and a mental status factor on which the remaining tasks have high loadings. These two factors are related to each other, suggesting that they can be understood as two aspects of general cognitive performance.

An aggregate score formulated as a simple summation of correct points achieves a reasonably normal distribution which is able to differentiate at the high and low ends of the performance range. For more detail on the cognitive measures, see papers by Herzog and Wallace (1996, 1997).

☐ Methodological Issues

Nonresponse and Noncoverage

The representative nature of a survey of older people is only achieved if every older person has a chance to be selected into the sample, and if every eligible sample member agrees to participate in the survey, or if those eligible persons who elect not to participate are a random subset of the total sample (Moser & Kalton, 1972). None of these conditions is met in the typical survey of the aged.

First, institutionalized persons are typically not included in the household sampling frame for community surveys; this is a form of noncoverage error. Data from the National Nursing Home Survey suggest that 65% of nursing home residents have one or more cognitive disabilities, a rate which does not appear to differ much by age (Van Nostrand, Miller, & Furner, 1993). Data from the Minimum Data Set also suggest that as many as half of all nursing home residents are cognitively impaired (Morris et al., 1994). In combination with the fact that 5% or more of the older population reside in nursing homes at any point in time, any prevalence rate of cognitive disability generated from a community survey would have to be increased by another 2% to 3% to account for the many cognitively impaired persons living in institutions.

Second, survey response rates may exceed 80% of all eligible persons, as was the case in our AHEAD survey, but more typically they are around 70% or even lower and tend to decrease with increasing age (Herzog & Rodgers, 1988a), raising the possibility of substantial nonresponse bias. This possibility is confirmed by findings indicating that nonrespondents tend to be in worse health and have lower cognitive ability than respondents. Although it is typically difficult to learn much about those who did not participate in the survey, in the regional survey called Michigan Generations study we made a special effort to collect such information from the interviewers and found that about one third of all older nonrespondents cited health reasons compared with less than 10% of young and middle-aged adults (Moles, 1987). Clearly, health problems are a much more important reason for nonparticipation among persons over 60 than among those who are younger. Note that in the Michigan Generations study we could not distinguish between physical and cognitive health problems.

Finally, in the longitudinal AHEAD survey we can investigate how cognitive performance measured in the first wave predicts to nonresponse status in the second wave (Table 1). Those Wave 1 respondents who became nonrespondents in Wave 2 (line 3) performed less well cognitively in Wave 1 than those who remained respondents in Wave 2 (line 1), suggesting that cognitive difficulties are a reason for subsequent nonresponse.

In the AHEAD survey we have taken steps to assess and possibly minimize the nonresponse bias. Thus, we are asking an informant (or proxy) respondent to participate if the eligible respondent is unable or unwilling to do so. For about one third of all such cases at Wave 1, we·

TABLE 1.   AHEAD WAVE 1 COGNITIVE PERFORMANCE, BY AHEAD WAVE 2 INTERVIEW STATUS

	Cognitive Performance at Wave 1			
	Immediate Recall (0–10)	Delayed Recall (0–10)	Serial 7s (0–5)	Mental Status (0–10)
Interview status at Wave 2:				
Self-respondents	4.8	3.4	3.2	9.1
Proxy-respondent	3.1	1.6	1.9	7.1
Nonrespondent	4.4	2.9	2.6	8.6
Deceased	3.8	2.3	2.4	8.1

Note. Table entries are means. All differences except the differences between nonrespondents and deceased on Serial 7s are statistically significant.

were able to interview an informant, and these responses are included in the response rate calculation, allowing for the 80% response rate rather than a 70% rate, if only self respondents had been included. In Table 1, respondents represented by a proxy in Wave 2 (line 2) had performed worse in Wave 1 than self-respondents and even nonrespondents, confirming the impression that proxy respondents often represent cognitively impaired respondents.

Whereas proxy answers are usually substituted for respondent answers to survey questions which deal with facts and opinions, it is not obvious how they may substitute for cognitive performance tests. We have used the Informant Questionnaire on Cognitive Decline in the Elderly (IQOCDE) scale developed by Jorm and his colleagues, which asks the informant to judge the eligible respondent on many aspects of memory and intelligence. Jorm's studies have shown that the scale differentiates those who are diagnosed as demented from those not so diagnosed (Jorm, 1994; Jorm and Jacomb, 1989). Using Jorm's scoring we identify 412, or about 46% of, demented respondents among those reported on by a proxy. This suggests again that an important reason for a proxy response is cognitive problems.

In order to learn more directly about the cognitive ability of those represented by a proxy, we attempted at Wave 2 to collect cognitive performance information on those eligible respondents otherwise represented by a proxy. Out of some 900 such respondents, about 100 were willing to try and about 60 completed the entire set of questions. Most likely, those respondents represent a positively selected subgroup of all respondents represented by a proxy. This information confirms the hypothesis based on the proxy and the Wave 1 information: sample members for whom proxy interviews were obtained performed much worse on cognitive tasks such as free recall, Serial 7s, and mental status-type tests than did self-respondents (Table 2).

In general, then, nonrandom losses due to nonresponse and noncoverage suggest that the most cognitively impaired people are likely to be underrepresented in a typical survey. If proper representation of the population is at issue, as it often is when one decides to use a survey, nonresponse bias deserves careful attention. Luckily, if proxy respondents are permitted, some of the most severely cognitively impaired respondents are not excluded from the sample.

Missing Data

Older respondents are also more likely to refuse to answer or avoid answering a survey question. And again, this may lead to lower effec-

TABLE 2.   AHEAD WAVE 2 COGNITIVE PERFORMANCE AMONG
RESPONDENTS REPRESENTED BY PROXY AND SELF-RESPONDENTS

	Respondents Represented by Proxy	Self-Respondents
Immediate noun recall (0–10)	2.3	4.8
Delayed noun recall (0–10)	1.5	3.5
Serial 7s (0–5)	1.8	3.1
Total cognitive score (0–35)	9.5	20.1

Note. Table entries are means.

tive response rates for specific questions and to bias in the resulting data if the respondents who fail to provide an answer are different from those who do give an answer. Like other national surveys, the AHEAD faced this problem of item nonresponse: In Wave 1, about 10% of all respondents refused to subtract 7s, and 3% to 4% refused to participate in the free recall test. These respondents scored significantly worse on the cognitive performance measures that they were willing to try (i.e., the remaining mental status-type items and a self-rating of memory) than did those who completed these tasks (Herzog & Wallace, 1997). This implies that prevalence estimates derived from a survey are further biased towards a cognitively well-functioning population by the missing answers from low-functioning respondents.

In the AHEAD we dealt with this problem by estimating likely performance scores on refused tests from performance on the nonmissing cognitive tests and from other personal characteristics. Using this imputation procedures, the resulting distribution of cognitive functioning included a slightly higher proportion of low-scoring individuals. Interestingly, when we used the imputed measures to estimate substantive relationships with risk factors and consequences (see below), the results differed little from results with unimputed measures (Herzog & Wallace, 1997).

Longitudinal Design

Longitudinal or prospective surveys represent the most powerful designs for investigating the causal linkages between cognitive performance and its precursors and consequences. Standard survey techniques require that identical questions be asked at each wave of a longitudinal survey in order to avoid confounding measurement change with substantive change (Cook & Campbell, 1979). This technique is inopportune when the measure is a memory or even a knowledge test because repeated exposure may improve performance over time. In the nationwide longitudinal Health and Retirement Survey (HRS) of 51- to 61-year-olds we found that the average number of nouns recalled from a list of 20 nouns increased by an average of about one half of a noun when the same list was presented again two years later (i.e., in Waves 1 and 2).

Part of the improvement in memory performance over time is likely to be due to the mere experience with the nature of the task which cannot be controlled, but part of it is likely to be due to the learning of the specific material. In order to control for the experience with the specific material, we constructed lists that contained different but equivalent nouns for an immediate and delayed free recall task in the AHEAD Wave 2 study. Following the rules of construction used for the single 10-noun list in AHEAD Wave 1, we selected one- and two-syllable nouns of high frequency (AA according to Thorndike & Lorge, 1944, except for one A noun per list) and high imagery and concreteness (6.0 or more according to the norms established by Paivio, Yuille, & Madigan, 1968). Nouns satisfying these conditions were then ordered by recallability according to the norms established by Rubin and Friendly (1986) and distributed to form six lists. We administered each form to a random subset of about 30 respondents in a telephone pretest.

The four lists selected for maximum equivalence in the pretest were then randomly assigned to respondents in counterbalanced sequence over the next four AHEAD waves such that (a) each respondent responds to each form only once, (b) each form appears equally often in each wave, and (c) each form follows each other form equally often at each wave. Data from the first administration of the four counterbalanced forms in AHEAD Wave 2 indicate that the four forms differ minimally from each other (Table 3), which is particularly impressive given the large sample sizes of about 1,500 respondents per form.

When we compare AHEAD Wave 1 data (using one recall list) with AHEAD Wave 2 data (using the four different but equivalent lists) for respondents who participated in both waves, unlike for the HRS, we find no overall improvement (data not shown). The lack of improvement, of course, could also be due to the older age of the AHEAD than the HRS respondents. We will be able to assess the importance of the manipulation more directly using data from future waves of HRS and AHEAD.

Another complication arises in longitudinal studies when questions refer to generally available information in order to test orientation or tertiary memory. If the requested information remains the same, respondents learn what is required and may even prepare for the

TABLE 3.   EQUIVALENCE OF NOUN RECALL LISTS IN AHEAD WAVE 2

	Mean	Standard Deviation	N
Immediate noun recall			
List 1	4.8[a]	1.9	1563
List 2	4.6[b]	1.9	1507
List 3	4.7[ab]	1.8	1485
List 4	4.8[ab]	1.8	1480
Delayed noun recall			
List 1	3.6[a]	2.2	1530
List 2	3.4[a]	2.2	1474
List 3	3.5[a]	2.1	1448
List 4	3.5[a]	2.2	1453

Note. The differences between means which share the same superscripts (a or b) are not statistically significant.

answers. An example from the AHEAD survey is that respondents remembered the requested definition of scissors and cactus. If the requested information changes over time, longitudinal changes are further confounded. A prime example is the question about the name of the president and the former president of the U.S. contained in many cognitive screens. In 1986, when we conducted the first wave of the Americans' Changing Lives (ACL) study, former president Carter was not well remembered because then-president Reagan was in his second term and Carter had had only one term as president. In 1989, when we conducted the second ACL wave, former president Reagan was better remembered because then-president Bush had just recently come into office, and Reagan had been president before him for two terms.

Standardization of Testing

Surveys are usually taken in a respondent's home by one of dozens of interviewers. Standardization of test administration is difficult in this situation. Despite careful training, interviewers may vary in exactly how they ask the survey questions and administer the cognitive tests, and the home environment may vary in how well it facilitates or interferes with the successful completion of the interview process. To illustrate, two brief examples are reported: the presentation of the nouns for the free recall test and the effect of overhearing test performance by another respondent in the household.

For the free recall test we trained about 100 interviewers of the AHEAD study to read the 10 nouns at a rate of 2 seconds per noun and impressed on the interviewers not to read any of the nouns more than once. In order to set up proper expectations among the respondents, we included these specifications in the standardized instruction to be read to the respondent. We checked the level of standardization of interviewer behavior achieved for the free recall test by tape-recording and coding of more than 60 (63) interviews randomly chosen across interviewers and study period.

The analysis shows (a) that most interviewers spent between 14 and 26 seconds reading the 10 nouns and (b) that about one quarter of them were asked to repeat or explain a word, a request that most of them honored. In fact, most outliers of time beyond the range of 14 to 26 seconds can be explained by interruptions caused by such a request. While we are gratified by the lack of major variation in presentation time, we have not yet determined how best to deal with the repetition of words. The accurate understanding of single, high-frequency nouns without context is inherently difficult, especially for an administration over the telephone, and therefore respondents' requests for clarification are likely to continue.

The second example of a standardization problem stems from the AHEAD design, which calls for both spouses to be interviewed. Because the AHEAD surveys older persons who are largely retired, both spouses are often found at home and cannot always easily be separated for the conduct of the interview. We suspected that the one spouse overhearing the cognitive testing of the other might have an unfair advantage.

When we compared the cognitive performance of the spouses who were interviewed first with those who were interviewed second, we found supporting evidence for our suspicion (Table 4). In AHEAD Wave 1 an advantage for the second respondent is evident for the delayed recall and the Serial 7s tests in the face-to-face situation. In the telephone situation, where overhearing is not as likely, the second respondent appears to be disadvantaged (except in the Serial 7s test), which is consistent with our informal observations that the less healthy spouse will often be interviewed last.

In AHEAD Wave 2 we attempted to minimize this contamination between spouses by including the spouses explicitly in the counterbalancing assignment such that spouses never get the same noun list in the same or even adjacent survey waves. Data for the noun recall tests in AHEAD Wave 2 show that our procedure worked: the second spouse now performs worse. Note that the second spouse still performs better in the Serial 7s and the mental status tests, which remained identical for both spouses.

TABLE 4. DIFFERENCES BETWEEN SECOND AND FIRST RESPONDENT IN THE SAME HOUSEHOLD IN AHEAD WAVES 1 AND 2 (MARRIED RESPONDENTS ONLY)

	Mode of 1st/2nd Respondent	
	Face to Face/ Face to Face	Telephone/ Telephone
Immediate noun recall (0–10)		
Wave 1	.16	−.42*
Wave 2	−.64*	−.65*
Delayed noun recall (0–10)		
Wave 1	.40*	−.23*
Wave 2	−.80*	−.71*
Serial 7s (0–5)		
Wave 1	.54*	.56*
Wave 2	.47*	.46*
Mental status (0–10/12)		
Wave 1	.14	−.06
Wave 2	.25*	.15

Note. Table entries are mean differences, adjusted for respondent age, education, and self-reported memory. *$p < .05$.

Mode Effect

Telephone surveys have become very popular because of cost advantages. A number of studies do not find any major differences in data quality between telephone and face-to-face surveys (Groves & Kahn, 1979; Herzog & Rodgers, 1988b). Nevertheless, concerns about telephone surveys of older people persist and are particularly prevalent with respect to cognitive performance tests which require a well-controlled and closely supervised administration and for which hearing difficulties could prove critical.

In order to formally test the effect of mode of administration on cognitive measures, a full mode experiment was built into the second wave of the AHEAD study in the following form. The original AHEAD design calls for a switch from a telephone to a face-to-face administration when a respondent turns 80. In the second and third waves of the AHEAD, respondents in the transition age range of 78 to 81 were randomly assigned to either a telephone or a face-to-face administration. In other words, one random half of respondents were assigned to make the transition to a face-to-face survey administration a wave earlier than the other random half, providing for an experimental manipulation of the mode assignment. The average cognitive scores obtained from respondents assigned to the telephone mode and those assigned to the face-to-face mode do not differ significantly (Table 5), indicating no reliable performance differences between respondents in telephone and face-to-face assignments. These analyses provide supporting evidence that the AHEAD cognitive performance scores are not affected by whether they are collected over the telephone or face-to-face.

Substantive Analyses Using the AHEAD Cognitive Measures

Finally, we return to the beginning of this chapter and the substantive issues that motivate the inclusion of cognitive performance measures in surveys. We start by describing some recent substantive analyses of predictors and outcomes of cognitive performance. In a first analysis we predicted general cognitive performance from a set of sociodemographic, health status, and health behavior characteristics by using multiple regression analysis. Because participants in laboratory experiments do not represent the entire older population, relatively little is known about how cognitive performance is distributed across subgroups of the American population. Our analyses were designed to address this issue. We found that age and educational differences were substantial; older people who were relatively young and well educated performed better cognitively than those who were relatively old and not well educated. Interestingly, income had an independent marginal effect, net of educational and age differences; those with higher incomes performed better than those with lower incomes. Health was also related to cognitive performance: self-reported health was strongly positively related to cognitive functioning, and occurrence of a stroke

TABLE 5. EXPERIMENTAL MODE ASSIGNMENT: COGNITIVE SCORES IN AHEAD WAVE 2 (RESPONDENTS AGED 79–82 ONLY)

	Mode	
	Telephone	Face to Face
Immediate noun recall (0–10)	4.52	4.49
Delayed noun recall (0–10)	3.23	3.12
Serial 7s (0–5)	3.02	2.94
Mental status items (0–12)	10.54	10.47

Note. Table entries are means. No mode differences are statistically significant.

was negatively related. Finally, alcohol consumption was related to cognitive functioning: respondents who consumed some alcohol functioned better than those who did not consume any alcohol. To summarize, the AHEAD data confirm some of the better known correlates of cognitive functioning in older age, e.g., age, educational attainment, and health, while at the same time contributing some new suggestive findings, such as the relationship between income and alcohol use with cognitive performance. For more detail see Herzog and Wallace (1997).

An issue of theoretical and policy interest is whether cognitive functioning plays a role in the day-to-day functioning of older adults in housework and self-care. In a second analysis using the HRS Wave 1 data, we observed a relationship between cognitive performance and difficulties experienced with instrumental activities of daily living (IADLs) and to some degree with activities of daily living (ADLs) when controlling statistically for illness, sensory impairment, and depressive symptoms (Wray, Herzog, & Park, 1996). This finding suggests that cognitive functioning plays a role in competence in housework and self-care, independent of health and depressive feelings. As expected, no such relationship was evident for mobility and strength limitations. In the AHEAD Wave 1, the relationship with ADLs and IADLs emerged in even stronger form. In other words, competence in activities which would appear to require some thinking and planning were clearly related to cognitive performance, whereas competence in activities requiring little thinking and planning were not related. These findings add further to the construct validity of the measures of cognitive as well as of day-to-day functioning in the AHEAD.

We conclude with a finding that bears on the methodological issue that underlies the use of cognitive performance measures in surveys: the role of cognitive functioning with respect to survey data quality. We asked a subsample of the AHEAD Wave 2 respondents a second battery of questions on difficulties experienced with ADLs and help received with them, in a different format from the core battery, at the end of the interview. The answers that respondents gave to the two sets of questions were generally but not always consistent. The frequency of inconsistent answers that a respondent gave was related to his or her performance on the cognitive tests in that those respondents with lower cognitive scores gave more inconsistent answers (Rodgers & Miller, 1997). In a multiple regression analysis that included demographic and health characteristics of the respondents as predictors, performance on the cognitive tests was a strong and highly significant predictor of the number of discrepant reports, both with respect to whether help was received with ADLs and with respect to whether the respondent had any limitation on ADLs. These findings indicate that those with poor cognitive status tend to give less reliable answers to questions about ADLs than those with high cognitive status.

☐ Conclusion

In conclusion, the substantive findings regarding correlates of cognitive functioning and the relationship between cognitive functioning and survey data quality provide a sense of construct validity to the survey measures of cognitive functioning developed for the AHEAD and HRS. At the same time, we have identified a number of sources of error related to methodological features of surveys. They include the nonresponse and missing data bias, and the difficulty of standardizing over respondents, over interviewers, and over longitudinal survey waves. While we have dealt successfully with some of these sources of error, we are still working on solutions for others. Successfully dealing with the latter will further improve the strength and validity of findings related to cognitive measures in survey research.

☐ Acknowledgments

Funding for this research was provided by grants UO1 AG12980 and RO1 AG02038. Appreciation is expressed to Joan Marty for assistance with the data analysis.

☐ References

Brandt, J., Spencer, M., & Folstein, M. (1988). The telephone interview for cognitive status. *Neuropsychiatry, Neuropsychology, and Behavioral Neurology, 1*,111–117.

Cook, T. D., & Campbell, D. T. (1979). *Quasi-experimentation: Design and analysis issues for field settings.* Chicago: Rand McNally.

Groves, R. M., & Kahn, R. L. (1979). *Surveys by telephone.* New York: Academic Press.

Herzog, A. R., & Rodgers, W. L. (1988a). Age and response rates to interview sample surveys. *Journal of Gerontology: Social Sciences, 43*, S200–S205.

Herzog, A. R., & Rodgers, W. L. (1988b). Interviewing older adults: Mode comparisons using data from a face-to-face survey and a telephone survey. *Public Opinion Quarterly, 47*, 405–418.

Herzog, A. R., & Wallace, R. B. (1996). Measurement of cognition in AHEAD: Methodological and substantive investigations. *Proceedings of the 25th Public Health Conference on Records and Statistics.* (DHHS Publication No. PHS 96-1214). Washington, DC: U.S. Department of Health and Human Services.

Herzog, A. R., & Wallace, R. B. (1997). Measures of cognitive functioning in the AHEAD study [Special Issue]. *Journal of Gerontology: Social Sciences, 52B*, 37–48.

Jorm, A. F. (1994). A short form of the Informant Questionnaire on Cognitive Decline in the Elderly (IQCODE): Development and cross-validation. *Psychological Medicine, 24*, 145–153.

Jorm, A. F., & Jacomb, P. A. (1989). The Informant Questionnaire on Cognitive Decline in the Elderly (IQCODE): Socio-demographic correlates, reliability, validity and some norms. *Psychological Medicine, 19*, 1015–1022.

Moles, E. L. (1987, November). *Perceptions of the interview process.* Paper presented as part of the symposium "Interviewing Older Adults", presented at the 40th Annual Scientific Meeting of Gerontological Society of America, Washington, DC.

Morris, J. N., Fries, B. E., Mehr, D. R., Hawes, C., Phillips, C., Mor, V., & Lipsitz, L. A. (1994). MDS cognitive performance scale. *Journal of Gerontology: Medical Sciences, 49*(4), M174–M182.

Moser, C. A., & Kalton, G. (1972). *Survey methods in social investigations* (2nd ed.). New York: Basic Books.

Paivio, A., Yuille, J. C., & Madigan, S. A. (1968). Concreteness, imagery, and meaningfulness values for 925 nouns. *Journal of Experimental Psychology, 76*(1, pt. 2), 1–25.

Rodgers, W. L., & Miller, B. (1997). A comparative analysis of ADL questions in surveys of older people [Special Issue]. *Journal of Gerontology: Social Sciences, 52B*, 21–37.

Rossi, P. H., Wright, J. D., & Anderson, A. B. (1983). Sample surveys: History, current practice, and future prospects. In P. H. Rossi, J. D. Wright, and A. B. Anderson (Eds.), *Handbook of survey research.* San Diego, CA: Academic Press.

Rubin, D. C., & Friendly, M. (1986). Predicting which words get recalled: Measures of free recall, availability, goodness, emotionality, and pronunciability for 925 nouns. *Memory and Cognition, 14*(1), 79–94.

Salthouse, T. (1997, February). *The pressing issues: A cognitive aging perspective.* Paper presented at the Conference on Cognition, Aging, and Survey Measurement, University of Michigan, Ann Arbor.

Thorndike, E. L., & Lorge, I. (1944). *The teacher's word book of 30,000 words.* New York: Teacher's College.

Van Nostrand, J. F., Miller, B., & Furner, S. E. (1993). Selected issues in long-term care: Profile of cognitive disability of nursing home residents and the use of informal and formal care by elderly in the community. *Vital and health statistics. Health data on older Americans: United States, 1992. Series 3: Analytic and epidemiological studies, No. 27.* Hyattsville MD: U.S. Department of Health and Human Services, National Center for Health Statistics.

Wray, L. A., Herzog, A. R., & Park, D. C. (1996, November). *Physical health, mental health, and function among older adults.* Paper session at Gerontological Society of America Annual Meeting, Washington, DC.

CHAPTER

Bärbel Knäuper

Age Differences in Question and Response Order Effects

Much of what we know about the living conditions, health care needs, or financial situation of older people is based on self-reports from survey interviews. However, numerous studies have shown that self-reports are highly context dependent. Minor changes in question or response format can result in major differences in the reported behaviors or opinions (Schuman & Presser, 1981; see Sudman, Bradburn, & Schwarz, 1996, for a comprehensive review). This can lead researchers and the public to draw dramatically different substantive conclusions about the opinions or behaviors under investigation.

Although a great number of results have been accumulated, a coherent theoretical model to account for context effects has long been lacking. Only recently have such models been proposed (e.g., Schwarz, Hippler, & Noelle-Neumann, 1992, 1994; Strack & Martin, 1987; Tourangeau & Rasinski, 1988). Drawing on psychological reasoning, these models aim to predict the emergence, size, and direction of context effects in surveys. Mostly developed in social cognition research, the models so far have neglected the role of sociodemographic variables such as respondent age, race or ethnicity, social class, or educational level. Rather, context effects were traced back to mental processes that are assumed to be identical for all social groups. The researchers assumed that the process by which the answers given to survey questions are influenced by questionnaire variables should not differ by social group, although people's answers may of course differ as a function of their social group.

Sociological survey researchers, on the other hand, have a long tradition of suspecting that the pattern and size of context effects differs by social group (e.g., Schuman & Presser, 1981; see also Alwin, this volume). Until now, attempts to identify such systematic variations concentrated mainly on respondents' educational level. It was assumed that people with a lower educational level were more susceptible to context effects (e.g., Krosnick & Alwin, 1987; Narayan & Krosnick, 1996; Schuman & Presser, 1981).

In the present chapter, it is argued that both positions, that is, the sociologist's attempts to trace context effects back to differences between sociodemographic groups, and the psychologists' neglect of these differences, are hampering the understanding of the real determinants of the emergence of context effects in surveys. A fruitful combination of both approaches is necessary in order to identify the common underlying cognitive mechanisms that mediate the occurrence of response effects in surveys. It is suggested that certain sociodemographic variables *stand for* differences in mental processes, which will be illustrated for the case of respondent age. Aging is strongly associated with changes in cognitive functioning, particularly reductions in cognitive and memory resources. It is argued that age differences in the susceptibility to context effects in self-reports are due to differences in the ability to process and store information in the survey situation.

☐ Answering Survey Questions: The Role of Working Memory Resources

What are the cognitive processes that are involved in responding to survey questions? Answering such questions involves the simultaneous operation of multiple tasks (cf. Strack & Martin, 1987; Tourangeau, 1984; see Sudman, Bradburn, & Schwarz, 1996, Chap. 3, for a more detailed discussion). Respondents need to understand the meaning of the question, retrieve relevant information from memory, form a judgment on the basis of the retrieved and other available information, format it to fit the provided response alternatives, and possibly edit the response with respect to social desirability. Accomplishing these tasks thus involves the parallel storage, retrieval, organization, evaluation, and manipulation of complex information. Undoubtedly, these processes require considerable amounts of cognitive capacity. In fact, the described cognitive processes and manipulations are typical for what has been labeled in cognitive psychology as *working memory*. Working memory refers to that part of our cognitive system that is responsible for comprehending new information, retrieving old information, and simultaneously executing storage processes (Baddeley, 1986). Because the cognitive tasks involved in answering survey questions are dependent on cognitive resources, it is suggested that working memory capacity is the crucial theoretical construct in the analysis of age-sensitive context effects in self-reports (see also Knäuper, 1997).

Cognitive aging research has convincingly demonstrated that working memory resources decline with age (e.g., Daneman & Carpenter, 1980; Salthouse, this volume; Wingfield, this volume; see Salthouse, Babcock, & Shaw, 1991, for a review). Older people can hold less information active in their working memory than younger people, and they have more difficulty performing multiple cognitive operations simultaneously. Studies on sentence and discourse comprehension have reliably found that most of the age-related variance in task performance can be accounted for by individual differences in working memory resources (e.g., Kemper & Kemtes, this volume; see Just & Carpenter, 1992, for a review). When the task extends beyond sheer comprehension (as survey questions do), older adults have been found to show impaired performance under conditions that tax cognitive resources (e.g., Connelly, Hasher, & Zacks, 1991). In sum, cognitive aging research suggests that older individuals encounter difficulties when complex tasks require more cognitive resources than they have available. As has been described above, answering survey questions involves complex judgment and memory processes, in addition to question comprehension, thus increasing the potential resource dependency of the survey tasks and the magnitude of age effects.

The age-related decrease in working memory resources has counterintuitive implications for the prediction of context effects in surveys: While certain types of context effects can be expected to decrease with increasing age, other types of context effects should increase with age. Thereby, the characteristics of the specific context effect and their interaction with the amount of working memory resources an individual has available at a given point in time determine which of these two possibilities will occur. Decreasing processing resources render it more difficult for older respondents to keep earlier information in their working memory. Therefore, older adults should be less able to remember information brought to mind by preceding questions, resulting in decreased question order effects. By the same token, however, they should find it more difficult to hold all response alternatives in the working memory and to elaborate on their implications, resulting in increased response order effects. Both these predictions and their assumed underlying cognitive processes will be described in turn below.

☐ Reduced Question Order Effects

It has long been known to survey researchers that the content of preceding questions can profoundly influence the answers given to subsequent ones (for reviews and examples see Payne, 1951; Schuman & Presser, 1981; Schwarz & Sudman, 1992; Tourangeau & Rasinski, 1988). Question order effects usually reflect that respondents use the information that is brought to mind by preceding questions in order to answer a subsequent one. Schwarz and Bless (1992) proposed a mental construal model of attitude judgment to predict the emergence, direction, size, and generalization of context effects in attitude measurement. In general, a preceding question may result in a similar response to a subsequent question (e.g., bringing something positive to mind results in a more positive judgment), or in a dissimilar response (e.g., bringing something positive to mind results in a more negative judgment). The former effect is usually referred to as "assimilation effect," while the latter is labeled "contrast effect."

Individuals do not retrieve all knowledge that may bear on the target that is to be evaluated. Rather, they rely on the subset of potentially relevant information that is most accessible at the time of judgment (see Bodenhausen & Wyer, 1987; Higgins, 1989). Questionnaire variables can affect what is temporarily most accessible. For example, this can be information that has just been used for answering a question. This information is particularly likely to still be in respondents' minds when a related question is asked later on. How the accessible information influences the judgment depends on the way it is categorized. Information that is included in the temporary representation that individuals form of the target category results in assimilation effects. For example, when being asked about their life in general, respondents may include information about their marriage satisfaction if the preceding question referred to their marriage. If they evaluated their marriage positively they might find their life in general more positive than if they had not been asked this question before (see Schwarz, Strack, & Mai, 1991). The same piece of information that elicits an assimilation effect may, however, also elicit a contrast effect. That is, accessible positive information may render a subsequent evaluation more negative. This is the case when the information is excluded from, rather than included in, the temporary representation formed of the target category. For example, if people are instructed not to allow their response to a preceding question about marriage satisfaction affect their general life satisfaction judgment, they will exclude it from the target of their life in general, and a contrast effect will emerge. Thus, if they evaluate their marriage positively and are then instructed to exclude this aspect from the evaluation of their life in general, they will appraise their general life satisfaction more negatively than if they had not been asked the marriage question before.

It is suggested that the size of assimilation and contrast effects is a function of the amount of working memory resources an individual has available for the judgment process. Since working memory resources decrease with age, the availability of information used previously should decay faster for older respondents than for younger respondents. In addition, they should have fewer cognitive resources from which to draw inferences on the basis of the activated information. Consequently, assimilation and contrast effects as a result of question order should be less pronounced for older than for younger respondents. Evidence supporting this assumption is presented further below.

☐ Increased Response Order Effects

Numerous experiments embedded in representative surveys over the past decades demonstrate that the order in which response alternatives are presented can profoundly affect the responses themselves. This has been shown even for the presentation of a comparatively small number of response alternatives, such as two or three items (for reviews and examples, see Schwarz & Hippler, 1991; Schwarz, Hippler, & Noelle-Neumann, 1992). Generally, response order effects can occur in either of two forms: primacy or recency effects. *Primacy effects* refer to the higher endorsement of the same response alternative if presented early in the list, whereas *recency effects* refer to the higher endorsement of the same item if presented late in the list. Recent models (Krosnick & Alwin, 1987; Schwarz, Hippler, & Noelle-Neumann, 1992) trace these effects to the differential elaboration that the various response alternatives receive, depending on their position in the list and the mode in which they are presented (i.e., auditory or visual).

In general, respondents endorse an alternative when it brings agreeable thoughts to mind, but do not endorse it when it brings disagreeable thoughts to mind. Response alternatives, however, can only induce agreeing or disagreeing thoughts if respondents can think about the implications of each response alternative. According to the elaboration accounts (Krosnick & Alwin, 1987; Schwarz, Hippler, & Noelle-Neumann, 1992), their opportunity to do so, however, is limited by the order and the mode (visual versus auditory) in which the response alternatives are presented. It is further assumed that the opportunity to elaborate is affected by limited cognitive resources of older adults in a specific and predictable way, as will be outlined below (see also Knäuper, 1997).

Visual Mode

First, suppose that the response alternatives are presented visually, either on a show card or in a self-administered questionnaire. In this case, respondents may spend most thought on the first alternatives they encounter. Their mind is already cluttered with these thoughts when moving on to subsequent items (cf. Krosnick & Alwin, 1987). If the first alternative elicits agreeing thoughts, they may endorse it without spending much thought on subsequent alternatives. Thus, a response alternative that elicits agreeable thoughts is more likely to be endorsed when presented early rather than late in a list, resulting in a primacy effect under visual presentation conditions. By the same token, the more respondents can think about a response alternative that elicits disagreeable thoughts, the less likely they are to endorse it. Hence, if such an alternative is presented early rather than late, it is less likely to be endorsed, resulting in a recency effect under visual presentation conditions.

Auditory Mode

If the response alternatives are read out loud to respondents (as is the case for all experiments presented here), the opportunity to think about each response alternative is constrained by the speed with which the interviewer moves on (Krosnick & Alwin, 1987). Hence, they can elaborate most on the last response alternative read to them because the interviewer pauses to wait for their answer. If this extended elaboration results in agreeable thoughts, alternatives presented later are more likely to be endorsed than earlier ones, resulting in a recency effect under auditory presentation conditions. By the same token, response alternatives that elicit disagreeing thoughts should be least likely to be endorsed when read last. In this case, the respondents should instead endorse earlier presented alternatives, resulting in a primacy effect. Given, however, that survey researchers usually present agreeable items in surveys, a dominance of recency effects can be expected when the alternatives are read out loud.

The Role of Working Memory Resources

Respondents with insufficient working memory resources should find it particularly difficult to hold all alternatives presented active in their working memory simultaneously and to elaborate equally on their implications. Hence, respondents with reduced working memory re-sources should elaborate even more on just the alternatives read first or last, depending on the mode in which the items were presented. For agreeable items, one should find increased primacy effects in a visual presentation mode and increased recency effects in an auditory pre-sentation mode.

☐ Summary of Theoretical Assumptions

Altogether, diverging predictions for the occurrence of age differences in context effects can be made based on the specific characteristics of these effects. While question order effects are expected to decrease with increasing age, response order effects are predicted to increase. Both these apparently diverging predictions are consistent with the working memory resources approach and reflect an interaction of working memory resources with the specifics of the two types of con-text effects. While question order effects are characterized by the im-pact that previous information exerts because it is still in the working memory, response order effects are characterized by the impact previ-ous information exerts because it is no longer in the working memory. Decreasing working memory resources render it more difficult for older respondents to keep earlier information in mind and to elaborate on their implications. This information can therefore influence responses to subsequent questions to a lesser extent. By the same token, how-ever, older respondents should find it more difficult to consider all response alternatives and should therefore select those alternatives presented early or late in the list because these are most likely to receive ex-tended elaboration.

In both cases, the age-related different susceptibility to context ef-fects can lead to profound misinterpretation of methods-induced dif-ferences as substantive differences in attitudes between age groups or generations. This chapter aims to illustrate this notion with selected examples. For this purpose, question and response order experiments originally conducted by Schuman and Presser (1981) were reanalyzed by age.

☐ Data and Analysis

The reported findings are based on reanalyses of data collected by Schuman and Presser (1981) between 1971 and 1980 when the authors conducted over 130 experiments in national representative samples of the U.S. population. The experiments were designed to test the effects of question form, wording, response order, context, and various other question features on attitude judgments in surveys. Most of the experiments were conducted in telephone interviews; only a minor portion were face-to-face interviews. Using a split-ballot experimental design, respondents were randomly assigned to one of two questionnaire forms (for details on the study designs, see Schuman & Presser, 1981). The examples reported here focus on Schuman and Presser's question order and response order experiments (presented in Chap. 2 of their book). All these experiments were conducted over the phone.

The analyses presented here are based on the same schema used by Schuman and Presser (1981). The responses to the two question forms are cross-classified separately for the various age groups and are then tested separately for statistical significance using the likelihood ratio χ^2. There is considerable variation in sample size between groups in the various experiments. In particular the "older respondent" group is regularly much smaller than the younger respondent group since older respondents were, of course, not oversampled for the original experiments. Thus, significance levels of the χ^2 statistics cannot be directly compared. As an additional measure of association, the Goodman-Kruskal gamma will therefore be reported as an estimate of magnitude, which controls for variations in sample size.

☐ Reduced Question Order Effects

First, different kinds of question order experiments that were originally conducted by Schuman and Presser (1981) were reanalyzed by respondent age. As outlined earlier, it was assumed that question order effects are less pronounced for older as compared to younger respondents.

Effects of a Previous Question Series

The first set of reanalyses was conducted to test the assumption that, in comparison to younger respondents, older peoples' responses to a question are less influenced by the context provided by a series of questions. As a first example, a question order experiment conducted by Schuman and Presser in the 1971 Detroit Area Study (DAS-71, Schuman & Presser, 1981, p. 34) was reanalyzed.

In this experiment, a standard item on subjective social class was placed at different positions in two questionnaire forms. In one questionnaire it appeared before an extended series of inquiries concerning the respondent's educational and occupational history (Form A). In the other form the social class question was asked after the education and occupation questions (Form B). Schuman and Presser expected that, if asked after the education and occupation questions, respondents would feel more pressure to bring their class identification into line with the information they had just given about their educational and occupational background than when these questions were not asked before. This should result in a stronger association between "objective" and "subjective" social class variables in the "after form" than in the "before form." Schuman and Presser also expected differences in the marginals for the subjective class question as a function of question order. Their results, however, revealed no differences in the association strength or in the marginals by question order.

Reanalyses by age were conducted to test whether existing question order effects might have been covered by analyzing the data for the entire sample and not breaking them down by respondent age. To do so, the data were analyzed separately for respondents below and those above 55 years of age. As can be seen in Table 1, the initially expected question order effect appears when the data of the younger respondents are analyzed separately. Younger respondents assigned themselves to a "higher" social class after answering questions about their educational and occupational history than when these questions were not asked before ($\chi^2 = 9.89, df = 3, p < .02$). Eight percent more respondents assigned themselves to the upper or middle class when questions about their educational and occupational history were asked before (see Table 1). As can be seen, however, there is no such order effect for the older group ($\chi^2 < 1$), with differences ranging only between 0.5% and 1.6%. In addition, question order affected the association between an objective measure of class (years of completed school) and the subjective measure of class only for younger respondents (see last row in Table 1). When the subjective class question was asked after questions about educational and occupational history (Form B), younger respondents showed a significant association between the completed years of school and their assignment to a subjective social class (Pearson's $r = -.22, p < .0001$). As expected, older respondents' answers to the objective and subjective measures were not associated ($r = -.04, p > .50$).

These results provide first evidence that older respondents' answers to questions might be less affected by previously asked questions than younger respondents' questions. In order to investigate whether this finding generalizes to other experiments, a similar question order experiment originally conducted by Schuman and Presser (1981) was

**TABLE 1. SUBJECTIVE CLASS EXPERIMENT: PERCENTAGE CHOOSING
SUBJECTIVE SOCIAL CLASS CATEGORIES BY QUESTION ORDER AND AGE**

Question: "A large community like the Detroit area is made up of many kinds of groups. If you had to place yourself in one of these groups, would you say that you are in the upper class, middle class, working class, or lower class?"

Subjective Class	Younger Respondents (21–54)			Older Respondents (55–91)		
	Form A	Form B	Diff.	Form A	Form B	Diff.
Upper class (%)	1.4	2.5	−1.6	4.0	2.5	1.5
Middle class (%)	44.3	51.2	−6.9	39.7	39.0	0.7
Working class (%)	49.9	42.5	7.4	51.5	53.1	−1.6
Lower class (%)	4.4	3.8	0.6	4.9	5.4	−0.5
Total %	100	100		100	100	
N	(n = 698)	(n = 687)		(n = 227)	(n = 241)	
χ^2	$\chi^2 = 9.89, df = 3, p = .02$			$\chi^2 = 0.93, df = 3, p = .83$		
gamma	−.15			.05		
Association "subj." with "obj." measure	$r = -.22, p < .001$			$r = -.04, p > .50$		

Note. Carried out in DAS-71 (see Schuman & Presser, 1981).

reanalyzed by age. This question order experiment had also been carried out in the 1971 DAS survey (Schuman & Presser, 1981, p. 48). It investigated whether different kinds of preceding questions about religious matters influenced responses to the question of whether the respondent's interest in religion had risen, declined, or remained the same over the past 10 to 15 years. In Form A of the questionnaire, the question was preceded by a number of items about comparable objective religious aspects such as church membership or church attendance. In Form B, the religious interest question was preceded by more subjective questions about belief in God and in life after death. Schuman and Presser expected that the subjective context would lead to more reports of heightened interest in religion. The authors found a significant question order effect, but opposite to that expected: Fewer respondents reported that their interest remained the same when the interest question followed the subjective belief questions ($\chi^2 = 7.29, df = 2, p < .05$).

Reanalyses of this experiment again revealed that age moderates the question order effect. The order effect is almost twice as large for younger as for older respondents. When compared to the objective context, the subjective context leads 10.1% more younger people to endorse decreased interest in religion. Only 5.1% more older respondents report decreased interest in religion after the subjective, in comparison to the objective, context. Again, the order effect is only significant for younger respondents (21–54 years of age, $\chi^2 = 9.25$, $df = 2$, $p < .01$), while older people's responses are not significantly affected by question order ($\chi^2 = 1.25$, $df = 2$, $p > .50$).

In sum, reanalyses of these two experiments provide the first evidence that older respondents are less affected in their responses to subsequent questions by previously asked questions. As described above, this decrease in the susceptibility to effects of question order may be attributed to age-related reductions in working memory resources. Due to reduced working memory resources, earlier questions are processed less deeply, and their content decays faster in working memory. Therefore, previous questions exert less of an impact on responses to subsequent questions.

An alternative explanation for the findings presented might, however, be that older respondents' self-assignments to a subjective class or their interest in religion are more stable or crystallized than those of younger respondents. This could also explain why their responses are less affected by context manipulations. Since no data on the degree of crystallization of the attitudes were collected in the original experiments, it is not possible to rule out this alternative explanation with the archival data available. But to increase the confidence in the claim that context effects are attenuated for older people, additional question order experiments were reanalyzed for which this alternative explanation appears less likely.

Two Related Questions: Assimilation Effects

The next set of reanalyses was carried out on experiments in which the order of two related questions was reversed. Schuman and Presser conducted one such experiment in July 1980 (Schuman & Presser, 1981, p. 29). In this so-called "reporter experiment," respondents were asked about their attitudes towards allowing Communist or American reporters into each others' countries and reporting the news back to their home country. The authors found that respondents are more likely to feel that Communist reporters should be allowed to come into the United States and report the news back to their home country after having responded to a question about allowing American reporters into

Communist countries. Similarly, respondents were less likely to allow American reporters into Communist countries after having answered the question on letting Communist reporters into the United States. Schuman and Presser assume that this consistency or assimilation effect occurs because respondents answer in terms of pro-American or anti-Communist sentiments, and the second question then immediately makes a norm of reciprocity salient. Respondents feel pressure to follow that norm and give a response that is consistent with their answer to the preceding question.

It should be noted that order effects for these kinds of question sequences should be obtained only when respondents (a) recognize that the preceding question is related to the subsequent question, (b) remember their answer, and (c) draw the respective inference. These cognitive tasks require considerable working memory resources. Again, drawing on evidence from the cognitive aging research that working memory resources decrease with age, it is assumed that older respondents show these kinds of assimilation effects to a lesser extent than younger respondents. Schuman and Presser's results were broken down by respondent age to test this assumption.

Table 2 shows the results of the reanalysis. As expected, only younger respondents (21–54 years) show the assimilation effect that Schuman and Presser had reported for the entire sample. Younger people's responses to the Communist reporter item is strongly affected by whether or not this question was preceded by the American reporter item. A total of 25.6% more respondents would allow Communist reporters to come into the United States after answering the same question for American reporters than when the Communist question was asked alone. Similarly, 21% fewer respondents would allow American reporters to come into the United States after answering the Communist reporter item first. Both question order effects are highly significant ($\chi^2 = 17.6$, $df = 1$, $p < .001$ and $\chi^2 = 13.2$, $df = 1$, $p < .001$, respectively). For respondents over age 55, no such question order effect is found. For all age groups over 55, the order in which the two questions are asked does not affect the responses (all χ^2 ns).

Again, we see that older respondents—presumably due to a lack in working memory resources—show less context-dependency in their responses than younger individuals.

Two Related Questions: Contrast Effects

For other question sequences in which two related questions were asked subsequently, Schuman and Presser found contrast effects when the

TABLE 2. REPORTER EXPERIMENT: PERCENTAGE SAYING "YES" TO EACH REPORTER ITEM BY ORDER AND AGE

	Respondent Age (Years)			
	18–54	55+	60+	65–93

Communist Reporter Item: "Do you think the United States should let Communist newspaper reporters from other countries come in here and send back to their papers the news as they see it?"

	18–54	55+	60+	65–93
Comm./Amer. (%)	55.1 (107)	48.0 (52)	38.2 (34)	40.0 (20)
Amer./Comm. (%)	80.7 (124)	52.6 (38)	43.3 (30)	28.6 (21)
Difference (%)	−25.6	−4.6	−5.1	11.4
χ^2, $df = 1$	$\chi^2 = 17.60$, $p < .001$	$\chi^2 = 0.18$, ns	$\chi^2 = 0.17$, ns	$\chi^2 = 0.60$, ns
gamma	−.54	−.09	−.11	.25

American Reporter Item: "Do you think a Communist country like Russia should let American newspaper reporters come in and send back to America the news as they see it?"

	18–54	55+	60+	65–93
Comm./Amer. (%)	61.5 (109)	58.0 (73)	53.1 (32)	55.6 (18)
Amer./Comm. (%)	82.5 (126)	73.5 (56)	65.4 (26)	58.8 (17)
Difference (%)	−2?.0	−15.5	−12.3	−3.2
χ^2, $df = 1$	$\chi^2 = 13.20$, $p < .001$	$\chi^2 = 2.17$, ns	$\chi^2 = 0.89$, ns	$\chi^2 = 0.05$, ns
gamma	−.50	−.34	−.25	−.07

Note. Carried out in SRC-80, July (see Schuman & Presser, 1981). Number of respondents in parentheses.

order of the two questions was reversed. In their "abortion experiment" (Schuman & Presser, 1981, p. 36, SRC-79), a question that provided a strong legitimization for an abortion was asked either before or after a "weaker" abortion question. Specifically, the following two questions were asked with the order of the questions reversed in two versions of the questionnaire:

Question A: "Do you think it should be possible for a pregnant woman to obtain a legal abortion if there is a strong chance of serious defect in the baby?" (strong legitimization);

Question B: "Do you think it should be possible for a pregnant woman to obtain a legal abortion if she is married and does not want any more children?" (weak legitimization).

The results for the overall sample showed that the weaker abortion question (Question B) received substantially more support (by 13%) when asked first than when asked after the stronger, child-defect item (Question A). The stronger item, on the other hand, was unaffected by question order. Thus, a contrast effect occurred, with the difference in the marginals between the two questions being larger when asked in the strong-weak order than when the questions were each asked first. This presumably reflects the fact that "not wanting any more children" appears as a less legitimate reason for an abortion when contrasted with "serious defects in the baby."

As expected, reanalyses of this experiment by age show that this question order effect is limited to younger respondents. Younger respondents (below age 55) show a strong and highly significant contrast effect for the weaker abortion question when the stronger one was asked before ($\chi^2 = 19.49$, $df = 1$, $p < .001$). The weaker, no-more-children question received 19.5% more support when asked first rather than when asked after the stronger child-defect question. As expected, no such question order effect was found for older respondents. As can be seen in Table 3, there is a linear decrease of the question order effect with increasing age. The difference between question order forms decreases from 14.8% when all respondents over 55 years of age are included in the analysis to –1.4% for respondents over 65 years of age.

Note that one would draw very different conclusions about the relationship between age and attitudes towards abortion depending on the order in which the questions were asked. One would conclude that older people are less supportive of legalized abortion when the general question is asked first, but that attitudes towards abortion are thoroughly independent of age when the general question is preceded by the specific one. Thus, the age-dependency of context effects would lead us to draw different substantive conclusions.

The last two reanalyses presented demonstrate that even for short

TABLE 3. ABORTION EXPERIMENT: PERCENTAGE SAYING "YES" TO EACH ABORTION ITEM BY ORDER AND AGE

	Respondent Age (Years)			
	18-54	55+	60+	65-93

Weak Abortion Question: "Do you think it should be possible for a pregnant woman to obtain a legal abortion if she is married and does not want any more children?"

	18-54	55+	60+	65-93
Weak/Strong (%)	69.1 (246)	63.0 (73)	57.7 (52)	48.6 (35)
Strong/Weak (%)	49.6 (244)	48.2 (56)	51.2 (41)	50.0 (30)
Difference (%)	19.5	14.8	6.5	-1.4
χ^2, $df = 1$	$\chi^2 = 19.49$, $p < .00$	$\chi^2 = 2.83$, $p < .09$	$\chi^2 = 0.39$, ns	$\chi^2 = 0.01$, ns
gamma	-.38	-.29	-.13	.03

Strong Abortion Question: "Do you think it should be possible for a pregnant woman to obtain a legal abortion if there is a strong chance of serious defect in the baby?"

	18-54	55+	60+	65-93
Weak/Strong (%)	88.2 (246)	87.7 (73)	84.6 (52)	80.0 (35)
Strong/Weak (%)	88.1 (244))	80.4 (56)	78.1 (41)	73.3 (30)
Difference (%)	0.1	7.3	-6.5	-6.7
χ^2, $df = 1$	$\chi^2 = 0.001$, ns	$\chi^2 = 1.28$, ns	$\chi^2 = 0.66$, ns	$\chi^2 = 0.40$, ns
gamma	.005	-.27	-.22	-.19

Note. Carried out in SRC-79, August (see Schuman & Presser, 1981). Number of respondents in parentheses.

question sequences (only one preceding question has to be held active in working memory to induce the effect), question order effects are attenuated for older respondents. This might appear least surprising in the particular case of the American/Communist reporter experiment given the semantically complex structure of the question. The Communist reporter item, for example, reads "Do you think the United States should let Communist newspaper reporters from other countries come in here and send back to their papers the news as they see it?" This is a complex issue which requires higher order mental reasoning to fully comprehend what is meant. Understanding and answering this question obviously require considerable amounts of working memory resources. However, social issues addressed in attitude questions are in most cases complex, with complicated inferences and various facets to consider. The questions about the legalization of abortion are a good example of this. The questions themselves seem simple, but the task of answering them goes beyond the sheer comprehension of the question. The various social implications need to be considered in order to come up with an informed response. In sum, it is usually not the linguistic or syntactic complexity that taxes respondents' working memory resources, but rather the cognitive implications that need to be drawn about the issue in question.

☐ Increased Response Order Effects

As has been demonstrated for question order effects, older people with reduced working memory resources can hold less information active in working memory at a certain point in time. They are therefore less affected by the order in which questions are presented in a survey. Due to reductions in their working memory resources, older respondents should also have difficulties in equally considering all response alternatives which are presented to them in a list and in elaborating on their implications. Instead, they may need to focus their attention on those response alternatives that they can still remember well. These should be alternatives which were presented first or last. Hence, while question order effects seem to decrease with increasing age, primacy and recency effects in response alternative lists should be more pronounced among older respondents.

To test this assumption Knäuper (1995, 1997) conducted a meta-analysis of all response order experiments carried out by Schuman and Presser (1981, Chap. 2). This meta-analysis convincingly demonstrated that older respondents indeed are more vulnerable to showing primacy and recency effects in response alternative lists. For 12 out of the 14 reanalyzed experiments, larger response order effects were obtained for older as compared to younger individuals. In some cases older respondents showed response order effects that were about six times as large as the effects displayed by younger respondents. Across all 14 experiments the mean absolute difference between response order conditions was about twice as large for older as for younger respondents (13.9% versus 6.6%; see Knäuper, 1997). Later, Smith and Bishop (1996; Bishop & Smith, 1997) conducted an even more comprehensive meta-analysis that confirmed Knäuper's findings. It can hence be concluded with some confidence that older respondents show stronger response order effects. Currently, laboratory experiments are underway to examine the cognitive processes that are assumed to underlie this age-related increase in response order effects (Schwarz, Park, & Knäuper, 1996). These experiments will allow a direct test of the assumption that reductions in working memory resources can account for the age differences in the size and direction of response order effects in surveys.

A differential susceptibility to the order in which response alternatives are presented can have profound effects on the inferences drawn from survey findings about age or generational differences in attitudes or behaviors, similar to what has been demonstrated earlier for question order effects. Below, two representative examples are presented that illustrate this for response order effects. Details of the meta-analysis of all experiments can be found in Knäuper (1997).

Recency Effects

As a first illustrative example, I draw on the divorce experiment that Schuman and Presser conducted in September 1979 (SRC-79, Schuman & Presser, 1981, p. 66) as part of a telephone interview. Respondents were asked either of two questions. The question was exactly the same for both groups, but the order of the last two response options was reversed. Specifically, respondents were asked: "Should divorce in this country be easier to obtain, more difficult to obtain, or stay as it is now?" The order of the last two response options was reversed in the two questionnaire forms so that in one form "stay as is" was the middle item, and in the other form "stay as is" was the last. The results showed that whichever alternative was presented last was endorsed significantly more than the one that was presented in the middle. For the alternative "stay as is," for example, the endorsement increased significantly—by 12%—when it was placed at the end rather than in the middle (see Schuman & Presser, 1981, p. 67).

A reanalysis of this experiment by age reveals a dramatic increase in the size of this response order effect with respondent age (for a detailed presentation of the results, see Table 4 in Knäuper, 1997). Among respondents younger than 55 years of age, the response alternative "stay as is" was chosen only 7.4% more often when presented last rather than in the middle of the response sequence. The response order effect for this group is not significant ($\chi^2 = 2.63$, $df = 2$, ns). The size of the response order effect, however, increases substantially with age. For respondents 55 years or older the difference between response orders is already 18.6%, and it rises up to 45.5% for respondents over 70 years of age. When "stay as is" is presented in the middle (Form B), only 22.7% of respondents over 70 years old choose it. In this case, most respondents choose the response alternative presented last ("more difficult," 68.2%). If "stay as is," however, is the alternative that is presented last (Form A), then most older respondents choose it for an answer (68.2%), and the "more difficult" response option is chosen by only 31.8% of the respondents. These findings demonstrate clearly that with increasing age respondents are more likely to choose whatever alternative is presented last.

Note that, similar to what has earlier been shown for question order effects, one would draw very different substantive conclusions about the relationship between age and attitudes depending on the order in which response alternatives are presented. When "more difficult" is presented last and "stay as is" is presented in the middle, older respondents apparently report more conservative attitudes towards divorce than younger respondents (68.2%, versus 36.4% of the youngest favoring more restrictive divorce laws). When, however, "more difficult" is presented in the middle, the responses are virtually identical (31.8% and 31.4%, for the oldest and the youngest respondents, respectively). This finding again illustrates that age-related changes in cognitive functioning may not only influence the emergence and size of context effects but result in different conclusions about age or generational differences in attitudes depending on the order in which response options are presented.

Primacy Effects

A final example serves to demonstrate that it is not necessarily the last item that is endorsed more often with increasing age. For Schuman and Presser's "adequate housing" experiment (Schuman & Presser, 1981, p. 68) primacy effects were found to increase with respondents' age. In this experiment, which was replicated in several surveys, respondents were read the following statement: "Some people feel the federal government should see to it that all people have adequate housing, while others feel each person should provide for his own housing. Which comes closest to how you feel about this?"

The order of the two response alternatives was reversed in the two versions of the questionnaire, i.e., one group of respondents heard the government statement first and the "each person" statement last, and the other group heard the government statement last and the "each person" statement first. Schuman and Presser—unexpectedly—found a primacy effect for this item. As shown in Table 4, this primacy effect is due in the first place to older respondents. The difference between response alternative order is only small and not significant for respondents below age 55 (4.9%; $\chi^2 = 1.12$, $df = 1$, ns). For older respondents, however, the order effect is substantial and significant. The difference in endorsement between response orders is 12.9% for respondents over age 55, 11.6% for those aged 60 and older, and 14.5% for those over age 65.

In sum, these illustrative examples demonstrate that the size of primacy and recency effects increases with age (for a systematic review and meta-analysis, see Knäuper, 1997). It is suspected that reductions in working memory resources require older respondents to focus their attention on either the first or the last response alternatives presented, rendering those alternatives most accessible and most clearly represented in their working memory. They are therefore more likely to be chosen for an answer than items presented in the middle of a response option sequence.

TABLE 4.   ADEQUATE HOUSING EXPERIMENT: PERCENTAGE ENDORSING THE GOVERNMENT RESPONSE ALTERNATIVE BY ORDER AND AGE

Form A. "Some people feel the federal government should see to it that all people have adequate housing, while others feel each person should provide for his own housing. Which comes closest to how you feel about this?"
Form B: "Some people feel each person should provide for his own housing, while others feel the federal government should see to it that all people have adequate housing. Which comes closest to how you feel about this?"

	Respondent Age (Years)			
	18–54	55+	60+	65+
Form A (%)	40.9 (235)	38.2 (68)	39.2 (51)	37.8 (37)
Form B (%)	36.0 (222)	25.3 (75)	27.6 (58)	23.3 (43)
Difference (%)	4.9	12.9	11.6	14.5
χ^2, $df = 1$	1.12, ns	2.76, $p < .10$	1.66, ns	2.02, $p < .16$
gamma	.10	.29	.26	.33

☐ Discussion

The important outcome of the presented reanalyses of question order and response order effects by respondent age is that response effects are not generally enhanced in older age, and data are not always more biased in older people, as has been suggested in the past (e.g., Andrews & Herzog, 1986). Consistent with research on memory and aging, certain response effects, namely question order effects, decrease with increasing age, resulting in less biased data. Other response effects, namely, response order effects, increase with respondent age, rendering survey responses of older people more biased due to the order in which response alternatives are presented in a list. For both kinds of context effects it was demonstrated that inferences about age-related differences in opinions or behaviors depend on the specifics of the questionnaire. While one would conclude that the behaviors or opinions of older people do not differ from those of younger people under one question or response order condition, one would arrive at the opposite conclusion under the other order condition. Hence, it is important to understand how age-related changes in cognitive functioning impact on the processes underlying self-reports in surveys. Without this understanding, one runs the risk of misinterpreting methods-induced differences as substantive age or generational differences, as has been demonstrated in the present paper. This, in turn, could lead to erroneous theoretical conclusions and applied recommendations.

While the evidence for an age-related increase in response order effects is strong and is by now supported by two extensive meta-analyses (Bishop & Smith, 1997; Knäuper, 1997), age differences in question order effects have until now been examined less thoroughly. Although the findings presented here are compatible with the outlined theorizing, the examples are selective and a meta-analysis of existing question order experiments is now needed in order to examine the assumptions separately for different classes of question order experiments. Question order effects are complex and possibly represent a number of distinct types of effects that are based on distinctly different psychological processes.

Indeed, although the claim was made in the present paper that question order effects should generally be less pronounced among older people, one could also reasonably argue that some question order effects should be more pronounced in older people. Cognitive aging research has shown not only that working memory resources decrease with age but also that older individuals have more difficulty inhibiting irrelevant information once activated (Hasher & Zacks, 1988). Other research has shown that older adults maintain primed information in memory longer (MacKay & Burke, 1990; Myerson, Ferraro, Hale, & Lima, 1992). The effects of activated knowledge structures may persist more profoundly in subsequent questions for older compared to young adults due to sustained activation (e.g., Hamm & Hasher, 1992; Hartman & Hasher, 1991; Myerson et al., 1992). To the extent that older respondents are less able to inhibit information activated previously, question order effects could be expected to be accentuated rather than attenuated for older relative to younger respondents. Whether, however, this activation advantage is of sufficient endurance to affect subsequent questions is an open issue and needs to be addressed in future experimental research. Possibly, an accentuation is only found when the information brought to mind is highly self-relevant and emotionally involving for older people, in which case it may elicit rumination and reminiscence (cf. Schwarz, Park, & Knäuper, 1996).

As these conjectures indicate, age-related differences in cognitive functioning raise theoretically informative questions about the emergence of context effects in self-reports. If we want to avoid misleading conclusions about age-related changes in attitudes and opinions and similar phenomena, we need a better understanding of age-related differences in the processes underlying self-reports. Future research will need to test the proposed assumptions under controlled conditions. Laboratory experiments are currently underway for this purpose (Schwarz, Park, & Knäuper, 1996). In these experiments, individual's working memory resources will be assessed with appropriate measures and it will therefore be possible to investigate directly the impact of reductions in memory resources on the susceptibility to context effects. This research will allow the specification of the cognitive functions that contribute to context effects in self-reports and the development of procedures that may minimize them.

☐ Acknowledgments

The reported research was conducted while the author was a visiting scholar at the Institute for Social Research, University of Michigan, and was supported by fellowships granted by the German Research Council and the Max Planck Society, Germany.

☐ References

Andrews, F. M., & Herzog, A. R. (1986). The quality of survey data as related to age of respondent. *Journal of the American Statistical Association, 81,* 403–410.
Baddeley, A. D. (1986). *Working memory.* Oxford, England: Clarendon Press.

Bishop, G. F., & Smith, A. E. (1997, May). *Response-order effects in public opinion surveys: The plausibility of rival hypotheses.* Paper presented at the conference of the American Association for Public Opinion Research, Norfolk, VA.

Bodenhausen, G. V., & Wyer, R. S. (1987). Social cognition and social reality: Information acquisition and use in the laboratory and the real world. In H.-J. Hippler, N. Schwarz, & S. Sudman (Eds.), *Social information processing and survey methodology* (pp. 6–41). New York: Springer-Verlag.

Connelly, S. L., Hasher, L., & Zacks, R. T. (1991). Age and reading: The impact of distraction. *Psychology and Aging, 6,* 533–541.

Daneman, M., & Carpenter, P. A. (1980). Individual differences in working memory and reading. *Journal of Verbal Learning and Verbal Behavior, 19,* 450–466.

Hamm, V. P., & Hasher, L. (1992). Age and the availability of inferences. *Psychology and Aging, 7,* 56–64.

Hartman, M., & Hasher, L. (1991). Aging and suppression: Memory for previously relevant information. *Psychology and Aging, 6,* 587–594.

Hasher, L., & Zacks, R. T. (1988). Working memory, comprehension, and aging: A review and a new view. In G. H. Bower (Ed.), *The psychology of learning and motivation* (Vol. 22, pp. 193–227). New York: Academic Press.

Higgins, E. T. (1989). Knowledge accessibility and activation: Subjectivity and suffering from unconscious sources. In J. S. Uleman & J. A. Bargh (Eds.), *Unintended thought* (pp. 75–123). New York: Guilford Press.

Just, M. A., & Carpenter, P. A. (1992). A capacity theory of comprehension: Individual differences in working memory. *Psychological Review, 99,* 122–149.

Knäuper, B. (1995, November). *Response effects in older age.* Paper presented at the meeting of the Midwest Association for Public Opinion Research, Chicago, IL.

Knäuper, B. (1997). *The impact of age and education on response order effects in attitude measurement.* Manuscript under review.

Krosnick, J. A., & Alwin, D. F. (1987). An evaluation of a cognitive theory of response-order effects in survey measurement. *Public Opinion Quarterly, 51,* 201–219.

MacKay, D. G., & Burke, D. M. (1990). Cognition and aging: A theory of new learning and the use of old connections. In T. M. Hess (Ed.), *Aging and cognition: Knowledge organization and utilization* (pp. 213–264). Amsterdam: North Holland.

Myerson, J., Ferraro, R. F., Hale, S., & Lima, S. D. (1992). General slowing in semantic priming and work recognition. *Psychology and Aging, 7,* 257–270.

Narayan, S., & Krosnick, J. A. (1996). Education moderates some response effects in attitude measurement. *Public Opinion Quarterly, 60,* 58–88.

Payne, S. L. (1951). *The art of asking questions.* Princeton, NJ: Princeton University Press.

Salthouse, T. A., Babcock, R. L., & Shaw, R. J. (1991). Effects of adult age on structural and operational capacities in working memory. *Psychology and Aging, 6,* 118–127.

Schuman, H., & Presser, S. (1981). *Questions and answers in attitude surveys.* New York: Springer-Verlag.

Schwarz, N., & Bless, H. (1992). Constructing reality and its alternatives: Assimilation and contrast effects in social judgment. In L. L. Martin & A. Tesser (Eds.), *The construction of social judgments* (pp. 217–245). Hillsdale, NJ: Erlbaum.

Schwarz, N., & Hippler, H.-J. (1991). Response alternatives: The impact of their choice and ordering. In P. Biemer, R. Groves, N. Mathiowetz, & S. Sudman (Eds.), *Measurement error in surveys* (pp. 41–56). Chichester, England: Wiley.

Schwarz, N., Hippler, H.-J., & Noelle-Neumann, E. (1992). A cognitive model of response order effects in survey measurement. In N. Schwarz & S. Sudman (Eds.), *Context effects in social and psychological research* (pp. 187–201). New York: Springer-Verlag.

Schwarz, N., Hippler, H.-J., & Noelle-Neumann, E. (1994). Retrospective reports: The impact of response alternatives. In N. Schwarz & S. Sudman (Eds.), *Autobiographical memory and the validity of retrospective reports* (pp. 187–199). New York: Springer-Verlag.

Schwarz, N., Park, D., & Knäuper, B. (1996). *Aging, cognition, and context effects in self-reports.* Grant proposal. National Institute of Aging.

Schwarz, N., Strack, F., & Mai, H. P. (1991). Assimilation and contrast effects in part-whole question sequences: A conversational logic analysis. *Public Opinion Quarterly, 55,* 3–23.

Schwarz, N., & Sudman, S. (Eds.). (1992). *Context effects in social and psychological research.* New York: Springer-Verlag.

Smith, A. E., & Bishop, G. F. (1996, May). *Standing the test of time: Aging and response-order effects.* Paper presented at the conference of the American Association for Public Opinion Research, Salt Lake City, UT.

Strack, F., & Martin, L. L. (1987). Thinking, judging, and communicating: A process account of context effects in attitude surveys. In H.-J. Hippler, N. Schwarz, & S. Sudman (Eds.), *Social information processing and survey methodology* (pp. 123–148). New York: Springer-Verlag.

Sudman, S., Bradburn, N. M., & Schwarz, N. (1996). *Thinking about answers: The application of cognitive processes to survey methodology.* San Francisco: Jossey-Bass.

Tourangeau, R. (1984). Cognitive sciences and survey methods. In T. Jabine, M. Straf, J. Tanur, & R. Tourangeau (Eds.), *Cognitive aspects of survey methodology: Building a bridge between disciplines* (pp. 73–100). Washington, DC: National Academy Press.

Tourangeau, R., & Rasinski, K. A. (1988). Cognitive processes underlying context effects in attitude measurement. *Psychological Bulletin, 103,* 299–314.

CHAPTER   Duane F. Alwin

Aging and Errors of Measurement: Implications for the Study of Life-Span Development

Measurement error has potentially serious consequences in the study of social behavior using sample surveys, regardless of the characteristics of the subject population. Because of the cognitive demands of some survey questions (see Sudman, Bradburn, & Schwarz, 1996), and given well-documented laboratory and survey results regarding declines associated with aging in some domains of cognitive functioning (see Herzog & Rodgers, 1989; Park et al., 1996; Salthouse, 1991, 1996; Schaie, 1990, 1993, 1996), it has been suggested that there may be identifiable differences in errors of measurement associated with the age of the respondent in actual surveys. Given the impact of levels of measurement error on the robustness of statistical analysis in social and behavioral research (Bohrnstedt, 1983; Bohrnstedt and Carter, 1971; Cleary, Linn, & Walster, 1970), if there are differences in measurement error across age groupings, it is important to take these differences into account in the analysis of data.

Despite the reasonableness of these expectations based on theories of cognitive aging, however, survey researchers studying older populations have generally not been able to demonstrate that there are serious age-related errors of measurement in routine applications of the survey interview. In one important study using comparisons of survey reports to administrative records, census counts, and maps, Rodgers and Herzog (1987) found few age differences in the accuracy in self-reports of factual material (e.g., voting behavior, value of housing, and characteristics of neighbors). They concluded that evidence to date "does not indicate that [problems of measurement error] are consistently more serious for older respondents than for any other age group" (p. 387). Similarly, research on the measurement of subjective variables has failed to show large differences in reporting errors by age, although it is sometimes the case that the oldest respondents (e.g., over the age of 60) are the least reliable (Alwin, 1989; Alwin & Krosnick, 1991b; Rodgers, Andrews, & Herzog, 1992).

The possibility that age is linked to the quality of measurement in surveys raises a number of additional questions. For example, it is important to ask whether the effects of age are monotonic or whether the decremental effects of aging occur only after a certain age, say age 60. Also, we need to know whether the possible measurement errors associated with aging are reflected in the measurement of all phenomena or whether they are linked specifically to the nature of the content being measured. In the analysis presented later in this chapter, I examine these issues for factual material and three types of subjective variables: attitudes, beliefs, and self-perceptions. Given the relevance of cognitive skills to survey measurement, one must also consider the extent to which other age-related phenomena are confounded with differences among age groups. For example, are differences in cohort experiences linked to cognitive development, and if so, how does one draw inferences about the unique role of aging with respect to comparisons of measurement errors across age groups? This chapter addresses how the differing cohort experiences relevant to cognitive development, particularly the differing schooling levels of respondents of different ages, contribute to the understanding of the link between age differences and errors of measurement by examining adjustments to reliability estimates based on the relationships among age, schooling, and reliability. The latter is important because there are many aspects of cohort experiences that are tied to schooling—both the amount of schooling and its quality—and these experiences are relevant to performance on cognitive measures. If cohort differences in schooling account for the lower reliability of older people in some content domains, then processes of aging would not represent a complete explanation.

The research presented here addresses these questions using data on the reliability of measurement in longitudinal studies of respondents in the 1956–58–60 and 1972–74–76 National Election Study (NES) panels. Using estimates of reliability for single survey questions, results are presented by age, educational level, and question content. An effort is made to control for educational level in drawing comparisons among age groups regarding propensities for measurement error using the classical "covariance adjustment" from the Analysis of Covariance (ANCOVA) statistical model. Before presenting these results, we first review the theoretical basis for the hypothesis that there are age differences in measurement error. Then we consider the possibility that age-related patterns of reliability are due to the influence of the significantly lower levels of education among older respondents.

☐ Age Differences in Error Measurement

Responses to survey questions are affected by a number of factors which produce errors of measurement. It is generally agreed that key sources of measurement errors are linked to aspects of survey questions, the cognitive processes of information processing and retrieval, the motivational context of the setting that produces the information, and the response framework in which the information is then transmitted (see Alwin, 1989, 1991b, 1995, 1997a; Alwin & Krosnick, 1991b; Andrews, 1984; Bradburn & Danis, 1984; Cannell, Miller, & Oksenberg, 1981; Groves, 1989; Hippler, Schwarz, & Sudman, 1987; Knäuper et al., 1997; Schwarz & Sudman, 1994; Strack & Martin, 1987; Tourangeau, 1984, 1987; Tourangeau & Rasinski, 1988). From the point of view of assessing survey measurement errors, there are essentially six critical elements of the response process that directly impinge on the reliability of survey measurement: (a) *content validity:* the adequacy of the question in measuring the phenomenon of interest; (b) *comprehension:* the respondent's understanding or comprehension of the question and the information it requests; (c) *accessibility:* the respondent's access to the information requested (e.g., do they have an opinion?); (d) *retrieval:* the respondent's capacities for developing a response on the basis of the information at hand, say from internal cognitive and affective cues regarding their attitude or level of approval; (e) *communication:* the respondent's translation of that response into the response categories provided by the survey question; and (f) *motivation:* the respondent's willingness to provide an accurate response. These factors play a role in affecting the quality of survey data, whether the question seeks information of a factual nature or whether it asks for reports of subjective states, such as beliefs and attitudes, but they are perhaps especially problematic in the measurement of subjective phenomena such as attitudes, beliefs, and self-perceptions.

These factors also play a role regardless of the characteristics of the subject population, but they are often theorized to be especially relevant to the response process for older respondents (see Herzog &

Rodgers, 1982). Theoretically speaking, age may be related to the response process with respect to each of the above critical factors. Specifically, with regard to *comprehension of the question*, it is well known that cognitive capacities for recognition of meaning and understanding concepts appear to decline in old age (see Salthouse, 1991; Schaie, 1993), and this may be the basis for declines in the reliability of survey reporting in old age (Andrews & Herzog, 1986).

With regard to *accessibility to requested information*, it appears that age is unrelated to the relative accessibility of factual information, as several studies show little difference in measurement errors (e.g., Rodgers and Herzog, 1987). However, with regard to subjective content, the obverse may be true. An example of this is Converse's (1964) famous example of "nonattitudes": respondents who do not have opinions or attitudes may feel pressure to respond to survey questions because they assume interviewers want them to answer, and because of cultural norms, they believe opinionated people are held in higher esteem than the ignorant and uninformed. According to Converse (1964), because respondents wish to conform to these expectations and project positive self-images, they frequently concoct attitude reports, making essentially random choices from among the offered response alternatives. Critics of this viewpoint (e.g., Achen, 1975) argue that measurement errors are not the fault of respondents' random reports, but primarily due to the vagueness of the questions. Whatever the case, older respondents may be more subject to these processes, since they may be less informed of current events and less likely to have attitudes about them. There is some support for this in studies showing that older respondents are more likely to answer "don't know" to survey questions (Gergen & Back, 1966; Ferber, 1966; Francis & Busch, 1975; Rodgers & Herzog, 1987). There is reason to expect, however, that this pattern was more prevalent for attitudes and expectations, and less so for factual content.

Retrieval of requested information is often viewed as one of the most serious elements of the response process, given the importance of both memory and cognitive processing in formulating responses to many survey questions. Age differences in memory have been widely documented, although research is often characterized by weak research designs based on limited samples. An exception to this is the study by Herzog and Rodgers (1989), which reports a clear, age-related decline in memory performance in a cross-sectional sample of the Detroit, Michigan metropolitan area. Obviously, when memory fails or when retrieved information is ambiguous or imprecise, there is a tendency to create measurement errors in approximating the "true" value. To the extent that there are communication difficulties associated with age, they are likely to be linked to the response framework offered the respondent in mapping retrieved information to the response categories provided. Older respondents may not be as facile as younger respondents with more difficult and complicated response schemes. Similarly, motivational differences among respondents could produce differences in measurement error, although it is not altogether clear that motivation per se varies by age. That is, older respondents may not be any more likely to "satisfice" than "optimize" in producing answers to survey questions (see Alwin, 1991b).

☐ Cohort Differences in Errors of Measurement

The empirical part of this study is concerned with the intersection of two findings: reliability differences by age and by education (Alwin, 1989; Alwin & Krosnick, 1991b). Specifically, we ask whether age variation in measurement reliability can be explained by differences among age groups in levels of schooling. In other words, are age differences in schooling experiences partly or totally responsible for measurement errors apparently linked to age? If they are, one needs to be cautious in drawing inferences about the causal role of processes of cognitive aging in producing measurement errors. This is, however, more than a statistical issue of making sure that adequate controls have been undertaken to rule out alternative hypotheses. The issue I raise is more fundamental: observations of differences among groups of different ages need not be evidence of anything having to do with processes of aging.

One of the difficulties with the attribution of differences in cognitive performance to aging is the fact that in such cross-sectional studies age is confounded with cohort (see Salthouse, 1991; Schaie, 1993). If cohort experiences were not important for the development of cognitive functioning, there would be no reason for concern, but there are clear differences among cohorts in aspects of experience that are relevant for cognitive scores, e.g., the nature and amount of schooling (Alwin, 1991a). There is a rather long tradition in sociology of theorizing about the role of historical time as a factor in socialization processes involved in the transition to adulthood. The German sociologist Karl Mannheim (1952) popularized the concept of "generation" to refer to the fact that growing up in different historical periods may have influences on individual characteristics; and the American demographer, Norman Ryder, brought Mannheim's work into greater focus by recasting the argument in terms of the more precise terminology of "cohort" and the social metabolism of "cohort replacement" (Ryder, 1965). But aging and cohort influences are difficult to disentangle, because within a one-time, cross-sectional study, age and birth year are perfectly correlated. It is possible, however, to directly measure aspects of cohort experiences that account for their impacts.

Thus, on logical grounds, before entertaining explanations of age differences in measurement errors involving the possibilities of the impact of aging and processes associated with it, one should probably try to rule out the role of different cohort experiences. Nearly 25 years ago, Matilda Riley (1973) warned that comparing different age groups could lead to an "aging" or "life cycle" fallacy. Cohort experiences are temporally prior to the overall experience of aging, so it is logical and necessary to rule out cohort differences among age groups that are creating a spurious association between age and reliability of measurement. This, of course, requires the specification of theoretically relevant cohort-related factors that are also related to measurement error. For example, are aging interpretations of age differences robust with respect to controls for variables which reflect cohort experiences linked to cognitive development and which are associated with errors of measurement? Specifically, several studies report that educational attainment is positively related to memory performance (Arbuckle, Gold, & Andres, 1986; Perlmutter, 1978; Herzog & Rodgers, 1989). Since cohorts differ systematically in their amount of schooling attained, it is natural to wonder whether cohort factors may be contributing spuriously to the empirical relationship between age and errors of measurement.

To put the issue somewhat more narrowly, to what extent are differences in response effects or measurement errors heretofore identified as linked to processes of aging really due to cohort experiences in exposure to schooling? Do age differences in reliability of survey reporting remain when we control for cohort differences in schooling? Schooling is one of the clear-cut differences among birth cohorts in contemporary society, with vast differences between those born at the beginning of the century and those born more recently. Schooling contributes to the reduction of survey errors, since more educated respondents, regardless of age, systematically produce fewer errors in survey responses (Alwin & Krosnick, 1991b). In order to control for schooling differences, I apply covariance adjustments of reliability estimates for age groups, adjusted for compositional differences in schooling. This exercise essentially equates the groups statistically in their exposure to schooling. Because schooling is strongly related to both age and reliability, some substantial changes are recorded. In addition, because of differences in reporting errors by the content of the information sought in surveys, it is important to control for the content and source of survey data. I therefore examine age differences in reliability in four content categories: (a) factual content, (b) beliefs, (c) attitudes, and (d) self-perceptions, controlling for differences in the educational experiences of cohort categories.

☐ Research Design and Statistical Estimation

The aim of this research is to estimate the errors of measurement in survey responses. This requires a clear definition of measurement error, a design for identifying components of error, and a model for estimating the specified quantities. There are a number of different ways in which one can approach the question of measurement error and estimate its effects. For example, one can compare age groups in the experimental effects of varying question forms (e.g., Knäuper, 1997). This approach, however, focuses on mean levels or biases between experimental categories and does not address the question of the contribution to measurement error variance. Another approach, one proposed previously (e.g., Achen, 1975; Alwin, 1989), formulates the problem of measurement error as a component of response variance, using information from variances and covariances in a within-subjects measurement design, specifically a repeated-measures design, which permits a focus on the reliability of measurement.

Two general design strategies exist for estimating the reliability of single survey questions: (a) the use of similar measures in the same interview, or (b) the use of replicate measures in reinterview designs (see Alwin, 1989; Marquis & Marquis, 1977). The application of either design strategy is problematic, and in some cases the estimation procedures used require assumptions that are not appropriate. Estimation of reliability from information collected within the same interview is especially difficult, owing to the virtual impossibility of replicating questions. Researchers often employ similar though not identical questions, and then examine correlation or covariance properties of the data collected. It is risky to use such information to estimate item reliability, since questions that are different contain specific components of variance, orthogonal to the quantity measured in common, and difficulties in being able to separate reliable components of specific variance from random error variance presents a major obstacle to this estimation approach. Such designs require relatively strong assumptions regarding the components of variation in the measures, notably that measures are *univocal* and have properties of *congeneric* measures (see Alwin & Jackson, 1979; Jöreskog, 1971).

A second approach to the estimation of the reliability of survey data uses a reinterview or panel design. Such designs also present problems in estimating reliability. For example, the test-retest approach using a single reinterview must assume that there is no change in the underlying quantity being measured (Lord & Novick, 1968; Siegel & Hodge, 1968). This is a problem in many situations, since with two waves of a panel study, the assumption of perfect correlational stability is unrealistic, and without this assumption little purchase can be made on the question of reliability in designs involving two waves.

Because of the problematic nature of the assumption of perfect stability, several efforts have been made to analyze panel surveys involving three waves, where reliability can be estimated under certain assumptions about the properties of the error distributions (see Heise, 1969; Wiley & Wiley, 1970). These are the models used in my subsequent analysis of reliability, so it is useful to describe this approach in somewhat more detail. Specifically, I employ a class of just-identified simplex models that specify two structural equations for a set of three over-time measures of a given variable y_t:

$$y_t = \tau_t + \varepsilon_t,$$
$$\tau_t = \beta_{t,t-1}\,\tau_{t-1} + \upsilon_t.$$

The first equation represents a set of measurement assumptions, indicating that (a) the over-time measures are assumed to be τ-equivalent, except for true attitude change, and (b) the measurement error is random (see Alwin, 1989; Jöreskog, 1970). The second equation specifies the causal processes involved in the change of the latent variable (e.g., an attitude) over time. This model assumes a lag-1 or Markovian process in which the distribution of the true variables at time t is dependent only on the distribution at time $t-1$ and is not directly dependent on distributions of the variable at earlier times. If these assumptions do not hold, then simplex models may be inappropriate. However, our previous analyses indicate that, as a first-stage analytic approach, this model is extremely valuable (see Alwin, 1989).

Estimates of these structural-equation parameters allow us to assess the reliability, as well as the stability, of the various measures analyzed here. In order to estimate such models, it is necessary to make some assumptions regarding the measurement error structures and the nature of the true change processes underlying the measures. All estimation strategies available for such three-wave data require a lag-1 assumption regarding the nature of the true change. This assumption in general seems a reasonable one, but erroneous results can arise if it is violated. The various approaches differ in their assumptions about measurement error. One approach (see Heise, 1969) assumes equal reliabilities over occasions of measurement. This is often a realistic and useful assumption, especially when the process is not in dynamic equilibrium, i.e., when the observed variances vary with time. Another approach to estimating the parameters of the above model is to assume constant measurement error variances rather than constant reliabilities (see Wiley & Wiley, 1970). This is often seen as a less restrictive set of assumptions than that made by the Heise (1969) approach, but it can produce erroneous estimates if the true variances increase or decrease systematically over time. Experience indicates, except for this case, that the two approaches almost always produce virtually identical results for standardized parameters (Alwin, 1989). In the following, I present results for Wave 2 estimates of reliability from the Wiley-Wiley (1970) model, which can be shown to be equal to Heise's (1969) estimate of reliability based on these same models.

One of the main advantages of the reinterview design is that, under appropriate circumstances, it is possible to eliminate the confounding of the systematic error component discussed earlier, if systematic components of error are not stable over time. Of course, estimation of reliability from reinterview designs makes sense only if one can rule out memory as a factor in the covariance of measures over time. Thus, the occasions of measurement must be separated by sufficient periods of time to rule out the operation of memory. In cases where the remeasurement interval is insufficiently large to permit appropriate estimation of the reliability of the data, the estimate of the amount of reliability will most likely be inflated.

☐ Data and Measures

Few studies meet the design requirements mentioned above because panel studies on nationally representative populations, with more than two waves of measurement, are extremely rare. Also, the remeasurement intervals are rarely distant enough to rule out memory as playing a large factor. However, several appropriate data sets do exist. Here I rely on two University of Michigan National Election Study Panels, developed in the 1950s and 1970s, which were linked to the biennial national NES cross-sections. To briefly explain the latter, every two years since 1952 (except 1954) the Survey Research Center of the University of Michigan's Institute for Social Research has interviewed a representative cross-section of Americans to track national political participation. In presidential election years, a sample is interviewed before the election and immediately afterward. In nonpresidential election years, only postelection surveys are conducted. Data are obtained from face-to-face interviews with national full-probability samples of all citizens of voting age in the contiguous United States, exclusive of military reservations, using the Survey Research Center's multistage area sample (see Miller et al., 1991). The sample sizes typically range between 1,500 and 2,000. On two occasions the NES conducted the long-term panel studies that are used here. One was conducted in 1956–58–60 and one in 1972–74–76. Of respondents interviewed in 1956, 1,132 were reinterviewed in 1958 and again in 1960 (see Campbell, Converse, Miller, & Stokes, 1971). The questionnaires used in the 1958 and 1960 panel studies were the same as those used in the 1958 and 1960 cross-sections, but there was considerable overlap between the 1956, 1958, and 1960 studies. Of the respondents interviewed in 1972, 1,320 were successfully reinterviewed in 1974 and again in 1976. Again, the questionnaires used in these reinterview studies were the same as those used for the cross-section samples interviewed at those times. There was also considerable overlap between the 1972, 1974, and 1976 surveys (Center for Political Studies, 1979).

The data utilized here are from all nonredundant variables available in these two panel studies at all three waves. This criterion is met by 255 variables. The main source of information on these variables was the respondent, including both self-reports and reports on other members of the household (e.g., household head or respondent's spouse). In addition, some information was obtained by the interviewer and some information was added to the data file by the survey organization, based on sampling information, which are not included here. In this analysis we focus solely on the self-report measures. Due to small numbers of cases in some instances and other problems with the data, we excluded some variables, resulting in 199 self-report measures for the present analysis.

These variables fall into four content categories.

1. *Facts*. Objective information regarding the respondent or members of the household (e.g., information on the respondent's characteristics, such as the date of birth, amount of schooling, amount of family income, and the timing, duration and frequencies of certain behaviors).
2. *Beliefs*. Subjective assessments of states and/or outcomes regarding the respondent or others (e.g., information on respondent's perceptions of how political parties stand on various issues).
3. *Attitudes*. Affective responses to particular objects or actors, assumed to exist along a positive/negative continuum of acceptance, favorableness, or agreement (e.g., attitudes on policy issues or about po-

litical leaders are frequently used and measured along a dimension of approval or disapproval).
4. *Self-Descriptions.* Subjective evaluations or assessments of the state of the respondent within certain domains (e.g., a common form of self-description in political studies is party affiliation, or assessments of interest in politics, or the extent to which they care about who wins an election).

In the case of facts, such objective information must often be estimated, in which case there is some ambiguity in the distinction between facts and beliefs. The major distinction here is that facts can presumably be verified against objective records, whereas beliefs are, by definition, a matter of personal judgment. Attitudes and self-descriptions are similarly often confused, since the latter can be thought of as attitudes toward one's self, but for present purposes, attitudes are those variables in which the object of the response was not the self.

☐ General Results[1]

The main purpose of this analysis is to examine differences in estimated reliability by the age of the respondents and to control observed differences in reliability for pre-existing differences in unique cohort experiences. Table 1 presents the reliability of measurement for self-reports in the NES panels by the content domain. There is uneven distribution of information across these classifications, which is an inevitable consequence of my secondary analysis approach. From these results it can be seen that the typical reliability for responses to self-report questions in these surveys is .54, which is not all that high. This means that for the typical self-report questionnaire item, approximately 46% of the response variance is due to random error sources. Of course,

TABLE 1. ESTIMATES OF RELIABILITY OF MEASUREMENT IN SELF-REPORTS BY QUESTION CONTENT: NATIONAL ELECTION STUDY PANELS, 1956–58–60 AND 1972–74–76

Content of Question	Number of Items	Reliability
Facts	64	.707
Beliefs	68	.411
Attitudes	43	.537
Self-Assessments	24	.466
Total: Self-Reports	199	.540

there is variability around this average, with some variables being measured with near perfect reliability and others being measured quite poorly (see Alwin, 1997b).

It seems self-evident that various domains of content may inherently differ in the extent to which they may be measured reliably. Indeed, there is an untested hypothesis in the survey literature that facts, all other things being equal, ought to be more reliably measured than is the case in the measurement of subjective variables (see Kalton and Schuman, 1982). Analyzing differences among respondent self-reports only ($n = 199$), these results indicate statistically significant differences (F-value of 26.25, with 3 and 184 degrees of freedom, $p <$ .0001), with the main source of the difference coming from the high level of reliability in the measurement of respondent facts. So, there is clearly support for the assumption that factual information can be more reliably measured in general.

☐ Schooling Differences in Reliability of Self-Reports

One of the central goals of this research is to test the hypothesis that if there are differences in measurement reliability by age, one possible explanation for this is the differences in the educational levels of younger vs. older respondents. Table 2 presents data on reliability estimates by

TABLE 2. RELIABILITY OF SELF-REPORTS IN ELECTION SURVEYS BY EDUCATION

		Self-Reports			
Schooling	N	Facts ($n = 47$)	Beliefs ($n = 51$)	Attitudes ($n = 31$)	Self-Perceptions ($n = 12$)
0-11 Years	435	.62	.37	.52	.37
12 Years	420	.63	.42	.55	.48
13–15 Years	169	.68	.40	.60	.53
16+ Years	221	.71	.48	.63	.5
Total	1245	.66	.42	.58	.49
b-coeff.		.032	.031	.037	.065
β-coeff.		.122	.199	.291	.248
F-ratio		.722	3.74	3.72	.944
p-value		.540	.012	.013	.428

levels of schooling within content categories of self-reports. Shown here is the relationship between education and reliability, which is basically linear with a correlation (given here as the b-coefficient) that varies between .12 and .25. The regression coefficients indicate that a two-year increase in education produces between a .03 and .06 change in reliability. Thus, college graduates report information in surveys at a level of reliability that is roughly .1 higher than that for high school graduates. In the case of measurement of attitudes and beliefs, these results are highly significant. The results for factual data are not significant, although the trend is clearly in the same direction. Similarly, the trend is present for self-perceptions, but due to the small number of questions in this category, the patterns are not statistically significant. Overall, however, there are educational differences in the reliability of self-reports. This evidence signals the possibility that cohort differences in education could play a role in patterns of reliability by age.

☐ Age Differences in Schooling

To reinforce the need for controls for education in assessing age differences in reliability, Table 3 presents data on schooling differences among the cohorts (or age groups) studied in the 1970s NES panels. Age is strongly related to level of education due to the influence of cohort factors. The standard deviation of education, years of schooling, in these data is about 3.2, so the oldest and the youngest differ by more than a standard deviation, on average about 4 years. Given the link between schooling and measurement reliability reported above (see

TABLE 3. BIRTH COHORT DIFFERENCES IN EDUCATION: 1972–74–76 NATIONAL ELECTION PANEL STUDY

Birth Cohort	Age[1]	N	Schooling[2]
1. 1947–1954	18–25	205	13.32
2. 1939–1946	26–33	227	12.72
3. 1931–1938	34–41	190	12.70
4. 1923–1930	42–49	204	12.18
5. 1915–1922	50–57	167	11.19
6. 1907–1914	58–65	147	10.54
7. <1906	66+	165	9.26
Total	18–97	1305	11.84

Notes. [1]Age in 1972. [2]Years of schooling completed in 1972.

Table 2), differences in the amount of schooling across age groups could explain any tendency in these data for older respondents to have lower reliability.

☐ Age Differences in the Reliability of Self-Reports

In Table 4, I present the relationship between age and reliability within each of the content categories considered: facts, beliefs, attitudes, and self-perceptions. This table presents both the unadjusted mean reliabilities by age (Column 1) and the adjusted mean reliabilities (Column 2). Considering the unadjusted reliability estimates first, note that these results confirm the hypothesis based on earlier research that there are few age differences in the reliability of reporting factual information (the older respondents are no more or less likely to produce greater errors of measurement), but in the case of beliefs, attitudes, and self-perceptions, the oldest age groups have systematically lower reporting reliabilities. These unadjusted results by age are, however, not statistically significant, although it is very clear that the oldest age group has the lowest reliability.[2]

TABLE 4.   RELIABILITY ESTIMATES FOR SELF-REPORTS IN ELECTION SURVEYS BY AGE GROUP: 1972–74–76 NATIONAL ELECTION PANEL STUDY

| | Reliability | | | | | | | |
| | Facts | | Beliefs | | Attitudes | | Self-Perceptions | |
Age Group	(1)[1]	(2)	(1)	(2)	(1)	(2)	(1)	(2)
1. 18–25	.71	.66	.42	.38	.63	.57	.53	.44
2. 26–33	.61	.59	.44	.42	.57	.53	.50	.45
3. 34–41	.75	.72	.44	.41	.58	.55	.49	.44
4. 42–49	.65	.64	.42	.41	.56	.55	.48	.46
5. 50–57	.71	.73	.47	.49	.62	.64	.47	.51
6. 58–65	.70	.74	.47	.51	.55	.60	.54	.62
7. 66+	.67	.75	.38	.46	.48	.57	.40	.57
Total	.68		.44		.57		.49	
Items	47		51		31		12	
F-ratio	.85	1.71	1.29	3.21	2.68	1.53	.19	.53
p-value	.64	.41	.09	.00	.46	.06	.99	.21

Note. [1]Column (1) contains unadjusted reliability estimates, column (2) contains estimates of reliability adjusted for cohort differences in education.

Thus, there is a clear pattern in the unadjusted reliabilities suggesting that those in the oldest age group may have more measurement errors in the measurement of nonfactual content. The question remains as to the source of these patterns and whether they may be due to differences in the schooling experiences of different cohort groups. Table 4, Column 2 presents the adjusted differences in mean reliability, once the greater reliability of educational groups and educational differences among cohorts (see Tables 2 and 3) are taken into consideration.[3] These adjusted reliability results show, however, that when we take into account the age-education and education-reliability relationships, the differences in age groups are reduced. In fact, in two cases the sign reverses, suggesting that there is generally a positive relationship between age and measurement reliability. This is a somewhat surprising result, given the strength of the theoretical hypotheses reviewed above regarding expectations of age differences in measurement reliability. In two cases, for attitudes and beliefs, the results show a significant relationship of age and reliability adjusted for differences in schooling. Clearly, the adjustment removed the distinctiveness of the oldest age group in both cases, generally indicating that once education differences among the age groups are removed, reporting reliability in the oldest age categories is no lower than in the younger groups, and it might actually be marginally higher in some cases.

☐ Life-Span Trajectories of Stability and Measurement Reliability

The results presented above indicate that, after adjustments for between-cohort differences in schooling, older respondents actually have higher reliabilities in the measurement of attitudes and beliefs. One hypothesis for why this is happening, the "aging stability" hypothesis (Glenn, 1980), is based on theories of life-span development of attitudes and beliefs which suggest that older respondents have more crystallized attitudes and beliefs. As a result, they are able to report their attitudes and beliefs with less error than is true for much younger respondents whose subjective states are still undergoing formation, and who therefore have a more difficult reporting task. Hence, for the measurement of some variables, younger respondents may produce less reliable data because they are reporting on states that are more likely to be undergoing change. To examine this possibility, we examined the life-span patterns of stability of attitudes and beliefs in the above analysis, using the latent variable structural equation model given above. These results are given in Table 5.

TABLE 5. AGE DIFFERENCES IN LEVELS OF STABILITY IN SUBJECTIVE
VARIABLES: 1950s AND 1970s NATIONAL ELECTION STUDY PANELS

Birth Cohort	Age	N	Attitude Stability	Belief Stability
1947–1954	18–25	205	.48	.39
1939–1946	26–33	227	.54	.41
1931–1938	34–41	190	.66	.53
1923–1930	42–49	204	.66	.44
1915–1922	50–57	167	.44	.40
1907–1914	58–65	147	.51	.33
<1906	66+	165	.52	.29
Total	18–97	1305	.54	.40

These results provide very little support for the hypothesis that patterns of higher reliability in older age in the measurement of attitudes and beliefs results from the greater crystallization of subjective phenomena in older age. There is little support for this because, as indicated in Table 5, rather than an aging-stability effect the pattern is one of midlife stability (see Alwin, 1994, 1997c). There is support for the idea that younger respondents have lower levels of stability, and that these levels increase with age, peaking and flattening out from ages 35–49. Thereafter, there is a decline in stability, returning to earlier pre-midlife levels. Thus, life-span levels of reliability, whether one considers either the unadjusted or adjusted figures given above, do not follow the same pattern as do life-span levels of stability.

☐ Conclusions

We began this chapter with the idea that, although there are strong theoretical reasons to expect that cognitive decrements known to accompany aging may impair reliable reporting of information in survey research, studies comparing rates of measurement error across age groups in actual surveys have generally not been able to demonstrate that aging is a major problem in routine use of surveys (e.g., Rodgers & Herzog, 1987). The conclusions of the present research seem to support this view, namely, that there is little support for the hypothesis that aging contributes to greater errors of measurement in older populations. In the analysis presented here, among factual measures, there are virtually no detectable differences in reliability by age. Among nonfactual measures, particularly measures of attitudes and beliefs, there is a clear pattern in the unadjusted reliabilities that those in the oldest age group may produce more measurement errors. However, when we take into account age-education and education-reliability relationships, the sign reverses and, if anything, for some domains of subjective measurement, there is generally a positive relationship between age and measurement reliability, with those respondents over 50 years having the highest reliabilities. The results of this exercise are rather surprising, since for some types of subjective variables, once age differences in cohort experiences are taken into account, reporting reliability appears to be highest in the oldest age groups. Thus, once age groups are statistically equated with respect to levels of schooling, and age differences in levels of schooling are taken into account, reliability of measurement increases with age, rather then decreases. These results call for further examination and replication before they can be generalized, but they do suggest other possible explanations for age patterns of measurement error. I would especially urge researchers studying age differences in measurement error to take schooling differences and other cohort experiences into account before concluding that cognitive decrements due to aging create problems for survey measurement. In the meantime, given the possibilities of measurement error differences among younger and older respondents in some domains, it is still important to examine life course events and processes independent of measurement error, where possible, employing methods of statistical analysis that confront these possibilities head on (e.g., Alwin and Krosnick, 1991a; Alwin et al., 1991; Alwin, 1997c).

☐ Endnotes

1. Details of this study are presented in another paper (Alwin, 1997b). In addition to the source and content of the information requested by a given question, it is possible to relate reliability to the characteristics of the question. For example, patterns of reliability vary according to the number of response categories provided and whether the response options are labeled.

2. As I have indicated elsewhere (Alwin, 1992), it is not appropriate to apply statistical tests to these differences in reliability, given that the sampling assumptions have not been met. That is, survey questions have not been sampled from a universe of such questions, and the items included are by no means independent of one another. Nonetheless, this offers a rough gauge of the extent of differences by age. With respect to the unadjusted reliability differences, in all cases here, however, a comparison of the oldest age group against all others produces highly significant results.

3. The adjusted reliability for the jth age group is as follows:

$$r^*_j = r_j - b_{rx} (\mu_{.j} - \mu_{..}),$$

where r_j is the unadjusted reliability for the jth age group, b_{rx} is the unstandardized regression coefficient in the regression of reliability on years of schooling (see Table 2), $\mu_{.j}$ is the mean level of schooling for the jth age group, and $\mu_{..}$ is the grand mean of schooling for the population. All estimates here are based on the 1970s NES panel data. Estimation was carried out within content categories, and thus the regression coefficient used in these calculations varied as a function of the content considered.

☐ Acknowledgments

Research reported here was supported by the following grants from the National Institute on Aging: "Stability of Individual Differences Over the Life-Span" (R01-AG04743-06) and "Aging and Errors of Measurement" (R01-AG09747-02). The author acknowledges the research assistance of David Klingel and the helpfulness of Regula Herzog in tracking down some of her unpublished results.

☐ References

Achen, C. H. (1975). Mass political attitudes and the survey response. *American Political Science Review 69*, 1218–1231.

Alwin, D. F. (1989). Problems in the estimation and interpretation of the reliability of survey data. *Quality and Quantity, 23*, 277–331.

Alwin, D. F. (1991a). Family of origin and cohort differences in verbal ability. *American Sociological Review, 49*, 784–802.

Alwin, D. F. (1991b). Research on survey quality. *Sociological Methods and Research, 20, 3–29.*

Alwin, D. F. (1992). Information transmission in the survey interview: Number of response categories and the reliability of attitude measurement. In P. V. Marsden (Ed.), *Sociological methodology 1992* (pp. 83–118). Washington DC: American Sociological Association.

Alwin, D. F. (1994). Aging, personality and social change: The stability of individual differences over the life-span. In D. L. Featherman, R. M. Lerner, & M. Perlmutter (Eds.), *Life-span development and behavior* (pp. 135–185). Hillsdale, NJ: Erlbaum.

Alwin, D. F. (1995, April). *The reliability of survey data.* Paper presented at an International Conference on Measurement Error and Process Quality, Bristol, England.

Alwin, D. F. (1997a). Feeling thermometers vs. 7-point scales: Which is better? *Sociological Methods and Research, 25*, 318–340.

Alwin, D. F. (1997b). *The reliability of survey data.* Unpublished paper. Institute for Social Research, The University of Michigan, Ann Arbor.

Alwin, D. F. (1997c, July). *The life-span stability of attitudes and beliefs.* Paper presented at the Workshop on the Development of Attitudes and Beliefs Over the Life-Span, Stanford University, Palo Alto, CA.

Alwin, D. F., Cohen, R. L., & Newcomb, T. M. (1991). *Political attitudes over the life-span: The Bennington women after fifty years.* Madison, WI: University of Wisconsin Press.

Alwin, D. F., & Jackson, D. J. (1979). Measurement models for response errors in surveys: Issues and applications. In K. F. Schuessler (Ed.), *Sociological methodology 1980* (pp. 68–119). San Francisco: Jossey-Bass.

Alwin, D. F., & Krosnick, J. A. (1991a). Aging, cohorts and the stability of socio-political orientations over the life-span. *American Journal of Sociology, 97,* 169–195.

Alwin, D. F., & Krosnick, J. A. (1991b). The reliability of survey attitude measurement: The influence of question and respondent attributes. *Sociological Methods and Research, 20,* 139–181.

Andrews, F. M. (1984). Construct validity and error components of survey measures: A structural modeling approach. *Public Opinion Quarterly, 46,* 409–442.

Andrews, F. M., & Herzog, A. R. (1986). The quality of survey data as related to age of respondent. *Journal of the American Statistical Association, 81,* 403–410.

Arbuckle, T. Y., Gold, D., & Andres, D. (1986). Cognitive functioning of older people in relation to social and personality variables. *Psychology and Aging, 1,* 55–62.

Bohrnstedt, G. W. (1983). Measurement. In P. H. Rossi, J. D. Wright, and A. B. Anderson (Eds.), *Handbook of survey research* (pp. 70–121). New York: Academic Press.

Bohrnstedt, G. W., & Carter, T. M. (1971). Robustness in regression analysis. In H. L. Costner (Ed.), *Sociological methodology 1971* (pp. 118–146). San Francisco: Jossey-Bass.

Bradburn, N., & Danis, C. (1984). Potential contributions of cognitive research to questionnaire design. In T. Jabine, M. Straf, J. Tanur, & R. Tourangeau (Eds.), *Cognitive aspects of survey methodology: Building a bridge between disciplines.* Washington DC: National Academy Press.

Campbell, A., Converse, P. E., Miller, W., & Stokes, D. (1971). *American Election Panel Study: 1956, 1958, 1960.* Ann Arbor MI: Inter-University Consortium for Political and Social Research.

Cannell, C., Miller, P. V., & Oksenberg, L. (1981). Research on interviewing techniques. In S. Lienhardt (Ed.), *Sociological methodology 1970* (pp. 389–437). San Francisco: Jossey-Bass.

Center for Political Studies. (1979). *The American National Election Series: 1972, 1974, and 1976, Volumes I & II.* Ann Arbor MI: Inter-University Consortium for Political and Social Research.

Cleary, T. A., Linn, R. L., & Walster, G. W. (1970). Effect of reliability and validity on power of statistical tests. In E. F. Borgatta and G. W. Bohrnstedt (Eds.), *Sociological methodology 1970* (pp. 30–38). San Francisco: Jossey-Bass.

Converse, P. E. (1964). The nature of belief systems in the mass public. In D. E. Apter (Ed.), *Ideology and discontent* (pp. 206–261). New York: Free Press.

Ferber, R. (1966). Item nonresponse in a consumer survey. *Public Opinion Quarterly, 30,* 399–415.

Francis, J. D., & Busch, L. (1975). What we know about "I don't knows". *Public Opinion Quarterly, 39,* 207–218.

Gergen, K., & Back, K. (1966). Communication in the interview and the disengaged respondent. *Public Opinion Quarterly, 30,* 385–398.

Glenn, N. (1980). Values, attitudes and beliefs. In O. G. Brim, Jr. and J. Kagan (Eds.), *Constancy and change in human development* (pp. 596–640). Cambridge, MA: Harvard University Press.

Groves, R. M. (1989). *Survey errors and survey costs.* New York: Wiley.

Heise, D. R. (1969). Separating reliability and stability in test-retest correlation. *American Sociological Review, 34,* 93–191.

Herzog, A. R., & Rodgers, W. L. (1982). *Surveys of older Americans: Some methodological investigations.* Final Report to the National Institute on Aging (AG02038). Survey Research Center and Institute of Gerontology, The University of Michigan, Ann Arbor.

Herzog, A. R., & Rodgers, W. L. (1989). Age differences in memory performance and memory ratings as measured in a sample survey. *Psychology and Aging, 4,* 173–182.

Hippler, H.-J., Schwarz, N., & Sudman, S. (1987). *Social information processing and survey methodology.* New York: Springer-Verlag.

Jöreskog, K. G. (1970). Estimating and testing of simplex models. *British Journal of Mathematical and Statistical Psychology, 23,* 121–145.

Jöreskog, K. G. (1971). Statistical analysis of sets of congeneric tests. *Psychometrika, 36,* 109–133.

Kalton, G., & Schuman, H. (1982). The effect of the question on survey responses: A review. *Journal of the Royal Statistical Association, 145,* 42–73.

Knäuper, B. (1997). *Age and response effects in attitude measurement.* Unpublished paper. Survey Methods Program, Institute for Social Research, University of Michigan, Ann Arbor.

Knäuper, B., Belli, R. F., Hill, D. H., & Herzog, A. R. (1997). *Question difficulty and respondents' cognitive ability: The impact on data quality.* Unpublished paper. Survey Methods Program, Institute for Social Research, University of Michigan. Ann Arbor, MI.

Lord, F. M., & Novick, M. L. (1968). *Statistical theories of mental test scores.* Reading MA: Addison-Wesley.

Mannheim, K. (1952). The problem of generations. In P. Kecskemeti (Ed.), *Essays in the sociology of knowledge* (pp. 276–322). Boston: Routledge & Kegan Paul. (Original work published 1927).

Marquis, M. S., and Marquis, K. H. (1977). *Survey measurement design and evaluation using reliability theory.* Santa Monica, CA: Rand.

Miller, W. E., and the National Election Studies. (1991). *American National Election Studies: Cumulative data file 1952-1990.* Center for Political Studies, Institute for Social Research, University of Michigan, Ann Arbor.

Park, D. C., Smith, A. D., Lautenschlager, G., Earles, J. L., Frieske, D., Zwahr, M., & Gaines, C. L. (1996). Mediators of long-term memory performance across the life-span. *Psychology and Aging, 11,* 621–637.

Perlmutter, M. (1978). What is memory aging the aging of? *Developmental Psychology, 14,* 330–345.

Riley, M. W. (1973). Aging and cohort succession: Interpretations and misinterpretations. *Public Opinion Quarterly, 37,* 35–49.

Rodgers, W. L., Andrews, F. M., & Herzog, A. R. (1992). Quality of survey measures: A structural modeling approach. *Journal of Official Statistics, 3,* 251–275.

Rodgers, W. L., & Herzog, A. R. (1987). Interviewing older adults: The accuracy of factual information. *Journal of Gerontology, 42,* 387–394.

Ryder, N. B. (1965). The cohort as a concept in the study of social change. *American Sociological Review, 30,* 843–861.

Salthouse, T. A. (1991). *Theoretical perspectives on cognitive aging.* Hillsdale, NJ: Erlbaum.

Salthouse, T. A. (1996). The processing-speed theory of adult age differences in cognition. *Psychological Review, 103,* 403–428.

Schaie, K. W. (1990). Intellectual development in adulthood. In J. E. Birren & K. W. Schaie (Eds.), *Handbook of the psychology of aging* (3rd ed., pp. 291–309). San Diego, CA: Academic Press.

Schaie, K. W. (1993). The course of adult intellectual development. *American Psychologist 49*, 304–313.

Schaie, K. W. (1996). Intellectual development in adulthood. In J. E. Birren & K. W. Schaie (Eds.), *Handbook of the psychology of aging* (4th ed., pp. 266–286). San Diego, CA: Academic Press.

Schwarz, N., & Sudman, S. (1994). *Autobiographical memory and the validity of retrospective reports.* New York: Springer-Verlag.

Siegel, P. M., & Hodge, R. W. (1968). A causal approach to the study of measurement error. In H. M. Blalock, Jr. & A. B. Blalock (Eds.), *Methodology in social research* (pp. 28–59). New York: McGraw-Hill.

Strack, F., & Martin, L. (1987). Thinking, judging and communicating: A process account of context effects in attitude surveys. In H.-J. Hippler, N. Schwarz, & S. Sudman (Eds.), *Social information processing and survey methodology* (pp. 123–148). New York: Springer-Verlag.

Sudman, S., Bradburn, N. M., & Schwarz, N. (1996). *Thinking about answers: The application of cognitive processes to survey methodology.* San Francisco: Jossey-Bass.

Tourangeau, R. (1984). Cognitive science and survey methods. In T. Jabine, M. Straf, J. Tanur, & R. Tourangeau (Eds.), *Cognitive aspects of survey methodology: Building a bridge between disciplines.* Washington DC: National Academy Press.

Tourangeau, R. (1987). Attitude measurement: a cognitive perspective. In H.-J. Hippler, N. Schwarz, & S. Sudman (Eds.), *Social information processing and survey methodology* (pp. 149–162). New York: Springer-Verlag.

Tourangeau, R., & Rasinski, K. A. (1988). Cognitive processes underlying context effects in attitude measurement. *Psychological Bulletin 103*, 299–314.

Wiley, D. E., & Wiley, J. A. (1970). The estimation of measurement error in panel data. *American Sociological Review, 35*, 112–117.

INDEX